SECOND EDITION

Case Histories of Deviant Behavior

An Interactional Perspective

GLORIA RAKITA LEON

CASE HISTORIES
OF
DEVIANT BEHAVIOR

SECOND EDITION

CASE HISTORIES
OF
DEVIANT BEHAVIOR

An Interactional Perspective

Gloria Rakita Leon
UNIVERSITY OF MINNESOTA

HOLBROOK PRESS, INC.
BOSTON

Library of Congress Cataloging in Publication Data

Leon, Gloria Rakita.
  Case histories of deviant behavior.

  Includes bibliographies and index.
  1. Mental illness—Cases, clinical report,
statistics. I. Title.
RC465.L44   1977   616.8'9'09   77-7790
ISBN 0-205-05847-7

TO MY FAMILY

CONTENTS

FOREWORD

The planning of a second edition is a time for rejoicing. Publisher and author have done their work well, the demand for the book remains high, and it is time to bring out the new edition. It is also a time for taking stock. Much has happened since *Case Histories of Deviant Behavior* first appeared three years ago. Events are moving at such a pace that what was a valid reflection of behavior therapy in 1974 has become incomplete and inadequate as a characterization of behavior therapy today. Dr. Gloria Leon, an astute observer as well as a skillful behavioral clinician, chronicles well this progression of events in the second edition of her book.

We have come a long way from the narrow S-R formulation of little more than a decade ago. Behavior therapy is becoming increasingly social learning theory oriented. Leading personality theorists such as Staats, Lazarus, Bandura, Rotter, and Mischel have all presented innovative variations, modifications, or extensions of what may be called the basic social learning theory model. With occasional notable exceptions, despite their major differences, all of these leading exponents of social learning theory share an allegiance to data, operational definition, and an awareness of the roles of reinforcement, modeling, and related concepts. It is this which really unites behavior therapists, regardless of orientation, technique, or clinical strategy. These developments are cogently illustrated—either explicitly or implicitly—in the various cases documented in this updated edition of *Case Histories of Deviant Behavior.*

It is no coincidence that the subtleties of the interactional process between the individual and the environment assume increasing importance in the thinking and clinical strategies of most of these sophisticated molders of the behavioral scene. The environment accounts for certain facets of the behavior of the individual and, in its turn, the behavior of the individual influences the responses of others in the social milieu. In all of these activities, cognitive variables play as yet only partially understood roles. Thus, different people may respond in a highly individualized and seemingly idiosyncratic fashion to what, at first blush, appear to be identical stimuli.

According to a survey conducted by Garfield and Kurtz (reprinted in the January 1976 issue of the *American Psychologist*), even in 1974 the main stream of clinical psychology was beginning to move in three cohering directions: towards increased acceptance of the theory and practice of behavior therapy; towards a greater reliance upon techniques derived from the Existential-Gestalt complex; and towards a growing respect for ideological and technological flexibility. A year later, writing in the same journal, Mahoney observes that clinical psychologists seem to be assimilating and integrating two approaches to psychotherapy once thought to be divergent and incompatible. One emphasizes behavioral techniques and the other focuses on cognitive and affective intrapersonal processes. Paul Wachtel—whose well articulated opinions I respect but, for the most part, find unacceptable—would probably view this as yet another indication of an imminent rapprochement, a philosophical integration between psychodynamic/mentalistic and behavioral/operationally defined therapeutic models. Not so. What it does suggest is, first, that technical eclecticism—in Lazarus' sense—is a viable and increasingly acceptable clinical procedure and that techniques derived from any source can be effectively integrated into the armamentarium of the therapist. Second, that cognitive and affective intrapersonal processes can be meaningfully and usefully subsumed under some form of behavioral rubric.

What we are really witnessing, perhaps sporadically in clinical psychology at large and in a concentrated and definitive fashion in behavior therapy, is a convergence of two seemingly divergent trends in our understanding of human behavior. These are, on the one hand, an emphasis upon the intrapersonal—stressing cognition, self-control and the inner person—and, on the other hand, an emphasis upon external influences—interpersonal factors, drugs, and a host of environmental and sociological variables. Increasingly, these two segments of an individual are seen to complement each other and, like the Roman god Janus, be the two parts of one vibrant entity.

These consequential developments are well reflected in this second edition of *Case Histories of Deviant Behavior*. While most of the original cases are wisely retained, additional chapters have been chosen to emphasize the increasing convergence of these two complementary trends. As one would expect from a clinician of Dr. Leon's caliber, this book is timely and sensitive to the prevailing *Zeitgeist*. It will, as she suggests, provide students of abnormal psychology with an alternative to the more traditional explanations of deviant functioning. But more than this, the book will serve to orient the behaviorally sophisticated clinician to current developments in behavior therapy. What is happening in behavior therapy is much more a reflection of a general trend in clinical psychology than many traditional psychotherapists care to admit. Dr. Leon has succeeded in holding up a larger and more searching mirror than she had possibly at first intended.

Dr. Leon is presenting case reports rather than case studies. Well conceived and purposively presented case reports can be of inestimable clinical value. As such, it is not necessary that they satisfy the much needed and exacting criteria established by Lazarus and Davison for the case study. It is also of little significance that the testing procedures and methods of therapy reported in some of these cases are different from those that a more rigorous behavior therapist might employ. *Viva la difference*—as long as the procedures are demonstrably effective!

The hallmark of behavior therapy is a sensitivity to orderly and data-based change regardless of theoretical orientation. It is hoped the third edition—and I am convinced that there will be a third edition—will present even further extentions of these developments. This book is clearly written, broad in its coverage, and responsive to major trends and influences. It might even represent the inauguration of a novel series in the progress of clinical behavior therapy as documented through the case report.

Cyril M. Franks
Professor and Director of Post
Doctoral Training

Graduate School of Applied and
Professional Psychology
Rutgers University
New Brunswick, New Jersey

REFERENCES

Garfield, S.L., and Kurtz, R. Clinical psychologists in the 1970s. *American Psychologist*, 1976, *31*, 1–9.

Lazarus, A.A., and Davison, G.C. Clinical innovation in research and practice. In A.E. Bergin and S.L. Garfield (Eds.), *Handbook of psychotherapy and behavior change*. New York: Wiley, 1971. Pp. 196–213.

Mahoney, M.J. Reflections on the cognitive-learning trend in psychotherapy. *American Psychologist,* 1977, *32,* 5–13.

Wachtel, P. *Psychoanalysis and behavior therapy: Toward an integration.* New York: Basic Books, 1977.

PREFACE
TO THE FIRST EDITION

This book was written to provide the student of abnormal psychology with an alternative to the traditional explanations of deviant functioning. The case history material in each chapter is analyzed from a social learning point of view, and the development of a particular pattern of behavior is assessed in relation to the individual's social learning history. Each method of therapy employed is discussed and evaluated, and a sampling of the relevant literature is reviewed.

The social learning approach suggests that one can understand the behavior of an individual by studying the reinforcement and modeling influences in that person's past and present social environments. While earlier learning theories have stressed the impact of the environment in determining an individual's behavior, the social learning approach focuses on the *interaction* between the individual and the environment. Not only does the environment influence the behavior of the individual, but the individual's behavior, in turn, influences the responses of others in the social milieu. Thus, a person may learn to behave in a highly aggressive manner through observational learning and experiencing a particular reinforcement history. However, other persons in the environment respond to an aggressive individual in a clearly different way than they respond to an extremely passive person.

Social learning theory may provide a reasonable alternative to psychodynamic explanations of particular disorders. A case in point is Wolpe and Rachman's reinterpretation (1960) from a social learning point of view of Freud's analysis of the development of a phobia in the classic case of Little Hans. Within the last fifteen years, theories and techniques of behavior therapy have emerged also as viable alternatives to psychodynamic or psychoanalytically oriented methods of treatment. An assessment of the client's currently existing interaction patterns would seem to be an important step in the process of selecting a particular technique of behavior modification. The goal of social learning oriented therapy would then be to aid the individual to modify his or her present social relationships, and to teach the individual how to relate to others in a more flexible and satisfying manner.

The case histories in this book were chosen to illustrate the symptom clusters traditionally associated with a particular diagnostic label. The diagnostic categories are generally in accord with the standard nomenclature of the American Psychiatric Association (DSM-II, 1968). The reader should recognize, however, that in reality many cases show mixed symptoms and do not fit perfectly into a given category.

The case studies include information about the individual's family history. Although knowledge of the person's past social relationships may not be particularly necessary to modify the present problem behaviors, this information can be extremely valuable to the student of deviant behavior, in demonstrating how behavior patterns develop and are modified over time.

In several of the cases, the testing procedures and the method of therapy employed were different from the techniques that a behaviorally oriented therapist might use. However, the information gained from these other methods was made available to the readers to illustrate the range of current techniques. Also, depending on the information available about a given case, some chapters have a greater emphasis on therapy procedures than do others. Finally, not all of the cases presented were therapeutic successes. It is apparent that there is a continued need for research in developing more effective therapeutic procedures for persons of varying socioeconomic and cultural backgrounds.

The cases in this book were based on information gained by permission from a number of clinics, institutions, and therapists. The chapters dealing with childhood disorders present data about mother-child interactions that were observed in a clinic setting, according to a standardized technique developed by the author (Leon, 1971; Leon and Morrow, 1972). In all of the cases, the names used were pseudonyms, and identifying details were changed to protect the anonymity of the persons involved.

The author wishes to thank Arnold Lazarus for his helpful comments on the several chapters he reviewed, and Ivan Mensh for his careful review of the entire manuscript. The advice of Karen Chamberlain, Alice Cottingham, Bernard Guerney, William Powell, Lillian Robbins, Michael Schulman, Teres Scott, Larry Silver, and Arlene Tucker is also gratefully acknowledged. Appreciation is expressed to Paul Conway, Holbrook Press editor, for his advice and encouragement.

The major part of the manuscript was typed by Veronica Curcione, and special thanks are in order for her skill and patience. The help of Janie Balak, Eileen Birnholz, and Anne Wolff is also appreciated.

GRL

REFERENCES

American Psychiatric Association. Diagnostic and statistical manual of mental disorders (2nd ed.) (DSM-II). Washington: American Psychiatric Association, 1968.

Leon, G. R. Case report. The use of a structured mother-child interaction and projective material in studying parent influence on child behavior problems. *Journal of Clinical Psychology*, 1971, *27*, 413–416.

Leon, G. R., and Morrow, V. Differing patterns of maternal behavioral control and their association with child behavior problems of an active or passive interpersonal nature. *Journal Supplement Abstract Service*, 1972, *2*, 136–137.

Wolpe, J., and Rachman, S. Psychoanalytic "evidence": A critique based on Freud's case of Little Hans. *Journal of Nervous and Mental Disease*, 1960, *131*, 135–148.

Introduction

In the period since the first edition of this book, a number of social learning theorists have included cognitive variables in their formulations and analyses of deviant behavior. Discussions of cognitive variables apparently have become socially acceptable in behavioral circles. However, Rotter (1954) presented a social learning theory that was cognitive in nature and contained concepts such as need value, the expectancy and probability value of a particular reinforcement occurring, the degree of the person's preference for a specific reinforcement, and differences between internal and external reinforcement. Rotter used the term "psychological situation" instead of the term "stimulus." He defined the psychological situation as the individual's selective response to both internal and external stimulation, in a way consistent with that person's unique experience. The effect of the environment on the individual was viewed as occurring through the expectancies for the reinforcement or punishment of specific behaviors that were aroused by particular environmental cues. These generalized expectancies were the key for understanding, predicting, and changing human behavior. Rotter, Chance, and Phares (1972) presented the application of this particular social learning conception of personality to the analysis of abnormal behavior and the understanding of the process of psychotherapy.

Bandura and Walters (1963) formulated a different type of social learning theory of personality development. They emphasized the crucial role of observational learning in the development of new response patterns, and felt that Rotter's form of social learning theory was inadequate to explain the occurrence of a response that had not as yet been learned, and therefore had a zero probability value of occurrence. Bandura and Walters also discussed the effect of reinforcement processes emanating from the social environment on the shaping and maintenance of both prosocial and deviant behaviors. Their emphasis was on the interactions between the individual and the environment, including the notion that the behavior of other persons in the social milieu is in turn influenced and modified by the responses emitted by the particular individual. Therefore, persons were not seen as merely passive recipients of environmental influences, but were viewed as actively engaged in reciprocal behavioral interactions with other persons. The writings of Lazarus (1971) and others reflect the application of a social learning theory focused on interpersonal relationships to behavioral analysis and treatment.

Bandura (1972) expanded on modeling theory, and his more recent explanation of observational learning includes cognitive factors such as attention, the symbolic coding and rehearsal operations governing retention processes, motor reproduction processes, and motivational processes. Bandura states that modeling influences operate through the information the model conveys, and that the observer acquires primarily a symbolic representation of the modeled event. Bandura rejected the notion that observational learning occurs as a specific stimulus-response association.

Mischel (1973) has presented a cognitive social learning theory of personality that draws from both Rotter's and Bandura's earlier formulations. He rejected the concept of personality traits and argued for behavioral specificity rather than personality consistency, i.e., that behavior is determined by specific conditions and not by enduring traits. However, he felt that the meaning and impact of a stimulus can be modified by cognitive transformations. Therefore, he emphasized the individual's behavioral and cognitive activities in relation to specific environmental conditions. Mischel does not view the phenomenon of expectancy as a generalized trait but, instead, focuses on the individual's expectancies about outcomes in specific situations and the associated subjective values of those outcomes. Thus, the individual behaves according to specific expectancies about the consequences of different behavioral possibilities in a particular situation. The effectiveness of reinforcement lies in its ability to modify behavior outcome expectancies. The interactions between the person and the environment are therefore mediated by the cognitive encoding and categorization of events and the individual's evaluation that behaving in a given manner will result in a particular outcome.

A behavioral conception of self-control is a related development in the greater interest of social learning theorists in cognitive variables. Thoresen and Mahoney (1974) discussed self-control as a process whereby the individual engages in overt and covert behaviors to alter the environment. These alterations, in turn, systematically modify other relevant behaviors. For example, a person who stops buying cigarettes, removes all of the ashtrays from the house, and says to himself or herself "smoking is bad," is engaging in self-control through changing the environment. Removing an ashtray and its associated cue to smoking then functions as an environmental alteration that could modify the frequency of the urge to smoke. These self-initiated behavior changes would then affect the individual's interactions with other persons in the environment in relation to smoking. The basic feature of this concept of self-control is that the individual is his or her own agent of behavior change. Recently, there has been a greater emphasis in the behavior therapy literature on self-management as a means of modifying behavior and maintaining behavior changes (e.g., Graziano, 1975; Mahoney, 1974). Certainly, the ultimate goal of many token reinforcement programs in schools, institutions, and in the home is for self-reinforcement to eventually become strong enough to maintain a behavior change.

Another development that has influenced social learning theory has been the growing interest in the role of constitutional factors in behavioral interactions (Gelfand, 1975; Wing, 1974). For example, innate differences in infant activity level, frequency of crying, and the sex of the child can affect the way parents and others initially respond to that infant. This response pattern in turn may establish and perpetuate a particular type of interaction pattern with that infant. The growing research evidence suggesting genetic or constitutional factors in the development of some types of psychotic disorders points to another type of biological "given" that can result in particular types of interactions with persons in the social milieu. However, the fact that not all children who are at high risk for the development of a particular disorder manifest that disturbance (Garmezy, 1974) suggests that the social learning process operates in conjunction with the biological variables that might influence behavior.

The new chapters in the second edition of this text demonstrate the increasing emphasis of social learning theorists on the interaction of biological and social processes. A different case of early infantile autism is presented, and additional chapters have been included on the topics of manic-depressive psychosis and schizophrenia. The inclusion of case studies of anorexia nervosa and obesity reflect the growing interest of therapists and students of deviant behavior in the eating disturbances.

As in the first edition, identifying details in the cases presented were changed to protect the anonymity of the persons discussed. All of the names used were pseudonyms.

I would like to thank Kelly Bemis, Irving Gottesman, and Ivan Mensh for their helpful comments on various chapters of this book. The diligence and skill of Maureen Boehm and Janet Peterson in typing the manuscript were invaluable. The cooperation of Paul Conway, Holbrook Press editor, was appreciated very much.

GRL

REFERENCES

Bandura, A. Modeling theory: Some traditions, trends, and disputes. In R. D. Parke (Ed.), *Recent trends in social learning theory.* New York: Academic Press, 1972. Pp. 35–61.

Bandura, A., & Walters, R. H. *Social learning and personality development.* New York: Holt, Rinehart, and Winston, 1963.

Garmezy, N. Children at risk: the search for the antecedents of schizophrenia. Part II: Ongoing research programs, issues, and intervention. *Schizophrenia Bulletin,* 1974 (Summer), No. 9, 55–125.

Gelfand, D. M. (Ed.). *Social learning in childhood* (2d ed.). Monterey, Calif.: Brooks/Cole Publishing, 1975.

Graziano, A. M. (Ed.). *Behavior therapy with children* (Vol. II). Chicago: Aldine Publishing, 1975.

Lazarus, A. A. *Behavior therapy and beyond.* New York: McGraw-Hill, 1971.

Mahoney, M. J. Self-reward and self-monitoring techniques for weight control. *Behavior Therapy*, 1974, *5*, 48–57.

Mischel, W. Toward a cognitive social learning reconceptualization of personality. *Psychological Review*, 1973, *80*, 252–283.

Rotter, J. B. *Social learning and clinical psychology.* Englewood Cliffs, N.J.: Prentice-Hall, 1954.

Rotter, J. B., Chance, J. E., & Phares, E. J. *Applications of a social learning theory of personality.* New York: Holt, Rinehart, and Winston, 1972.

Thoresen, C. E., & Mahoney, M. J. *Behavioral self-control.* New York: Holt, Rinehart, and Winston, 1974.

Wing, J. *Early childhood autism* (2d ed.). London: Pergamon Press, 1974.

PART ONE

CHILDHOOD DISORDERS

$2o^2$

1

Early Infantile Autism— The Case of Jimmy Peterson

Five-year-old Jimmy Peterson was brought by his parents to an inpatient child psychiatry diagnostic unit at a large city hospital. The family's local physician referred the youngster to the hospital for intensive evaluation of his hyperactivity and failure to develop communicative speech. The parents readily agreed to a three-week hospital admission so that a coordinated team of specialists could evaluate their son. Mr. and Mrs. Peterson indicated that Jimmy was impossible to manage, was not toilet trained, said only a few words, and generally screamed or gestured to make others aware of what he wanted. They had been concerned about his lack of speech for some time and welcomed the inpatient evaluation when it seemed clear that the youngster was not going to "outgrow" his various speech and behavior problems. They shared with the staff their feelings of frustration, sadness, and disappointment in Jimmy's poor and puzzling development.

Jimmy was an attractive, well-built youngster of normal height and weight. The Peterson family was white, and lived on a farm in the Midwest. Mr. and Mrs. Peterson were in their middle 30's. Jimmy had one older sister, Michelle, who was 10 years old at the time of the evaluation. She was described by her parents and the referring physician as "perfectly normal" and doing well in school. There were no persons with a history of mental illness on either side of the parents' families.

DEVELOPMENTAL BACKGROUND

Mrs. Peterson reported that she had had a normal pregnancy with each of her children and could not recall any birth complications or postnatal problems. Jimmy had had the usual childhood diseases and the parents reported that there were no particular medical problems or high fevers during or subsequent to these illnesses. Jimmy had never had a serious head or body injury.

The Petersons could recall nothing unusual in Jimmy's early physical development, except that he showed no clear hand preference and still used his right or left hand with equal frequency. They felt that in general his motor development was normal as compared to the progress of his older sister. However, he was extremely active and had a very short attention span. The parents attributed the fact that Jimmy was not toilet trained despite a great deal of effort on Mrs. Peterson's part to the fact that he would not sit still long enough to be trained. They felt that Jimmy's lack of interest in pleasing his parents also was a factor. Mrs. Peterson indicated that Michelle had been toilet trained by the time she was two and a half years old. Mrs. Peterson had tried the same methods of frequent placement on the potty and praise for elimination with Jimmy, but with no success. She indicated that she still tried to place Jimmy on the potty from time to time, but essentially had given up hope of training him for the present time.

The Petersons agreed that Jimmy's behavior always had seemed different. Mrs. Peterson related that Jimmy never had let her hold him close and, even as an infant, he would arch his back, cry, and struggle to get out of her arms. He never stretched out his arms to be held, nor had he ever smiled in recognition when family members walked into a room where he was. He also had never engaged in the typical infant babbling and cooing. Mrs. Peterson indicated that she had become quite concerned when Jimmy passed his second birthday and still had not developed any speech other than shrill cries. The family physician had suggested that Jimmy just might be slower than average in developing language, and that the parents should make an extra effort to try and talk to him. He also referred them to a speech therapist who found it impossible to test Jimmy because of his high activity level.

At age three, Jimmy occasionally said a few words, but these words appeared unrelated to ongoing activities in his immediate vicinity. Efforts by family members to get him to repeat the word he had just uttered, or to imitate new words were unsuccessful. Jimmy began to smile occasionally, but the smiles were unpredictable and did not appear to be in response to behaviors by other persons in the family. Further, it was not possible to get Jimmy to smile with regular frequency. He did not follow directions and he generally did not appear to pay attention to other persons. Mrs. Peterson said that Jimmy seemed to relate only to "things" or objects, not to people. At present, he spent a great deal of time at home spinning a toy, rhythmically banging an object, or rocking back and forth in a chair. He often masturbated while rocking, and sometimes sucked on his fingers at the same time.

Jimmy had progressed somewhat in language skills between the ages of three to five. He was able to say approximately 20 words, but he still tended to gain attention principally through gestures, pulling on someone's arm, or emitting a shrill cry. He showed a greater tendency to smile to appropriate social stimuli than he had previously, and his attention span seemed to have increased somewhat. However, he continued to spend a great deal of time apparently aimlessly walking about the house. He actively ran, hit, clawed, or cried if someone tried to hold him or dress him. He also strongly resisted sitting at the table throughout an entire meal.

THE OBSERVED INTERACTION

Jimmy was observed in a structured interaction situation with his mother. This standard interaction was developed by the author as a means of observing, in a clinical setting, the kinds of home behaviors parents complain about when they bring their child to a guidance clinic (Leon, 1971; Leon and Morrow, 1972). The Observed Interaction begins with a ten-minute free play period, followed by the parent and child working cooperatively on a series of tasks. These tasks and puzzles were devised in a manner so that both parent and child must work together in order to complete the requirements of the situation. The mother was told that she and her child would be observed from behind a one-way mirror.

In the free play situation, Jimmy wandered about the playroom, much as he had during the parents' just completed conference with a hospital social worker, psychologist, and psychiatrist. Mrs. Peterson sat in a chair in a corner of the playroom, smiled occasionally at Jimmy when his glance crossed hers, and watched him move around the room. After several minutes, she got up and attempted to involve her son in some cooperative play with wooden blocks. She spoke to Jimmy in an apparently cheerful tone of voice, but he did not answer her and he moved to another part of the room. Mrs. Peterson made several other comments to him during the free play period but he appeared oblivious to his mother's conversation.

When it was time to begin the task of doing a jigsaw puzzle together, Mrs. Peterson led Jimmy over to a chair beside her. However, almost as soon as he sat down, Jimmy got up again and continued wandering around the room. Mrs. Peterson then got up and firmly, although not in a harsh manner, took Jimmy by the arm and brought him back to the chair. Jimmy began to whine and emit shrill cries, flap his hands, and eventually wiggled out of his mother's grasp. Several minutes later, Mrs. Peterson again called Jimmy over to the table. He came over, stood by the table, and watched as his mother explained and demonstrated how to fit together two pieces of the puzzle. Jimmy watched his mother's demonstration for a moment and then began to handle the puzzle pieces and spin them on the table. However, he subsequently put the two pieces of the puzzle together, and smiled fleetingly when his mother praised him.

Mrs. Peterson later attempted to get Jimmy to hold the basket puzzle (the next task in the standardized Observed Interaction procedure) so that she could string some rods through the basket spaces. She walked over to Jimmy, verbally instructed him to hold the basket, and then placed the basket in his hands. However, Jimmy's response was to push the basket back at her. Mrs. Peterson then completed the task by herself and, when finished, sat quietly in her chair and observed Jimmy's wanderings around the room until the session was over. Jimmy made no apparent attempt to communicate in words with his mother during the session.

During the interaction procedure, Mrs. Peterson engaged in numerous attempts, both verbally and nonverbally, to involve Jimmy in games or in the required task procedures. She appeared comfortable with Jimmy, and did not exhibit signs of anger when he refused to interact with her. She usually was unsuccessful in gaining Jimmy's cooperation during the session. Generally, he wandered around the room, giving one the impression that he was alone. Attempts to interact with him seemed almost an intrusion on this aloneness. However, several positive signs were noted: Jimmy did respond occasionally with a smile to his mother's praise, and he had successfully imitated his mother's demonstration of how to fit two pieces of the puzzle together.

HOSPITAL EVALUATION

Jimmy separated readily from his parents and did not cry or struggle when he was brought to the children's unit of the hospital for the three-week evaluation period. The staff attendant attempted to lead Jimmy over to a play area, but he pushed her away and remained standing in the middle of the room. He soon began walking about the large day room, but his movements seemed restless and aimless rather than exploratory. Jimmy was quite silent and expressionless, and only began screaming and hitting out at others when someone attempted to interfere with his wanderings.

MEDICAL AND NEUROLOGICAL ANALYSIS

There were no abnormalities found on the physical examination nor on various routine and specialized laboratory tests. No abnormalities were noted in reflex responses or in other areas of function evaluated on the neurological examination. However, an electroencephalogram demonstrated positive findings and was interpreted as "a moderately abnormal record." There were indications of both a generalized cerebral dysfunction as well as localized dysfunctions in the parietal and frontal areas of the brain. Specialized hearing tests indicated that Jimmy's auditory acuity was within the normal range.

PSYCHOLOGICAL AND LEARNING ANALYSIS

Jimmy was seen by Dr. S., a psychologist who had had a great deal of experience in evaluating nonverbal children. She noted that Jimmy formed eye contact with her, but this contact did not last long and was not a result of her request that Jimmy look at her. However, he did sit down at a small table when Dr. S. asked him to, and he began looking at and manipulating the test materials. He also occasionally smiled in response to praise. Jimmy made sounds fairly frequently, often with what could be interpreted as signs of pleasure, demand, or protest.

The youngster's arm and body movements as he sat in the chair were fairly continuous although not extremely rapid. Gross and fine motor coordination generally appeared quite adequate. He tended to look away from the activity he was engaged in, although Dr. S. noted that it was sometimes possible to redirect his attention back to the test materials. Despite his fleeting attention, Jimmy demonstrated that he understood the concepts of shape, size, and color, and that he was able to function on some tasks at an age-appropriate level.

Jimmy was seen also by a person trained in special education. Dr. V. noted that the youngster used specific strategies to shut Dr. V. out from demanding that he perform on various tasks: Jimmy would look away from the table, push the test objects away, and get out of his chair. These strategies seemed attentive, planned, and very goal-directed. Jimmy appeared to exhibit a strong negativism and resistance to cooperate and interact with others, and these behaviors clearly would interfere with his performance level and his opportunities to learn new tasks. The youngster readily worked for a candy reinforcer when the task was an easy one and did not require him to communicate, but the effectiveness of the reinforcer decreased significantly when increased demands were made on him to communicate and cooperate. However, Jimmy demonstrated some skills and intellectual functioning within the normal range for his age.

The consensus of the persons who had observed Jimmy's behavior for the three-week period on the ward and in the various testing situations was that he manifested many of the behaviors associated with the syndrome of early infantile autism. The parents were advised to allow Jimmy to remain at the hospital for at least three to four months. The children's unit was structured as a therapeutic milieu and Jimmy would have the opportunity to learn more appropriate social skills through the application of reinforcement techniques. Also, Jimmy could attend half-day sessions at a school for autistic children associated with the hospital. Mr. and Mrs. Peterson readily agreed to this recommendation, and both parents expressed the hope that Jimmy could be helped in some way to eventually function better in his home environment.

HOSPITAL TREATMENT PROGRESS

Jimmy was not placed on any medications to control his deviant behaviors. A cooperative program was initiated between the children's unit and the school for autistic children and Jimmy spent the morning at the school and resided on the unit the rest of the time. He was worked with on a one-to-one basis at the school, with the initial aim that of breaking through his negativism by shaping him to establish a close, affectionate relationship with his teacher. The academic tasks such as teaching him to draw a line, fitting toys together, or exchanging named objects were seen as a vehicle for promoting cooperation and overcoming his initial negativistic response to those around him.

During the first week of the school program, Jimmy was allowed to wander around the room while carrying various objects, but his teacher would occasionally call him over to her to perform simple tasks. Once he had carried out these tasks, he was allowed to wander off again. The strategy was to teach him new behaviors through successive small steps, but to make this interference in his habitually isolated response pattern as unstressful as possible. The teacher also made efforts to increase his physical contact with her. She forcibly picked him up, swung him around, and held him as much as possible. His tolerance for the amount of time he would accept contact with her increased over the week.

The teacher also held Jimmy on her lap during the teaching periods and thus directed his attention to the work materials. When Jimmy focused his gaze on a task and then succeeded in carrying it out correctly, she hugged him and gave him lavish praise. Social approval and hugs were the sole reinforcers used. If Jimmy tried to get out of his teacher's lap during their short work periods, she forcibly constrained him by holding him, and remained holding him throughout the tantrum that ensued. In this manner, Jimmy learned that his tantrums would not result in his being allowed to continue his solitary wanderings. The teacher's verbal behavior and positive affect while hugging Jimmy were quite different in quality from the matter-of-fact manner in which she restrained him and said "no" when he was in the midst of a tantrum. Therefore, Jimmy eventually was able to learn to discriminate between various types of physical contact.

Over a period of several months, Jimmy made consistent progress in learning academic skills and in following directions. He also imitated and later repeated words he had learned, and smiled more frequently. His first move with persons was no longer to escape. He showed greater enjoyment in being with other persons, and eventually sought others out from time to time in order to play with them.

On the hospital ward, Jimmy was reinforced with praise for developing self-help skills and for cooperating in getting dressed. He was taught by means of active holding and social praise to stay at the dining room table with the other children. Also, the staff attendant assigned to work with him gradually taught and reinforced him with particularly favored foods for eating with a spoon and for eating a greater variety of foods. A toilet training program was initiated that was an expansion of the procedure reported on by Pumroy and Pumroy (1965). Jimmy's behavior was shaped so that he spent some time each day in the proximity of the toilet. During specified periods of time when he might be likely to urinate, he was given a piece of candy once every minute and praised whenever he was within one foot of the toilet. Several days later, he was given the candy and verbal praise for each minute he actually sat on the toilet, and eventually, only after urinating. Therefore, the goal of teaching Jimmy to urinate in the toilet was accomplished through small steps that were successive approximations of the target behavior.

Eventually, Jimmy spent less time in isolated activities such as wandering around the room or rocking in a chair. He more frequently sought out social interaction with the other children and adults, and he also initiated physical contact with adults, such as handholding or hugs. He exhibited a greater overt response to what was going on around him and began to establish more frequent and prolonged eye contact with others.

PLACEMENT AND FOLLOW-UP

Over the course of Jimmy's hospitalization, Mr. and Mrs. Peterson were given specific instructions in how to interact with him in a manner similar to the methods used in the school and hospital. Near the time of the youngster's discharge, the teacher spent a weekend with Jimmy at the Petersons' home and demonstrated to them the specific techniques she had used to establish cooperation and reinforce language skills in the classroom. Arrangements also were made to enroll Jimmy in a special program in a school system near the Petersons' home, and the local teachers visited the school for autistic children and observed and practiced the procedures used there.

One year after discharge from the hospital, the parents and teachers reported that Jimmy was making slow but continued progress in speaking in sentences. They also indicated that he was more socially responsive than he previously had been, and easier to take care of. A follow-up visit by the hospital staff confirmed that although one could not consider Jimmy as "normal," he clearly had made substantial progress in language skills and in becoming more positively oriented toward other persons.

DISCUSSION

Jimmy's behavior resembled the kinds of behavior patterns that have been considered part of the syndrome of autism. Kanner (1943) employed the term *early infantile autism* to describe a group of children who were brought for evaluation because they appeared to be feeble-minded. In a number of the cases, there had also been a question of whether the child suffered from auditory impairment. However, Kanner reported that the children's cognitive potentialities and hearing ability were not defective, but only masked by a basic disorder. This disorder was a disability, seen from the beginning of the child's life, in relating in the usual manner to other persons and situations. The child's behavior was described as governed by an obsessive desire for the maintenance of sameness that no one but the child could disrupt. Changes of routine or in the placement of objects often were extremely disturbing to the child and could result in a tantrum until the sameness was restored. It was also noted that the autistic child related to persons as objects rather than as human beings. If someone tried to take a block or other object away from the autistic child, the child would struggle and become angry with the person's hand, rather than with the person, per se.

Kanner stated that the case histories of these youngsters indicated that the child attempted to shut off stimuli impinging from the outside environment. The child appeared to be preoccupied with the manipulation of objects in a stereotyped manner, or absorbed in self-stimulatory activities such as masturbation and rhythmic rocking. The youngster did not seem to respond to environmental stimuli unless these stimuli intruded in the form of someone disrupting the child's routine. Language, when present, was not used to convey meaning to other persons, although many of the youngsters were able to repeat certain words or phrases over and over, or echo words that another person was saying to the child (echolalia).

Kanner (1972) also observed that the autistic children he diagnosed and treated came from families with highly intelligent parents. A great deal of obsessiveness was noted in the family background. Kanner felt that there were very few parents of autistic children who could be described as warmhearted, and the parents' marital relationship was seen as a cold and formal one. Kanner stated that there was a strong relationship between the various types of childhood psychoses and parental attitudes of coldness and perfectionistic behavior. He felt that these parental interaction patterns had a more consistent and higher correlation with early infantile autism than did the factors of heredity, body build, or metabolic dysfunction. However, Kanner stated that one could not overlook the possibility of a constitutional predisposition to autism, although he strongly felt that the parental interaction patterns were more important causative factors.

In discussing severe emotional disorders of early childhood, Mahler (1952) made a distinction between early infantile autism and a pattern that she termed symbiotic infantile psychosis. She stated that the latter disturbance occurs at a somewhat later point in the child's development than the autistic syndrome. Mahler theorized that symbiotic infantile psychosis represented a desperate effort to avert the severe anxiety of mother-child separation. In both types of disorders, she pointed to the disturbed relationship between mother and child, rather than focusing on heredity or metabolic dysfunction as causative factors.

Ferster (1961) presented a learning theory analysis of the development of the syndrome of autism. He analyzed the kinds of behaviors the parent engaged in while interacting with the child, and the effect of the parent's behavior in shaping the child's behavior. The typical activities of the autistic child were viewed as the result of the child learning that these particular behaviors will bring parental attention, while a wider variety of behaviors will bring no reinforcement.

Ferster described the parents as exhibiting a prepotent behavioral repertoire. This was defined as a pattern in which the behaviors and activities of the parent are strongly dominant over most activities of the child. The parent is primarily engrossed in his or her own activities and spends as little time as possible interacting with the child. The parent's needs and interests therefore continually take precedence over the needs and interests of the child. In this type of situation, the child gains parental attention primarily when he or she forcibly intrudes on the parent's repertoire. The child soon learns that the most effective way of intruding is by engaging in primitive, negative behaviors such as screaming and temper tantrums. When the child engages in quieter, more socially acceptable behaviors, the parent does not pay attention to the child. Positive behaviors therefore remain low on the child's response hierarchy or are extinguished entirely. This results in the child eventually exhibiting a severely impoverished behavioral repertoire, with a limited number of behaviors in which the child reliably engages.

Lauretta Bender (1952) discussed the general syndrome of childhood schizophrenia and did not specify early infantile autism or symbiotic psychosis as qualitatively different types of disorders. She considered childhood schizophrenia as basically a biological disturbance, manifested by poor physiologic functioning in all organ systems. She stated that these youngsters revealed pathology at every level and in every area of integration and patterning within the central nervous system. Included were the vegetative, motor, perceptual, intellectual, emotional, and social areas of functioning.

Rimland (1964) also considered autism as basically a biological rather than an interpersonal disturbance. He speculated that the reticular formation in the brain may possibly be the site of a lesion or injury caused by hyperoxia (an excess of oxygen) soon after birth or in early infancy. It was also hypothesized that there might be a genetically determined susceptibility to damage caused by an excess of oxygen. Rimland suggested that the symptoms of autism such as the aloneness, the preservation of sameness, and the inability to relate new stimuli to remembered experience were caused by this hypothesized lesion.

Recent research developments have suggested that autism can be differentiated from childhood schizophrenia, and that the basic handicaps of autism may be produced by organic rather than emotional factors (Wing, 1970). Difficulties in comprehension, in the use of verbal and nonverbal language, and in processing sensory input appear to be critical deficits with a probable neurological basis. Therefore, current theory and research have concentrated on the cognitive handicaps of these children rather than the postulated secondary overlay of emotional disturbance.

An epidemiological study of children ages eight to ten carried out in Britain (Lotter, 1966; 1967) found a relatively greater incidence of neurological and other abnormalities in a group of youngsters with marked autistic behavior as compared to other groups of children. This finding has been pointed to in support of the theory of an organic etiology of autism. The overall ratio of boys to girls with autism in the Lotter study was 2.6 to 1. Rutter and Lockyer (1967) and Rutter, Greenfeld, and Lockyer (1967) reported on a five-to-fifteen year follow-up study of a group of children with the diagnosis of "infantile psychosis." The majority of these youngsters manifested psychotic development in early infancy, and probably would have been labeled as autistic if present-day criteria for the diagnosis of autism had been employed. Contrary to Lotter's findings, none of the psychotic children manifested strong signs of neurological impairment at the physical examination upon hospital admission. However, over a quarter of the children manifested a probable to a strong likelihood of brain damage at the follow-up. (The strength of these findings is tempered somewhat by the fact that Rutter and his colleagues conducted almost all of the physical examinations, and the possibility of inadvertent examiner bias in the diagnosis of organic difficulties cannot be ruled out.) In terms of social adjustment, the psychotic children at follow-up in the Rutter, et al study were functioning at a more adverse level than the control group of nonpsychotic, hospitalized children. All but 8 percent of the psychotic group were in some type of institutional or special setting. The investigators also found that the child's initial score on an intelligence test was the most important factor related to later favorable outcome. However, the opportunity to attend school, irrespective of initial level of disturbance, also was associated with a higher probability of receiving a good adjustment rating at adolescence.

The discrepancy between the studies by Lotter, and by Rutter, et al on the initial manifestation of neurological problems might have been due to a stricter diagnostic criterion for autism or infantile psychosis in the investigation by Rutter and his colleagues. However, the fact that so many of the youngsters in the Rutter, et al study later showed signs of brain damage suggests that some type of organic impairment is a significant factor in autism. Hanson and Gottesman (1976) reviewed the research evidence on possible genetic factors in the development of early infantile autism and in childhood schizophrenia. They concluded that it was more likely that biological, but not genetic factors, were etiologically significant in early infantile autism as compared to childhood schizophrenia.

Jimmy Peterson's life history illustrates many of the characteristics of early infantile autism viewed from an organic rather than a psychogenic perspective. In contrast to Kanner's descriptions of the parents of autistic children, numerous contacts with the Petersons suggested that they were warm, interested persons, with a genuine affection for both of their children. Their older child had developed normally, was doing well in school, and apparently was comfortable with her peers and with adults. The parents reported that they had a good relationship with each other, and no unusual family crises occurred at the time Jimmy was born nor in his early years. Both parents agreed that Jimmy had been a "special" child, different from birth on, and that he had never responded to physical contact or social stimuli in the way that their older child had. As Jimmy grew older, his lack of language development and possible cognitive deficits became more evident. As he matured, the gap grew wider between his intellectual and language performance and that of other children the same age. Although he gave evidence of some age-appropriate intellectual functioning, in most intellectual skills his performance was well below the norm for his age level.

Jimmy's poor language skills may have been due in part to deficits in the input and processing of sensory information. The focal abnormalities noted on the electroencephalogram also suggest the possibility of some specific type of cerebral dysfunction. This dysfunction could possibly be a contributing factor to the type of unevenness of performance noted in many autistic children. For example, some autistic youngsters demonstrate the ability to count, choose colors, or imitate words if their attention is focused on the task, but they show a difficulty in spontaneously naming these colors or engaging in simple sentence conversations when their attention is not specifically directed to the task. The aversion to physical contact and interactions with other persons might also stem in part from an inability to integrate the various sources of incoming sensory stimulation.

These sources of multiple sensory input could be a combination of tactile, visual, auditory, and kinesthetic sensations. The difficulty in understanding one's environment and responding appropriately to it through verbal and nonverbal communications might make a generalized withdrawal from that environment extremely reinforcing. The reinforcing properties of this withdrawal could account for the development of the autistic aloneness. Repetitive behaviors such as rocking or rhythmically spinning objects could acquire a strong reinforcing value if these activities are the few that the child can control. The often-noted hand flapping of autistic and some retarded children when frustrated could also function as a learned response that reduces frustration or aversive arousal because of the reinforcement derived from the rhythmic movements.

A social learning analysis of the behaviors manifested in early infantile autism can be reconciled with an organic theory if one views many of the emotional and social difficulties noted in autistic children as learned responses secondary to a basic biological deficit. Thus, one may not know the specific etiology of the processes that initially caused the child to engage in temper tantrums, rhythmic rocking, and solitary play. A further unknown may be the specific processes that prevented the youngster from developing appropriate language skills. However, these maladaptive behaviors become further reinforced and increase in response strength through their effect on the environment. Engaging in a temper tantrum results in being left alone, and not speaking prevents one from going through the difficult and perhaps confusing process of learning how to talk and communicate through words and sentences. The longer the child develops without speech the more established this pattern becomes. From a Piagetian viewpoint, the amount of practice in developing sensory images to process information determines the amount of cognitive development that occurs. Therefore, youngsters who have not acquired language skills by age five or six may be unable to "catch up" and develop complex language skills at a later time. The inability to make up this lost developmental time occurs because they never learned and practiced the cognitive processes necessary to formulate basic concepts.

It should be kept in mind that an effective treatment program need not explain the etiology of a disorder. However, it is clearly important that systematically used behavioral techniques could extinguish some of the autistic behaviors Jimmy manifested, and gradually increase his response repertoire of prosocial behaviors. Jimmy's teacher and the ward personnel demonstrated and rewarded him for small steps of behavior change. This procedure led ultimately to the youngster's development of newly learned behavior patterns and proved quite effective in teaching Jimmy academic and self-help skills. A dramatic decrease in tantrums and an increase in his academic attainment resulted from the technique of holding him, waiting until his tantrum subsided, and then continuing with the demand that he perform a given task. In this manner, the adult did not reinforce him for his tantrum behavior by allowing him to be left alone or by giving up the demands for new learning. The patience and skill his teacher and the staff of the children's unit demonstrated in gradually establishing a relationship with him resulted in Jimmy's eventually gaining greater reinforcement in interacting with others than in being left alone. This dramatic behavior change initially was accomplished by forcibly intruding on his isolation, not allowing him to withdraw, and then giving him a great deal of social reinforcement for interacting with others. Gradually, physical contact with persons became associated with other reinforcing events, and the aversive properties of approaching people and being hugged extinguished over time.

An important part of the treatment program was to actively teach the parents and the local school personnel who would be working with Jimmy the specific techniques that had been employed to change his behavior. Walder and Hirsch (1969) reported successful results in teaching the parents of autistic children how to use behavioral techniques to modify their own child's negative behaviors and to increase the response strength of positive behaviors. An effective program for training parents to interact with and teach their autistic children was reported also by Schopler and Reichler (1971). On the other hand, a follow-up of autistic children who had been involved in an intensive behavior modification program indicated that those children who were institutionalized after the treatment program ended reverted back to their pretreatment autistic behaviors (Lovaas, Koegel, Simmons, and Long, 1973). Therefore, the importance of continuing with the same methods of teaching Jimmy such as reinforcing social behaviors, ignoring negative ones, and forcibly intruding on his isolation were stressed to the parents and the school. It did not seem likely that the progress he had made at the hospital and special school would generalize or be maintained in the natural environment without continuing these techniques at home.

Social learning processes appear unlikely to have caused Jimmy's autistic behavior syndrome. However, the systematic application of the techniques of reinforcement, imitation learning, and procedures for the extinction of negative behaviors clearly helped Jimmy to function in a more verbally communicative and prosocial manner. With intensive effort from persons in his home environment, it is hoped that the youngster's slow but continuous progress will be sustained.

REFERENCES

Bender, L. *Child psychiatric techniques.* Springfield, Ill.: Thomas, 1952.

Ferster, C. B. Positive reinforcement and behavioral deficits of autistic children. *Child Development*, 1961, *32*, 437–456.

Hanson, D. R., & Gottesman, I. I. The genetics, if any, of infantile autism and childhood schizophrenia. *Journal of Autism and Childhood Schizophrenia*, 1976, 6, 209–234.

Kanner, L. Autistic disturbances of affective contact. *Nervous Child*, 1943, 2, 217–250.

Kanner, L. *Child psychiatry*. (4th ed.) Springfield, Ill.: Thomas, 1972.

Leon, G. R. Case report. The use of a structured mother-child interaction and projective material in studying parent influence on child behavior problems. *Journal of Clinical Psychology*, 1971, 27, 413–416.

Leon, G. R., & Morrow, V. Differing patterns of maternal behavioral control and their association with child behavior problems of an active or passive nature. *Journal Supplement Abstract Service*, 1972, 2, 136–137.

Lotter, V. Epidemiology of autistic conditions in young children. I. Prevalence. *Social Psychiatry*, 1966, 1, 124–137.

Lotter, V. Epidemiology of autistic conditions in young children. II. Some characteristics of the parents and children. *Social Psychiatry*, 1967, 1, 163–173.

Lovaas, O. I., Koegel, R., Simmons, J. Q., & Long, J. S. Some generalization and follow-up measures on autistic children in behavior therapy. *Journal of Applied Behavior Analysis*, 1973, 6, 131–166.

Mahler, M. S. On child psychosis and schizophrenia; autistic and symbiotic infantile psychosis. *Psychoanalytic Study of the Child*, 1952, 7, 286–305.

Pumroy, D., & Pumroy, S. The systematic observation and reinforcement technique in toilet training. *Psychological Reports*, 1965, 16, 467–471.

Rimland, B. *Infantile autism*. New York: Appleton-Century-Crofts, 1964.

Rutter, M., Greenfeld, D., & Lockyer, L. A five-to-fifteen-year follow-up study of infantile psychosis: II. Social and behavioural outcome. *British Journal of Psychiatry*, 1967, 113, 1183–1199.

Rutter, M., & Lockyer, L. A five-to-fifteen-year follow-up study of infantile psychosis: I. Description of sample. *British Journal of Psychiatry,* 1967, *113,* 1169–1182.

Schopler, E., & Reichler, R. J. Parents as cotherapists in the treatment of psychotic children. *Journal of Autism and Childhood Schizophrenia,* 1971, *1,* 87–102.

Walder, L. O., & Hirsch, I. Training mothers in groups as reinforcement therapists for their own child. *Proceedings of the 77 Annual Convention of the American Psychological Association,* 1969, *4,* 561–562.

Wing, L. The syndrome of early childhood autism. *British Journal of Hospital Medicine,* Sept. 1970, 381–392.

2

Habit Disturbance and Negative Behaviors—The Case of Carl Moore

Carl Moore was seven years old and in the second grade when he and his parents were initially seen at a family counseling center. They were referred to the clinic by a local physician because of problems with Carl's toilet habits: wetting his pants every day and each night, and soiling three to four times a week. The parents also reported that they felt the youngster tended to act in an effeminate manner, and that he was extremely negativistic and refused to comply with any of their requests.

Carl appeared for the initial evaluation dressed in a suit and tie, and his brown hair was neatly combed. There was nothing in his mannerisms, gait, or tone of voice indicating the effeminate behavior of which his parents complained.

The family was white and of upper middle class background. The father owned a prosperous retail store, and the Moore family lived in a large home in the suburbs.

DEVELOPMENTAL BACKGROUND

Carl was the third of five children. At the time the family was seen, Carl was seven years old, and his two older brothers, Douglas and Frank, were 13 and 12, respectively. Carl has two younger sisters, Susan, who was four, and Cathy, age one and a half.

Mrs. Moore described all of her pregnancies as difficult, but particularly so when she was pregnant with Carl. On the orders of her obstetrician, she frequently had to remain in bed for up to a week at a time because of uterine bleeding. Although this had happened an average of two or three times with the other children, Mrs. Moore estimated that she had spent a total of at least four weeks in bed during her pregnancy with Carl. There were no difficulties reported, however, during Carl's delivery and birth.

Mrs. Moore stated that after Carl's birth, she had felt tired and depressed, particularly after arguments with her husband. Both she and her husband had wanted a girl and were very disappointed when Carl was born. Mrs. Moore said that she had been more disappointed than her husband because she greatly desired to have a daughter to counteract the "male emphasis" in her home.

Carl's general developmental progress appeared normal. Mrs. Moore reported that he was a good baby and there were no special problems. He walked and spoke simple words at 9 months of age. He was bottle fed, then began to drink from a cup when he was approximately 13 months old.

The mother indicated that she began toilet training Carl when he was between 13 and 14 months old. She followed the same procedure with all of her children: she would place the youngster on a potty several times a day, stay in the room with the child when possible and read stories to him or her until either elimination occurred or the child got up from the potty and refused to sit any longer. Carl was able to remain dry during the daytime when he was about two and a half years old. He was also able to control his bowels at this time and to use the potty for elimination. Mrs. Moore reported that by three years of age, Carl was able to remain dry throughout the night.

When Carl was three years old, Susan was born. Although there was a transitory problem at this time with Carl occasionally wetting his pants during the daytime, this pattern did not persist. Mrs. Moore said that she was too busy with Susan to make a fuss the few times Carl had an "accident," so she would tell him "no, no" and help him change his pants, without too much additional comment. She did not tell Mr. Moore about the wetting episodes, since they were so infrequent and soon stopped entirely.

Carl's toilet habits reportedly remained good until Mrs. Moore started toilet training the youngest child, Cathy, about six months prior to coming to the clinic. Quite suddenly, according to Mrs. Moore, Carl started wetting his pants every day and every night during sleep. He also began having bowel movements in his pants approximately three times a week. Two episodes of wetting occurred at school, but all of the remaining times the wetting and soiling occurred when Carl was at home or outside playing. Carl showed no apparent embarrassment or discomfort and tended to ignore the situation or deny that elimination had occurred. When confronted by his mother or siblings, he frequently stated that he did not realize that he had eliminated in his pants. Mrs. Moore generally cleaned up after Carl, rather than asking him to do this for himself. Both parents tended to react to the situation by shouting at Carl and ridiculing him by calling him a baby. Often both mother and father spanked Carl in response to a wetting or soiling incident.

Carl was taken to an urologist and hospitalized for two days for tests to determine whether there might be a physical basis to his elimination difficulties. All of the tests were negative and the urologist suggested that the child be referred for psychological evaluation.

SOCIAL HISTORY

The father and mother both described their marital situation as one of frequent discord. Mr. Moore, who was in his late 30's, reported that at times his wife was openly antagonistic to him. He stated that she often tended to "put down" his accomplishments, irrespective of whether they related to his successful business or to something he had made around the house. He felt that Mrs. Moore was unwilling to give him support in any of his efforts at work or in disciplining the children.

Mrs. Moore was also in her late 30's at the time the family visited the counseling center. She stated that she felt resentful of her husband because he was seldom home, and that when he was present, he tended to interact with her and with the children in an autocratic fashion. She also reported that Mr. Moore would issue commands which he expected the family to comply with immediately, and would shout at his wife or spank the children if his orders were not carried out at once. Mrs. Moore felt that she had to take her children's side in their disputes with the father, because she judged his demands and his frequent use of physical punishment to be unreasonable.

The parents very rarely went out together on social occasions. They had few friends, and neither Mr. nor Mrs. Moore had relatives who lived in the immediate vicinity.

Both parents indicated that Carl seemed to be more of a problem than the other children. Mrs. Moore said that, until the past year, Carl had frequently provoked fights with his older brothers. These arguments usually ended with either Douglas or Frank hitting Carl, and Carl then coming to the mother in tears. Mrs. Moore usually did not intervene, but rather told the boys to settle their disputes among themselves. She reported that it was very difficult to get Carl to do the things she asked of him. Until recently, when she told him to pick up his toys or get his jacket on to go outside, he had usually said "no," and had run out of the room.

Within the year prior to the initial clinic visit, Carl's behavior pattern gradually changed. Carl did not interact with his brothers as often as he had previously. He also lessened his defiant behavior in relation to maternal requests. Mrs. Moore related that Carl's usual response when she asked him to do something had now become one of noncompliance rather than overt opposition. When asked to perform a household chore such as making his bed or straightening up the family room, Carl never said "no," but he somehow never got around to doing what was asked of him either. He would continue to say "in a minute" or he would disappear to some other part of the house. Eventually, Mrs. Moore ended up doing the job herself, or occasionally she asked one of the older boys to do the chore instead. Mrs. Moore would often complain about Carl's behavior to the father, but then would step in to protect Carl when his father began spanking him.

Mrs. Moore felt that Douglas and Frank were on the whole more cooperative than Carl. She did report, however, that at times Douglas and Frank were defiant of her requests. The mother responded to this by threatening to tell their father when he got home. If Mr. Moore found out about the episode, he would then administer physical punishment to either Douglas or Frank. Mrs. Moore did not tend to intercede in this punishment as much as she did with Carl.

The mother stated that it was easier dealing with Douglas and Frank than with Carl because at least she knew where she stood with the two older boys. If she asked Douglas or Frank to do something they did not want to do, they would just tell her "no," instead of saying nothing and disappearing, as was Carl's pattern. The two older boys, however, usually tended to comply with the mother's requests. Douglas' and Frank's chief area of conflict in interpersonal relationships appeared to be their aggressive interactions with Carl.

Susan and Cathy seemed to have a much more positive relationship with their parents. Four-year-old Susan was described by both Mr.

and Mrs. Moore as "not too much of a problem." The mother expressed satisfaction that she had given birth to a daughter, after having three boys in a row. Mr. Moore also stated that he was pleased to have a daughter. Because Susan was so much easier to care for after the difficulties with the boys and particularly Carl, the parents were also pleased with the birth of their youngest daughter, Cathy.

Susan tended to comply with the mother's requests and received a great deal of praise from Mrs. Moore for acting like a "good girl," rather than noisy or rowdy like the boys. Mr. and Mrs. Moore frequently commented on how cute and lady-like Susan acted. The mother reported that she rarely had to   l at Susan to get her to obey, and Mr. Moore could remember only two incidents when he had spanked her. Both situations, as described by Mr. Moore, involved episodes where Susan began hitting her younger sister, Cathy. The mother corroborated these events. She stated that she had witnessed the situations and had interceded at the time the dispute took place and had made Susan stop. The mother did not administer a spanking but waited and told the events to Mr. Moore who then spanked Susan.

Cathy was one and a half, "into everything" in the house, and in need of a great deal of supervision because she was so active. Mrs. Moore frequently asked Carl to watch Cathy to see that she did not get into trouble. Carl seemed to enjoy being with Cathy and Susan rather than with his older brothers.

Mrs. Moore began toilet training Cathy six months prior to the clinic visit. She would place Cathy on the potty, and then sometimes read to her for 15 or 20 minutes in hopes that she would eliminate while her mother interested her in a story. Although Cathy was active at other times, she sat quietly on the potty while Mrs. Moore was there with her and reading to her. As soon as Mrs. Moore left the room, Cathy would also get up and walk out of the bathroom. Toilet training had not as yet been accomplished.

Carl's brothers presently refused to play with Carl because he "acted like a sissy or a girl," and because he wasn't interested in sports or rough and competitive games. Carl enjoyed playing house with his sister Susan, and frequently assumed the role of mother or female teacher in their games of pretend. Carl did not have any male friends at school or in the neighborhood. His only friend was a neighborhood girl a few months older than he was.

During the period when Carl began to have problems with elimination, his brothers were quite hostile to him. They tended to ridicule him until he started to cry, or else they refused to interact with him in any manner. The parents did not usually respond to the teasing, except at times to agree with what the brothers were saying. Susan also began to make fun of Carl and call him "stupid" and "baby," and played with him much less than she used to. The only family member with whom Carl seemed to have a warm relationship was one and a half year old Cathy. Although he occasionally teased her, on the whole he appeared to enjoy playing with her. Carl and Cathy played together with blocks and dolls, and he also would gently push her on a small bike or help her ride on a rocking horse.

The effeminate behavior that the parents complained of seemed related primarily to Carl's choice of female playmates and his preference for quiet fantasy games, particularly those in which he could play a feminine role. Mrs. Moore tended to respond with amusement to Carl's feminine role play activity, although she also stated that Carl was acting like a sissy. The mother encouraged Carl to play with Cathy because this gave her more free time, since Cathy was so active and in need of almost continuous supervision. Mr. Moore usually responded to Carl's play activity with ridicule, much as Douglas and Frank did. However, Mr. Moore did not tend to encourage Carl to play more active or competitive games, and Carl rarely went with his father to any sporting events. Occasionally, Mr. Moore would take Douglas and Frank to a baseball game, but when he asked Carl if he wanted to go too, Carl would always say "no." Mr. Moore did not attempt to persuade Carl to change his mind. As the elimination problem continued, Mr. Moore stopped asking Carl to accompany him anywhere, although he still took the older boys with him from time to time.

PSYCHOLOGICAL EVALUATION

Carl was given a battery of psychological tests in order to gain more information about the nature of his difficulties. He was seen by a male psychologist who introduced himself to Carl and his mother in the waiting room. The youngster accompanied the examiner to the testing room, but only after he had gained information about exactly where his mother would be while he was being tested. Carl did not attempt to converse with the psychologist either while walking down the corridor, or in the testing room. He answered the examiner's questions in a very brief manner and seldom looked directly at him. Carl spoke in a soft voice and did not make any attempts to explore the room or ask questions about the various testing materials. There were no indications of effeminate behavior.

Carl's performance on an intelligence test administered to him indicated that his overall intellectual functioning was in the bright normal range. There was some discrepancy between the relatively higher scores he gained on the subscales measuring verbal ability and abstract reasoning, and the relatively lower scores he received on the subscales measuring coordination and the ability to use concepts dealing with spatial relationships. His relatively higher performance in the verbal area was probably reflective of an interest pattern involving school work, reading, and fantasy play, rather than one of interest and experience in manipulating tools or building objects.

Carl was asked to make up stories from cards in the Tasks of Emotional Development (TED) series. Each of these cards shows a scene involving peers or family members in some type of interaction. The cards are moderately ambiguous in that there are a number of different descriptions that an individual can give for what appears to be happening in the card scene. The traditional rationale for using cards of this type is that when confronted with an ambiguous situation where there are no clear cut right or wrong answers, the individual will "project" his own needs and problems into the responses he gives to the test stimuli (Murray, 1933). The cards can also be interpreted as providing information about current social interaction patterns.

Carl did not reply as rapidly to the cards as he had to the intelligence test material. He repeatedly asked if he could switch to other tasks, and he gave quite short descriptions to a number of cards presented to him. He also indicated that he could not think of anything to say on three of the cards presented. Several of the story themes elicited from Carl involved passive noncompliant behavior directed toward the parents. Other stories centered on rivalry among siblings for the parent's affection and attention.

The passive noncompliant interactions which Carl related on some of the card stories tended to be quite similar to the type of behavior the mother complained about in her interview with the social worker. Carl told a story about a child being asked by his mother to clean his room. The child continually told his mother "later," and never actually carried out this chore. This story was very much like a real life incident that his mother had related.

The stories Carl gave were quite sparse and matter-of-fact in light of his bright normal intellectual ability and his relative superiority in the verbal area. The psychologist concluded that Carl was inhibited in expressing any type of emotion, and that the youngster was uncomfortable in situations where he was not sure exactly what was expected of him. At these times, Carl apparently tried to respond in as minimal a fashion as possible.

THE OBSERVED INTERACTION

Mrs. Moore and Carl entered the playroom together, and both listened as the psychologist explained the procedure for the structured interaction.

During the ten minute free play period, Mrs. Moore sat in a chair and watched Carl's play activities. Carl looked about the room and picked up a toy gun. He held it for a moment, then put it down and started looking through a box with small toys in it. The youngster occasionally picked up a play object such as an animal puppet or toy accordian and showed it to his mother, commenting "look at this," or "this is neat." Mrs. Moore's response was a short "hmm." She tended to ignore the child's presence, and communication between the two was quite limited. There were only a few times during the free play period when she conversed with Carl. In one of these instances, she told him to speak more quietly when he started to comment in a loud tone of voice about his success in shooting darts from a dart gun. Mrs. Moore also told Carl he was becoming too noisy when he began hitting an inflated clown and saying "pow" with each hit. Carl did not play with the doll house or with any of the dolls in the room.

At the signal that the free play period was over, Carl and his mother began working on the questionnaire. Mrs. Moore asked each question in a matter-of-fact tone of voice, and wrote down Carl's responses. A number of times she disagreed with an answer Carl gave. For example, in response to the question "What do you usually do if you are the first one up in the morning?", Carl said, "play downstairs, until everyone else is up." Mrs. Moore said, "No, you don't. You start making noise and wake everybody up." She then proceeded to write down what she said rather than what Carl had said.

Following completion of the questionnaire, mother and child worked together on a jigsaw puzzle. Although instructed to work together cooperatively, Mrs. Moore set about doing the puzzle by herself. Carl literally had to grab pieces of the puzzle out of his mother's hands in order to complete the part of the puzzle he was working on. When finished, Mrs. Moore commented approvingly on her own performance, but ignored the work done by her son.

The final activity was the basket puzzle. In order to successfully finish this task, the child has to hold a wire basket completely steady while the mother threads some rods through the mesh and bolts them in place. Carl held the basket reasonably steady, but complained a number of times that he was getting tired of just standing there. Mrs. Moore ignored these comments and firmly told Carl to hold the basket up when Carl changed position while standing. Mrs. Moore again expressed satisfaction about her own performance when the task was finished, but failed to comment on her son's role in helping her.

In general, Mrs. Moore tended to ignore any questions Carl asked her, or said, "I don't know," irrespective of whether these questions pertained to the play materials, activities mentioned on the questionnaire, or clinic procedures. The mother manifested either neutral or negative affect in her interactions with Carl, and Carl in turn tended to exhibit a pattern of passive complaints rather than open defiance of his mother's commands.

COURSE OF PSYCHOTHERAPY

Mr. and Mrs. Moore were seen together in counseling sessions once a week. Carl was also seen weekly in play therapy with a male therapist. The choice of a male therapist for Carl was based on the notion that he needed a warm and accepting male figure with whom to identify.

Carl had participated in nineteen play therapy sessions when treatment was recessed for the summer vacation. At the end of this time period, the therapist felt that Carl had made substantial progress in becoming more open and expressive in his play activities and in his relationship with the therapist. The therapist reported that Carl was able to handle competition more adequately by the end of the year; he no longer insisted on winning every game played. The youngster continued to express to the therapist his liking for school because in this situation he knew that there was a definite right or wrong answer. Carl felt that in his relationships with people, much of the time he was not sure how to behave.

An initial counseling plan had involved helping the parents set up a behavior modification program for dealing with Carl's elimination problems. However, the parents reported some difficulty in observing and tallying specific behaviors, and the behavior modification procedure was temporarily suspended. The Moores tended to spend more time talking about their own personal and marital problems than they spent talking about their children's problems. This was encouraged by their therapist under the assumption that many of Carl's difficulties derived from his parents' interpersonal difficulties. At the end of the first year of treatment, the parents reported that Carl still soiled and wet his pants, and that they were still unable to handle his negativistic behavior. The parents seemed to accept the observation made early in therapy that Carl's problem was not one of effeminacy as much as one of difficulty in engaging in competitive activity. They were told that these problems would be dealt with in play therapy. The issue of effeminacy as a problem in and of itself was not brought up again by the Moores.

Carl and his parents returned for a second year of therapy. The same social worker continued to see the parents, while a female therapist now saw Carl weekly in play therapy. The play therapy sessions still revolved around the theme of competition, with Carl beginning to express a concern about accidents happening, and how one cannot always control the things that happen in life. Carl's relationship with the female therapist was quite mixed. He frequently insisted to his parents that he did not want to come to the clinic, although once there, he appeared to enjoy the sessions.

During the second year of therapy, the parents were given more specific instructions about how to use behavior modification procedures to lessen the frequency of soiling and wetting. There was a marked decrease in this problem once positive reinforcement was systematically used whenever elimination occurred in the toilet. The parents also focused more specifically on their reactions to Carl's negative behavior. They began to give him more social approval and attention for positive behaviors, rather than berating him for acting in a nonassertive manner, or allowing him to get involved in some other activity before he completed a job asked of him. However, the bulk of the sessions with the parents continued to be a discussion of their own personal difficulties.

After two years of treatment, the Moores felt that some progress had been made in helping Carl with his problems. They decided that they would like to try to deal with the family situation without outside help. The social worker and psychologist concurred, and therapy was terminated at this point.

DISCUSSION

There are a number of elements which influence whether a given behavior pattern is labeled as a problem, or as abnormal behavior. Ullmann and Krasner (1969) have defined deviant behavior as a function of the behavior itself, the social context in which the particular behavior occurs, and the presence of an agent of society who observes the behavior and performs the labeling.

The parental complaint that Carl behaved in an effeminate manner can be analyzed in relation to this social labeling process. Carl manifested an interest pattern that involved a preference for quiet, noncompetitive games, an enjoyment in playing house and at times playing the part of the mother, and a preference for female rather than male companions. Most parents would probably tolerate these behaviors for a time in a three year old boy. They would also not become too concerned if these play behaviors occurred infrequently, perhaps in a social context where the youngster could not find anyone else in the neighborhood to play with other than his sisters or female peers. However, at some point related to the age of the child and the pervasiveness of this behavior in many different types of social situations, the parents, older siblings, and perhaps a teacher as well applies the label "effeminate" or "sissyish" to this behavior. The behavior is then considered abnormal.

An issue worth pursuing is whether Carl's play interests were a reflection of an attempt to resolve the Oedipus complex by assuming a feminine identification, or whether Carl enjoyed quiet play activities with girls because he had found this type of behavior reinforcing in the past. The Oedipus complex is a Freudian concept suggesting that the boy between the ages of three to six is torn by sexual strivings for the mother and intense hostility and fear of the father. The father is seen as a strong and threatening competitor for the mother's love, and therefore someone who could harm the youngster if he continues to strive for the mother's affection.

A psychoanalytic analysis of Carl's difficulties might suggest that because the father was so competitive and castrating in his interactions with his son, Carl was unable to resolve the Oedipus complex by identifying with the father-aggressor. As a result, he was not able to achieve a masculine identification. The youngster found it safer to stop competing with the father for the mother's love, and he therefore assumed a feminine, noncompetitive behavior pattern through identifying with the inconsistently protective mother.

A social learning analysis of the same situation would explore the particular patterns of interaction that occurred in Carl's life experiences, in order to find out why playing with girls in noncompetitive situations was such a highly reinforcing activity. From Carl's social history, we learned that he had two older brothers who were quite active and fairly aggressive in their interactions with him. Carl attempted to model his behavior after that of his brothers and to act in an assertive or aggressive manner. However, this behavior was not reinforced because his brothers were able to maintain a dominant role through their greater physical strength. When Carl tried to compete with them, they taunted him and called him "sissy," or if he cried when they hit him, they called him "cry baby."

Frank and Douglas showed discrimination learning in their aggressive behavior toward different family members. They learned that if they were defiant of parental requests they would be punished, but if they aggressed against Carl nothing would happen. Carl, on the other hand, was punished by his brothers and received no support from his mother when he interacted aggressively with Frank and Douglas. Carl was also unsuccessful in acting aggressively with other boys his own age. Further, if he aggressed against Cathy or Susan, he was punished by his father. The discrimination training that Carl received was that he would not be rewarded for acting in an aggressive manner, but that reinforcement could occur when behaving nonaggressively.

Carl did not experience a consistently warm or supportive relationship with either of his parents. Mrs. Moore tended to intercede when her husband began spanking Carl, after she had complained about Carl's behavior. From Carl's point of view, his mother was therefore both a source of punishment and a source of gratification. The Observed Interaction showed that the mother also interacted in either an indifferent or competitive manner with Carl. She did not allow him the satisfaction of mastering the puzzle they were working on together, nor did she either praise him or show an interest in any of his activities in the playroom.

Carl's relationship with his father was also quite mixed. Mr. Moore spent very little time at home with his children when Carl was growing up. His primary role seemed to be that of punisher for the daily transgressions of the children. Mrs. Moore set her husband up in this role by presenting a chronicle of the children's misdeeds to him upon his arrival at home, with the expectation that he would deal with these problems by physically punishing the wrongdoers. The mother therefore transformed the father's arrival home into an extremely aversive event for the children. Mr. Moore concurred with this arrangement, and as a result, his presence frequently was an unpleasant stimulus for the children.

In contrast to his own situation, Carl was able to observe the parents' more positive behavior in relation to his younger sisters. His sister Susan was praised for acting like a "good girl" and the parents gave her a great deal of social approval for showing traditional feminine interests and for acting in a nonaggressive manner. When Carl played quiet games with his sister, he did not get into any difficulties with his mother, and therefore avoided being punished by the father. His mother also encouraged him to keep his youngest sister amused. It was only after this behavioral pattern had become established for some time that the parents labeled Carl's behavior as "effeminate," "sissyish," or "babyish." It is clear, however, the Carl was avoiding punishment and gaining reinforcement for acting in this way.

The question arises as to whether or not Carl's "effeminate" behavior should have been modified. The definition of what is acceptable masculine and feminine behavior in a given society is strongly determined by the sexual role stereotypes of that society. In our culture, the stereotype of masculine behavior does not include an acceptance of boys showing interest in dolls, playing house, or acting in a submissive manner. This type of behavior, however, does conform to the traditional stereotype of appropriate feminine behavior.

The judgment of the professional persons dealing with the Moore family was that it was not their function to change Carl's behavior to conform to a masculine sexual stereotype that does not allow for growth and free expression (Friedan, 1963; Greer, 1971). Rather, it seemed more appropriate to help Carl to have greater flexibility in his relationships with others, by teaching him the social skills necessary to interact with male peers in the more traditional male-oriented games. However, it seemed important to encourage him to feel that he was not a sissy if he played with girls at times. Since acting in a submissive, nonassertive manner in all social situations is not helpful for personality development, it was felt that Carl should be reinforced for acting in a more assertive manner. The counseling sessions with the parents that related to Carl's play interests did not focus on changing "effeminate" behavior, but dealt with how to help provide Carl with alternative ways of behaving.

Carl's elimination problems appeared when his mother started toilet training his youngest sister. Although nocturnal enuresis is not uncommon in seven year olds, daytime wetting and bowel incontinence at this age are more infrequent and traditionally have been considered a manifestation of a psychotic or prepsychotic process (Ginott and Harms, 1965). In Carl's case, psychological testing plus two years of play therapy failed to reveal an underlying thought disturbance or severe pathology.

Carl was able to observe that his sister, during the process of her toilet training, was gaining a great deal of attention fron the mother. Mrs. Moore read stories to Cathy and entertained her as long as she remained on the potty. The mother was expressing a great deal of interest in her daughter's eliminative functions, and this occurred at a time when Carl was receiving very little social approval for any of his behavior. Although Carl had several incontinent episodes prior to the present situation, Mrs. Moore did not reinforce these occurrences with negative attention, and the elimination problem stopped. Carl's incontinence at the time of Cathy's toilet training served the function of diverting a great deal of attention to him. Negative attention was more reinforcing than just being ignored by the family. The fact that the elimination problems continued for almost a year and a half suggests that Carl was able to gain very little positive reinforcement or social approval at home for engaging in other types of behaviors. A dramatic decrease in incontinence occurred only when the parents consistently began a behavior modification program aimed at rewarding Carl for eliminating in the appropriate place. Most important, they also learned to give him social approval for positive behaviors that had previously gone unnoticed.

The negativism that the parents complained about when they brought Carl for evaluation was related to the nonassertive behavioral pattern the youngster adopted. When his mother asked him to make his bed and he said "no!", he was inviting punishment. If he continued to respond "in a minute" each time his mother asked, quite often nothing would happen. In the counseling sessions, the parents began to learn how to set limits so that they were not reinforcing noncompliance, and at the same time, they were also taught to give Carl social approval for acting in a positive manner.

The method of treatment used in this case is worthy of discussion. The author does not agree that play therapy in a clinic setting is the treatment of choice for youngsters with behavioral-emotional difficulties. The process of a therapist seeing a child once a week and then returning him to an essentially unchanged home environment appears to be an ineffective treatment plan. Even though the parents were also being seen, the sessions with the parents during the first year of treatment were devoted primarily to their own marital problems, rather than to how their marital problems affected their interrelationships with their youngsters.

In the author's opinion, a more effective treatment strategy would have involved not seeing the child at all, but working intensively with the parents. The latter could then have been helped to understand the reinforcement contingencies operating in the home, i.e., which behaviors they were reinforcing through attention and social approval and how these reinforcement patterns shaped the types of behaviors in which their children were engaging. By dealing with the parents, one might have avoided the remission of elimination problems that occurred when Carl found out that the play therapy was to be discontinued. A number of studies with parents of neurotic and psychotic children have shown that the parent can be an effective therapist in modifying the problem behaviors of the child (Bijou, 1965; Wahler, Winkel, Peterson, and Morrison, 1965; Zeilberger, Sampen, and Sloane, 1968).

Many times parents receiving counseling for their children will bring up episodes from their own past or from their present life situation. For therapy to be most effective, the therapist should help the parents to relate these episodes to current problems with their child. The focus of the sessions is then on the child's behavioral difficulties. The therapist is in a position to suggest to the parents alternative ways of responding, and the therapist can socially reinforce the parents for changing their behavior with the child and with each other. The parents will also be reinforced when they change their typical response patterns to the problem child, by the positive changes they observe in the child. The child thus becomes more of an agent of gratification to the parents than he was before. In Carl's case, as the parents began to notice and reinforce the more socially acceptable behaviors that he engaged in, he began to be more likeable to them. They in turn were able to respond to him in a more loving way than they had previously, and the parents also began to be more aware of the feelings and behaviors of their marital partner. The entire emotional tone of the interactions began to change, and it was the parents, with the therapist's help, who were able to begin modifying the problem behaviors of their child.

Ideally, the role of the therapist vis à vis the parents should be one of an educator, rather than a curer (Guerney, Stollak, and Guerney, 1971). Hopefully, the lessons that the parents learn on how to handle problem behaviors in one child will generalize to their relationships with their other children. In order to accomplish this goal, it is important for the therapist to continue to focus on the role of the parents in the development of behavioral difficulties in the child, and on how the parents can modify the child's problem behavior. A model of the therapist as a teacher, rather than a curer of the sick, seems most appropriate to this conception of the therapeutic process.

REFERENCES

Bijou, S. W. Experimental studies of child behavior: normal and deviant. In L. Krasner & L. P. Ullmann (Eds.), Research in behavior modification. New York: Holt, Rinehart & Winston, 1965. Pp. 56–81.

Friedan, B. The feminine mystique. New York: Dell Publishing Co., 1963.

Ginott, H., & Harms, E. Mental disorders in childhood. In B. B. Wolman (Ed.), Handbook of clinical psychology. New York: McGraw-Hill, 1965. Pp. 1094–1118.

Greer, G. The female eunuch. New York: McGraw-Hill, 1971.

Guerney, B., Stollak, G., & Guerney, L. The practicing psychologist as educator—an alternative to the medical practitioner model. Professional Psychology, 1971, 2, 276–282.

Murray, H. A. The effect of fear upon estimates of the maliciousness of adult personalities. Journal of Social Psychology, 1933, 4, 310–329.

Ullman, L. P., & Krasner, L. A psychological approach to abnormal behavior. Englewood Cliffs, N.J.: Prentice-Hall, 1969.

Wahler, R. C., Winkel, G. H., Peterson, R. F., & Morrison, D. C. Mothers as behavior therapists for their own children. Behavior Research and Therapy, 1965, 3, 113–134.

Zeilberger, J., Sampen, S. E., & Sloane, H. N., Jr. Modification of a child's problem behaviors in the home with the mother as therapist. Journal of Applied Behavior Analysis, 1968, 1, 47–53.

3

Minimal Brain Damage— The Interaction of Processes of an Organic and Social Nature

Beth Goldberg was five and a half years old when her parents brought her to a local guidance clinic for evaluation. The parents complained of difficulty in disciplining the child, and now that the youngster was enrolled in kindergarten, the teacher was also having disciplinary problems. The kindergarten teacher reported to the parents that Beth was easily distracted, inattentive, and hyperactive. The teacher also noticed a number of visual-motor difficulties suggestive of a possible perceptual problem. At the teacher's suggestion, the parents made an appointment at the guidance clinic.

The Goldberg family was white and of lower middle-class background. At the time of evaluation, the father was employed as the manager of a service station. The family owned a small three-bedroom home, where Beth shared a room with her four-year-old sister. The youngest member of the family was a brother, who at the time was one and a half years old.

DEVELOPMENTAL HISTORY

Mrs. Goldberg reported that her pregnancy with Beth was uneventful and that she felt quite well during this time. The period of labor and

43

delivery, however, was extremely difficult. The labor lasted a duration of approximately twenty hours, and forceps were used to deliver the child. When Beth was born, the umbilical cord was wrapped around her neck, and the obstetrician's report indicated that the youngster was slightly blue in color, indicating anoxia (lack of oxygen). The infant was placed under intensive care for the first 48 hours of life. No other symptoms occurred, and the parents were able to bring Beth home from the hospital on the fifth day. Mrs. Goldberg stated that there were no unusual circumstances during the pregnancy and birth of the other two children.

A report from the pediatrician noted that the youngster had shown continual developmental progress, but at a slower than average rate. Beth was not able to sit unaided until she was 9 months old, and she began crawling at 13 months of age. The onset of walking was at 19 months, also somewhat later than average. Beth spoke single words at 20 months and did not speak in sentences until she was approximately 2 years and 9 months old. At the time of evaluation, her speech occasionally tended to be difficult to understand. Beth was bottle fed until 13 months of age, and according to her mother, toilet training was completed with great difficulty when the child was 3 years old. Mrs. Goldberg indicated that Beth still wet her bed at night on occasion, but this did not occur very frequently.

When Beth was 2 years old, there were four different episodes when she fell on her head. These events occurred over a two month period, and she reportedly landed on her brow each time. On the first occasion, she fell out of a shopping cart at the supermarket and the other times she fell down stairs or off a chair at home. Beth did not lose consciousness, nor did she have any long term symptoms after these falls. She was taken to her pediatrician when she fell out of the shopping cart, and the pediatrician reported that there was no evidence of a concussion. The child has not had any episodes of high fever, convulsions, or severe illness.

SOCIAL HISTORY

Beth was the result of a planned pregnancy. Her parents indicated that they had been hoping for a boy, but were no more than momentarily disappointed with the birth of a daughter. Their major concern immediately after the youngster's birth was whether or not she had been harmed by the difficult labor and delivery. When Beth responded well in the hospital, and the parents were able to take her home at the usual time, the parents were reassured that she was unharmed. The pediatrician felt that Beth had overcome the difficulties experienced at birth, and he saw no evidence of impairment at that time.

As Beth grew older, her development was somewhat slower than average, but was not grossly retarded. The parents were not unduly concerned, because there was continuing evidence of developmental progress. Since Beth was the first born, there were no other children to compare her with for the first year and a half of her life. As the eldest, Beth had always been ahead of her siblings in overall progress.

Mrs. Goldberg reported that Karen, who is 1½ years younger than Beth, appeared to be catching up with Beth in ability. Karen had begun to recognize and copy letters, and was able to catch a ball, tie her shoes, and build objects with blocks at least as well as Beth.

The parents related that they were extremely pleased when their son Harmon was born, because they had greatly desired to have a boy. The youngster was one and a half at the time of the interview, and the parents stated that he was a special delight. They indicated that they tended to focus a great deal of attention on him, perhaps at times to the exclusion of the two older daughters.

Mrs. Goldberg felt that her chief problem with Beth was that her daughter would not cooperate with her. She stated that it was very difficult to get Beth to follow any instructions, and spankings and shouting appeared to have no effect. Mrs. Goldberg reported that Beth had frequent temper tantrums characterized by screaming and kicking her feet and occasionally holding her breath. The mother felt that these episodes occurred primarily when she insisted that Beth do something that the youngster did not want to do, such as pick up her toys, put her coat on by herself, or refrain from fighting with one of the other children. Mrs. Goldberg's response to Beth's tantrums was to threaten to spank her, or yell at her to stop. Beth usually ignored her mother's threats, so eventually she did receive a spanking.

The mother indicated that she became very exasperated because Beth was so active and constantly running around the house. When Beth played outside, Mrs. Goldberg said that she had to be constantly alert as to Beth's whereabouts, because she never played in one place for any length of time. Mrs. Goldberg complained of Beth's inability to sustain play activity, whether inside the house or outside, for more than a few minutes at a time. According to the mother, Beth quickly tired of whatever activity she was involved in, and would then begin doing something else. As a result, there was a constant litter of toys that Beth had scattered about and which she refused to pick up.

Mr. Goldberg indicated regret that he could not spend more time at home with his family than he did. His job required long working hours, and many times when he was short of help, he worked seven days a week. When he got home, he often was too tired to interact with the children for any length of time. The parents stated that their marital relationship was harmonious, although Mr. Goldberg's long working hours left little opportunity to do things together. Both parents agreed that the primary responsibility for disciplining the children rested with the mother. Mr. Goldberg said that he reprimanded or spanked Beth occasionally if his wife indicated that Beth had been particularly difficult and destructive with some toys or household objects.

Mrs. Goldberg felt that most of her interactions with Beth were unpleasant. She said that because Beth was so active, the youngster was constantly getting into trouble. Therefore, the mother was required to continually discipline her so that she did not get completely out of control. Mrs. Goldberg also stated that she had a constant fear that Beth would be kidnapped, because Beth showed as much friendliness to strangers as to people she knew. Beth did not appear to be shy or inhibited in the presence of persons she did not know, but would start talking to anyone.

Mrs. Goldberg explained that there was a great deal of friction between Beth and her sister Karen. Karen was beginning to become more assertive, and there were frequent fights between the two girls. These disputes were usually about toys that both children wanted to play with or different programs that each wanted to watch on television. Karen would not follow Beth's directions and Beth then resorted to hitting Karen. Karen's customary response was to come crying to her mother. Mrs. Goldberg usually handled the situation by intervening and letting Karen get her way, on the assumption that Beth was older and therefore should be more responsible. Both girls were punished if they interfered with their brother's activities or disturbed him when he was sleeping. Mrs. Goldberg felt that on the whole, Karen was much more likely than Beth to mind her, and Karen seemed to enjoy playing with Harmon more than Beth did.

Although there were a number of children in the neighborhood who were Beth's age, Beth usually played alone. She tended to play with other youngsters for short periods of time, but then would often get into a fight with one of them. Beth's response to the dispute was to wander off by herself and engage in some other activity.

SCHOOL PROGRESS

Beth had been attending kindergarten for four months prior to the clinic evaluation. Her teacher noticed that the child was having trouble performing tasks that most five-year-olds were able to do quite easily. For example, Beth found it extremely difficult to cut out figures from a sheet of paper and paste them in a given manner on another piece of paper. The youngster's drawing skills were also well below her age level, as was her ability to build objects with blocks or copy letters or numbers with some degree of accuracy. When the teacher tried to help Beth after she performed poorly on a task, Beth usually walked away.

The teacher reported that Beth was overactive, constantly distracted, and unable to maintain one activity for an extended period of time. She also noted that Beth tended to run into or over objects that were in her way. The teacher suggested to the parents that the youngster be taken for a psychological evaluation in order to gain more information about the nature of her difficulties at school. The teacher thought that it might be advisable to place Beth in a special class in first grade, but that decision would not be made until the outcome of the evaluation was known.

Both parents were quite concerned about the problems their daughter was having in kindergarten and immediately followed through with the teacher's suggestion that Beth be taken for a psychological evaluation. The parents also took Beth for an eye examination, and the ophthalmologist indicated that Beth's vision was normal for her age.

PSYCHOLOGICAL EVALUATION

Beth was an active, neatly dressed youngster with brown hair and eyes, who appeared to be somewhat small for her age. She separated easily from her mother and walked with the psychologist to the testing room. Dr. S. offered Beth his hand as the two of them walked down the corridor, and she readily held his hand and talked to him. The youngster did not ask any questions about where her mother would be while she was being seen.

Upon entering the testing room, Beth immediately began to pick up objects lying on the shelf and started to look at the materials in some of the boxes. Dr. S. asked Beth to sit in a chair next to the table, and she sat down for a moment, but then got up and came over to stand next to the examiner. The psychologist against asked Beth to go back to her seat, so they could begin the first of the activities they would be working on together. Beth complied with his request.

There were two testing sessions with Dr. S., and on both occasions, Beth tended to manifest a short attention span. She quickly lost interest in one task and would begin to ask questions about something else. She was easily distracted, in that any noise extraneous to the testing room commanded her immediate interest and attention. Subsequent to the distraction, it was difficult for the examiner to get Beth to divert her attention back to the task that she was working on. The youngster also tended to get up and wander around the room quite frequently, and a number of times asked to leave the room to get some water or to go to the bathroom. Her speech was generally intelligible.

Dr. S. conversed with Beth and gave her a number of tests in order to gain more information about her difficulties. Some of the hypotheses he wished to evaluate were the possibility of mental retardation, neurological impairment, maturational lag, or problems resulting from social-behavioral factors.

The results of an intelligence test indicated that Beth was functioning at a mental age level of 4 years, 1 month. This was approximately a year and a half below her chronological age, and technically placed her at a borderline level of functioning. However, her performance revealed a great deal of scatter, i.e., she failed some items that were easy for her age, while she passed other, more difficult items. Beth performed at her age level on the vocabulary subtest and on questions dealing with the ability to form verbal concepts. Her performance, however, was much weaker on those items involving perceptual or motor skills. Beth had trouble with tasks such as stringing beads in a particular pattern or order, recognizing geometric figures, and remembering and being able to describe objects that were no longer in front of her.

The youngster also manifested an inability to visualize objects in space and execute tasks involving fine motor coordination. For example, when Beth was asked to draw some pictures of various persons, she was unable to draw a closed circle for the head, and she drew arms and legs that were joined at inappropriate places to the body. She wrote her name with the letter "B" reversed, and she wrote the letter "A" upside down. Dr. S. noted that Beth's gross motor coordination in tasks such as walking and reaching for objects was adequate for her age, but she consistently had difficulty when fine motor skills were called for. Her performance on these tasks was below her age level. An example of the problem with fine motor coordination was Beth's inability to place a small doll on a toy chair without the doll falling off.

Beth's response to the Tasks of Emotional Development (TED) cards revealed expressions of sibling rivalry, and also feelings of worthlessness because of a perceived lack of ability to do the tasks expected of her. The youngster pictured the mother on the cards as always angry because of demanding something the child was not able to do.

In light of the youngster's case history, distractibility, poor attention span, and visual motor problems, she was diagnosed as minimally brain damaged. Mental retardation and maturational lag were ruled out due to the fact that Beth's disability was not consistent in all areas of functioning, and because she possessed verbal comprehension commensurate with her age level. Her emotional difficulties seemed in large part a reaction to her frustration at being unable to perform certain tasks as well as those persons around her expected her to. The negativistic behavior that the parents and teacher complained of was probably due to an inability to comprehend instructions, as well as fear of failure.

NEUROLOGICAL EXAMINATION

A neurological consultation was obtained at the time of the clinic evaluation. The neurologist reported that Beth's electroencephalogram (EEG) was normal for her age level. There was no evidence of generalized irregularities in brain functioning nor of any abnormality localized in a specific area of the brain. Reflex development and motor coordination were below age level, but were not grossly abnormal. The neurologist noted the difficulty in fine motor coordination and the perceptual problems, and on this basis, agreed with the diagnosis of minimal brain damage.

THE OBSERVED INTERACTION

Beth and her mother entered the playroom and Mrs. Goldberg listened as the psychologist described the interaction procedure. Beth immediately began to explore the room and enthusiastically commented on the toys she found. Her exclamations did not appear to be directed to either her mother or Dr. S. After several minutes, Mrs. Goldberg firmly told Beth to be quiet so that she could hear what Dr. S. was saying. Beth continued to handle the toys in the room, but did not speak as loudly as before.

The youngster spent the entire free play period wandering from one toy or game to the next, and she did not play with any particular object for longer than a few minutes. Her play activity took on a pattern of looking at the pieces of a game such as a checker set, and then moving the pieces around in the box. With each succeeding motion, the pieces banged together harder and harder, until eventually some fell on the floor. Beth then left this game and walked over and looked at another object. The youngster briefly handled some puppets and then later a dart gun, but did not play with these toys in any way other than by holding them in her hand or banging them on the table. Beth punched the inflated clown a number of times and laughed as the clown moved back and forth. However, it was difficult for Beth to accurately aim at the clown and hit it, unless she stood quite close to it.

There was virtually no verbal communication between mother and child during the free play period. Beth laughed and made comments throughout the time interval, but these comments did not seem to be directed to her mother. Mrs. Goldberg did not react verbally to the content of what Beth was saying, and the youngster did not ask her mother any questions. Mrs. Goldberg sat in a chair next to the table and silently watched what Beth was doing. When Beth's exclamations or play activity became too loud, Mrs. Goldberg said "shh," or "You're making too much noise," and Beth responded by lowering her voice level for a while.

Mrs. Goldberg called Beth over to the table when the free play period ended. Beth complied, listened to her mother's instructions for filling out the questionnaire, and then got up from the table and began playing with a toy telephone. Mrs. Goldberg again told Beth to sit down, and the youngster returned to her chair for a moment but then got up once more. Mrs. Goldberg repeated her statement that Beth sit down, and Beth said "no." The mother got up from her chair, took the child by the hand, and brought her back to the table. She then asked Beth for an answer to the first questionnaire item. Beth replied, and while Mrs. Goldberg was writing down the answer, the youngster got up and looked in the sink. Mrs. Goldberg did not ask Beth to sit down again while they were working on the questionnaire, but directed the remaining questions to wherever Beth happened to be at the moment. Beth answered the questions asked of her, and the few times she said "I don't know," her mother accepted this answer and wrote it down. Beth sat down at her mother's request when the latter put the picture puzzle on the table. Mrs. Goldberg explained to Beth that the two of them had to solve the puzzle together. Beth held some of the pieces in her hand and pushed other pieces around on the table, but did not attempt to join any of the parts. Her mother did not repeat the instructions to Beth nor did she demonstrate how the pieces should fit together. Mrs. Goldberg began working on the puzzle herself, and did not say anything when Beth left the table. The mother continued working alone until the puzzle was completed.

Mrs. Goldberg then got up from the table and asked Beth to come with her to the cabinet to help with the basket puzzle. Beth went over to the cabinet, and her mother handed her the wire basket and told her to hold it steady. Beth held the basket approximately four minutes, but she did not hold her arms still and the basket moved somewhat. Mrs. Goldberg indicated to Beth several times that she was not holding the basket steady enough, but these instructions did not produce any change. The mother then helped Beth to brace the basket by holding it with one hand while she strung the rods through the mesh, but she was unsuccessful in steadying the basket by this procedure. Beth began to complain that the basket was too heavy for her, and eventually Mrs. Goldberg said "All right. I'll do it here," and put the basket on the table and completed the task in this manner. She did not say anything to Beth when she was finished, but sat down in a chair and without comment, waited for the examiner to return.

It was evident from the interaction procedures that Mrs. Goldberg tended to communicate with her daughter primarily when the latter was engaged in loud or disruptive activities. Mrs. Goldberg did not make much effort to teach Beth how to do the various tasks, and she carried out the joint procedures herself when Beth's attention became focused on some other object in the room. Beth was not encouraged or reinforced for cooperating with her mother.

COURSE OF THERAPY

Dr. S. met with the parents and explained that the results of the psychological evaluation and the information received from the various consultants all pointed to a diagnosis of minimal brain damage. The parents were informed that this condition could have occurred as a result of the difficult labor and delivery, although many other youngsters diagnosed as minimally brain damaged do not have a history of any unusual problems or head injuries. They were further told that usually one cannot point to a definite circumstance as being the cause of this disorder, so the diagnostic judgment tends to be based primarily on the information gained from the psychological evaluation and the school report.

Dr. S. was careful to point out that the findings did not mean that Beth would be unable to understand classroom material or make progress in school. It did indicate, however, that she would have difficulty with visual-motor skills such as those involved in eye-hand coordination, and there would be problems in areas requiring fine motor control. Most important, the parents would need help in learning to recognize the behavior that was a result of neurological impairment, and not expect Beth to behave at a level that she was incapable of performing at. It was also suggested that the parents could benefit from guidance in how to help Beth make use of her abilities, and in how to deal with her behavior problems.

Dr. S. recommended that Beth be placed in a class for children with learning disabilities when she entered first grade, so she could receive special instruction geared to her perceptual problems. Mrs. Goldberg and Beth were also offered the opportunity to receive therapy at the clinic, and the nature of the therapy was described.

Mr. and Mrs. Goldberg were quite upset to hear Beth's problems described in terms such as minimal brain damage. Mrs. Goldberg particularly was shocked to find out that what she had been viewing solely as a behavior problem had a physical basis to it. The parents were somewhat reassured when Dr. S. emphasized that Beth's difficulties were not of a completely incapacitating nature, that she was not mentally retarded, and that she would be able to make progress in school. The parents agreed to the recommendation that Beth be placed in a special class the following year, and they also made arrangements for the mother and child to participate in the therapy program.

Beth and her mother were introduced to a unique form of treatment called filial therapy. This method of therapy was devised by Dr. Bernard G. Guerney, Jr. (Guerney, 1964; Stover and Guerney, 1969; Fidler, Guerney, Andronico, and Guerney, 1969), and involves the mother performing play therapy with her own child. A group of mothers who will be participating in filial therapy are initially taught the technique by observing a trained professional. The professional therapist engages in play therapy with one of the children from the group of participants, while all of the mothers observe behind a one-way mirror. The therapist then discusses with the group the specific techniques that were used and emphasizes that the mother must allow the child to lead in the play. The child is free to do whatever he or she wants to in the play sessions except for a few carefully defined limits. For example, the child is not allowed to hit or hurt the parent or stab the inflated doll with a sharp instrument.

An important process in filial therapy is for the mother, as therapist, to be accepting of whatever feelings the child wishes to express through play. The child is thus allowed to express positive as well as negative feelings, and the mother learns to accept and reflect these emotions. In this manner, the child will begin to feel more trust in the parent, and will feel that the parent is more sensitive to and has more trust in the child.

The mothers learn the technique of reflection of feelings through teaching sessions, by repeatedly observing the professional therapist, and then by taking turns performing play therapy with their child while the others watch. The observers have the opportunity to provide suggestions and comments immediately after the practice sessions. When the technique is learned, the therapy is carried out by the mother once a week in a designated place in the home, using a standard set of toys and equipment. The mothers also continue to have weekly group meetings where they observe one of the members and her child in a play session. Following the observation, the mothers meet with the group therapist to discuss their observations and to bring up any problems they may be having with their children.

Filial therapy has been particularly helpful for mothers who have difficulty communicating with their youngsters, and who find it hard to express positive emotions to them. Research findings indicate an increase in ratings of maternal empathy after the mothers have been involved in filial therapy for a period of time (Guerney, Stover, and De Meritt, 1968).

When Beth was evaluated at the clinic, a filial therapy group was just being formed for brain damaged youngsters. Beth and her mother appeared to be good candidates for the program, since Mrs. Goldberg had such great difficulty in expressing or communicating positive feelings toward her daughter. Mrs. Goldberg and Beth participated in the program for 14 months.

Mrs. Goldberg initially stated that she felt awkward and self-conscious engaging in play therapy with Beth, but eventually she was able to become more sensitive to and accepting of her daughter's feelings. Mrs. Goldberg's comments in the group sessions showed that she had a greater understanding of how Beth felt when stressful episodes occurred at home or at school.

Beth reportedly looked forward to the weekly play sessions where she could have her mother's undivided attention. The youngster was able to play out feelings of frustration and impotence that occurred when she was expected to perform tasks or behave in a manner that was beyond her capacity. She also began to show evidence of an enhanced self-concept, in the sense of a greater feeling of adequacy or ability to master the environment. The higher self-esteem probably occurred because she was able to gain parental approval and later self-reinforcement for engaging in activities where she was able to perform well.

A great deal of the group discussion centered on problem behaviors that occurred in the home. The therapist helped the mothers to focus on differentiating between the behaviors that a given child could be expected to perform, in contrast to behavioral expectations that were beyond the child's capability. The relationship of the child to other children in the family was also discussed, and numerous examples of friction among siblings were brought up for group comment.

Along with the ongoing filial therapy program, the therapist outlined behavior modification techniques for the parent to use in dealing with some of the child's problem behaviors. The addition of reinforcement techniques was an adaptation of the filial therapy procedure specifically for youngsters with cerebral dysfunction. It is important to note that many problems, such as hyperactivity which had an organic basis, were modified through the use of rewards and social approval for less active behavior.

The mothers were able to give each other social support in trying new behavior modification techniques, and it was helpful for them to be with others who had similar types of problems. The mothers learned from each other that many of the behavior problems secondary to brain damage or dysfunction were modifiable through the systematic use of reinforcement procedures.

Therapy with the Goldberg family was terminated by mutual agreement after 14 months. At that time, Mrs. Goldberg was much more consistent and loving in her interactions with Beth, and Beth was manifesting markedly fewer behavior problems at home. The youngster was progressing well in a class for children with learning disabilities, and the teacher reported that there were no particular behavior problems at school.

Periodic phone calls to the family over the next several years indicated that Beth was continuing to make good progress in her special class, and there were no unusual behavior difficulties at home.

DISCUSSION

This case illustrates two important points. First, parental expectations may be unrealistic in light of a child's abilities, and second, behaviors which are due to cerebral dysfunction can be modified through changing the parent-child interactions. In the case presented, the parents were able to learn that some of the performance expectations they had for their daughter were unrealistically high. Yet within this broad framework, the child was able to make continued academic progress, and she was able to adhere to specific standards of behavior that were set up by the parents.

The diagnosis of minimal brain damage is often difficult to prove or disprove. The neurological and perceptual signs may be of a suggestive nature rather than precisely manifested. The label can also be a wastebasket category for professionals who see some type of dysfunction, but are unable to pinpoint an exact cause or etiology. It should also be noted that the meaning and implications of the diagnosis are extremely confusing and frightening to many parents.

Since the symptoms of minimal brain damage are often ambiguous, one is usually not able to say with certainty exactly how the posited damage occurred (Yacorzynski, 1965). Many of the commonly accepted indicators of cerebral damage are also found in individuals who do not manifest organic pathology. For example, an abnormal electroencephalogram could be a sign of cerebral dysfunction, but generalized abnormal brain activity may also be found in children with behavioral problems (Klinkerfuss, Langa, Weinberg, and O'Leary, 1965; Werry, 1968). A birth history of prolonged labor by the mother and a difficult delivery does not automatically mean that the child will suffer brain damage. Many children go through a complicated birth without manifesting any long term after effects. Therefore, parents who have just been told that their child is suffering from minimal brain damage may justifiably ask, "Where is the damage?" or, "How did the damage

occur?" The professional is then placed in the difficult and contradictory position of trying to convey to the parents that there were no clear
cut indications of brain damage, but rather, there were signs of neurological dysfunction.

The term "minimal brain damage" may therefore be an inappropriate description for many of the youngsters who are given this
label. Research on children with problems similar to Beth's has been
carried out by L. B. Silver (1971 a, c). His findings indicate that the
majority of these youngsters do not have abnormal EEG patterns nor
do they evidence other neurological signs such as abnormal reflexes. His
research also shows that one rarely finds any information in the child's
history which suggests that damage to the central nervous system
occurred during the fetal or post-delivery development period. Silver
therefore questions the use of the label "minimal brain damage" to
describe these youngsters and proposes the term "neurological learning
disability syndrome" as an alternative. Many of these youngsters respond to drug therapy with a lessening of hyperkinetic and distractible
behavior (Silver, 1971b). Thus, a consultation with a physician is also
important in cases involving severely hyperactive behavior.

When meeting with the parents, one can point to the specific
perceptual-motor difficulties noted in the child, and explain that the
diagnosis was arrived at on the basis of these particular indicators. The
fact that the teacher is usually one of the first persons to notice the perceptual problems could also be discussed. It would seem that the
most important information conveyed to the parents, however, is that
the child is hampered in daily functioning because of a neurological
dysfunction which is often manifested in learning and behavioral problems. As McCarthy and McCarthy (1969) pointed out, the identification of the child's specific learning problems and the development of
educational techniques to alleviate these difficulties may be of more
practical importance to the child than demonstrating a hypothetical site
of brain injury. Dealing with the youngster's behavior problems is also a
primary concern.

In Beth's case, one was able to observe a number of the signs
commonly associated with the syndrome traditionally labeled as minimal brain damage. First, the history of the difficult labor and associated
anoxia would cause one to be alert to the possibility of future problems. The series of four falls that occurred when Beth was approximately two years of age were most likely a result of an already present
visual-motor problem, rather than the cause of that difficulty. The falls

occurred at an age when the youngster was still learning to walk. This "accident proneness" was probably reflective of a difficulty in synthesizing visual and motor information which was consistently seen throughout Beth's development.

Beth's reported friendliness, indiscriminate to friends or strangers, may also be reflective of her perceptual problems. Just as she had difficulty discriminating between a six-sided and eight-sided figure, it may also be that she was unable to visually differentiate, at first glance, the persons she knew from those whom she did not know.

Beth manifested a phenomenon commonly seen in children with neurological dysfunction. She was able to perform well in certain but not all areas of functioning. Although unclear speech can be a symptom of cerebral dysfunction, Beth's verbal ability was adequate for her age level in spite of the fact that it was occasionally difficult to understand a given word that she was saying.

Children with learning disabilities are often under great pressure for achievement because the parents may not realize that the youngster is experiencing any problems. The mother may view the youngster's difficulties as stemming from the fact that the child "won't mind," and she responds to the child on this basis. Therefore, the child may be punished for being too noisy or destructive or for not finishing a chore that was started, when in fact, it is extremely difficult for the child to perform that task. The parents thus may shout at, criticize, or spank the child for something that is not within the child's capacity to carry out.

Further, other siblings may ridicule the youngster for being clumsy or for constantly getting into trouble. The child then becomes more and more frustrated, and begins to feel that he or she is "bad," or that no matter what one does, one will be criticized for that action. The child may then respond by having a temper tantrum which becomes more severe the longer it lasts, because of the youngster's difficulty in controlling or inhibiting a behavior once it begins. The same type of phenomenon (disinhibition) can be seen in the child with substantiated brain damage who gradually becomes wilder and more destructive while playing with some toys or games.

It is particularly difficult for a youngster who is having problems accomplishing tasks that he or she is unable to perform to have a younger sibling close in age. The other child may be rapidly catching up in ability to the impaired child, and the latter may then be unfavorably compared to the younger sibling.

In evaluating the results of the filial therapy program, improvement can be seen in a number of areas. Irrespective of the benefits derived from allowing Beth to express her feelings in play, the technique also allowed the interpersonal relationship between mother and child to become more positive and rewarding. The mother was spending a period of time each week giving her undivided attention to her daughter's play activities, and the child began to relate to the mother in a manner other than by having tantrums and arguments. The mother in turn began to respond to the child with more positive affect and the interaction between them became more enjoyable. The mother also became more sensitive to the child's feelings and more empathic with her. These attitudes were not specific to the play sessions, but from the mother's report, generalized to events that occurred during the rest of the week. The entire emotional tone of the mother-child interactions gradually changed with therapy.

The mothers' group sessions also proved to be beneficial. The participants learned that there were other persons who had similar problems, and thus were able to receive social support from each other. The mothers were also taught behavior modification techniques which they could apply to their children's problem behaviors. The successful use of these procedures again changed the interpersonal relationship with the child from a punitive and critical one to one of reward and praise. Associated with this change, the home environment became a setting where standards of behavior were clearly defined and realistically attainable.

Beth showed good progress in her disabilities class and was able to learn quite well once specialized techniques were used to compensate for her perceptual problems. One cannot overemphasize how important it is to the child to experience frequent success and praise. The child's feelings of mastery and self-image as a worthwhile, competent person are dependent on the individual's life experiences and influence the approach to future learning situations.

Psychologists and educators speak of the upper limits of a child's ability, or use the term "intellectual potential." However, no one can say with certainty exactly how great that potential is, or to what heights a particular child can progress. Rosenthal and Jacobson's study (1968) of teacher expectancy indicated that when a teacher believed a child had promising intellectual potential, that child showed better academic progress than did another equally intelligent child who was not given the good potential label.

One cannot accurately predict that the intellectual progress of a neurologically impaired child will rise to a given point and no higher. The parents and the school personnel must deal directly with the intellectual and behavioral disabilities these children are experiencing, but in so doing, they do not have to condemn these youngsters to an inferior status. On the contrary, it is possible to give these children the opportunity to reach greater levels of development than was ever previously expected of those with neurological learning disabilities.

REFERENCES

Fidler, J. W., Guerney, B. G., Andronico, M. P., & Guerney, L. Filial therapy as a logical extension of current trends in psychotherapy. In B. G. Guerney (Ed.), *Psychotherapeutic agents: new roles for nonprofessionals, parents, and teachers.* New York: Holt, Rinehart, & Winston, 1969. Pp. 47–55.

Guerney, B. G. Filial therapy: description and rationale. *Journal of Consulting Psychology,* 1964, *28,* 304–310.

Guerney, B. G., Stover, L., & De Meritt, S. A. Measurement of empathy in parent-child interaction. *Journal of Genetic Psychology,* 1968, *112,* 49–55.

Klinkerfuss, G. H., Langa, P. H., Weinberg, W. A., & O'Leary, J. L. Electroencephalographic abnormalities of children with hyperkinetic behavior. *Neurology,* 1965, *15,* 883–891.

McCarthy, J. J., & McCarthy, J. F. *Learning disabilities.* Boston: Allyn & Bacon, 1969.

Rosenthal, R., & Jacobson, L. *Pygmalion in the classroom.* New York: Holt, Rinehart, & Winston, 1968.

Silver, L. B. A proposed view on the etiology of the neurological learning disability syndrome. *Journal of Learning Disabilities,* 1971, *4,* 123–133. (a)

Silver, L. B. The neurological learning disability syndrome. *American Family Physician,* 1971, *4,* 95–102. (b)

Silver, L. B. Familial patterns in children with neurologically based learning disabilities. *Journal of Learning Disabilities*, 1971, *4*, 349–358. (c)

Stover, L., & Guerney, B. G. The efficacy of training procedures for mothers in filial therapy. In B. G. Guerney (Ed.), *Psychotherapeutic agents: new roles for nonprofessionals, parents and teachers.* New York: Holt, Rinehart & Winston, 1969. Pp. 534–544.

Werry, J. S., Studies on the hyperactive child. *Archives of General Psychiatry*, 1968, *19*, 9–16.

Yacorzynski, G. K. Organic mental disorders. In B. B. Wolman (Ed.), *Handbook of clinical psychology.* New York: McGraw-Hill, 1965. Pp. 653–688.

4

Aggressive Behavior in Association with a Disadvantaged Environment

Oswald Williams was 11 years old when his mother brought him to a community guidance center. The family was black and at the lowest socio-economic level. The mother was a 36-year-old widow, and she and her eight children were living in a public housing project. The family had been on welfare for the past five years. A welfare worker in the district where the family lived referred Mrs. Williams to the center.

Mrs. Williams was primarily interested in an evaluation of her son's intelligence. She had questions about the accuracy of his placement in a special class for children of borderline or retarded intelligence, where he had remained since the second grade. Oswald also had difficulties related to his frequently unprovoked aggressive behavior both at school and at home. The aggressive behavior occurred in interactions with peers and teachers, as well as with his mother and siblings.

Oswald appeared for the initial interview in faded, neatly pressed trousers and shirt. He seemed to be somewhat small for 11 years of age. He sat close to his mother in the waiting room, but separated readily from her when asked to go with the psychologist for the testing session.

DEVELOPMENTAL BACKGROUND

Oswald was the fourth child in a family of five boys and four girls. An older brother had died two years previously at the age of 15 as the result of an accident. At the time the family was seen, the eldest sister was 15, his brother Percy was 13, and Oswald was 11. The younger siblings included two brothers, ages 10 and 4, and three sisters, ages 8, 7, and 5.

Oswald was born prematurely during his mother's eighth month of pregnancy. The delivery progressed without complications and the youngster was placed in an incubator for three weeks. Oswald weighed four pounds at birth, and was released from the hospital in his mother's care five weeks after he was born. His weight at that time was approximately 5 pounds, 4 ounces.

Mrs. Williams reported that Oswald was the only one of her children who was born prematurely. The other children were all born full term and had fairly uneventful infancies. Oswald, however, required a great deal of extra care as an infant. Because he was born prematurely and was quite small when brought home, Oswald was often hungry and required food every two or three hours the first three months of his life.

Oswald's early life was accompanied by a number of illnesses. At four months of age he was hospitalized with a diagnosis of meningitis, and was released from the hospital after a one month stay with no apparent aftereffects. He contracted pneumonia before the age of two and was treated at home. Mrs. Williams noted that Oswald had always been more susceptible to colds than had the other children.

The mother reported that Oswald began to walk unaided at 18 months, which is slightly later than average, although within normal limits. He began to speak words when he was two years, and according to the mother began stuttering at three years of age when he stopped sucking his thumb. Oswald continued to have episodes of stuttering and his speech was always unclear. The stuttering became more pronounced when he was involved in emotionally charged situations. Toilet training was started at about one and a half years of age and completed a year later. However, Mrs. Williams related that Oswald continued to wet his bed occasionally until he was 9 years old.

The youngster had always been somewhat small for his age and on the slender side, although he ate regularly, and according to his mother, enjoyed his food.

SCHOOL HISTORY

Oswald entered first grade when he was 6 years old. In May of that school year he was referred to the special education department because of "partial lack of communication and reading impairment." The youngster was given the Stanford-Binet intelligence test, which is individually administered. On the basis of his performance on this test, his intellectual functioning was considered to be at the retarded level (I.Q. below 70). At the start of the next school year, he was placed in a special class for educable youngsters, i.e., those children who are judged to be able to profit from classroom instruction presented at a slower rate than usual.

In light of Oswald's premature birth and multiple illnesses in childhood, the teacher at the school referred him to a neurologist. An electroencephalogram was given in order to determine whether there were any signs of neurological impairment. The results were inconclusive, and the neurologist diagnosed the youngster as mildly retarded.

Subsequent intellectual evaluations with other tests during Oswald's second year of school resulted in his being classified in the category of Borderline Intelligence (I.Q. 70–80). Oswald has continued in a special class throughout his school career.

SOCIAL HISTORY

The Williams family suffered an extremely traumatic event 2 years prior to the visit to the guidance center. Mr. Williams and the eldest son were riding in an automobile that another car crashed in to, and both father and son were killed. Mrs. Williams related that she and the children were stricken with grief and shock for a number of months, and only with great difficulty accustomed themselves to getting along without the father and elder brother.

Mrs. Williams described her husband as a loving and devoted father, and a strict disciplinarian. He had been employed as a laborer but was frequently out of work because jobs were in short supply in the area where they lived. Mrs. Williams was used to having her husband make most of the family decisions, and found it extremely difficult to take over the entire burden of family responsibility after her husband's death.

Mrs. Williams indicated that even before the deaths occurred, she was quite anxious and concerned about her children's whereabouts and activities. After the accident, this concern deepened, and Mrs. Williams tried to have knowledge of where each child was at every moment. She stated that if one of the children was even five minutes late getting home from school, she became acutely anxious and set out on foot to look for that child. She also reported that when she went out to the supermarket or to a church activity, she called home every 10 or 15 minutes to make sure the children were all right and that they were home and still being supervised by the eldest daughter. Mrs. Williams rarely went out in the evening until she recently began working.

Part of this mother's concern about her children's activities was of a long-standing and quite realistic nature. The Williams family lived in a low-income public housing project in an area where robberies and crimes of violence were a frequent occurrence and drug pushers and addicts were in abundance on the streets. Mrs. Williams's anxiety about the children walking alone in the daytime or in the evening appeared well founded in light of the environmental hazards prevalent in the area where they lived.

The family's income level had always been marginal. When the family grew in size, they were often on welfare to supplement the father's earnings. Until her husband's death, Mrs. Williams had stayed home and cared for the youngsters. After therapy began, she started working several evenings a week as a cleaning woman in an office building.

Mrs. Williams reported that she tended to rely on her husband to set limits and take the initiative in disciplining the children. She stated that Mr. Williams was also concerned about where the children were, and would spank them if they were late in getting home or if they did not obey him. Since the father was periodically out of work and home all day, he was able to supervise the children's activities quite closely. The children were administered physical punishment frequently, but Mrs. Williams indicated that the father was never abusive with the children and, therefore, they respected him. Mrs. Williams tended to yell at the children when they disobeyed her, and threatened to tell the father about the children's misbehavior. The mother felt that the children were equitably disciplined, and it did not appear to her that any one child was singled out for a greater amount of punishment.

After the father's death, Mrs. Williams continued to discipline the children primarily by shouting at them. She stated that she constantly had to yell at the children, and that they tended to ignore her. She felt that the children were in control of her emotions, because they could get her very anxious or very angry in a moment's time, depending on what they were doing. Mrs. Williams reported that lately she had to resort to physical punishment more often in order to get the children to mind her. Spankings seemed to be effective in getting the younger children to comply. However, she was worried about whether in the future she would be able to control the older children, particularly the boys. Mrs. Williams felt that when Percy and Oswald got older and larger, they would not continue to allow their mother to hit them. She was afraid that eventually they would begin to strike her back, and then she would have absolutely no control over them.

Mrs. Williams was also worried about her eldest daughter's behavior. Janice was 15 years old and her mother was constantly worried that she was keeping company with a crowd of friends who would have a bad influence on her. The school reported that Janice was absent from class from time to time, and Mrs. Williams was afraid that her daughter might be tempted to begin shoplifting, or that she might get into some difficulty related to sexual activity.

Mrs. Williams had recently formed a friendship with a man who lived with his mother in the same housing project that she lived in. He was in his early 40's, and had never been married. Mr. Adams visited the Williams family and spent the night there on the weekends. Mrs. Williams felt that the children enjoyed Mr. Adam's visits. She had given her friend permission to discipline the children, and occasionally he spanked one of them for misbehavior. Mrs. Williams said that the children were more likely to obey Mr. Adams than her, and she was grateful that she could rely on him to help her with the children.

From the mother's report, it appeared that Oswald and his siblings were experiencing a great deal of friction in their relationships at home and at school. Mrs. Williams continually and ineffectually shouted at the children or hit them, and the children quite frequently fought among themselves. Oswald and his 10-year-old brother Leroy were constantly fighting because Leroy wore Oswald's clothes without asking Oswald for his permission. Leroy was one year younger, but taller than Oswald. Their verbal disputes quickly turned into punching matches, necessitating intervention by Mrs. Williams or one of the older siblings. Mrs. Williams tended to respond to these episodes by yelling at the boys. The boys would ignore her, and quite frequently the fighting would erupt again.

Oswald also fought with his 13-year-old brother Percy, but their disputes did not result in drawn out fights. Percy was quite a bit larger than Oswald, and after Percy hit Oswald a few times, Oswald would back off and the fight then ended. Oswald fought with his younger brothers and sisters also, and hit them when they got into arguments with him. However, Oswald occasionally played games with his younger sisters, and when he did get into arguments with them, he did not punch them as hard as he did Percy and Leroy.

Since the family was living together in a four-room apartment, the children were quite frequently in each other's way, and fighting often ensued. When Oswald's brothers and sisters got angry at him, they often teased him about his stuttering and mimicked him. This made Oswald even angrier and he tried to hit the person who was imitating him. When he began shouting at the child he was fighting with, he stammered even more.

Mrs. Williams left Janice in charge of the children when she was out of the house. Oswald was not likely to listen to Janice, but he usually did not go outside without her permission.

Oswald spent a great deal of time watching television, and did not play very often with the neighborhood children. This was partly a result of his mother's attempts to keep the children home after school or outside under her supervision. Also, the neighborhood children made fun of Oswald when he began to stutter, and because Oswald was physically small for his age, he was usually unsuccessful in his attempts to beat up the boys who were teasing him.

At school, Oswald, Percy, and Janice were in frequent trouble with the teacher and were often sent to the principal's office because of disciplinary problems. Shortly before coming to the guidance center, Janice, Percy, and Oswald were all on suspension at the same time from their respective classes. The suspensions occurred because of similar complaints of not listening to the teacher, walking out of the classroom, and in Percy and Oswald's case, fighting with other boys while class was in session.

Oswald's teacher sent a report to the guidance center stating that the youngster was in frequent difficulty in class because he did not comply with the teacher's requests. For example, Oswald refused to obey the teacher when asked to go back to his seat after he got up and grabbed something that belonged to another child. He continued doing whatever activity he was engaged in at the moment. The teacher stated that he had often observed Oswald engaged in unprovoked physical or verbal aggression against one of his classmates, and that lately this problem had increased in severity. Recently, Oswald lit matches in class, and when he took some papers and attempted to start a fire in the hallway, he was suspended from school for two weeks. This episode had occurred two months prior to the visit to the guidance center. In addition, Oswald had been suspended several times for periods of from three days to two weeks, for turning over chairs in class, fighting with other youngsters, and refusing to wait in the principal's office.

Despite these behavior problems, Oswald had been progressing somewhat in class. He had learned to read at a beginning second grade level and could do simple arithmetic problems. However, the teacher reported that Oswald stuttered when emotionally aroused. He also tended to stutter in response to the teacher asking him a question in class that he did not know the answer to.

PSYCHOLOGICAL EVALUATION

Oswald was interviewed and tested by a female psychologist. When she came to the waiting room to meet Oswald, he quickly got up without glancing at his mother, and followed the examiner to the testing room. Oswald was very quiet and did not initiate any conversation. He sat in a chair throughout the testing session, and was very cooperative. He briefly answered the questions asked of him, and stuttered only when the topic turned to the difficulties he was experiencing with his siblings, and the disciplinary problems he was having at school.

At times it was hard to understand the youngster. He frequently substituted one sound for another, such as the "f" sound in place of the "th," and the "d" sound in place of the "t." These substitutions were consistent, so that the examiner was able to catch on to the youngster's speech pattern after listening to him for a while.

Oswald was given a battery of tests administered over two testing sessions. The particular tests were chosen to enable the psychologist to gain information about the youngster's current intellectual and academic functioning, and about areas of behavioral or emotional problems. Oswald was also given a number of tests to assess perceptual-motor functioning, in order to ascertain whether there was any evidence of neurological impairment.

Oswald's performance on the intelligence test at age 11 was consistent with the scores he had received on tests given five years previously. The youngster scored in the range of borderline intelligence. He manifested a slight superiority in tasks involving spatial concepts in comparison to those dealing with abstract verbal skills. An assessment of reading and arithmetic ability indicated that Oswald was performing at a beginning second grade level. This was consistent with what one would expect in terms of his age and intellectual functioning.

The test results did not indicate any signs of neurological impairment or brain damage. Oswald was able to perform tasks measuring visual motor ability, visual memory, and auditory discrimination at a level commensurate with his overall intellectual functioning.

The youngster was given a number of cards from the TED series and was asked to make up a story about the scene depicted on each card. His responses indicated that he had mixed feelings about the desire to assert himself and be independent, and the wish to be dependent and seek the mother's protection. A conflict of this nature is quite typical for youngsters who are close to adolescence.

The maternal figure that Oswald described in the stories was a woman who frequently resorted to physical punishment in order to get her child to obey. The youngster made numerous references in his stories to a boy who gets "beat up" by the mother for some transgression such as breaking a window, not cleaning his room, or not doing his homework. The mother, however, was also pictured as a person who genuinely cared about her son, even though the boy was described as physically hurting after some of the punishments administered by the mother. Adult males were generally described as passive figures showing little influence in the boy's life.

Another theme of the projective stories was the fear of physical harm from peers. The boy on the pictures was described as playing ball or games with other youngsters, but many times the boy was fearful that something would happen and he would get beat up. Oswald also described some calamity or accident suddenly befalling a group of children playing together.

THE OBSERVED INTERACTION

Mrs. Williams and Oswald entered the playroom with the psychologist and were given the procedure instructions for the Observed Interaction. During the free play period, Mrs. Williams sat rather stiffly in a chair while Oswald walked around and explored the room. Mrs. Williams appeared to be somewhat uncomfortable in the surroundings; she frequently told Oswald to hush when he spoke in a moderately loud tone of voice, and she picked up the procedure card a number of times and re-read the instructions for the interaction. Oswald rarely conversed with his mother during this period. He spent most of his time shooting darts at the ceiling and walls or hitting the inflated clown. Oswald expressed a great deal of glee when a dart hit a ceiling light, and his mother responded to this by telling him to stop shooting at the light as he might break something. There was a gradual increase in the frequency of shooting darts over the course of the free play period, and the verbal accompaniment to each shot also became louder. Oswald showed an increase in the intensity of pummeling and jumping on the clown as the session progressed, and he began to ignore his mother's pleas to play quietly.

Mrs. Williams called Oswald over to the table when it was time to begin work on the questionnaire. It took a long time to complete this task as Oswald did not remain seated for very long; he got up a number of times and played with objects in the room. Mrs. Williams had to ask him several times to come back and sit down before he eventually did so. The mother had difficulty reading some of the questions and deciding with Oswald on an appropriate response.

Mother and child initially worked on the jigsaw puzzle together. After several minutes, Oswald got up from the table and began to wander about the room, ignoring his mother's requests to come back and work on the task. Following a number of unsuccessful efforts to get Oswald to work with her, Mrs. Williams slowly and methodically finished the puzzle by herself.

Oswald cooperated with his mother for several minutes on the last task, the basket puzzle. However, he soon began to complain that he was tired just standing there and holding the basket. His mother rather sharply told him that he had better stand there and hold the basket if he knew what was good for him. In response, Oswald held the basket more steadily until the task was finished, but he still complained about being tired just standing there.

The youngster gave evidence of a short attention span during the interaction, and he also showed a gradual increase in verbal and motor activity as he became more engrossed in play activity. As the interaction session progressed, he tended to ignore his mother's attempts to get him to cooperate, until she spoke firmly to him and conveyed a threat of punishment. Mrs. Williams did not attempt to teach Oswald how to perform the various tasks.

COURSE OF PSYCHOTHERAPY

The social worker who interviewed Mrs. Williams and the psychologist who saw Oswald jointly met with the mother. They told her that on the basis of the tests given, it appeared that Oswald was in an appropriate school placement. There were no indications from the tests of a higher intellectual potential. In order for the youngster to make the most satisfactory progress, they recommended that he be kept in a special education class, and not put in a regular class. The slower pace of the special class seemed to be better suited to his intellectual functioning. They also discussed with Mrs. Williams Oswald's orientation toward physical punishment. They suggested that both she and the youngster could benefit by coming regularly to the center for therapy. Mrs. Williams agreed, and a male therapist was chosen for Oswald in an effort to give the youngster a nonpunishing male figure to model his behavior after. Mrs. Williams also came for weekly sessions with a male social worker. These sessions were oriented around teaching the mother adequate skills for dealing with her children's behavioral difficulties.

The mother was also told that it would be helpful for Oswald to receive speech therapy. It was felt that Oswald would be less likely to get into fights based on taunts about his speech, if he had help in controlling his stuttering and modifying his unclear speech pattern. Mrs. Williams agreed to this suggestion, and numerous efforts were made over a five month period to enroll Oswald in a speech therapy class. Because the family had no funds for private help, public agencies were the only places that were contacted. This proved to be an exercise in frustration, as the few facilities available, including Oswald's school, consistently reported that either their enrollments were filled, or there was no staff person free who could take on an extra case. In spite of repeated efforts by the center staff, it was impossible to place the youngster in a speech therapy class.

The psychotherapy sessions with Oswald generally centered around an attempt to build a friendship with the boy. In the more structured testing session with a woman, Oswald's speech was fairly understandable except when personal topics were discussed. In contrast, the male therapist had extreme difficulty in conversing with the youngster. Oswald did not initiate any conversation, and minimally answered the therapist's questions or comments. Oswald also tended to stutter a greal deal when conversing with the therapist, and the latter found it extremely difficult to understand the boy. The therapy sessions were therefore oriented around building up a relationship through non-verbal means, and Oswald appeared to enjoy coming to the guidance center. He played cards, checkers, or darts with the therapist, went for walks with him, and the two of them routinely stopped off at the snack bar for a soft drink.

Mrs. Williams met weekly with the social worker. She expressed a desire to receive counseling, but cancelled her appointments or else just failed to appear on an average of one out of four sessions. On the occasions when she failed to come, Oswald missed his counseling session also.

Mrs. Williams was able to bring up issues for discussion with the therapist. She freely expressed her frustrations in trying to discipline so large a family and her fears that some harm would befall her children. The therapist attempted to get the mother to see that physical punishment and shouting were ineffective means of dealing with her children. He explored with her specific incidents that had occurred at home, and using these incidents, pointed out how she rarely gave approval or attention for positive behaviors, but instead tended to focus primarily on her children's disruptive behaviors.

Mrs. Williams complained that she felt constantly anxious and upset, and would express these feelings by yelling at the children. The therapist suggested that Mrs. Williams spend some time out of the house engaged in activities that did not include the children. Mrs. Williams began to go to some church activities occasionally. With the therapist's support, she was able to limit her calls home to once an hour, instead of telephoning every 15 minutes, as she had previously done.

Mrs. Williams desired to provide her family with more comforts than she could obtain from the welfare checks she received, and was encouraged to obtain a part-time job. Although she preferred to work during the day, the only job she could find was as a cleaning woman several evenings a week. Mrs. Williams reported that after she started working, she felt more relaxed than she had in a long time. She was pleased that she was able, from time to time, to get away from her difficulties with her children. The therapist continued to confront the mother with the ineffectiveness of her attempts to discipline the children, and he used examples from some of the events that occurred in the Observed Interaction. He also urged her to actively change her customary modes of interaction with the children, instead of just complaining about their behavior. He gave her concrete suggestions for alternative ways that she could interact with them, based on the principle of giving social approval for positive behaviors, instead of attention primarily for negative behaviors.

Even though Oswald appeared to have a pleasant relationship with his therapist, the youngster was getting into more and more difficulty at school and had been suspended a number of times. It was decided that it would be useful to set up a systematic program to modify his behavior in the school setting. With the concurrence of the mother and teacher, Oswald's therapist met with the teacher and worked out a behavior modification program. The program involved rewarding Oswald with a token from the teacher each time he worked quietly at his seat for a 15 minute period. Oswald would then take the tokens home to his mother and she would cash them for him, with each token being worth a penny.

Both the mother and teacher agreed that this approach was workable and Mrs. Williams was told that she could discuss the progress of the procedure during her therapy session the following week. However, Mrs. Williams called and cancelled her next two appointments, and then stopped calling the center entirely. The program in the school could not be carried out without the mother's cooperation, and with the family ceasing their contacts with the guidance center, it was not possible to continue to intervene in the school situation. Mrs. Williams made no further attempt to contact the center. Letters sent to her were not answered.

DISCUSSION

Treatment progress in this case was quite variable. Both Oswald and his mother came to the guidance center for weekly sessions over a period of five months. However, Oswald had extreme difficulty in communicating with his therapist, and this dearth of conversation served the function of diverting attention away from a discussion of his behavioral difficulties. Mrs. Williams terminated the visits at a point when the therapist was pressing her to make some specific changes in her behavior at home with the children.

Mrs. Williams spent a great deal of time in therapy complaining about the problems she was having. When the therapist encouraged and instructed Mrs. Williams in how to take active steps to change her interactions with the children, she did not follow through. It may be that once she found some interests outside of the home and felt less anxious, her motivation for changing her behavior with the children lessened. Even though Oswald's difficulties at school were becoming increasingly more serious, his behavior at home was no worse than usual. Mrs. Williams appeared to have become adapted to a situation where there was a great deal of fighting and shouting going on in the home, and may have been relieved that it was no worse.

It seems important at this point to briefly review some of the research that has been done on the attitudes of lower socio-economic class individuals toward receiving help for emotional problems. There have also been a number of studies on the nature of mental health services to the poor, and the attitudes of the professional persons delivering these services. This information may help provide for a more meaningful discussion of whether there were any alternative procedures which might have been more effective in aiding the Williams family.

Hollingshead and Redlich (1958) found that persons of lower socio-economic status were more likely to frame emotional problems in physical rather than psychological terms. These individuals were therefore more likely to seek and receive some sort of somatic therapy such as pills or treatments, rather than verbal psychotherapy. In the Williams' case, their appearance at a guidance clinic was related primarily to a desire to re-evaluate Oswald's school placement, rather than seeking help with emotional problems.

Our mental health services to the poor have been quite limited and relatively ineffective. The sobering studies by Hollingshead and Redlich, and the Midtown Manhattan Study (Srole, Langner, Michael, Opler, and Rennie, 1962) clearly showed that there is a preponderance of severe emotional disorders in individuals of the lower socio-economic strata, and very few facilities that can prevent or treat problems other than by providing custodial care.

The emergence of the community mental health movement seems to be a first ray of hope in treating families like the Williams, who manifest multiple difficulties in several family members, and who are unaccustomed to seeking help in the more traditional mental health facilities, assuming these facilities are available. The studies of the Joint Commission of Mental Illness and Health (*Action for Mental Health*, 1961) were instrumental in the passage by the federal government of the Community Mental Health Centers Act of 1963. These studies showed the need for facilities for the prevention and care of emotional disorders located in the area where the person lives. The studies also showed the need for more effective care for persons already in mental institutions.

The Williams case presents a number of important problems that sometimes occur in dealing with individuals who have a different racial, economic, and cultural background than the persons working with them. Previous research has indicated that not only do lower socio-economic class clients feel uncomfortable in expressing themselves verbally to a middle class therapist (Hollingshead and Redlich), but the therapist also feels ill at ease, less empathic, and less optimistic about the success of psychotherapy with persons whose life experiences have been markedly different from his or her own (Strupp, 1960; Strupp and Williams, 1960; Wallach and Strupp, 1960; Carson and Heine, 1962). Perhaps if Mrs. Williams could have been seen in a storefront mental health center, located in the community where she lived and staffed by trained para-professionals indigenous to that community, she would have had more of a feeling that someone realistically understood her problems. Then she might have been able to change her behavior toward her children so that the home situation was not one of continual friction.

This may appear to be a rather simplistic solution, but the issue may be clarified if one views the mother as a person overwhelmed by personal and absolutely realistic environmental stresses. The death of her husband and eldest son left her in a situation where, in her middle 30's, she was faced with the primary responsibility of caring for and providing guidance to eight children. Further, she was living in a dangerous neighborhood where her children were constantly prone to some sort of harmful influence. To compound this situation even further, Oswald functioned in school at a borderline level of intelligence, and was taunted for his slowness and his speech problems. The school that he went to did not provide him with speech therapy, and had large numbers of children in one classroom. The teacher was apparently unable to deal with the disciplinary problems that ensued except by suspending the offending child from school. This, of course, put the child back out on the street, and caused him to get even further behind in school. The family was also clearly in need of a continually present stepfather, who could provide a good role model for the youngsters and share in the raising of the children.

One may legitimately ask, "What can really be done to help this mother?" The answer is not easy, and labeling the mother as unmotivated for treatment is perhaps unfair. It may have seemed useless to Mrs. Williams to continue coming to receive help for one problem, when all of the other problems facing this family were so overwhelming and difficult to solve. As long as Oswald was not behaving any worse at home and Mrs. Williams was feeling less anxious, perhaps she felt that this was the best she could hope for.

A mental health aide indigenous to that community might have been able to suggest more practical help, such as where to get a larger place to live so that the children were not constantly together and irritating one another. Perhaps Mrs. Williams could have undergone some special job training in order to find work during the daytime, or someone could have worked more consistently with the school to alleviate some of Oswald's difficulties there. However, the problems of the adverse environmental circumstances this family was forced to live in are not an issue that can be solved by one mental health professional or one agency. The latter is a problem for our entire society.

The genesis of Oswald's aggressive behavior pattern can be understood in part as an attempt to imitate or model the type of behavior that he had observed to be successful in his environment. The youngsters who were able to fight and defend themselves did not tend to get beat up by others. According to a writer who grew up in Harlem (Brown, 1965), one of the ways of attaining status in the local community and in school was by being able to fight. Also, if one is more aggressive than the other children, then one can strike first and thereby prevent others from taking one's money or possessions.

In Oswald's home, a similar type of situation occurred. His mother was ineffectual in her attempts to prevent fighting, so each child's place in the pecking order was determined by whom he or she could beat up. The only way that Oswald could stop his brothers and sisters from teasing him or taking things that belonged to him was to fight with them. Aggressive behavior was therefore an extremely dominant response in his behavior repertoire, in part because the persons in the environment failed to reward alternate behaviors.

In terms of family role models, all of the children observed their father engaging in a great deal of physical punishment. After his death, Mrs. Williams increased the frequency with which she resorted to physical punishment. However, hitting one of the children further modeled aggressive behavior. Although physical punishment had an immediate suppressive effect on aggression, it did not lessen the probability that the child would again act aggressively at a future time. Mrs.

Williams did not use deprivation of privileges as a punishment. This procedure might have been more effective because the child learns that the penalties or consequences for various negative behaviors last over a longer duration than the time period involved in getting a spanking. Mrs. Williams also did not tend to comment on or reinforce more socially appropriate behaviors. Since she tended to respond to the children primarily when they engaged in disruptive behaviors, positive behaviors did not become more frequent.

Oswald's aggressive behavior in school served the function, in part, of diverting attention from his poor academic performance and his speech problems. Perhaps Oswald could have received more of a feeling of competence and academic mastery if he had been taught with a programmed text, so that he could learn in small, easy steps, with a frequent experience of success. It is unfortunate that the mother did not follow through with the modification program the therapist set up with the teacher. However, positive behavior change might have occurred in the school setting if the behavior modification program had been structured so that the reinforcement was provided directly by the teacher. This system might have resulted in a diminishment of aggressive behavior at school and the emergence of more socially appropriate behaviors.

A token economy system in the classroom could have been of benefit to many members of the class. The rising popularity and obvious effectiveness of token reinforcement programs for dealing with disruptive behavior (O'Leary and Becker, 1967; Hall, Panyan, Rabon, and Broden, 1968; Phillips, 1968; Zimmerman, Zimmerman, and Russell, 1969; O'Leary and Drabman, 1971) may eventually put an end to the self-defeating practice of suspending or expelling from school those youngsters who are discipline problems.

Although Oswald scored fairly consistently over the years on the intelligence tests given him, one could question the validity for this youngster of results obtained from tests that have been standardized on essentially white middle-class populations speaking a different vocabulary and undergoing different life experiences. One wonders how many middle-class youngsters would be classified as borderline or retarded in intelligence if they had to be evaluated on a test using Black English and consisting of questions about situations they have had little experience with. The difficulty is that once a child gets labeled as deficient in intelligence and put in a special class, he is learning less and less each year in comparison to what a child in a regular class is learning. After five or six years in a situation like this, it is virtually impossible for a child to catch up. Irrespective of any speculation about whether Oswald was fairly categorized when he first entered school, at the time Oswald was evaluated at the center, he was better off in a special class. Being far behind in a regular class and teased for this would not have helped his problems in school.

From the standpoint of therapy, it may be too harsh to say that the Williams case was a failure, but it certainly was not a success. The mental health field has just begun to grapple with the problem of reaching the disadvantaged members of our society who are faced with a multitude of problems, many of them outside their own personal control. Let us hope that eventually we will be able to reach these persons, and that they will have better control over their own destiny.

REFERENCES

Brown, C. *Manchild in the promised land.* New York: MacMillan Co., 1965.

Carson, R. C., & Heine, R. W. Similarity and success in therapeutic dyads. *Journal of Consulting Psychology,* 1962, *26,* 38–45.

Hall, R. V., Panyan, M., Rabon, D., & Broden, M. Instructing beginning teachers in reinforcement procedures which improve classroom control. *Journal of Applied Behavior Analysis,* 1968, *1,* 315–322.

Hollingshead, A. B., & Redlich, F. C. *Social class and mental illness.* New York: Wiley, 1958.

Joint Commission of Mental Illness and Health, *Action for mental health.* New York: Basic Books, 1961.

O'Leary, K. D., & Becker, W. C. Behavior modification of an adjustment class: A token reinforcement program. *Exceptional Children,* 1967, *33,* 637–642.

O'Leary, K. D., & Drabman, R. Token reinforcement programs in the classroom: A review. *Psychological Bulletin,* 1971, *75,* 379–398.

Phillips, E. L. Achievement Place: Token reinforcement procedures in a home-style rehabilitation setting for "pre-delinquent" boys. *Journal of Applied Behavior Analysis*, 1968, *1*, 213–224.

Srole, L., Langner, T., Michael, S., Opler, M., & Rennie, T. *Mental health in the metropolis: The midtown Manhattan study* (Vol. 1). New York: Mc-Graw-Hill, 1962.

Strupp, H. H. Nature of the therapists's contribution to the treatment process. *Archives of General Psychiatry*, 1960, *3*, 219–231.

Strupp, H. H., & Williams, J. V. Some determinants of clinical evaluations of different psychiatrists. *Archives of General Psychiatry*, 1960, *2*, 434–440.

Wallach, M. S., & Strupp, H. H. Psychotherapists' clinical judgments and attitudes towards patients. *Journal of Consulting Psychology*, 1960, *24*, 316–323.

Zimmerman, E. H., Zimmerman, J., and Russell, C. D. Differential effects of token reinforcement on instruction-following behavior in retarded students instructed as a group. *Journal of Applied Behavior Analysis*, 1969, *2*, 101–112.

PART TWO

ADOLESCENT AND ADULT DISORDERS

5

Phobic Behavior in a College Student—An "Irrational" Fear of Spiders

Joyce Ryan phoned for an appointment at a university counseling center because she had become increasingly upset and embarrassed about her longstanding fear of spiders. She indicated that her only problem was this fear, and that she was baffled by the panic reaction which ensued when she saw a spider.

When Joyce came to the counseling center for evaluation, she was a 20-year-old college junior, majoring in English literature. She lived in a dormitory on the school campus and saw her family during vacation periods and occasionally on week-ends.

SOCIAL HISTORY

Joyce was the middle child in a family of three children. Her older sister, Barbara, was 24 years old and had been married for two years at the time Joyce was seen. A younger brother Ted, 17, was a senior in high school.

Joyce was raised in a comfortable, white middle-class environment. Her father had earned an M.S. in chemistry, and worked for a large chemical concern. Mrs. Ryan was a housewife, with interests centering primarily around home activities. Barbara always received higher grades in school than Joyce did, and Joyce felt that her older sister had been continually held up as an example for her to emulate. However, even though Joyce was an above average student, she never was able to match her sister's academic performance.

When Joyce was growing up, her relationship with her sister and brother was one of frequent discord. She and Barbara fought continually, and Barbara usually won the dispute because she was older. Joyce described an incident that occurred when she was 10 or 11 and had dressed up in some of Barbara's clothes. When her sister saw her, she became very angry and began ridiculing Joyce, calling her "stupid" and "baby." Joyce in turn began to kick Barbara, and Barbara tried to remove the blouse and hair band that Joyce had on, which belonged to Barbara. In the process, the blouse got torn and Barbara then went crying to her mother. Mrs. Ryan was downstairs, and although she had heard the dispute, she had not attempted to intervene. The result of the incident was that Mrs. Ryan complained to her husband about the episode when he got home, and Joyce then got a spanking from her father. Barbara was not punished and Joyce felt this was unfair. She said that if Barbara had asked her to give the items back instead of calling her names, she would have given them back to her.

Joyce related that she was never able to get along well with her sister, and even though Barbara was now married, she still did not feel very close to her. Joyce did not experience a close emotional bond with her brother Ted, either. Because Ted was three years younger than she, Joyce felt that they never had much in common. Ted always seemed to be the "pesty little brother" who was constantly disturbing her things, just as she was always involved with Barbara's possessions. When they were younger, she and Ted often ended up a dispute by punching each other. Mrs. Ryan usually did not intervene, and if Mr. Ryan heard about or observed the fight, he tended to encourage Ted to defend himself, but did not interfere in any other way.

Joyce felt that her parents had a reasonably happy marital relationship. Mr. Ryan was the person who made the decisions in the family, and he generally assumed a protective role toward his wife. Mrs. Ryan looked to her husband for advice and guidance on many daily situations. Mr. Ryan appeared to be interested in matters involving the home and children, and willing to take the time to consider the situation and express an opinion.

Mr. Ryan was often involved with activities related to his job, and he frequently brought work home with him in the evenings. Although Mr. Ryan took an interest in his daughters, he interacted more with Ted than with the two girls. He bought Ted a chemistry set when the latter was quite young and encouraged him in this area. Ted learned a great deal about chemistry from his father and Mr. Ryan was quite pleased that his son was planning to major in chemistry in college.

Joyce indicated that it had always been difficult for her to confide in either of her parents, in spite of the fact that she knew that they meant well. Mrs. Ryan never seemed able to give Joyce any advice. When Joyce brought up problems about peer interactions or difficulties at school, Mrs. Ryan's usual response was "Don't worry. It'll work out all right." Mr. Ryan always seemed preoccupied with other matters, and Joyce did not seek out her father for advice.

Mrs. Ryan, in a number of areas, did not set an example for her children of competent behavior. She tended to defer most of the decision-making to her husband, and she also referred the children to him if they had any questions about their homework assignments. Further, she was afraid of insects, and if there was an insect in the house, she usually called on either Barbara or Ted to get rid of it. Mr. Ryan tended to express amusement at his wife's fears, and made a joke of these events.

Joyce could not relate any specific event as being the origin of her fear of spiders. She said that she remembered being teased by neighborhood children because of this fear, and that several times some of the neighborhood boys had caught a spider to tease and scare her. She felt, however, that her fear occurred prior to these childhood teasing episodes. For as long as she could remember, she felt uneasy when there was a crawling spider or some other insect nearby. If she saw a spider in the same room that she was in, she would run out and get someone to remove it. When younger, she often began to cry when confronted with a spider. At the time of evaluation, she reported that she still became panic-stricken when she saw a spider.

PRESENT STATUS

Joyce felt that her current level of functioning was quite satisfactory except for her unexplainable fear of spiders. She was baffled by the intense anxiety she experienced when she saw a spider, and troubled because the anxiety would not subside until she got away from the phobic stimulus. Although the most intense anxiety response occurred in relation to spiders, Joyce became quite anxious when she saw other insects as well. Joyce recognized that she was reacting with extreme anxiety to something which would not harm her, but she said that she could not control the anxiety response.

The client also described a number of current habit patterns that could be categorized as obsessive in nature. She reported that she worried a great deal about pending examinations at school and had recurring doubts about whether she would be able to answer the questions asked on the exam. She realized that these thoughts were not very realistic, because she generally studied a great deal and did quite well on exams. Nonetheless, she was still bothered by these doubts. Joyce also found it difficult to make decisions, ranging from which of two dresses to buy, to what major to follow in college. She tended to ruminate among a number of alternative possibilities, and usually was able to come to a decision only when some other person intervened and suggested a choice to her.

Joyce described her present relationship with her family as an ambivalent one. She said that she missed her parents and siblings when she was away at school. However, when she was home, she frequently became moody over seemingly trivial events, and then preferred to stay in her room. Her parents recognized these moods and generally did not attempt to interact with her during these episodes. When Joyce's affective state changed, she would then come out of her room. Neither she nor her parents made any mention of the incident, or tried to find out what had precipitated the emotional occurrence.

On the whole, Joyce felt that college life was a pleasant experience. She had a good academic record, though her cumulative grade point average was not as high as Barbara's had been. Joyce found it difficult to make friends, but she did have one close girl friend that she met at school, and the two were roommates. Joyce said that she was able to confide in her roommate when she was troubled with various school or family problems. Her friend had initially made the suggestion that Joyce contact the counseling center, and Joyce went along with this suggestion.

Joyce had not dated very often in college until ten months previously, when she met her present boyfriend. Larry also came from a white middle-class environment, and they met on campus. They soon began to go out together quite frequently, and they had an understanding that neither would date anyone else. Larry was the first boy that Joyce had sexual relationships with and she felt somewhat anxious about the anticipated parental response should her parents find out about this activity. Although from time to time they discussed the possibility of eventually getting married, both felt that they were not ready to take this step within the near future. Larry was unsure of his plans after college graduation and Joyce was also uncertain about what she wanted to do after she finished college.

Joyce reported that she was embarrassed by her panic reaction at seeing a spider when she was with her boyfriend. However, he appeared to think it was cute and enjoyed playing the role of defending Joyce from the insect.

PSYCHOLOGICAL EVALUATION

Joyce, an attractive young woman, appeared for the initial interview dressed in the standard campus attire of jeans and a shirt. Joyce sat in a chair in the waiting room, with her hands tightly clasped together. She immediately jumped up from her chair when Dr. K. appeared. Joyce responded briefly to his comments as they walked down the corridor to an interview room, but the client did not initiate any questions or conversation.

Joyce described her problems and current life situation during the interview. At times, the psychologist asked specific questions of the client, or directed the conversation to other topics in order to gain more detailed information about the difficulties Joyce was experiencing. The client was quite emphatic in stating that her major interpersonal problem was her fear reaction to spiders and she wanted psychological assistance primarily for solving that particular problem.

Dr. K. administered a selected group of subtests from an intelligence test. The subtests were given in order to gain a general estimate of intellectual functioning, and were also used as a rough screening device for possible thought disorders. Joyce was also given the Thematic Apperception Test (TAT). Many of the cards on this test depict an individual in either a solitary or interpersonal situation. The card scenes are rather vague, so that each person tends to give a somewhat different story of the events transpiring on the cards.

Joyce also was asked to complete a number of self-administered inventories, including the Fear Inventory (Wolpe and Lazarus, 1966), and the Minnesota Multiphasic Personality Inventory (MMPI). The Fear Inventory was originally designed to measure the intensity of fear in various situations. The information gained can then be used to construct anxiety hierarchies for systematic desensitization therapy.

Joyce's verbal comments and her performance on the various tests suggested that she approached the testing situation with extreme uncertainty. She frequently qualified her responses with comments such as "this may not be right, but . . . ," or "I'm not sure, but I think." She also exhibited a tendency to give long and overly detailed answers or descriptions, and showed a meticulous concern for small details on the figures that she drew.

The client scored in the superior intellectual range. There was no evidence on any of the tests of thought disturbance or poor reality testing suggestive of psychotic functioning. The responses generally indicated an extremely anxious individual who centered much thought and activity around a concern with insects. The area of greatest fear was in situations with crawling insects or spiders.

Several themes emerged from the responses given by the client on the TAT. Joyce described a number of family situations suggestive of sibling rivalry, or of a child attempting to get parental attention. Social situations with peers were described as being uncomfortable because of a lack of certainty about how to interact with others, particularly when expressing one's feelings. As a result, both positive and negative emotions were kept to oneself and not communicated.

The responses to the personality inventory and the profile drawn from these responses corroborated the other test findings. The client's profile indicated a phobic and excessively indecisive individual, who experienced difficulty in communicating with others.

COURSE OF THERAPY

Joyce appeared to be reasonably comfortable in her present social environment even though she was having some difficulty in relating to other persons. The psychological test results were consistent on the whole with the client's stated treatment goal of receiving help for her fear of spiders. The behavior therapy technique of systematic desensitization therefore seemed to be well suited for treating the client's phobic behavior.

Joyce readily accepted the recommendation of desensitization treatment, and agreed to come to the counseling center twice a week for half hour sessions. Dr. K. made it clear that if Joyce felt the need to discuss other problems, these issues could be brought up after each desensitization session.

The therapist determined that Joyce was amenable to systematic desensitization by testing whether she had the ability to clearly visualize scenes, and whether the anxiety-provoking scenes eventually used in treatment generated anxiety when visualized without relaxation. Joyce was taught the procedure of relaxation during the initial treatment sessions, and was asked to practice this technique at home each day. The client and therapist also devoted the early therapy sessions to constructing an anxiety hierarchy. An anxiety hierarchy is a list of scenes centering around a common anxiety-provoking theme. The scenes are ordered according to the client's report of the amount of anxiety generated by each individual scene.

Dr. K. and Joyce worked very closely on establishing a hierarchy centering around the theme of a fear of spiders. The client was instructed to list a number of scenes, and then make a comparative judgment of the amount of anxiety the imagination of each scene generated. The final list reflected a step-by-step progression in the amount of anxiety the client judged each scene to evoke.

The client stated that her fear of other insects was similar to, although somewhat weaker than, her fear of spiders. Since the anxiety hierarchy was constructed specific to the theme of a fear of spiders, an evaluation was to be made at a later time to ascertain whether spider desensitization also generalized to other insects. If generalization did not occur, separate hierarchies would then be constructed for other insects.

The anxiety hierarchy eventually arrived at was the following, presented in a descending order of anxiety arousal:

1. Spider crawling on client's arm
2. Spider touching client's arm
3. Spider next to client's arm
4. Spider approaching client's arm on arm rest
5. Client watching spider near arm rest
6. Spider crawling up arm rest
7. Spider standing still at chair leg
8. Spider crawling toward chair client is sitting on
9. Spider moving around at far end of room
10. Spider standing still at far end of room
11. Spider crawling around in next room
12. Spider standing still in next room

Once the hierarchy was constructed, the actual desensitization sessions commenced. Dr. K. instructed Joyce to relax and imagine the last scene on the hierarchy. After about eight seconds, the client was instructed to terminate visualization. Joyce was then asked whether she had experienced any anxiety while visualizing the scene, and she reported that she had felt mildly anxious. The therapist then instructed the client to relax again and to visualize the same scene for a number of seconds. This procedure continued until the client was able to picture the scene without anxiety arousal. At this point, the next scene on the hierarchy was worked on. Each new session started with the last scene that was mastered at the previous session. This scene was repeatedly visualized under relaxation, until the client was able to picture the scene without feeling anxious. Only then did the client proceed to the next item.

After each desensitization session, Joyce usually brought up other personal problems that she wanted to talk over with Dr. K. The latter pointed out to the client typical behavior patterns Joyce used in interacting with others, and also discussed the consequences of her behavior on those around her. Joyce was given support and social reinforcement for changing the interaction patterns that were creating problems for her, such as her relationship with her family and her difficulty in expressing her feelings.

Joyce progressed through all of the items on the hierarchy in a three-month period. She reported that the desensitization had also generalized, so that she no longer had an anxiety reaction to any type of insect. Joyce was quite pleased with the results of the therapy program. The alleviation of the fear of confronting spiders was associated with a lessening of other anxieties and doubts. Joyce reported that she was now able to approach social situations from a positive point of view, instead of a feeling of apprehension about whether she would see a spider and have a panic reaction.

Follow-up information was obtained one year after the completion of systematic desensitization therapy. The client indicated that there had been no recurrence of her phobic reaction to spiders and other insects, nor had any other phobic symptoms developed. She reported that she felt more at ease in interpersonal relationships than she had felt prior to therapy. Joyce was doing well academically and she still maintained a close relationship with her boyfriend.

DISCUSSION

Freud (1938) explained the phobic reaction state as being constituted in order to prevent anxiety from breaking out. According to the

American Psychiatric Association's diagnostic manual, a phobia is defined as a fear which is displaced to the phobic object from some other object of which the patient is unaware (DSM-II, 1968). Kutash (1965) similarly wrote that the pathologically feared object is symbolic of an unconscious underlying fear. The anxiety is focused on the phobic object because the particular phobia is less anxiety provoking than the underlying fear. As a result, the person can function quite freely, as long as the phobic situation is avoided. The assumption is made that therapeutic intervention aimed at removing the symptom without uncovering the repressed material will result in the development of yet another symptom. This process is termed symptom substitution.

Recent behavior therapy outcome studies cast doubt on the notion that symptom removal necessarily results in the formation of another symptom. Baker (1969) reported on a follow-up study of a behavior therapy program with enuretic children. He found that the treatment was effective in eliminating the problem of enuresis, and significant additional improvement in social functioning occurred once the symptom was removed. Nolan, Mattis, and Holliday (1970) reported on the outcome of two different types of symptom oriented treatments. Phobic individuals in a systematic desensitization program showed a decline in fear and other social problems after treatment. Youngsters who were treated with operant behavior modification procedures maintained or showed additional improvement six months after therapy was terminated. In both treatment programs, symptom substitution did not occur.

Mowrer, in his two-process theory of avoidance learning (1947), presented an alternative theoretical approach for understanding the phobic reaction. Although Mowrer's early formulations were based on experimental research with animals, the generalizations made from his studies appear to be relevant to human as well as animal behavior. Phobic behavior was viewed as a special case of avoidance learning. Two processes take place in avoidance learning: one involving classical conditioning, and the other involving instrumental learning processes. The first event in avoidance learning is the conditioned emotional response (CER), which occurs through classical conditioning procedures. When there is a contiguity or association in time between a neutral stimulus and an emotionally arousing event, the emotion that was elicited by the painful event (the unconditioned stimulus) becomes associated with the neutral stimulus. The neutral stimulus therefore becomes a conditioned stimulus eliciting the same type of response as occurs after presentation of the unconditioned stimulus. For example, a child who got hurt while playing in a small room could subsequently develop a phobia of small rooms because of the association of two functionally unrelated events, the injury and being in a small room. The small room becomes a conditioned stimulus when responses similar to the emotions experienced from getting injured (the unconditioned response) also begin to occur in the presence of the previously neutral stimulus. The sight or thought of a small room therefore results in a conditioned emotional response consisting of the elicitation of fear or anxiety responses.

The second step in avoidance learning is a process of instrumental conditioning. Through trial and error, the organism learns to perform a response to the conditioned stimulus that results in a reduction of the CER. The escape or avoidance behavior is therefore an instrumental response maintained because of the reinforcement associated with fear reduction. The avoidance (phobic) behavior becomes a highly over-learned response because of the continued reinforcement derived each time there is a reduction of the CER.

After a period of time, the individual learns to avoid the conditioned stimulus even before the CER occurs. According to Mowrer, this is the reason why it is so difficult to unlearn the phobic behavior. A response cannot extinguish unless it appears and is not reinforced. The avoidance response does not extinguish because the person does not stay in the phobic situation long enough for the CER to dissipate in that situation. Anxiety reduction and extinction would eventually occur after the individual has had a chance to experience the phobic situation a number of times without any painful consequences occurring. However, if the person is in the situation for a short period of time and then escapes while still experiencing anxiety, the anxiety does not extinguish, but may become conditioned to additional environmental stimuli associated with the phobic event.

Implosive therapy (Stampfl and Levis, 1967) was also inspired by learning conceptions regarding the nature of anxiety. This technique was based on the assumption that the phobic reaction would extinguish if the person forced himself or herself to intensely imagine the phobic situation and allowed the full extent of anxiety to rapidly occur. As in Mowrer's theory, it was assumed that extinction would result when the individual experienced the anxiety without any actual negative consequences occurring.

The technique of systematic desensitization was also based on the procedure of having the client experience the anxiety associated with the phobic situation. However, with systematic desensitization, the person was exposed to only small amounts of anxiety at a time.

Therefore a gradual development of responses other than anxiety could occur to the previously phobic stimulus.

There has been much controversy in the recent literature concerning the learning processes involved in systematic desensitization. Wolpe stated that the crucial process is one of counterconditioning; i.e., through relaxation training, responses antagonistic to anxiety become conditioned or paired to the cues previously eliciting anxiety (Wolpe, 1969). Relaxation therefore takes the place of anxiety and functions as an inhibitor of anxiety.

Other researchers have reported results suggesting that key elements in the desensitization process may be cognitive set, cognitive rehearsal, or a gradual extinction of anxiety, rather than the counterconditioning of antagonistic relaxation responses to the visualized scenes. Questions have also been raised about the necessity of scene visualization, and whether relaxation training must be employed at all. A good discussion of the research and issues involved in "how" desensitization works can be found in the chapter by P. J. Lang in C. M. Franks' *Behavior Therapy* (1969).

Another learning theory formulation of phobic behavior centers around the principles of imitation or observational learning (Bandura & Walters, 1963). These authors have presented evidence from many sources indicating that individuals can learn new responses merely through having the opportunity to observe others perform these behaviors. It is therefore possible that one of the ways that a phobic behavior can be learned is through exposure to another person who is exhibiting a fear or avoidance response. In this manner, a child can learn to fear dogs without ever having had an unpleasant experience with a dog, if the child has observed someone else avoiding dogs and then imitates this behavior. The avoidance response will have a high probability of being subsequently maintained, if the child is given attention and other social reinforcement for exhibiting this fear.

In analyzing the origin of Joyce's phobic reaction, it is evident that she had ample opportunity to observe her mother engage in phobic behavior toward insects. Mrs. Ryan modeled this fear reaction and exhibited anxiety reduction when the aversive stimulus was removed. Joyce was reinforced for imitating her mother by the maternal solicitude she received when expressing fears similar to those her mother exhibited. Mr. Ryan socially reinforced phobic behavior in both his wife and daughter by amusedly indulging their fears and playing the role of protector.

Mr. Ryan did not reinforce Ted for engaging in phobic behavior, probably because specific fears are considered more in keeping with feminine role stereotypes and are therefore reinforced more with girls. A boy engaging in the same type of behavior is labeled a "sissy," or seen as manifesting effeminate behavior. According to Joyce's account of her childhood, Ted was not given social attention for exhibiting a fear of spiders, and he did not imitate this behavior. For Ted, social approval was contingent on imitating a number of behaviors considered more in keeping with the male role, such as an interest in chemistry.

An interesting issue is why Joyce developed a phobia while her sister Barbara, also female and also observing the mother, did not. It seems likely that Barbara had a larger behavioral repertoire than Joyce did, from which to gain social reinforcement. We know that Barbara was older and therefore had more skills than Joyce. She was also more assertive and got better grades in school. These skills would therefore broaden the behaviors Barbara had available to her that resulted in social reinforcement. Joyce, being younger, could not match her sister's accomplishments at the same moment in time when Barbara performed these activities. She was therefore continuously presented with a model who was achieving at a level which Joyce could not match. However, one of the ways that Joyce was able to gain attention was by expressing a fear of insects.

There is increasing evidence that the opportunity to observe another person engaging in phobic behavior results in an imitation of that behavior (Bandura and Walters, 1963). Research findings also show that emotions can be vicariously instigated by observing a model's emotional responses to a feared object. The vicarious learning of emotional responses has been demonstrated in a series of studies by Berger (1962). An observer viewed a subject who supposedly received an electric shock each time a buzzer sounded. After a number of trials, the observer began to display a conditioned galvanic skin response to the sound of the buzzer. Berger's research clearly showed that emotional responses can be vicariously conditioned, merely through observing another person's emotional response. The observers had not personally undergone the aversive shock situation, but nonetheless began to exhibit a vicariously instigated emotional response after a short period of time.

Although Joyce did not remember experiencing an anxiety provoking event associated with spiders, it does not necessarily follow that she was repressing a traumatic episode. A synthesis of the principles of avoidance and observational learning theories can provide an alternative explanation for the client's behavior. Through observing her mother's fear of spiders, Joyce learned not only the phobic behavior, but the emotional response as well. The client therefore developed an anxiety response when confronted with the phobic object, and the conditioned emotional response subsided only when she engaged in avoidance or escape behavior. Irrespective of whether the avoidance learning occurred directly or through observation, the functional relationship between avoidance behavior and anxiety reduction appears to be the same. In Joyce's case, the phobic problem persisted until adulthood primarily because the anxiety reduction associated with escape or avoidance served to maintain this behavior. The factor of social reinforcement through the attention she received is also important.

The removal of the phobic symptom did not result in the appearance of a new symptom, nor were there any indications of a deterioration of behavioral functioning. On the contrary, the removal of the phobia resulted in greater feelings of self-confidence and competence. The client no longer found it necessary to approach each social situation with a plan about what to do in case she encountered a spider or other insect. Instead of serving as a means of binding up anxiety, the phobic response in Joyce's case functioned to make a greater number of interpersonal situations anxiety provoking. After going through the desensitization process, Joyce experienced a marked lessening of feelings of anxiety. She was able to unlearn the phobic response and be reinforced for engaging in more competent and pleasant modes of social interaction.

In addition to a fear of spiders, Joyce also exhibited many obsessive-compulsive patterns. After treatment, Joyce reported that the obsessive ruminations involved in decision making had lessened also. The greater feelings of self-confidence associated with successful mastery of the phobic problem had apparently made it easier for Joyce to feel more confident in other areas.

It is not unusual to find an individual manifesting several types of neurotic response patterns. Both phobic and obsessive-compulsive symptoms were seen in Joyce's case. Although there are diagnostic categories for mixed symptoms, it is often difficult to achieve agreement between any two diagnosticians on a particular diagnosis (Sandifer, Pettus, and Quade, 1964). In general, classic cases falling into a clear-cut diagnostic category are relatively infrequent. A great many of the individuals undergoing psychological evaluation exhibit mixed neurotic trends or even a combination of neurotic and psychotic patterns.

Joyce stated during the initial evaluation that she wanted help primarily with her fear of insects. This comment could have been interpreted as a sign of defensiveness suggesting that she would be a poor therapeutic risk. On the other hand, the client was communicating a desire to be treated primarily for the situation that was causing her the most discomfort. She perhaps made a quite realistic appraisal that her other problems were within her present coping ability. When the symptom causing her the most discomfort was removed through behavior therapy, Joyce was then able to quite accurately report an improvement in interpersonal functioning.

The difficulties the client described in communicating with others and in interacting with her parents were not explored at great length during the therapy sessions. The student might perhaps ask, "Was this client really helped in therapy?" The response to this question is in large part a value judgment. From a psychodynamic, insight-oriented point of view, the evaluation of the success of therapy would most likely be primarily negative. The client was still faced with a number of personal difficulties, the underlying cause of the disorder had not been dealt with, and she had not achieved insight into the reasons for her behavior.

A behaviorally oriented therapists, on the other hand, would probably view this case as a success. The therapy had achieved its goal of removing the phobic symptom, and there was also a general improvement in interpersonal functioning. Symptom substitution had not occurred, and although the client continued to have a number of "hang-ups," she was also experiencing much greater satisfaction in her life situation. Further, the treatment had been accomplished fairly quickly and at much less expense to the client, compared to the length and cost of verbal psychotherapy.

A total restructuring of personality did not occur during treatment, nor did the client have the opportunity to bring up repressed childhood memories. A question worth pondering is whether these latter procedures are necessary in order to help persons with psychological problems. Because symptom oriented therapies have more limited goals, these methods of treatment may result in improved functioning in a shorter period of time. Clearly, it was not necessary for Joyce to deeply explore her childhood memories in order to be helped to function more adequately at the present time.

REFERENCES

American Psychiatric Association. *Diagnostic and statistical manual of mental disorders.* (2nd ed.) (DSM–II.) Washington: American Psychiatric Association, 1968.

Baker, B. L. Symptom treatment and symptom substitution in enuresis. *Journal of Abnormal Psychology,* 1969, *74,* 42–49.

Bandura, A., & Walters, R. H. *Social learning and personality development.* New York: Holt, Rinehart & Winston, 1963.

Berger, S. M. Conditioning through vicarious instigation. *Psychological Review,* 1962, *69,* 450–466.

Freud, S. *The basic writings of Sigmund Freud.* New York: Modern Library, 1938.

Kutash, S. B. Psychoneurosis. In B. B. Wolman (Ed.), *Handbook of clinical psychology.* New York: McGraw-Hill, 1965. Pp. 948–975.

Lang, P. J. The mechanics of desensitization and the laboratory study of human fear. In C. M. Franks (Ed.), *Behavior therapy: Appraisal and status.* New York: McGraw-Hill, 1969. Pp. 160–191.

Mowrer, O. H. On the dual nature of learning–a reinterpretation of "conditioning" and "problem solving." *Harvard Educational Review,* 1947, *17,* 102–148.

Nolan, J. D., Mattis, P. R., & Holliday, W. G. Long-term effects of behavior therapy: a 12 month follow-up. *Journal of Abnormal Psychology,* 1970, *76,* 88–92.

Sandifer, M. G., Pettus, C., & Quade, D. A study of psychiatric diagnosis. *Journal of Nervous and Mental Diseases,* 1964, *139,* 350–356.

Stampfl, T. G., & Levis, D. J. Essentials of implosive therapy: a learning theory-based psychodynamic behavioral therapy. *Journal of Abnormal Psychology,* 1967, *72,* 496–503.

Wolpe, J. *The practice of behavior therapy.* New York: Pergamon Press, 1969.

Wolpe, J., & Lazarus, A. A. *Behavior therapy techniques: A guide to the treatment of neuroses.* Oxford: Pergamon Press, 1966.

Reactive Depression— "I Die A Little When I Cry"

A young woman called a local counseling center on the advice of the physician at the company where she worked. Angela Savanti was 22 years old, lived at home with her mother, and was employed as a secretary in a large insurance company. She stated that she had had passing periods of "the blues" before, but her present feelings of despondency were of much greater proportions. She was troubled by a severe depression and frequent crying spells, which had not lessened over the past two months. Angela found it hard to concentrate on her job, had great difficulty falling asleep at night, and had a poor appetite. She said her depression had begun after she and her boyfriend Jerry broke up two months previously.

Angela was dressed neatly when she appeared for her first interview. She was an attractive girl, but her eyes were puffy and ringed with dark circles. She answered questions and related information about her life history in a slow, flat tone of voice, which had an impersonal quality to it. She sat stiffly in her chair with her hands in her lap, and moved very little throughout the entire interview.

The client stated that the time period just before she and her boyfriend terminated their relationship had been one of extreme emotional turmoil. She was not sure whether she wanted to get married to Jerry, and he began to demand that she decide either one way or the other. Mrs. Savanti did not seem to like Jerry and was very cold and aloof whenever he came to the house. Angela felt caught in the middle and unable to make a decision about her future. After several confrontations with Jerry over whether she would marry him or not, he told her he felt that she would never decide, so he was not going to see her anymore.

Angela stated that she was both relieved and upset that Jerry had forced the issue and essentially made the decision for her. She did not attempt to contact him, but became increasingly depressed. She had stayed home from work several times during the past month and had just sat around the house and cried.

FAMILY BACKGROUND

Angela came from a working class family of Italian origin. Her only sibling was a sister Doreen, two years younger than she. Both sets of grandparents emigrated from Italy, and her parents were born in the United States. The Savanti family lived in a neighborhood of predominantly Italian ethnic composition and maintained ties to their relatives in the area. Both of the paternal grandparents died when the client was quite young, and Angela's mother and father separated when Angela was 11 years old. Mr. Savanti had moved to another city, and he had never sent money to support the family, nor had he been heard from since his departure. Mr. Savanti had worked as a store salesman when he lived with the rest of the family. After he left, Mrs. Savanti got a job in a factory, and she has worked there ever since.

Angela indicated that she and her sister usually got along fairly well, but they had never confided in each other. The client said that she had always had trouble expressing her emotions, and she felt that Doreen probably had the same problem. When they were younger, the only social activities they participated in together were going to church or visiting relatives. Doreen preferred playing outdoor games with boys and girls, while Angela was less active and spent more time around the house. Doreen usually got better grades in school than Angela did, and Mrs. Savanti always pointed out this difference in their report cards.

Angela stated that her childhood was a very unhappy period. Her father was seldom home, and when he was present, her parents were constantly fighting. Sometimes the arguments became quite severe and her father would throw things and shout. Mrs. Savanti usually became sullen and withdrawn after an argument, refused to speak to her husband, and became uncommunicative with her daughters. Angela remembered that many times as a child she was puzzled because it seemed that her mother was angry at her, too. Sometimes after an argument, Mrs. Savanti told her daughters that she had ruined her life by marrying their father.

Although Mr. Savanti had a poor relationship with his wife, he appeared to take some interest in his daughters. He occasionally accompanied the rest of the family to church on Sundays, and later dropped his wife off at her parents' house while he took the girls to a park or movie. Angela could not remember her mother ever expressing an interest in going somewhere with just Mr. Savanti and the girls. Angela recalled, however, that her father could not be relied on. Many times he did not arrive to take the girls on promised outings and he came home late in the evening instead. He always had an excuse for why he had not come, but he did not appear to understand how disappointed Angela and Doreen were.

Angela remembered very clearly the events that occurred at the time that her father left the family. It was Angela's eleventh birthday, and her mother had baked a cake for her and invited Angela's grandparents over for dinner. Mr. Savanti was supposed to be home after work, and they delayed dinner for about a half hour. When he did not appear, they ate without him. Mrs. Savanti did not make any comments about her husband, but her parents made a number of disparaging remarks about Mr. Savanti's reliability.

Angela reported that she felt worse and worse each time one of her grandparents made a remark, but she tried not to show them how disappointed she was. She also began to worry about whether some mishap had befallen her father, as he had promised her the day before that he would be sure to be home on time for her birthday. She made a comment to her mother expressing concern about why her father had not come home, but Mrs. Savanti abruptly changed the subject. When Angela went to bed that evening, her father still had not appeared. She remembered that she had difficulty falling asleep, because she was both disappointed and worried about where her father was.

Later that night, Angela was awakened by the sound of her parents arguing. She heard her mother accusing her father of being with another woman. Neither mentioned the fact that Mr. Savanti had not come home as promised for Angela's birthday. The argument increased in intensity, and Doreen woke up, also. They eventually heard their father say that he was moving out, because he did not want to live with someone who was not interested in him. Mrs. Savanti said nothing further, and Mr. Savanti packed his clothes and left the house. Doreen and Angela made no comment to each other, nor did they get out of bed and talk with Mrs. Savanti. This was the last contact they had with their father.

Angela recalled that she had felt very guilty when Mr. Savanti left. It seemed that if it hadn't been for her birthday, her parents would not have gotten into an argument and her father would not have gone away. She revealed that whenever she thought of her father, it was always with a feeling that she had been responsible in some way for his leaving the family. Angela had never communicated this feeling to anyone, and her mother rarely mentioned his name.

Angela described her mother as the "long-suffering type." She said that Mrs. Savanti expressed the belief that she had sacrificed her life to make her children happy, and the only thing she ever got in return was grief and unhappiness. Angela related that her mother rarely smiled or laughed and did not converse very much with the girls. She appeared to be most comfortable when they just left her alone and did not talk to her. When Angela and Doreen began going out on dates, Mrs. Savanti never asked them if they had had a good time, but instead, commented on how tired she was because she had waited up for them. She would make disparaging remarks about the boys they had been with and about men in general.

After Mr. Savanti's departure, Angela's mother went to work in a factory near their house. Angela felt that Mrs. Savanti had taken a menial job, and that her mother had a number of skills and was qualified for some other type of work. Mrs. Savanti indicated that she did not want any other job, but nevertheless, she would come home from work each day quite tired and complain about how hard she had worked. She would then put on her robe, cook dinner, and spend the evening watching television. If the girls tried to converse with her, she told them that she was tired and just wanted to be left alone. On the week-ends, Mrs. Savanti generally went over to her parents' house, and she spent her time there in the same manner—fairly uncommunicative, unkempt in appearance, and seated in front of the television set.

Angela said that she liked her grandparents, but now that she was older, it was no longer any fun going to their house. She felt that their ideas were old-fashioned, and she had very few interests in common with them. Her grandparents and mother were very religious, and it seemed that there were always religious overtones to any discussions with them. Angela reported that she was having a great many doubts about her religious faith and beliefs, and these doubts were especially troubling to her around the time she stopped seeing Jerry.

At the time of the clinic visit, Doreen was attending a community college and was occupied with school activities and part-time work. Angela had decided to take business courses in high school, and she reported that she enjoyed her job as a secretary. Both Angela and Doreen lived at home, but each pursued a separate path, except for going to church with their mother on Sunday.

SOCIAL HISTORY

The client indicated that she had always had a number of children to play with, and she also had several friends when she was a teenager. She recalled, however, that it had always been very difficult for her to share her feelings with her friends and tell them about events that were troubling her. Angela considered two of the girls she worked with as her good friends. Nonetheless, she found it hard to tell them much about her relationship with Jerry, or about her feelings of despondency after the breakup.

Angela had dated a number of boys when she was a teenager. She said that she had preferred going out with a group of persons to being alone with one boy, since she did not feel so compelled to carry on a conversation when she was part of a group. Mrs. Savanti was not very friendly to any of her daughters' friends, and Angela indicated that whenever someone came to the house, she felt embarrassed by her mother's untidy appearance and distant manner.

Angela had met Jerry at a party two years previously, when she was 20 and he was 23. She liked him from the first time they met, but she was very careful not to give any indication that she was attracted to him. She said that she was afraid Jerry would not be interested in her, or would not treat her as well if he knew that she liked him.

Angela described Jerry as a talkative and friendly person, of similar ethnic background. She said that he, too, had difficulty expressing his feelings, and many times he resorted to kidding around as a means of avoiding emotional expression. They dated off and on for a number of months and then started to go steady. They continued to go out only with each other until the time of their breakup.

Jerry began to talk about getting married six months prior to when they stopped dating. He said that he had a good job and he wanted to marry Angela. Angela, however, was very ambivalent about what she wanted to do. She enjoyed being with Jerry, but she was troubled by her mother's indifference toward him. Mrs. Savanti made numerous comments to the effect that all men are nice before they get married, but later their true nature comes out.

Angela was confused about her feelings toward Jerry and about his feelings toward her. She was not sure whether she loved Jerry, but she knew she would be unhappy if they stopped seeing each other. When she asked Jerry how he felt about her, he became annoyed and said that it was obvious what his feelings were, because he wanted to marry her.

Angela never told Jerry about the events that occurred at the time her father left the family, nor about her fear that if she did not know exactly what Jerry's feelings were toward her, she would end up in a situation similar to her mother's. Angela was not able to talk these issues over with Doreen, either. She felt that Doreen was living in a completely different world, and that the people Doreen met at college were quite different from the persons Angela associated with.

Angela revealed that she had often been troubled with depressive moods. During high school, if she got a lower grade in a subject than she had expected, her initial response was one of anger, followed by depression. She began to think that she was not smart enough to get good grades, and she blamed herself for studying too little. Angela also became despondent when she got into an argument with her mother or felt that she was being taken advantage of at work. However, these periods of depression usually lasted only about a day, and passed when she became involved in some other activity.

The affect that she experienced when she broke up with Jerry was much more severe in intensity and duration. She was not sure why she was so depressed, but she began to feel as if it were an effort to walk around and go out to work. It became difficult for her to initiate a conversation with others, and many times her lips felt as if they were stiff, and she had to make an effort to move them in order to speak. Angela found it hard to concentrate, and she began to forget things she was supposed to do. It took her a long time to fall asleep at night, and when she finally did fall asleep, she sometimes woke up in the midst of a bad dream. She felt constantly tired, and loud noises, including conversation or the television, bothered her. She preferred to lie in bed rather than be with anyone, and she often cried when alone.

At the point where Angela's depressive state was beginning to seriously interfere with her job, she decided that she had better see the company physician. She asked the doctor to prescribe something to help her sleep, so she would not be so tired and could concentrate better. The physician suggested that Angela receive some professional help with her problems and she was referred to a counseling center in the area.

PSYCHOLOGICAL EVALUATION

Angela was seen by Dr. H., a clinical psychologist. He established good rapport with his client, and although she was hesitant at first, she eventually began to talk more freely about the events related to her breakup with Jerry. She repeatedly stated how difficult it was for her to understand her feelings, let alone express them to someone else.

Angela cooperated during the psychological testing, and attempted to do each task asked of her. However, she did not answer any question spontaneously, and it usually took her several seconds before she gave a response. She was also somewhat slow in her motor behavior, such as putting the pieces of a puzzle together or arranging blocks in a pattern.

The client scored in the average range of intelligence. The long reaction times to verbal stimuli and the slowness of her motor responses suggested an impairment in intellectual functioning. This slowness in verbal and motor behavior is consistent with the performance observed in persons who are depressed. The client's affect, as interpreted from the test material, was constricted and controlled. She appeared to react strongly to some of the events occurring around her, but she controlled her emotions so that others were not aware of how she felt. She was troubled with a strong feeling of depression and a difficulty in sustaining interactions with other persons.

A theme which emerged on several of the tests referred to a person who had an unrealistically high level of aspiration, who was extremely self-critical. As a result, this person labeled her accomplishments as poor or mediocre, no matter how hard she tried. She was constantly plagued with feelings of inadequacy, self blame, and anger, because she was unable to live up to her high standards of performance.

Maternal figures were depicted as controlling and lacking in empathy and warmth. The client described a scene where a woman was forcing her daughter to perform a chore that the mother did not want to do herself. The mother did not understand or care that the daughter was not willing to do the task, and the daughter eventually complied with the mother's wishes.

Male figures were described as nice, but not to be counted on. Part of the blame for this unreliability was placed with the woman the man was interacting with. The assumption was made that she had the ability to modify the man's behavior, so any blame for the man's failings had to be shared by the woman as well.

There were no indications of psychotic thought processes during the interviews or on the test material.

COURSE OF PSYCHOTHERAPY

The counseling center that Angela went to was staffed by a number of persons who were trained in client-centered therapy. The consensus of the staff was that Angela would benefit from this particular method of therapy because of her long standing-difficulty in expressing and accepting her feelings, and her unrealistically high level of aspiration. Angela agreed with the recommendation that she enter into a therapy program, and she met twice a week with Dr. H. for a period of ten months.

The role of the therapist in client-centered therapy is to attain the internal frame of reference of the client, and to indicate to the client that the therapist is able to understand and perceive as the client understands and perceives (Rogers, 1951). Conveying this total understanding will result in the client being able to experience himself or herself as a person having positive as well as negative emotions. The client can then accept all of these feelings without guilt, having experienced that the therapist has been able to acknowledge and respect the entire range of the client's feelings.

The therapist must provide a warm and accepting emotional climate, so the client will eventually trust the therapist and feel free to bring up the events that are causing the emotional discomfort. Rogers uses the terms "empathy" and "unconditional positive regard" to describe the attitudes that the therapist should have in relation to the client (Rogers, 1961). Empathy is defined as the ability to take on the client's internal frame of reference and experience the same feelings that the client is experiencing. The therapist must also be able to convey unconditional positive regard, i.e., acceptance and love for the client as an individual. Rogers feels that only in this atmosphere of empathy and unconditional positive regard will the client eventually learn self-acceptance. Through self-acceptance, the client's self-esteem is raised and the client becomes able to proceed toward greater self-actualization (the full realization of one's potential).

In client-centered therapy, the direction of each therapy session is determined by the client. The therapist does not ask questions or give advice, but deals only with those matters that the client brings up. Angela found it difficult to take an active role in the interactions with the therapist during the initial therapy sessions, but eventually she learned to be more assertive and bring up the issues that were troubling her. Dr. H. focused on reflecting the feelings that Angela was expressing, and on helping Angela to clarify how she felt when particular events transpired.

It became apparent to the client that one of the reasons why she had difficulty in dealing with her emotions was that she felt a great deal of hostility toward many of the persons she cared for. She feared that if she expressed her angry feelings, she would lose the love of these persons. Angela eventually was able to deal with the fact that she had felt very angry at her father each time he had disappointed her, and that she was also angry with Jerry for terminating their relationship.

When her father did indeed desert her, one of the reasons why Angela felt guilty was because she thought that in some way he must have known that she was angry. Angela began to see that she was following a behavior pattern that was similar to her mother's. Angela also kept her feelings to herself and assumed a self-sacrificing attitude.

The client realized that she set unrealistically high standards of performance for herself and others, making it inevitable that she would be disappointed. She expected that both she and Jerry would be totally open and expressive with each other, and she then felt inadequate and confused when they did not achieve this type of relationship. She began to deal with her fear that there is always a loss of caring and affection after several years of marriage, and she became more aware of the characteristic ways she interacted with others.

Angela's depression eased as she began to make progress in therapy. A few months before the termination of treatment, she and

Jerry resumed dating. Angela discussed with Jerry her greater comfort in expressing her feelings and her hope that Jerry would also become more expressive with her. They discussed the reasons why Angela was ambivalent about getting married, and they began to talk again about the possibility of marriage. Jerry, however, was not making demands for a decision by a certain date, and Angela felt that she was not as frightened about marriage as she had previously been.

Therapy was terminated after ten months because Dr. H. was moving to another city. Both Dr. H. and Angela agreed that substantial progress had been made in therapy. Angela made no further effort to contact the counseling center.

DISCUSSION

Angela's despondency when she broke up with her boyfriend could well be considered a normal response to a stressful environmental event. The diagnosis of reactive depression was made on the basis of the intensity and duration of the affective response, i.e., the depression was more severe and more prolonged than the reaction of a normal person under similar circumstances (English and Finch, 1964). (The issue of definitions of normal and abnormal behavior is discussed in detail in Chapter 11.)

A common feature of reactive depression is that the person is unhappy and has lost the pleasure usually derived from every-day activities. Reactive depression is classified as a neurotic disorder because the individual is able to function in society and carry out ordinary activities reasonably well. In psychotic depressions, the person is highly incapacitated and unable to function.

Sigmund Freud wrote a paper in 1917 entitled *Mourning and Melancholia* (1959) that had an important influence on the development of a psychological formulation of depression. In this paper, Freud posited that melancholia or depression was a result of three factors: the loss of a love object, ambivalence (i.e., love as well as hatred for the love object), and a regression of libido into the ego. He further stated that the self blame seen in the clinical picture of depression is a result of reproaches against a love object being shifted on to the patient's own ego.

Psychoanalytically-oriented writers agree that the essential dynamic of depression is the turning of hostile impulses originally directed against other persons back upon the self (Alexander and Shapiro, 1952; English and Finch, 1964). The regression of libido into the ego means that the positive energies of the individual are withdrawn from other persons. The individual loses zest for life because interests are focused on the self, rather than on other persons or events in the environment.

Hofling (1968) took a more eclectic approach to the etiology of depression, and noted that a characteristic of many types of depression is an uncertainty about one's personal worth, and a marked lowering of self-esteem. The verbalization of these feelings of low esteem functions to evoke expressions of reassurance from others that one is indeed a worthwhile person.

There is increasing evidence of changes in biochemical functioning in depressed individuals. The chemical basis for depression appears to be related to a deficiency of serotonin, norepinephrine, and dopamine, all important biochemical agents necessary for brain functioning (Coppen, 1971; Gershon, Bunney, Goodwin, Murphy, Dunner, and Henry, 1971). However, the relationship of emotional states to biochemical factors in body functioning is not known at the present stage of scientific knowledge. The direction of a cause and effect sequence is therefore also hypothetical, i.e., whether emotional changes produce biochemical changes, or vice versa. Furthermore, it is possible that biochemical factors may be more important in the etiology of psychotic than in neurotic depressions.

A social learning explanation of depression suggests that this state may occur when a deprivation of positive reinforcement is the antecedent for a period of aversive emotional arousal. Ferster (1965) proposed that depression is due to a withdrawal of positive reinforcement, resulting in a suppression and reduction in the ongoing behavioral repertoire. The lessening of the amount of behavior that is emitted is therefore a consequence of the loss of major sources of reinforcement. Lazarus (1968) described a behavior therapy technique based on having the depressed individual imaginally project himself or herself a number of months into the future, and think of the positive reinforcers available at that future time. Supporting the hypothesis of depression as a consequence of inadequate reinforcement, Lewinsohn and Libet (1972) found that there is an association between a low rate of positive reinforcement, and the intensity of depression.

Seligman (1974) has suggested a learned helplessness model of depression. On the basis of analogue studies with animals, he proposed that the initial reaction to a stressful situation is anxiety. However, if the organism is unable to control the stressful situation, a learned helplessness or depression develops. In support of this hypothesis, Miller and Seligman (1973) found that depressed persons had a lesser tendency than non-depressed persons to expect success or reward in an activity in which they were engaging, thus suggesting that learned helplessness had become an expectancy or belief system.

In reactive depression, the individual may be responding to a deprivation of positive reinforcement that is permanent, such as the death of a loved one, or temporary, as in failing an important examination or losing one's possessions in a fire. Because of the nature of some environmental circumstances, there is very little the person can do, on a short-term basis, to reinstate the recent loss of positive reinforcement. One can take a failed course over again or rebuild a destroyed house, but the immediate situation remains unchanged. The individual then becomes emotionally aroused in response to the deprivation of customary sources of reinforcement and the cognitive evaluation of helplessness.

The depressive affect may also be associated with the inability to verbalize the state of aversive emotional arousal in the environment where the events occurred. In a circumstance perpetrated by other persons, as in being denied a job or a promotion, one may be blocked from directly verbalizing one's angry feelings because the other person is in a position to retaliate. Thus, labeling and directly verbalizing one's emotions could result in the occurrence of another negative contingency or punishment. In other situations, the agent of the frustration may not be available for the person to direct his or her anger.

Verbalization may take place in an environment where the discriminative stimuli are different from where the deprivation occurred, such as telling a member of one's family about an adverse event that happened at work. The verbalization of feelings therefore ensues in a nonpunishing environment functionally removed from where the loss of reinforcement occurred. Verbalization in this environment will not result in a reduction of the arousal state unless the verbalization is related to attempts at problem solving. On the other hand, the arousal may be further sustained by each recollection of the negative interactions that took place.

When a person engages in activities designed to be distracting from his or her problems, there may be a temporary feeling of relief due to a lowering of the level of chronic emotional arousal. However, as soon as the distraction passes, the person is again confronted with the same problems, and the depressive state recurs. If the activity the person is engaging in is in some way problem solving and not just a distraction, then there may be a more permanent alleviation of the depressive affect. The depression will eventually dissipate over time with the availability and use of alternate sources of reinforcement.

Many persons have been taught that whatever happens to them is their own fault. An individual with this type of history may be extremely self-critical and manifest a lowering of self-esteem as a result of a deprivation of positive reinforcement. One will then observe the often-noted clinical picture of the affectively depressed person who is also tormented by feelings of worthlessness and self-blame (Beck, 1967).

Bandura (1972) wrote that individuals engage in self-reward or self-punishment depending on whether their performance matches or falls short of their self-imposed standards. Marston (1964) suggested that the depressed individual may set a low criterion for negative self-reinforcement. Increasing the frequency of positive self-reinforcement by changing unrealistic standards of behavior would appear to be an important step in treating problems of depression. Related to this hypothesis, Jackson (1972) reported a decline in depression in a woman who was taught to administer positive self-reinforcement such as complimenting herself for completing various activities.

The development of Angela's generalized low level of self-esteem can be traced in part to her observations of her mother's behavior. Mrs. Savanti continuously interacted in a manner that suggested that she thought she was a worthless person, one who was taken advantage of by others, and who suffered in a physically taxing job so she could support her children. Angela imitated her mother's behavior, and she began to think of herself as inadequate, too. She also learned to refrain from expressing her feelings and communicating her problems to others.

Angela was rarely reinforced for any of her accomplishments at school, but she gained her mother's negative attention for what Mrs. Savanti judged to be poor performance at school or at home. Mrs. Savanti repeatedly told her daughter that she was incompetent, and any mishaps that happened to her were her own fault. She therefore received attention from her mother primarily when her mother was criticizing her. When Mr. Savanti deserted the family, Angela's first response was that somehow this event was her fault. From her mother's past behavior, Angela had learned to expect that in some way she would be blamed. At the time that Angela broke up with her boyfriend, she did not blame Jerry for his behavior, but she interpreted this event as a failing solely on her part. As a result, her level of self-esteem was lowered still more.

The type of marital relationship that Angela saw her mother and father model remained her concept of what married life is like. She generalized from her observations of her parents' discordant inter-actions to an expectation of the type of behavior that she and Jerry would ultimately engage in. Angela demanded that Jerry conform to her definition of acceptable interpersonal behavior, because of her belief that otherwise their marriage would not be a mutually reinforcing relationship. However, Angela set such high standards for Jerry's be-havior that it was inevitable that she would be disappointed.

Angela's initial fears of marital unhappiness were probably well founded. Before Angela entered psychotherapy, both she and Jerry were highly noncommunicative with each other. One of the results of therapy was that Angela was able to exhibit greater assertiveness and express her feelings more openly, and she, in turn, was able to reinforce Jerry's verbal behavior when he expressed his feelings. Thus, the nature of their relationship changed, with each person reinforcing the other for improved communication.

Angela was reacting to a crisis period in her life experience at the time that she became depressed. She was at a point where she was being asked to make a decision that had far-reaching ramifications. The difficulty in deciding about marriage was exacerbated by the fact that the client was also having doubts about her religious faith, and inter-preted the fact that she had these doubts as another indication that she was not a good person. The conflict about religion was related to a belief that if she lost her faith, she would also be deprived of the social reinforcement that was associated with her childhood. Being with her family at church on Sundays was an established family pattern that had continued since childhood.

Angela's uncertainties intensified when she was deprived of the major source of positive reinforcement she had, her relationship with Jerry. Despite the fact that she was overwhelmed with doubts as to whether she should marry him or not, she had gained a great deal of gratification through being with Jerry. Whatever feelings she had been able to express, she had shared with him, and with no one else. Angela labeled Jerry's termination of their relationship as proof that she was

4

not worthy of another person's interest. As a result, she became quite depressed.

Psychotherapy provided Angela with the opportunity to learn to express her feelings to the persons she was interacting with, and this was quite helpful to her. Most important, she was able to generalize from some of the learning experiences in therapy, and modify her behavior in her renewed relationship with Jerry. Angela still had much progress to make in terms of changing the characteristic ways she interacted with others, but she had already made a number of important steps in a potentially happier direction.

REFERENCES

Alexander, F., & Shapiro, L. Neuroses, behavior disorders and perversions. In F. Alexander & H. Ross (Eds.), *Dynamic psychiatry.* Chicago: University of Chicago Press, 1952. Pp. 117–139.

Bandura, A. Modeling theory: some traditions, trends, and disputes. In R. D. Parke (Ed.), *Recent trends in social learning theory.* New York: Academic Press, 1972. Pp. 35–61.

Beck, A. T. Depression: *Clinical, experimental and theoretical aspects.* New York: Harper and Row, 1967.

Coppen, A. Biogenic amines and affective disorders. In B. T. Ho & W. M. McIsaac (Eds.), *Advances in behavioral biology* (Vol. 1). *Brain chemistry and mental disease.* New York: Plenum Press, 1971. Pp. 123–133.

English, O. S., & Finch, S. M. *Introduction to psychiatry* (3rd ed.). New York: W. W. Norton, 1964.

Ferster, C. B. Classification of behavioral pathology. In L. Krasner & L. P. Ullmann (Eds.), *Research in behavior modification.* New York: Holt, Rinehart, & Winston, 1965. Pp. 6–26.

Freud, S. *Collected papers* (Vol. 4). New York: Basic Books, 1959.

Gershon, E. S., Bunney, W. E., Goodwin, F. K., Murphy, D. L., Dunner, D. L., & Henry, G. M. Catecholamines and affective illness:

Studies with L-DOPA and Alpha–Methyl–Para–Tyrosine. In B. T. Ho & W. M. McIsaac (Eds.), *Advances in behavioral biology* (Vol. 1). *Brain chemistry and mental disease.* New York: Plenum Press, 1971. Pp. 135–161.

Hofling, C. K. *Textbook of psychiatry for medical practice* (2nd ed.). Philadelphia: Lippincott, 1968.

Jackson, B. Treatment of depression by self-reinforcement. *Behavior Therapy,* 1972, *3,* 298–307.

Lazarus, A. A. Learning theory and the treatment of depression. *Behavior Research & Therapy,* 1968, 6, 83–89.

Lewinsohn, P. M., & Libet, J. Pleasant events, activity schedules, and depressions. *Journal of Abnormal Psychology,* 1972, *79,* 291–295.

Marston, A. R. Personality variables related to self-reinforcement. *Journal of Psychology,* 1964, *58,* 169–175.

Miller, W. R., & Seligman, M. E. P. Depression and the perception of reinforcement. *Journal of Abnormal Psychology,* 1973, *82,* 62–73.

Rogers, C. R. *Client-centered therapy.* Boston: Houghton Mifflin, 1951.

Rogers, C. R. *On becoming a person.* Boston: Houghton Mifflin, 1961.

Seligman, M. E. P. Depression and learned helplessness. In R. J. Friedman & M. M. Katz (Eds.), *The psychology of depression: Contemporary theory and research.* New York: Wiley, 1974. Pp. 83–113.

7

Anxiety Neurosis— The Case of Richard Benson

Richard Benson, age 38, applied to a psychiatrist for therapy because he was suffering from severe and overwhelming anxiety which sometimes escalated to a panic attack. He had been treated for this problem in a private psychiatric hospital, but several weeks after his release, the severe anxiety symptoms recurred and he decided to seek outpatient therapy. During the times when he was experiencing intense anxiety, it often seemed as if he were having a heart seizure. He experienced chest pains and heart palpitations, numbness, shortness of breath, and he felt a strong need to breathe in air. He reported that in the midst of the anxiety attack, he developed a feeling of tightness over his eyes and he could only see objects directly in front of him (tunnel vision). He further stated that he feared that he would not be able to swallow.

Mr. Benson indicated that he had been anxious most of his life, but it was only since his promotion at work six months ago that the feelings of anxiety became a severe problem. The intensity of the anxiety symptoms was very frightening to him and on two occasions his wife had rushed him to a local hospital because he was in a state of panic, sure that his heart was going to stop beating and he would die. His symptoms were relieved after he was given an injection of tranquilizer medication.

Mr. Benson had had a chronic problem of bladder and kidney infections when he was a child, but he had had no further incidence of these infections since the age of 11. Nevertheless, he had continued his childhood practice of always making sure that he knew exactly where a bathroom was located whenever he was in an unfamiliar place. He indicated a fear that he would wet his pants if he could not find a bathroom immediately when he had an urge to urinate. The client stated that he still felt extremely anxious when he did not have direct access to a bathroom, but over the past few months his anxiety had become more intense and had generalized to many other circumstances.

FAMILY HISTORY

Mr. Benson was white and came from an urban, working class environment. Both of his parents were born in the United States, and he was an only child. The client indicated that his parents' marriage was not a happy one, and he recalled their continual arguments. His mother and father separated when he was 8 years old and he had not seen his father since. His mother obtained a job in a restaurant when her husband left the family and she had continued to work as a waitress.

The client revealed that he had always been a fearful youngster. He often played with other children in the neighborhood when he was growing up, but he rarely fought back if one of the children started picking on him. All through the elementary grades, he had been extremely afraid of going to school and his mother had to force him to go each day. His fear stemmed from the fact that there were no bathrooms near his classroom and he was afraid that he would wet his pants in class if he suddenly had to urinate.

The client stated that he had had difficulty controlling his bladder when he had a bladder or kidney infection, and urination at that time was extremely painful. He indicated that several times in school he had partially wet his pants because the teacher had not immediately allowed him to go to the bathroom. He had been intensely concerned that the other children would notice that his trousers were wet and would then make fun of him. Subsequent to these episodes, he experienced an overwhelming need to urinate whenever he was in a place where a bathroom was not available. This pressure would not abate until he actually did urinate.

The client said that his mother had been extremely nervous for as long as he could remember. He also revealed that she was never demonstrative with her affection, but he regarded her as a devoted mother and he expressed fondness for her. She was extremely concerned about his physical health and she always made sure that he got enough sleep. She rarely administered physical punishment and she usually reprimanded him verbally when he misbehaved. Mrs. Benson closely supervised her son's play activities and he was left in the care of a relative when his mother went to work.

Mr. Benson indicated that by the time he was a teenager, he had learned to live with his anxiety about urinating involuntarily. His family physician wrote a note to the school principal stating that it was imperative that Richard be allowed to go to the bathroom whenever he felt the need. Permission was granted and this greatly lessened his fear of being confined in a classroom.

The client had several friends during adolescence and he sometimes associated with girls as part of a large group. However, he did not participate very often in social activities at school and he usually stayed home on the weekend or else visited relatives with his mother.

YOUNG ADULTHOOD

Mr. Benson had obtained an office job in a large investment corporation after he graduated from high school and had worked for that company ever since. His wife was employed as a secretary at the same corporation and they became acquainted at work.

The client's wife came from a large family and she had a number of relatives living in the area. She was the only girl that Mr. Benson had dated for any length of time, although she had gone out with several young men before they met. They decided to get married about a year after they started dating each other. They began saving their money and two years later they were married.

Mr. Benson described his relationship with his wife as a harmonious one. He said that both he and his wife were sexually inexperienced when they first married, but he indicated that there had been no problem in their marriage due to sexual concerns. He further stated that his wife was very understanding about his discomfort in situations where there was no bathroom available and she usually helped him to locate rest room facilities in any new place they were in.

The major area of disagreement between the Bensons involved their children, a son who was 10 and a daughter 7 at the time of evaluation. The client commented that he tended to be somewhat overprotective with them, but his wife believed in pushing the children into various activities so they would not be afraid of new situations. For example, when Richard Jr. was in first grade, Mrs. Benson arranged for him to walk to and from school with some other children in the neighborhood. Mr. Benson, however, felt that his wife should take Richie to school herself because his son was too young to be entrusted to the care of other youngsters. Mrs. Benson was convinced that the children could be relied on to help Richie cross the few streets to the school and after much further discussion, the client acceded to his wife's wishes.

Mr. Benson indicated that a struggle took place each evening because Cheryl refused to go to bed until it was her older brother's bedtime. The client considered himself more lenient than his wife in matters of disciplining the children and he said that he did not feel that it was worth the nightly struggle to insist that Cheryl go to bed at a specified hour. However, his wife felt that Cheryl was tired and cross the next day when she went to bed at the same time as Richie. Cheryl quickly learned to appeal to her father for help in staying up later, although, with a great deal of reluctance, he eventually backed up his wife's demands that Cheryl go to bed.

The client stated that these problems were relatively minor. He generally enjoyed the warmth of his family and he felt that his wife and children derived pleasure from being with him, too. They often went together on outings or to visit relatives and these events were quite pleasant, as long as he knew that rest room facilities were close by.

Mr. Benson and his wife had a number of friends and they also saw their relatives quite often. The client said that before the recent onset of severe anxiety symptoms, he was an easygoing person who was able to converse well with others. However, he stated that he usually gave in to the wishes of other persons because he did not like to argue. He felt that he was being pushy and overbearing if he tried to change another person's opinion or influence a friend's behavior in some way. For example, if he were discussing politics with someone and the latter disagreed with his opinion, he immediately attempted to change the subject and tried to avoid discussing the issue any further.

The client considered his ability to get along smoothly with others an important occupational asset, and he believed that this ability was a factor in his recent promotion to a more responsible position. He indicated, however, that he often felt angry and helpless because he continually acceded to the wishes of others, but the thought of freely expressing his opinions made him feel quite anxious.

PRESENT PROBLEM

Mr. Benson reported that soon after he was promoted to a new position, his anxiety symptoms had markedly intensified. He was confronted with greater job responsibilities requiring immediate decisions and he was no longer able to spend most of the working day at his desk. He had to meet with persons in their offices and he was sometimes involved in conferences in unfamiliar buildings that lasted an hour or more. It was more difficult for him to find a bathroom in his immediate vicinity and if he did not locate a rest room before he began conferring with someone, he felt an overwhelming need to urinate. He was extremely fearful that he would embarrass himself by wetting his pants and he eventually had to make some excuse in order to leave the conference and urinate in a rest room.

The client revealed that he had also begun to feel trapped when someone engaged him in conversation, and he occasionally experienced a sensation of panic. Even if he knew the location of a bathroom, he did not feel that he was free to leave the room as long as someone was talking to him. He also feared that he would be trapped in his car by heavy traffic, or that his car would stall in a tunnel or on a bridge.

Mr. Benson had been treated by the same family physician for a number of years. Periodic testing indicated that the intense urge to urinate was not caused by infections or other physical problems. The physician prescribed tranquilizer medication and recommended psychiatric help if the anxiety symptoms became more severe. However, Mr. Benson went back to his family physician when the somatic symptoms reached the terrifying point when it seemed as if he were having a heart attack. Despite the fact that he was already being maintained on tranquilizers, these symptoms did not lessen until he was given an injection of a supplementary dose of this medication.

As the anxiety symptoms became more severe and persistent, the client began to worry about when another acute anxiety attack would occur and this apprehension made him more anxious still. He expressed a general concern about his physical well being and he became extremely sensitive to any fluctuations in his breathing or difficulties in swallowing. He began to note the location of doctor's offices and hospitals in whatever vicinity he happened to be in and he became extremely anxious if medical help were not close by.

Mr. Benson reported that he had derived great enjoyment from bicycle riding with his children on the weekend. However, he became more and more reluctant to go cycling because many of the trails the children urged him to go on did not have bathroom or medical facilities available. Mr. Benson felt that he would be a poor example to his children if he urinated in the woods and he was extremely concerned about being close to a hospital. He eventually gave up cycling even on familiar trails with hospitals near by, because he was afraid that the rest room facilities would be in use if he had a sudden urge to urinate.

Mr. Benson stated that he could not fight off his constant feelings of anxiety and he was unable to control his behavior when the anxiety symptoms occasionally spiralled to a panic attack. He could not sit still when he felt acutely and painfully anxious and the only way he could find relief from his symptoms was to go home and pace back and forth in his yard. Gradually, he stopped perspiring and the rapid heart rate and other somatic symptoms subsided as well. He went back into the house as soon as he felt calmer, but after a half hour the symptoms often reappeared and the anxiety episode started all over again. At that point, the only way he could bring the anxiety attack under control was to contact his physician for a tranquilizer injection.

After suffering through an episode of severe anxiety, the client said that he was unable to eat and he could not go to work the next day. He took a sick leave from his job five weeks after the anxiety attacks began, because he was intensely anxious in most interpersonal situations. He found it difficult to be out of the house even during the short time it took to do an errand at a neighborhood store and he therefore tried to stay home as much as possible. The client reported that his wife had been quite tolerant of his fears up to that time, but she was becoming annoyed by the frequency and inconvenience of the anxiety symptoms.

With the help of his physician and the encouragement of his wife, Mr. Benson admitted himself to a psychiatric hospital for more intensive treatment. He felt that he was going downhill in his struggle to control his anxiety and he was well aware of the changes in his life situation that had resulted from the disabling anxiety symptoms.

HOSPITALIZATION RECORD

Mr. Benson was diagnosed as suffering from anxiety neurosis. He was administered tranquilizer medication four times a day and the dosage level was gradually reduced as the anxiety symptoms lessened. He was seen several times a week by a psychiatrist who explored with him the childhood origins of the anxiety reaction. They also discussed the relationship of the anxiety symptoms to the current work situation.

Reading materials, cards, and games were available in the hospital and the staff encouraged Mr. Benson to relax and converse with the other patients. Bathroom facilities were easily accessible on the ward and in other areas of the hospital. After he had been hospitalized for two weeks, the anxiety symptoms diminished and he was able to converse with others without feeling trapped.

Mr. Benson was discharged from the hospital one month after his admission. He stated that he felt greatly improved both physically and psychologically and was ready to return to work. He was continued on tranquilizer medication and he was also advised to continue psychiatric treatment on an outpatient basis. Mr. Benson said that he did not immediately follow through with the therapy recommendation because he was able to function well in his social milieu as long as he took the medication regularly. However, after several weeks he noticed that the anxiety symptoms were beginning to intensify once more and he became extremely concerned that he would have a recurrence of the severe anxiety attacks he had suffered prior to hospitalization.

Mr. Benson then made an appointment to see a local psychiatrist who was skilled in behavior therapy techniques.

PSYCHOLOGICAL EVALUATION

Dr. C. interviewed the client and he asked Mr. Benson to complete a number of self-administered tests. Mr. Benson behaved in a friendly and cooperative manner, although he appeared quite tense and anxious. He sat stiffly in his chair, with each hand tightly grasping the chair arm. Several times, he exhibited a startle reaction when a question was directed to him. He spoke at length about his problems and he said that he was distressed because he felt helpless in coping with his mounting feeling of anxiety.

Mr. Benson was asked to describe himself and he replied that he was a fearful person who was most anxious to get over these fears so he could live life to the fullest. He said that he was constantly thinking about getting well and was extremely upset by the fact that he was unable to overcome his fears.

Some of the tests administered to the client were different from the projective tests often employed by psychodynamically oriented diagnosticians. The assumption in using projective tests such as the Rorschach and the Thematic Apperception Test is that the responses to these ambiguous stimuli will reflect varying levels of the individual's unconscious processes. However, the usefulness of a given test is highly dependent on the particular diagnostician's assessment of the relevance of the information gained. If the goal of therapy is to modify presently existing behavior problems, then assessment procedures that give knowledge about current interactions may provide the most useful type of data. On the other hand, the therapist's approach to treatment may be based on the conviction that the processes requiring change are forces within the unconscious psyche of the individual. Then, the most important kind of information to collect may be projective test responses presumed to reflect these unconscious processes.

Since the therapist treating Mr. Benson was primarily interested in present interactions, the client was administered the Fear Inventory and the Assertion Scale (Wolpe and Lazarus, 1966), and several other self administered tests. Mr. Benson also completed the Minnesota Multiphasic Personality Inventory (MMPI), in order to gain information about the nature of his symptoms and the deviance of these symptoms from the population norm.

The client's test responses on the Fear Inventory could be grouped into several themes: a fear of physical harm, fear of interpersonal aggression, and a fear of being trapped. For example, the client reported a high intensity of fear in the following situations: "Prospect of surgical operations," "Becoming nauseous," "One person bullying another," "The sight of fighting," "Journeys by train," and "Being in an elevator."

The Assertion Scale responses indicated that the client had great difficulty behaving in an assertive but nonaggressive manner and he showed a tendency to avoid expressing his feelings. These tendencies were illustrated by the client's "yes" answers to the following items: "Are you inclined to be overapologetic?" "Do you usually keep your opinions to yourself?" "Do you usually keep quiet for the sake of peace?" "Is it difficult for you to compliment and praise others?"

The MMPI results also gave evidence of an individual who is troubled by a high level of anxiety and somatic preoccupation. There was no indication of thoughts or behavior suggestive of psychotic processes. The personality inventory results generally confirmed the diagnosis of anxiety neurosis.

COURSE OF THERAPY

Dr. C. felt that the most effective treatment procedure was one that directly modified the highly generalized anxiety response that was so distressing and limiting to the client. Further, it seemed important that Mr. Benson broaden his behavioral repertoire through learning how to act in a more assertive manner. By means of assertive training, he could be provided with more effective and satisfying social skills.

The therapist initially employed systematic desensitization with relaxation to condition the client to respond without anxiety to stimuli that were usually anxiety provoking. (See Chapter 5 for a full explanation of the systematic desensitization process.) An anxiety hierarchy was established, based on the fear elicited in situations where a bathroom was not available. After relaxation training was completed, the client was instructed to relax and visualize the scene on the anxiety hierarchy that provoked the least amount of anxiety. However, although the client could visualize quite clearly the various images on the anxiety hierarchy, this technique did not prove effective in reducing anxiety in real life situations. This procedure may not have been successful because the anxiety response was elicited by so many environmental stimuli, including numerous types of social situations.

Dr. C. then initiated a program aimed at modifying the anxiety response in the client's everyday environment, rather than in the therapist's office. This in vivo (real life) desensitization technique was also focused on situations where rest-room facilities were not immediately available. The client was given a number of assignments that were graded according to the amount of anxiety elicited and he was told to carry out these tasks in a step-by-step fashion. He worked on the least anxiety provoking task until he could perform that behavior without anxiety, and only then did he proceed to the next assignment.

Mr. Benson was first instructed to ride his bicycle along familiar roads with known bathrooms. He was told to stop at each rest room, go in and comb his hair, but to try not to urinate. Through mastering each task in succession, after several months he was able to cycle alone along unfamiliar trails. He reported that he did not feel anxious, nor did he feel the need to stop at a rest room. The client also succeeded eventually in cycling with other persons, without experiencing anxiety or the urge to urinate. Throughout this time period, Mr. Benson received a great deal of social reinforcement from his family and the therapist for each assignment that he successfully carried out.

After the client began to make some progress in traveling greater distances from bathroom facilities, implosive therapy was employed to modify his fear of social embarrassment. This problem had not been specifically dealt with in either of the systematic desensitization procedures. During implosive therapy (Stampfl and Levis, 1967), the therapist minutely describes scenes that are intensely anxiety provoking to the client. The latter is instructed to imagine, in the most vivid detail possible, the sights, sounds, and tactual experiences of those anxiety provoking situations. The client is encouraged to reach a high level of anxiety and to maintain this level until the described scene no longer elicits anxiety. Stampfl and Levis postulated that the reduction in anxiety occurred through the process of extinction.

Mr. Benson participated in several four to five hour sessions in which the therapist flooded him with continuous overwhelming images of being trapped alone and with other persons and urinating in his pants. These images were continually and vividly presented until the client no longer felt anxious during their visualization. This procedure proved highly effective in lessening the client's fear of embarrassment in social situations and the extinction of anxiety generalized to events outside of the therapist's office.

Through assertive training, the client learned broader interpersonal skills so he did not have to continually act in a submissive manner and then become anxious or angry. The therapist modeled more effective and assertive ways of dealing with the interpersonal difficulties that occurred at work and Mr. Benson then role played these new behaviors under the guidance of the therapist. Other interpersonal problems were discussed and evaluated from the standpoint of the submissive way in which the client habitually responded to social interactions. Alternative behaviors were then suggested and practiced.

Mr. Benson displayed a continuous improvement in his interpersonal functioning during treatment and there was a marked decline in his chronic anxiety level. After two years in therapy, he no longer felt trapped in situations where a bathroom was not available and he therefore was not as concerned about being embarrassed in front of other persons. He had not had a panic attack in almost two years and he had been able to go camping with his family in an area where there were no hospitals close by. The client was also functioning quite well at work and he reported that he found new pleasure in interacting with his family and other persons. Although he still took tranquilizer medication from time to time, these occasions were quite infrequent.

DISCUSSION

Anxiety neurosis

> "is characterized by anxious over-concern extending to panic and frequently associated with somatic symptoms . . . anxiety may occur under any circumstances and is not restricted to specific situations or objects" (DSM-II, 1968, p. 39).

Sigmund Freud originally delineated this chronic state of anxiety as a specific syndrome, which is called "angstneurose" (Jones, 1963). He described a condition of morbid anxiousness that was inappropriate to external circumstances and associated with every activity the person engaged in. This apprehensive expectation was manifested by a general restlessness, irritability, and feeling of worry. Ernest Jones (1963) wrote that the mental and physical symptoms of anxiety neurosis were an exaggeration of the normal physiological accompaniments of fear and therefore a perversion of the fear instinct.

Freud's initial theory of anxiety neurosis postulated that the underlying cause of the anxiety symptoms was excessive and unrelieved sexual tension. He stated that that sexual instinct became deflected in its aim and was then manifested physically and mentally as morbid anxiety. Jones stated unequivocally that anxiety neurosis would not occur in persons whose sexual needs were being gratified. Jones also wrote that the most effective type of treatment for anxiety neurosis was one that corrected the sexual disturbance.

Psychodynamic theorists, such as Adler, Horney, Fromm, and Sullivan, disputed Freud's contention that all neuroses originated from a real or, as Freud later added, an imagined sexual trauma. Each of these theorists proposed an alternative basic problem as the underlying cause of neuroses. However, there does appear to be a consensus among psychodynamic theorists that anxiety symptoms are due to the lack of specific defense mechanisms for controlling this affect (Noyes and Kolb, 1963). As a result, the anxiety remains diffuse or "free floating" and the individual is in a continual state of anxious expectation.

Psychoanalytic theory makes a distinction between fear and anxiety. A response to a realistic, objective danger is defined as a fear reaction, while anxiety is viewed as an apprehension about expressing one's forbidden instinctual impulses. Learning theorists tend to label a particular emotional reaction as fear if the response occurs in relation to a specific environmental stimulus. Anxiety is often defined as a reaction to a variety of threatening or noxious cues, or to less clearly defined environmental stimuli. However, fear and anxiety are not seen as qualitatively different entities (Lazarus, 1972), and the physiological component of the fear or anxiety response is considered to be the same.

Behavior theorists view neurotic reactions as learned behaviors that are acquired in the same way that other behaviors are. Wolpe (1962) stated that neurotic reactions are learned responses to anxiety that can be eliminated only through unlearning. Anxiety neurosis was interpreted as a process involving the conditioning of the anxiety response to a large number of stimuli frequently encountered by the individual. The maladaptive responses were initially learned in conflict situations or in other situations that elicited intense anxiety, and the anxiety response then generalized to a number of other environmental stimuli.

Wolpe stated that neurotic habits followed the principle of primary stimulus generalization. The intensity of the neurotic reaction in a given situation would then be determined by the degree of similarity between the present stimulus and the original conditioned stimulus. Bandura (1969) cited evidence demonstrating that the emotional responses elicited by a particular stimulus often generalized to other cues on the same physical or semantic dimension as the original stimulus. As a result of this conditioning process, it would be possible for the individual to experience continual or "free floating" anxiety.

Wolpe (1969) asserted that therapy should be specifically aimed at modifying the maladaptive conditioned response. He considered the procedures of reciprocal inhibition and the counterconditioning of the anxiety response to be crucial processes for unlearning neurotic reactions. Thus, the technique of systematic desensitization was originally based on the principle of counterconditioning a relaxation response to inhibit and take the place of the anxiety response. However, this viewpoint of how systematic desensitization functions has been challenged by other behavior therapists (e.g., Lazarus, 1971).

In anxiety neurosis, the anxiety response is a highly overlearned and generalized behavior pattern that is manifested in many kinds of situations. Therefore, severe anxiety may often be associated with a low frequency of sexual activity, but this finding does not necessarily imply that unrelieved sexual tension is the cause of the anxiety symptoms, as psychoanalytic theorists have stated. The clinical observation that anxiety neurotics manifest a lower frequency of sexual gratification may be due to the inhibition of sexual behavior by anxiety responses antagonistic to sexual arousal. This point can be demonstrated by Wolpe and Lazarus's technique (1966) of eliciting sexual arousal as a means of inhibiting anxiety.

Social learning theorists have expanded on the initial behavioral formulation of neurotic reactions as learned habits. The social learning approach stresses the importance of social reinforcement and observational learning in the acquisition and maintenance of adaptive as well as maladaptive behaviors. A functional relationship is postulated between given behavior patterns and reinforcement and modeling processes in operation in the individual's social environment.

Lazarus (1971) discussed the importance of social learning factors in the acquisition of neurotic behavior. He stated that it is too simplistic and mechanistic to consider neurotic symptoms merely as simple, learned or conditioned habits. According to Lazarus (1972), the treatment of neurotic symptoms requires the unlearning or relearning of interpersonal as well as situational sources of anxiety. For therapy to be most effective, it is often necessary to go beyond the modification of specific maladaptive behaviors and deal with the interpersonal context in which a problem is manifested. The interpersonal conditions maintaining a particular pattern of behavior must therefore be evaluated and changed. Lazarus suggested that the therapist should be skilled in a wide variety of techniques, so the procedures used in an individual case can be accommodated to the needs and problems of that particular client.

Knowledge of the past history of an individual is important in understanding personality development and in analyzing how a specific behavior was learned. However, that knowledge may not be particularly relevant in teaching a troubled individual alternative and more adaptive ways of dealing with the environment. The most fruitful and efficient approach to treatment may therefore be one that focuses on modifying the interaction patterns in the present environment that are maintaining the particular maladaptive behaviors. A given behavior problem can therefore be analyzed from the standpoint of how the individual's behavior determines the manner in which that person interacts with others, and conversely, how the behaviors that the person has learned to emit affect the way others respond to one.

Richard Benson's problems can be understood within a social learning framework if one evaluates the interpersonal as well as the situational factors influencing the development of his symptoms. Due to the childhood occurrence of severely discomforting physical symptoms, the client was classically conditioned to respond with anxiety to cues of bladder distention. The painful bladder and kidney infections and the associated pain during urination made this naturally occurring event highly aversive. Because of a fear of urinating involuntarily, the anxiety response generalized and included all situations where a bathroom was not immediately available. A great many social situations therefore became cues for anxiety because of the anticipated embarrassment that would result from involuntary urination.

It is likely that the conditioned anxiety response eventually would have extinguished when the client was a youngster if this response pattern had not been so generalized and so strongly reinforced by anxiety reduction. As the bladder infections became less frequent and eventually terminated, the anxiety associated with the possibility of uncontrolled urination should also have dissipated. However, the anxiety response had become classically conditioned to a great many physiological and environmental stimuli, and seeking closer proximity to a bathroom and urinating became an instrumental response that reduced anxiety in a variety of interpersonal situations. Each repetition of this behavioral sequence was followed by anxiety reduction, which further strengthened the avoidance conditioning process. Eventually, interpersonal anxiety in and of itself became a stimulus for the instrumental response of seeking a bathroom.

Although the client was deficient in assertive skills, he was able to get along well with his co-workers, and he apparently possessed the intellectual ability necessary to do his job well. He was able to function without overwhelming anxiety as long as he stayed within the self-imposed restrictions of his social environment, i.e., close to bathroom facilities. However, he began to experience intense anxiety and then panic reactions when his job responsibilities made it impossible for him to restrict his mobility. Mr. Benson was highly motivated to succeed in his new job position, and he attempted to perform well, despite the severe symptoms which eventually generalized beyond the work environment.

The client spent four weeks in a psychiatric hospital. This separation from the environment that was so anxiety-provoking was initially beneficial to him. However, while he was in the hospital, he did not learn any new skills that could take the place of his maladaptive behavior patterns. After he returned to his social milieu, there was a gradual recurrence of the severe anxiety symptoms, probably because he was confronted again with the same environmental problems.

The behavior therapy approach was apparently effective because the anxiety symptoms and the behaviors resulting from anxiety cues were directly dealt with. The highly overlearned anxiety response and the conditioned avoidance reaction showed marked evidence of extinction during the in vivo desensitization procedures. As the client succeeded in carrying out the tasks required of him, he was reinforced for this behavior by the social approval of others and by the self-gratification that came from a new sense of mastery and competence.

The flooding procedures were effective in alleviating some of the interpersonal aspects of the client's anxiety. Through vividly imagining a number of highly feared situations without these events actually taking place, the fear of involuntary urination and social embarrassment was extinguished. In addition, assertive training helped the client to learn more flexible interpersonal skills so he no longer responded in a submissive manner to all types of social situations.

It is clear that the client was intensely uncomfortable and distressed by his anxiety symptoms. However, the strength of the conditioning process made it virtually impossible for him to modify these responses, without therapeutic intervention addressed specifically to extinguishing these behaviors. The client realistically expressed a feeling of helplessness about controlling his symptoms, because the anxiety responses were not under voluntary control. The reduction in chronic anxiety level was therefore highly reinforcing to the client, as was his success in gradually changing his typical behavior patterns.

With the alleviation of the anxiety symptoms and the acquisition of additional social skills, there was a concomitant expansion in the client's social relationships. He was able to interact more effectively with others and to receive more gratification from interpersonal situations. The conditioning processes in existence since childhood had been modified by therapeutic intervention.

REFERENCES

American Psychiatric Association. *Diagnostic and statistical manual of mental disorders* (2nd ed.) (DSM–II). Washington, D.C.: American Psychiatric Association, 1968.

Bandura, A. *Principles of behavior modification.* New York: Holt, Rinehart, & Winston, 1969.

Jones, E. *Treatment of the neuroses.* New York: Schocken Books, 1963.

Lazarus, A. A. *Behavior therapy and beyond.* New York: McGraw-Hill, 1971.

Lazarus, A. A. Phobias: broad spectrum behavioral views. *Seminars in Psychiatry,* 1972, *4,* 85–92.

Noyes, A. P., & Kolb, L. C. *Modern clinical psychiatry* (6th ed.). Philadelphia: Saunders, 1963.

Stampfl, T. G., & Levis, D. J. Essentials of implosive therapy: A learning-theory-based psychodynamic behavioral therapy. *Journal of Abnormal Psychology,* 1967, *72,* 496–503.

Wolpe, J. The experimental foundations of some new psychotherapeutic methods. In A. J. Bachrach (Ed.), *Experimental foundations of clinical psychology.* New York: Basic Books, 1962. Pp. 554–575.

Wolpe, J. *The practice of behavior therapy.* Oxford: Pergamon Press, 1969.

Wolpe, J., & Lazarus, A. A. *Behavior therapy techniques. A guide to the treatment of neuroses.* Oxford: Pergamon Press, 1966.

8

A Life of Compulsive Rituals—The Case of Ruth Langley

Ruth Langley was 30 years of age when she sought the help of a behavior therapist. She had been in treatment since childhood with a succession of therapists who had used other treatment methods. The client had read about some recent developments in the field of behavior modification, and after a period of indecision, she made an appointment to see Dr. M.

Ruth was extremely thin. She sat rigidly in her chair, with her hands tightly folded, and she maintained an expressionless gaze and tone of voice. She revealed that she was troubled by a longstanding feeling of contamination which compelled her to carry out cleansing activities numerous times each day. She stated that she became intensely uncomfortable if she noticed any dirt on her person or in her immediate environment, and she responded to this feeling by thoroughly washing her hands and arms. If she detected some dirt in her house, she was compelled to completely and methodically scrub her apartment, in addition to showering in a rigidly specified manner. The client reported that she also felt contaminated after going to the bathroom and after doing housework or cooking, and again, she was compelled to thoroughly wash herself.

Ruth complained that her life was extremely restricted because she was spending most of her time engaged in some type of behavior she felt driven to carry out. In addition, each ritual activity was becoming more involved and time consuming. At the time of the interview, she was washing her hands at least three or four times an hour, showering six or seven times a day, and thoroughly cleaning her apartment at least twice a day.

The client was white and came from a Protestant, upper socioeconomic class background. Ruth was unmarried and she lived alone in a studio apartment. She had an independent income which provided her with comfortable financial support, and she spent her free time painting. However, she had done very little art work over the past few years, because her time had been so occupied with the performance of the various ritualistic behaviors.

CHILDHOOD BACKGROUND

The client indicated that her parents had an extremely superficial marital relationship. Mr. Langley was often away on extended trips, and her parents pursued their own separate interests. They usually interacted with each other in a polite and formal manner, although Ruth said that occasionally she had heard them arguing. When Mr. Langley was at home, he sometimes invited friends of the family over for dinner. However, Ruth felt that her mother did not really enjoy being with other persons, and Mrs. Langley also seemed more at ease when her husband was not at home.

Ruth described her mother as a cold and distant person, who was always involved primarily with her own interests. The client felt that her mother preferred the company of her horses and dogs to human companionship. Mrs. Langley typically spent most of her time alone, and only on rare occasions did she attend a social function. Ruth could not recall her mother ever hugging or kissing her, and Mrs. Langley tended to be very critical of Ruth when they were together. Mrs. Langley has been in some form of psychotherapy ever since Ruth could remember.

Ruth said that she was always very excited and happy when her father was at home. They laughed and had fun together, and they often spent some time horseback riding. She always felt keenly disappointed when he abruptly departed after being home for just a few days, even though he typically left in this manner and would then be gone for an indefinite period.

Ruth was an only child, and she grew up in the care of a succession of governesses. She described her family's large house as a very quiet and lonely place, with no other children close by for her to play with. When she was a child, she sometimes sought out the companionship of persons on the household staff, but the employees tended to relate to her in a very formal manner.

Ruth stated that the persons who took care of her consistently discouraged her from running around in spontaneous play, and they always made sure that she was immaculately clean. Mrs. Langley was highly critical of Ruth and her caretakers if her daughter was less than perfectly well groomed. The client said that her father was not as concerned about her appearance around the house, but if there were company present, he too expected her to look impeccably neat.

SCHOOL HISTORY

Ruth attended private day schools throughout her school career. She generally did not participate in games or play activities at school, and she particularly tried to avoid any kind of physical contact with the other children. She indicated that she was concerned that she would get dirty if she got too involved in play activities.

Ruth did not have any friends during adolescence, nor did she attend social functions at school. The behavior rituals she engaged in were quite noticeable by this time, and her classmates often ridiculed her because she repeatedly washed her hands in a specified manner, or walked around the school grounds in a precise and unvarying pattern.

The client received adequate grades in school and she excelled in her art courses. She enjoyed painting, and her teachers and the other students often made favorable comments about her work. Ruth stated that she was more comfortable while she was painting than at any other time in her daily existence.

SYMPTOM HISTORY

Ruth had engaged in ritual behaviors for as long as she could remember. She recalled that the persons taking care of her encouraged her to perform these behaviors, so she would keep clean and be occupied in some type of activity. By the time she was four or five years old, she had already developed a complex play sequence which involved putting all of her dolls in exactly assigned postures. She would raise a particular doll's arm to a certain angle and she would then point its legs in a given direction. She then placed each of her many dolls in other specified positions. When all of the dolls were arranged in this manner, she moved each of them in turn to another part of her room, where she established a different pattern of doll placement and position. She repeated this sequence four or five times, organizing each placement somewhat differently from the previous one. She also repeated in order certain words and phrases, such as "good doll," "bad doll," as she engaged in this play activity. Ruth remembered that she became extremely uneasy if she was interrupted in the middle of the doll-placing ritual, and she continued to feel uncomfortable until she was able to complete the entire sequence.

Ruth indicated that she experienced a strong feeling of satisfaction when she carried out the minute details of the ritual she was engaged in, and as she grew older, she developed many other stereotyped patterns of behavior. Before going to bed, she went through a set procedure of placing her pillow, blankets and various objects in her room in a particular spot, and she repeated specific phrases as she carried out this activity. When she got up in the morning, she arranged her pillow and blankets in yet another position and she moved the objects in her room to other assigned placements. If she did not complete the ritual each day in exactly the same manner, she experienced intense anxiety until she was able to do so.

Since childhood, Ruth had also engaged in complicated ritual activities related to procedures of cleanliness. She washed herself several times each day according to a set pattern. If it seemed as if she had soiled her clothing in any way, she repeated the washing sequence and changed her clothes as soon as possible. In the course of her activities at school and at home, it was often necessary to touch books or objects that she considered unclean. As a result, she was repeatedly compelled to wash her hands, with the thoroughness of the procedure depending on what she had been in contact with.

The client was ten years old when she was taken to a mental health professional for the first time. Her teacher had indicated to her that the time and attention she devoted to repetitive behaviors was interfering with her classroom performance. Ruth presumed that the school personnel had also advised Mrs. Langley that Ruth needed professional evaluation, because she was taken to a therapist soon after

Mrs. Langley attended a conference at school. The client has periodically been in some form of therapy ever since, initially in play therapy, and as she grew older, in some form of verbal psychotherapy. However, the ritual behavior did not lessen, despite these therapeutic efforts.

PRESENT FUNCTIONING

Following her graduation from high school, Ruth occupied herself by painting and taking art courses. She said that there was no one her age she felt particularly close to, and she did not participate in social activities with either men or women. When she did converse with others, the topic of conversation usually centered on the subject of art. Ruth indicated that she did not feel comfortable discussing other topics.

The client moved into her own apartment when she was 21 years old, and since that time, she saw her family only infrequently. She said that she enjoyed living alone because she was able to arrange her living space as she liked, without worrying that someone else would disturb her room arrangement or bring dirt into the room. Further, she was now free to buy and prepare only those foods which she considered healthful and free of contaminants.

The client stated that she was not bothered by all types of uncleanliness and disorder. She categorized aspects of her environment as "good dirt" and "bad dirt," and she did not engage in rituals in response to "good dirt." For example, she did not experience a compulsion to clean herself if she became spotted while painting, and there was no feeling of contamination when she ate foods she regarded as healthful.

Ruth had an almost constant feeling of contamination for the past two years, which compelled her to increase the extent of her compulsive behavior. However, she could not associate any particular event with the increasing severity of her ritualistic behaviors. At the time of evaluation, Ruth engaged in a complicated procedure of washing her hands that was especially thorough after urinating or defecating. She scrubbed each finger in order, and she carefully washed between her fingers. She then washed both sides of her hands and eventually she scrubbed her arms. She carried out this procedure with soap, and then she repeated the sequence with a strong disinfectant. Following these steps, she dried her hands with a large number of disposable paper towels. Next, she thoroughly scrubbed the toilet and sink in a specific manner, and then she repeated the hand washing procedure. If she still felt contaminated, the ritual included taking a shower as well, according to a set sequence. The client also washed herself in this stereotyped manner after cooking and housecleaning, but she varied the thoroughness of the process according to how dirty she felt.

Ruth stated that she felt frustrated and tired most of the time, due to the amount of effort involved in these rituals. She experienced a great deal of pain in her hands because the outer layer of skin was virtually rubbed off. Nonetheless, she felt compelled to thoroughly wash her hands and repeatedly clean her apartment each time she felt that she or her environment was contaminated in some way.

Although Ruth was in extreme discomfort because of the burden of these compulsions, she could not rest until she went through all of her daily rituals. She was forced to awaken at four in the morning and work for a minimum of six hours, just to get through her personal and household chores for the morning. However, she generally repeated part of the cleaning sequence at least four additional times a day.

Ruth revealed that she had engaged in masturbation since she was a child, and this behavior had increased in frequency over the past few years. She felt that she was doing something that was harmful and disgusting, but she could not prevent herself from engaging in this practice. Because she then felt unclean, she was forced to perform numerous rituals such as taking a shower, thoroughly scrubbing her hands, and changing her pajamas and bed linens. Her nightly rest was continually interrupted by these elaborate rituals, since she usually masturbated when she went to bed.

PSYCHOLOGICAL EVALUATION

The client was asked to complete a number of self-administered psychological inventories. She took an unusually long time to fill out the test material, and she indicated that it was often difficult for her to decide on the most accurate answer.

The Minnesota Multiphasic Personality Inventory (MMPI) results indicated an above normal elevation of the scales measuring psychotic and obsessive-compulsive thoughts and behavior. These findings suggested that the client sometimes engaged in cognitive processes and behavior that were quite deviant from the societal norm. There were also indications that she occasionally had difficulty distinguishing between reality and fantasy, because she was confused by unusual thoughts.

The client rated a series of items on the Fear Inventory (Wolpe and Lazarus, 1966) according to the degree of fear elicited by each situation or object. She indicated extreme discomfort in interpersonal situations where there was the possibility of an aggressive encounter. For example, she rated the following items as elicitors of strong fear: "one person bullying another," "tough-looking people," "angry people," and "the sight of fighting." Ruth also expressed a strong fear of "large crowds," "losing control," and "looking foolish," circumstances that in some way might draw attention to her. The client further indicated specific fears of dirt, mice, and spiders.

The test results therefore suggested that Ruth was hampered in her daily functioning by severe anxiety in social situations, as well as in situations related to dirt or uncleanliness. She seemed to fear that she would become anxious in interpersonal situations and lose control of herself. The compulsive, ritualistic behavior appeared to function as a means of preventing this loss of control.

COURSE OF THERAPY

Dr. M. indicated to Ruth that she believed in the client's sincerity in wanting to change her behavior, because of Ruth's continuing efforts to seek help from professional persons. The therapist further stated that she did not believe that Ruth enjoyed suffering, but she felt that Ruth had been unable to find an effective means of eliminating her compulsive behavior patterns.

Dr. M. employed the techniques of modeling and in vivo desensitization to modify Ruth's fear of contamination, and the client was given relaxation training over a number of sessions. Ruth then observed and carried out a series of tasks aimed at the desensitization of her fear of urine contamination. The therapist asked Ruth to go to the bathroom and bring back a sample of her urine. Next, Dr. M. instructed Ruth to sit in an easy chair in a state of relaxation, and while she relaxed, the therapist diluted one drop of urine into each of five large buckets of water. Dr. M. then directed Ruth to continue in a relaxed state, while the therapist immersed her hands in one of the buckets. Ruth was told that it was only necessary for her to watch the therapist and she would not be asked to imitate Dr. M.'s behavior until she felt completely ready to do so. The therapist repeated the hand immersion procedure in each of the other buckets, and she again instructed Ruth to maintain a state of relaxation.

During the third therapy session, Ruth was able to imitate the behavior of the therapist, and she immersed her hands in a bucket of water containing one drop of urine. During subsequent sessions, stronger concentrations of urine were added, and again Ruth was able to proceed with the hand immersion tasks after she had practiced relaxation for several minutes.

When the client had mastered the contact with urine without becoming anxious and feeling unclean, she was desensitized to other feared contaminants, such as perspiration and mucous. The client reported that the rituals in the home environment resulting from contact with these substances were greatly reduced following the in vivo desensitization procedures with the therapist.

Since the ritualistic behaviors took up so much of the client's daily activities, this problem was dealt with almost exclusively during the beginning treatment sessions. When there was progress in eliminating a particular behavior sequence, such as showering after hand washing, Dr. M. and Ruth began to work on reducing other segments of the stereotyped behaviors. Ruth was asked to designate which of the remaining rituals would be easiest to give up, and she was then given a daily homework assignment relevant to that ritual. These assignments took the form of directions to flush the toilet one time less after use, or to expend one roll less of paper towels each day for drying her hands. As a result, Ruth gradually began to give up increasingly greater portions of her compulsive behaviors.

The client reported her progress to the therapist, and the latter provided social reinforcement for the successful completion of these tasks. As her relationship with the therapist strengthened, Dr. M. repeatedly told Ruth that she did not have to engage in these compulsive behaviors and, with practice, she would not feel anxious when she refrained from performing a particular ritual.

The therapist also instructed Ruth to record all of the activities she engaged in on one particular day each week. She was also asked to make a notation of the thinking associated with her various activities during that day. The records thus provided information about the environmental stimuli that elicited ritualistic behavior, and they also furnished details about the few relationships that Ruth had with other persons. The information on the records also served as a gauge of progress in therapy. Dr. M. used the client's activity record to point out to her the cold and formal way she interacted with other persons. Part of each session was devoted to a behavioral analysis of the effect of the client's behavior on other persons, and how the behavior of others influenced Ruth's interactions.

After the client had been in treatment for ten months, Dr. M. suggested that Ruth participate in group therapy sessions in addition to individual therapy. Because the client had made progress in eliminating a great many of her ritualistic behaviors, it now seemed appropriate to provide her with the opportunity to practice social interactions in a supervised group setting. Ruth would then have the opportunity to gain social approval for relating to others without engaging in stereotyped behaviors.

Ruth continued to make progress in narrowing the frequency and the scope of her compulsive rituals. She reported that there was a marked reduction in the number of objects in the environment that elicited a feeling of contamination. She also showed an improvement in interacting with other persons, due to the reduction in the time spent in ritualistic behaviors and the concomitant acquisition and practice of more effective social skills. She was now able to converse with others about topics other than art, and for the first time in many years, she sometimes initiated a conversation.

DISCUSSION

Obsessive compulsive neurosis was described in the American Psychiatric Association's diagnostic manual as a disorder characterized by the intrusion of unwanted thoughts or actions that the individual is unable to stop (DSM-II, 1968). The person experiences strong anxiety and distress if these thoughts or behaviors are interrupted before they are completed. Obsessions were defined as unwelcome repetitive thoughts, often foolish or antisocial, that intrude on the individual. Compulsions refer to overt, ritualistic behaviors that the person feels driven to carry out, or else anxiety occurs. The individual may consider these thoughts or acts as irrational and absurd, but nonetheless he or she feels that engaging in the thought or act will in some way prevent an unknown catastrophe from happening (Cameron, 1963).

The obsessive compulsive individual has been characterized as a cold, intellectualizing, and rigid person who has difficulty reacting to others in a spontaneous manner (English and Finch, 1954). The individual approaches social interactions and problem situations from an intellectual point of view, devoid of affect. The obsessive compulsive may also exhibit a behavior pattern marked by excessive cleanliness, extreme orderliness, and tendencies toward stinginess.

According to psychoanalytic theory, obsessive compulsive neurosis is a disorder which stems from difficulties encountered in childhood, particularly during the anal stage of development (English and Finch). It was postulated that the parents of the obsessive compulsive individual were unduly harsh and demanding during the toilet training period, and because of the parents' punitiveness, the child developed unresolved feelings of intense hostility. The function of the thoughts and rituals was to undo and neutralize unacceptable aggressive and sexual id impulses. During adulthood, the neurosis was manifested by these obsessions and compulsions, which continued to serve as defense mechanisms for keeping the primitive id impulses concealed even from oneself.

Cameron (1963) analyzed from a psychodynamic point of view a case of a young woman's obsessive compulsive handwashing. He pointed out a familiar theme in obsessive compulsive disorders: intense emotional ambivalence, preoccupation with contamination, and the use of defensive countermeasures, i.e. the handwashing behavior. Cameron felt that an important feature of the case he described was the combination of intense love and hatred that was centered on the mother and father. Because of incomplete or defective repression, there was an overuse of the defense mechanism of reaction formation, i.e., the individual acted too clean or good, in order to deal with unconscious impulses to soil or to be evil. The purifying handwashing ritual was therefore interpreted as an attempt to undo the harmful thoughts directed to other persons. The extremely painful nature of the continual handwashing was viewed as a retaliatory self-punishment for having evil thoughts and impulses.

Maher (1966) presented an analysis of the obsessive compulsive behavior pattern that falls within a social learning framework. He characterized the obsessive compulsive individual's rituals as reparation or atonement behaviors. He noted that after a child commits a transgression, the parents generally demand that the child perform a reparative response such as saying "I'm sorry." The child may be deprived of parental forgiveness and affection until the desired reparative response occurs, while the performance of the atoning response will be reinforced by renewed parental approval.

When unrealistically high standards of behavior are set by the parents, it is extremely likely that the child will commit numerous transgressions. If the parents reinforce the child for making a reparative response after each designated offense, these atoning responses will occur with great frequency and they will also result in anxiety reduction. Therefore, rigid parents, through the high standards they set, may create a situation in which they frequently reinforce the child for making a reparative response.

The sequence of punishment, anxiety, and specific reparative behaviors thus becomes established through numerous repetitions. These responses may show stimulus generalization and eventually occur in circumstances unrelated to the original learning experiences, or in situations where the individual is merely expecting punishment. Certain types of obsessive thoughts can function in the same manner as reparative responses and also result in anxiety reduction. Maher wrote that the hand washing compulsion does not necessarily have to be viewed as symbolic of the cleansing of guilt. This behavior can be interpreted simply as an overlearned anxiety reducer associated with thoughts or actions that may have no logical connection to the handwashing act itself.

Some compulsive rituals can be viewed as reparative behaviors, such as repetitive handwashing or methodically placing the objects in one's room in a certain order. Other ritualistic behaviors may be responses that generalized from an initial reparative behavior. However, it is possible that many obsessive compulsive behaviors are the result of a chance pairing of a particular response and the occurrence of anxiety reduction. The given response may therefore be functionally unrelated to the reduction of anxiety. However, through superstitious conditioning, the response will increase in frequency if that particular behavior continues to be reinforced by anxiety reduction.

The obsessive compulsive behavior pattern may become intensified at critical points in the individual's life if that person's behavioral repertoire does not include alternate ways of coping with anxiety provoking situations. When confronted with additional environmental stresses, the obsessive compulsive individual may exhibit an increase in the frequency of the overlearned ritualistic behaviors, because these behaviors have reduced anxiety in the past. If the person has never learned more flexible social skills, he or she will probably respond with anxiety whenever there is a change in the customary social environment, and an increase in obsessive compulsive behaviors will then result.

The development of the obsessive compulsive personality pattern may also be related to a general pattern of parental inflexibility, rather than resulting from specific practices in regard to toilet training and feces, as psychoanalytic theory states. Sears, Maccoby, and Levin (1957) found that mothers who were rigid in toilet training their children were also demanding and punitive in their general approach to socialization procedures. These mothers tended to suppress the child's aggressive behavior and they were extremely punitive when the child engaged in sex play. Sexuality and bowel habits were equated by the parents as comprising a general area of modesty.

Rigid toilet training practices by the parent may therefore be one of a number of inflexible behaviors that the child is exposed to which play a role in shaping the obsessive compulsive behavior pattern. A parent who reinforces his or her child for conforming to a rigid toilet training schedule may also be likely to reward the child for general cleanliness, the suppression of affect, and the absence of sexual exploration. The parent will then chastise and punish the child when these standards of appropriate behavior are not adhered to, and the child will eventually learn to conform to the parent's criteria of acceptable behavior. As the child grows older, he or she will have the further opportunity to observe the parent's rigid moral standards, and one or both parents will again provide social approval when the youngster imitates these values and behaviors.

An analysis of the parent's role in the development of a deviant behavior pattern must also include an evaluation of whether the child viewed the parent as a positive reinforcing stimulus. When a parent interacts with a child in a generally warm and loving manner, then parental attention will function as a positive reinforcer. However, if a parent consistently responds to a child in a critical and harsh manner, then the child will be positively reinforced by receiving no attention from that parent.

Ruth Langley's mother attended to Ruth primarily by criticizing her when she was not meticulously clean. Therefore, receiving no attention from her mother was a positively reinforcing situation for Ruth. In addition, the persons taking care of her learned very quickly that if Ruth was neat and subdued in emotional expression, they also would escape Mrs. Langley's disapproval. These persons therefore actively reinforced the youngster for acting in a quiet and orderly manner. Mr. Langley was more affectionate and approving of Ruth's spontaneous behaviors, but he was seldom home. Thus, he was not a consistent reinforcing agent in Ruth's life, nor was he a continuous model of more socially outgoing behavior.

Mrs. Langley's attitude toward toilet training procedures was no doubt just as rigid and disapproving as her attitude toward dirt in general. It is likely that she elicited a great deal of anxiety in Ruth and her caretakers when her inflexible socialization standards were not adhered to. Ruth began to expect disapproval for untidiness, and she found that the anxiety provoked by this expectation was reduced when she took pains to keep herself clean. Her concern for self-cleanliness generalized to a concern for cleanliness and orderliness in her total environment. Thus, her doll playing activities and bedtime rituals became methodical and stereotyped, and any deviation from this routine produced intense anxiety until the ritual could be completed in appropriate sequence.

It can therefore be seen that Ruth's compulsive behavior pattern was not the result of rigid toilet training practices per se. Her deviant behavior was the consequence of a general adult disapproval of emotional expression and the reinforcement by these socializing agents of inflexible, ritualistic behaviors. Ruth's behavior rituals also served an important time-filling function because she was alone so much. Through trial and error, she found that performing time-consuming rituals gave her something to do that would not bring disapproval from the persons around her.

As Ruth grew older, her primary means of interacting with other persons was in relation to conversations about her paintings and art work. She did not label paint smears on her person as "bad dirt," because she received attention and approval from persons at school and in her social milieu for this activity. She also received gratification from the process of creating a painting, and she continued to engage in this activity when she was not encumbered by time-consuming rituals.

Ruth's deficiency in social skills became increasingly more apparent as she reached adulthood. She was unable to establish a lasting relationship with any one individual, and she learned to gratify her sexual needs through masturbation. The intensification of self-stimulatory behavior at this time period might have been due to the anxiety provoked by the realization that she was growing older and there was little prospect of any improvement in her life situation.

The client's behavior at the time of evaluation was highly deviant in many respects. Although obsessive thought patterns were not prominent in her case, she experienced intense and discomforting anxiety when she was unable to immediately carry out a ritualistic behavior. The signs of psychotic thought processes and behaviors displayed on the psychological tests may have been in large measure a reflection of the intense daily involvement in these compulsive rituals. As the extent and the time-consuming nature of the rituals diminished, it is probable that the deviance manifested on the test material would also diminish.

The client's obsessive compulsive behavior was modified by behavior therapy techniques similar to those employed in the treatment of phobias. While the phobic individual typically learns to reduce anxiety by avoiding a situation or object, the obsessive compulsive individual learns to reduce anxiety by thinking certain phrases or performing given acts.

Desensitization procedures have been shown to be effective in treating phobias (Paul, 1969) and obsessive compulsive disorders (Walton and Mather, 1963). Walton and Mather employed in vivo desensitization procedures in treating a woman who was a compulsive handwasher. During the course of treatment, she was asked to carry out a series of tasks that were graded according to their potency to evoke handwashing behavior. This technique was similar to the in vivo desensitization procedures utilized in treating Ruth. Walton and Mather's client showed an extinction of anxiety and compulsive behavior in relation to dirt when the desensitization training was completed. The authors felt that an important variable in behavior change was the extinction of anxiety, irrespective of whether one is dealing with phobic or ritualistic behaviors.

The therapy procedures employed in modifying Ruth Langley's behavior also resulted in the extinction of anxiety to feared contaminants. However, there was an additional, extremely important feature of her therapy program. She was guided in learning more socially useful skills for relating to other persons through participating in group therapy. Ruth was eventually able to learn how to communicate with others more effectively, and in a way that was more personally satisfying. Although Ruth had already modified a great many of her problem behaviors, it was evident that she would continue to benefit from additional therapy aimed at increasing her interpersonal behavioral repertoire.

REFERENCES

American Psychiatric Association. *Diagnostic and statistical manual of mental disorders.* (2nd ed.) (DSM–II). Washington: American Psychiatric Association, 1968.

Cameron, N. *Personality development and psychopathology.* Boston: Houghton Mifflin, 1963.

English, O. S., & Finch, S. M. *Introduction to psychiatry.* New York: W. W. Norton, 1954.

Maher, B. A. *Principles of psychopathology.* New York: McGraw-Hill, 1966.

Paul, G. L. Outcome of systematic desensitization. II. Controlled investigations of individual treatment, technique variations, and current status. In C. M. Franks (Ed.), *Behavior therapy.* New York: McGraw-Hill, 1969. Pp. 105–159.

Sears, R. R., Maccoby, E., & Levin, H. *Patterns of child rearing.* New York: Harper & Row, 1957.

Walton, D., & Mather, M. D. The application of learning principles to the treatment of obsessive-compulsive states in the acute and chronic phases of illness. *Behavior Research and Therapy,* 1963, *1,* 163–174.

9

The Development of Anorexia Nervosa— "I Just Want to Lose a Few Pounds"

Janet Caldwell was 14 years old and in the eighth grade. She was five feet, two inches tall and weighed 62 pounds at the time of her admission to the psychiatric unit of a local general hospital. Janet began dieting at the age of 12 when she weighed 115 pounds and was chided by her family and friends for being "pudgy." She continued to restrict her food intake over a two-year period, and as she grew thinner, her parents became increasingly more concerned about her eating behavior. She was hospitalized after outpatient treatment by the Caldwell's family physician proved ineffective in arresting her continuous weight loss.

Janet was the middle child in a family of three children. At the time of admission, her older sister was 17 and a senior in high school, and her brother was 12. Her parents were of Protestant, middle-class background, and the family attended church regularly. Mr. Caldwell said that his work as an engineer kept him quite busy, but he tried to spend as much time with his family as he could spare from his heavy work load. Mr. and Mrs. Caldwell described their marriage and family life as reasonably happy, although they were quite concerned about the intractability of Janet's weight loss and her inability to resume a more normal eating pattern.

FAMILY BACKGROUND

Janet was initially interviewed at the hospital by a psychiatry resident. She was extremely emaciated in appearance, and her skin was stretched tight over the bony skeleton of her face and arms. She spoke rapidly with a clipped, staccato intonation, and she frequently shifted position in her chair. Janet characterized her family as one in which high performance expectations were the rule. Each of the children was strongly encouraged to do as well as he or she could at school. Mr. Caldwell frequently pointed out to them that he usually brought papers home from his office to work on in the evening because he felt that it was also important for him to do the best possible job he could in any activity in which he was involved.

Janet indicated that she got along reasonably well with her brother and sister. She said that she sometimes fought with her sister about whose turn it was to perform certain chores around the house, but these disputes were not too frequent or severe. Each of the girls had her own room and circle of friends. However, they generally shared confidences about persons they liked and social activities they were involved in. Both of them enjoyed listening to and talking about the rock music they played on the family stereo. Janet said that her younger brother was a nuisance and very untidy, and she sometimes felt annoyed because he was pampered by her parents and seemed to receive a great deal of attention from them. However, she stated that she usually tried to avoid arguing with her brother and generally did not interact with him very frequently.

Janet described her mother as more involved with the children in day-to-day matters than her father was, and more lenient in disciplinary matters. Typically, Mrs. Caldwell talked and pleaded with the children when she wanted them to change their behavior in some way, while Mr. Caldwell tended to be more stern and more likely to issue directives that he expected the children to obey immediately. Janet indicated that she and her siblings generally did not disobey their father. However, if possible, they went to their mother first for permission to engage in various activities with friends, since she was more likely to say yes to their requests than their father was.

The expression of emotions such as anger, fear, or unhappiness was not encouraged at the Caldwell home, and the children were told by their parents that they were being childish if they verbalized strong feelings of any kind. The usual parental approach to dealing with emotional issues was to sit down and spend a great deal of time talking about the precipitating events that led up to a particular emotional feeling or outburst. However, expressing strong feelings was considered to be a sign of immaturity. The parents did not provide sexual information to their children nor were sexual issues discussed in the home.

SOCIAL HISTORY

It had always been fairly easy for Janet to make friends. She usually went out with a circle of three or four girlfriends with whom she had become particularly close over the past few years. She reported that she was quite active and enjoyed participating in sports and other activities with her friends. She also attended school and church functions at which boys her age were present, but she had not gone to any activity with just one boy. As her weight loss became quite severe, she and her peers tended to withdraw from interactions with each other.

Janet achieved an "A" average in school over the two years prior to hospitalization. She indicated that she always got good grades in school, even when her weight loss was quite severe. However, she had to work hard and spend a great deal of time studying in order to do well in school. She frequently became anxious before examinations because she was afraid that she would not do as well as others expected her to, and she would try to cope with these feelings by studying even harder. Nonetheless, she indicated that she has willingly put in the effort to get good grades and she felt gratified by her academic achievement.

A separate interview with the parents confirmed the information Janet had communicated.

SYMPTOM HISTORY

Mrs. Caldwell indicated that nothing unusual occurred during her pregnancy with Janet, and delivery and birth were also quite normal. The mother recalled that Janet's development proceeded at about the same rate as had the development of the other children in the family. There were no problems related to Janet's appetite or eating patterns as a child. Both Mr. and Mrs. Caldwell said that they had been somewhat surprised when Janet became slightly overweight at puberty, around the time when she began menstruating. They recalled that the family had mildly teased Janet about her weight, but stopped doing this when it appeared that she was upset by their comments.

Janet also felt that her weight problem began at the time of puberty. She said that her family and friends had supported her efforts to achieve a ten-pound weight loss when she first began dieting at age 12. Janet did not go on any special kind of diet. Instead, she restricted her food intake at meals, generally cut down on carbohydrates and protein intake, tended to eat a lot of salads, and completely stopped snacking between meals. At first, she was quite pleased with her progressive weight reduction, and she was able to ignore her feelings of hunger by remembering the weight loss goal she had set for herself. However, each time she lost the number of pounds she had set for her goal she decided to lose just a few more pounds. Therefore she continued to set new weight loss goals for herself. In this manner, her weight dropped from 115 pounds to 88 pounds during the first year of her weight loss regimen.

Janet felt that, in her second year of dieting, her weight loss had continued beyond her control. Her menstrual periods had stopped shortly after she began dieting, and this cessation coincided with the point at which she began to lose weight quite rapidly. However, since her menses had occurred on only two or three occasions, she was not concerned about the cessation of her periods until the past year when her weight loss and change in appearance had become quite noticeable. Janet stated that she began to feel ugly and scared by her continuing weight loss during the last year. She also was bothered by the stares she received from her classmates and from strangers. She became convinced that there was something inside of her that would not let her gain weight. She revealed that she did not feel hungry and the thought of food disgusted her. She often felt nauseated even after eating a small portion of food. Janet commented that although there had been occasions over the past few years when she had been fairly "down" or unhappy, she still felt driven to keep active and move around a great deal, just as she felt driven to keep on dieting. As a result, she frequently went for walks, ran errands for her family, and spent a great deal of time cleaning her room and keeping it in a meticulously neat and unaltered arrangement.

When Janet's weight loss continued beyond the first year, her parents insisted that she see their family physician, and Mrs. Caldwell accompanied Janet to her appointment. Their family practitioner was quite alarmed at Janet's appearance, and prescribed a high-calorie diet. Janet said that her mother spent a great deal of time pleading with her to eat, and Mrs. Caldwell planned various types of meals that she thought would be appealing to Janet. Mrs. Caldwell also talked a great deal to Janet about the importance of good nutrition. Mr. Caldwell, on the other hand, became quite impatient with these discussions and tended to order Janet to eat. Janet then would try to eat something, but often became tearful and ran out of the room because she could not swallow the food she had been ordered to eat. The youngster said that she often responded to her parents' entreaties that she eat by telling them that she indeed had eaten but they had not seen her do so. She often listed foods that she said she had consumed which in fact she had flushed down the toilet. She estimated that she only was eating about 300 calories a day.

Mrs. Caldwell indicated that Janet had appeared quiet and withdrawn, in contrast to her generally active and cheerful disposition, at the time she began dieting. Mrs. Caldwell recalled that Janet was having difficulties with her girlfriends during that period and Janet had mentioned that it seemed as if her friends were making excuses to avoid coming over when she invited them. Janet became very critical of her girlfriends, and Mrs. Caldwell felt that Janet behaved in an argumentative and stubborn manner with them. On occasions when Janet knew that some friends were coming over to the house, she drew up ahead of time a detailed plan of activities for them that encompassed the entire time period they had planned to spend at her house. She then became angry and uncomfortable if the girls did not want to engage in these activities or did not wish to do so in the order and the amount of time Janet had allotted to each activity. In general, Janet seemed less spontaneous and talked less with her family and others than she had during any previous period that her parents could recall.

At the time of her first appointment with the family physician, Janet said that she recognized that her weight loss was too severe, but it was impossible for her to eat more. Despite the entreaties and threats of her parents and family physician over the next few months, she continued to lose weight. Janet and her family then agreed with the advice of their physician that Janet should be hospitalized for treatment in an inpatient setting.

PSYCHOLOGICAL EVALUATION

Janet was administered the Minnesota Multiphasic Personality Inventory (MMPI), a multi-item, paper-and-pencil personality assessment instrument, and a number of projective tests. There were no signs of thought disturbance or severe emotional disorders manifested on any of these measures. All of the scale scores on the MMPI were within normal limits, although reflecting a tendency toward sexual immaturity, concerns about one's body, a denial of problems, and a relatively high reported activity level. The projective tests suggested conflicts about dependence vs. autonomy, i.e., ambivalent feelings about growing up and achieving independence from one's parents and family. Another prevalent theme that emerged was suggestive of depression, e.g., stories on the Thematic Apperception Test (TAT) about sadness, rejection, and unhappy and unsatisfying interpersonal relationships. Janet manifested a process of denial and undoing in her stories on the TAT cards. She frequently related a story that suggested an unhappy ending but, in the last sentence of her description, arbitrarily said that everything was going to turn out all right. She also told stories with stated unhappy endings and then changed the story resolution at the last moment to a happy one.

The psychological processes of denial and undoing were consistent with her behavioral tendencies to change or undo her weight status by dieting, engaging in a high level of activity to deny hunger and undo the weight-gaining effects of food consumption, and minimizing the threat to her health posed by her severe weight loss. However, although the processes of denial and undoing were evident in Janet's responses to the test stimuli and in her behavior, one cannot justifiably state that these particular characteristics were sufficient etiological factors in the manifestation of the anorexia nervosa syndrome. Further, the conflicts Janet expressed in relation to independence and separation from one's family are quite typical of the ambivalent struggles exhibited by adolescent youngsters and were not indicative of serious personality disturbance.

COURSE OF HOSPITAL TREATMENT

Soon after admission to the hospital, Janet was placed on a behavior modification program aimed at changing her eating behavior. Previous experience with anorexic patients at this particular hospital indicated that reinforcing either the amount of food eaten or a change in eating habits did not produce normal eating patterns. Conversely, this treatment strategy appeared to reinforce restricted food intake because of drawing attention to the fact that the person was not eating. Therefore, the specific goal of Janet's treatment program was to reinforce only weight gain and not deal at all with her behaviors in relation to food. A contract was set up before hospitalization in which Janet signed a consent form signifying her agreement to participate in a program in which she had to gain at least one-half pound per day in order to earn and accumulate points for specified privileges. At first, the privileges consisted of time outside of her room, which was barren except for a bed, table, and chair. Janet was weighed each morning and, if she did not meet the minimal weight gain requirement for that day, she remained alone in her room with the door closed until she was weighed again the following morning. On the days when Janet did not meet her weight gain requirement, there were no comments made by the staff as they placed Janet's meals in her room on a tray. The tray was removed 45 minutes later, again without staff comment. This program had been described in detail to Janet's parents and their written consent was also obtained prior to Janet's admission to the hospital.

Janet ate her meals alone in her room during the initial stage of hospitalization. However, she was allowed to eat in the dining room with the other patients after she had made progress in gaining weight. As a result of sustained weight gain, Janet was able to earn points for privileges on and off the ward such as exercise activities, movies, outings, and other social events. Janet was also seen in individual therapy by a female therapist several times a week throughout the time she was hospitalized. These sessions were not held on days when Janet failed to meet her minimal weight requirement. Janet and Dr. C. talked about Janet's typically dependent, passively manipulative, or overly conscientious way of relating to other persons. Alternative, more socially flexible ways of interacting with others were discussed and sometimes role-played. These sessions also included an exploration of fairly typical adolescent concerns about sexuality, being able to express one's feelings openly, and asserting oneself without attempting to control other persons.

Janet manifested a continuous increase in weight during the first few weeks she was in the hospital. At this point, family therapy sessions were held with Dr. C. and included all the members of the Caldwell family. These sessions explored each family member's responses to Janet's eating behavior. The methods they could use for ignoring noneating were evaluated as well. The therapy sessions also covered other family interaction issues such as the expression and sharing of strong feelings and concerns, and a discussion of the kinds of opportunities for independent behavior within the family system that could be available to the youngsters as they grew older.

Janet remained in the hospital for ten weeks. She continued to make fairly steady progress in gaining weight over the course of hospitalization, and she weighed 89 pounds at the time of her discharge. There were only five occasions over the ten-week period when she had failed to earn a point for minimum weight gain. Janet stated at the time of her discharge that she now felt happier and more self-confident than she had in a long time. She also indicated that eating no longer disgusted her, nor did she feel as if there were something inside of her preventing her from eating. She also felt that she would be able to maintain her eating behavior when she returned home.

ETHICAL ISSUES OF TREATMENT

Before instituting any type of treatment involving possibly aversive procedures, it is extremely important for ethical and moral reasons that the patient understand and freely consent to that particular treatment program. Ethical and legal considerations suggest that the program also should be evaluated and approved by an objective review board. The creation of review boards has been associated with a recent civil rights development establishing patients' advocates to insure the rights of persons committed to various institutions for treatment or custodial care. Treatment professionals in hospitals and other institutional settings therefore have been obliged to become more sensitive to the issues of patients' rights, including not only the patient's right to treatment (Wyatt and Stickney, 1971; cited in Mental Health Law Project, 1973), but his or her right to refuse treatment (Cohen, 1971). Procedures related to the appointment of guardians to sign consent for emergency and other treatment procedures, in cases in which the patient is deemed mentally incompetent to make that decision, are currently being discussed in many states. These issues are extremely complex and not completely resolved at present. However, the attempt to set down specific legal guidelines to insure the full rights of persons in hospitals and institutions is clearly a positive sign.

FOLLOW-UP

Janet was seen periodically by Dr. C. over the next year and a half. An initial problem during the first few weeks at home was that Janet again began losing weight. Therefore, Janet and her parents came in for a counseling session with Dr. C. aimed at setting up a specific contract and token system that could be carried out at home. The use of a contract system for weight gain in the natural environment proved quite effective, and the contract contingency arrangements were gradually withdrawn as Janet's eating behavior stabilized at home and she neared an appropriate weight for her age. However, an important part of the treatment strategy was to prevent the possibility of continued weight gain until the point of obesity. Therefore, at a specified point in the program, Janet was given social reinforcement by the family and therapist for the control of food intake and weight level instead of the consumption of large quantities of food. The specifics of the contract conditions were carefully monitored and adjusted by the therapist in conjunction with Janet and her parents. Dr. C. also explored with Janet any difficulties the latter might be experiencing in family and social relationships.

Janet reached and maintained a normal weight level and also reported that she was happy in her peer relationships and was doing well in school. She had a number of comfortable relationships with boys her own age, and she attended dances and other social activities with her friends. However, she no longer felt the pressure to keep doing something every minute of the day. Janet's menstrual periods had returned, and she did not exhibit anxiety or unusual conflicts in discussing sexual matters. Mr. and Mrs. Caldwell confirmed Janet's account of her improved and satisfying social relationships, and indicated that Janet's food consumption only infrequently was a problem. They felt that Janet sometimes tested the limits of their control over her activities, but they did not feel that this behavior was unusual or different from the behavior of their other children.

The prognosis appears good that Janet will be able to maintain a normal eating pattern. Favorable factors in her history were the fact that she came to a decision that she wanted help with her eating problem, and that she felt ugly and ashamed of her appearance and was bothered by the stares of other persons. She also did not manifest the self-induced vomiting and periodic eating binges often found in persons who exhibit a recurrence of the anorexic pattern.

DISCUSSION

Anorexia nervosa is classified in the American Psychiatric Association's Diagnostic and Statistical Manual (DSM-II, 1968) under Special

Symptoms—Feeding Disturbance. This designation is used for individuals whose disturbance is manifested by discrete, specific symptoms that are not the result of organic illness or other kinds of disorders. A number of psychologists and psychiatrists have discussed anorexia nervosa (literally, lack of appetite due to "nervous" reasons) under the category of a psychosomatic disturbance (e.g., Coleman, 1976). However, since there is no clear evidence of an emotionally mediated lack of appetite in this disorder, the designation of a special symptom or habit disturbance in relation to food intake appears more accurate.

The refusal of food is a symptom that can be associated with a variety of types of deviant behavior, such as hysteria, hypochondriasis, schizophrenia, and depression. Halmi and Sherman (1975) adapted a number of the criteria for the diagnosis of anorexia nervosa presented by Feighner, Robins, Guze, Woodruff, Winokur, and Munoz (1972). The adapted criteria are: an onset between the ages of 10 and 30 years; weight loss of at least 25 percent of original body weight resulting in the individual being at least 15 percent below normal weight; and a distorted, implacable attitude and behavior toward eating, food, or weight. This attitude overrides hunger, reassurance, or threats. A further sign designated by Feighner, et al. is no known psychiatric disorder or medical illness. For females, the criteria also include amenorrhea of at least three months' duration unless the symptoms occur before the onset of menses, with no known medical illness that could account for the amenorrhea. Anorexia nervosa occurs primarily in adolescent and young adult females. Estimates of incidence in males varies between 3 percent to 10 percent (Bemis, 1976). The death rate associated with anorexia nervosa has been estimated at 10 percent to 20 percent.

A characteristic of many anorexics is a desire for an extremely thin appearance. A strong need for thinness, rather than a diminishment or cessation of hunger, appears to be an important aspect of this disorder. Persons diagnosed as suffering from anorexia nervosa often maintain an avid interest in food and may not experience a true loss of hunger and appetite (Bemis, 1976). Therefore, a phobia of gaining weight or of taking in food seems to best characterize this eating disturbance. The food intake of anorexics is severely restricted and may average only 200–500 calories per day. On the other hand, some individuals also may manifest periods of uncontrolled excessive eating without satisfaction (bulimia). Self-induced vomiting may follow these episodes and may also occur after periods in which the individual feels that he or she has consumed too much food. A poorer prognosis has been found for persons who periodically engage in binge overeating and in self-induced vomiting.

Anorexics have been described as extremely manipulative in relation to their eating behavior and their avoidance of gaining weight, and they often exert a tremendous amount of control over their families or hospital personnel. Other persons easily become entangled in frustrating efforts to prepare foods the anorexic says that he or she would like to eat, or become involved in persuading or cajoling the individual to eat the food that has already been prepared. It is not uncommon for anorexics to lie about the amount of food they have eaten or hide food they told others they had consumed. The marked hyperactivity noted in many anorexic individuals serves to burn calories and thus avoid weight gain.

A number of the symptoms of anorexia such as tension, irritability, emotional lability, sexual disinterest, and preoccupation with and dreams of food are similar to the symptoms that were observed in persons participating in studies of semi-starvation (Schiele and Brozek, 1948). Therefore, instead of positing some type of psychodynamic explanation for these symptoms, the behaviors could be accounted for by the severe nutritional deprivation the person is undergoing.

The clinical literature is reasonably consistent in describing the behavior of anorexic individuals before the onset of severe weight loss as obsessive-compulsive, intelligent, conscientious, and shy or reserved (Bemis, 1976). Perfectionist strivings also were noted quite frequently by a number of clinicians. Writing from a psychodynamic perspective, Hilde Bruch (1970a, b) has posited that primary anorexia nervosa is caused by deficient ego development manifested by a disturbance in body identity including a lack of a sense of ownership of one's body. An inability to discriminate between the signals of various bodily urges also was noted. Bruch felt that these difficulties occurred because of a very early disturbance in mother-child interactions. The anorexic syndrome therefore was a manifestation of the individual's feelings of being overpowered by reality demands in which the fragile sense of self is undermined (Bruch, 1973). Since the onset of the anorexic symptoms is commonly at puberty, a number of theorists have suggested that conflicts about sexuality are associated with the refusal to take in food. Traditional psychoanalytic writers such as Waller, Kaufman, and Deutsch (1964) have described anorexia nervosa as a constellation centering around the symbolization of pregnancy fantasies and a symbolic denial of the childhood fantasy of oral impregnation by the father.

A great deal has been written in the psychoanalytic literature about the common association in females of the cessation or arrested onset of the menses and the onset of anorexia nervosa. The details of Janet's history are not suggestive of a sexual trauma nor any other kinds of sexual concerns atypical of twelve-year-old girls. On the other hand, physiological explanations of the menstrual factor are inconclusive since previous research indicates that amenorrhea often occurs in the early stages of weight loss (Halmi, 1974). Therefore, it may not be tenable to posit that the physiological changes associated with severe weight loss are the cause of the menstrual disturbance. At this time, the specific relationship between anorexia nervosa and amenorrhea is unclear and has not been fully explained by either psychogenic or physiological theories. In addition, whether there is some physiological factor contributing to the overwhelming incidence of anorexia nervosa in females is also unknown at present.

Behavioral formulations of anorexia nervosa have focused on an analysis of environmental reinforcement patterns and issues of avoidance behavior (Blinder, Freeman, and Stunkard, 1970; Leitenberg, Agras, and Thomson, 1968). However, the behavioral literature generally has emphasized the development of effective treatment procedures and has not been highly concerned with theoretical explanations of the onset and course of anorexia nervosa.

The obsessive-compulsive, perfectionistic, and intellectually striving behavior patterns that Janet manifested prior to and during her period of severe weight loss are similar to the premorbid histories of many individuals diagnosed as anorexic. There were few specific precipitating factors noted at the onset of the weight loss other than a concern about being overweight, some mild teasing by family and peers, and the encouragement of these persons to begin dieting. The episodic depression and aloofness Janet exhibited during the period of symptom onset were not atypical of the fluctuations in mood experienced by many youngsters at the time of puberty. However, her growing concern about dieting and losing weight became an overriding issue that eventually dominated her life existence. It is therefore not surprising that her peers grew less interested in interacting with her as her energies became more centered on the desire for thinness and as her physical appearance began to change markedly with weight loss. The scheduling of her friends' activities when they visited her seems to be one aspect of the generalized obsessive behavior pattern she manifested at that time, and further served to alienate her peers. Janet's typically high activity level also increased in intensity with her efforts at dieting and might have served as a distraction from thoughts of food and conflicts about eating.

The anorexic individual gains an extremely powerful hold over family interactions because the severe weight loss poses an extremely critical health problem. Therefore, Janet's parents and other family members easily became enmeshed in a struggle over persuading her to eat. It would seem inevitable that Mr. and Mrs. Caldwell would eventually begin differing with each other about the techniques they should use to induce Janet to stop dieting and to start eating regularly. Further, this added attention to and controversy over her eating behavior contributed to the control Janet had over her family and reinforced her non-eating behavior.

An interesting issue in Janet's case is the fact that during the second year of her weight loss she was not gaining a great deal of reinforcement from being thin. She was appalled by her physical appearance and wanted to stop losing weight, but she was unable to start eating normally. She indicated that she was disgusted and nauseated by consuming even small quantities of food. Psychological testing indicated adequate reality testing. There was no evidence of the severity and bizarreness of thought disturbance seen in schizophrenic disorders that could explain her feelings of disgust in relation to food. From a social learning perspective, one can conceptualize the difficulty Janet had in terminating her dieting behavior as the result of a conditioned aversion to food due to avoidance learning. The approach to or consumption of food initially might have resulted in severe anxiety about gaining weight. Anxiety reduction then occurred with the avoidance of food (or in the case of some individuals, with self-induced vomiting). Thus, the anorexic pattern became established as a food phobia because of the association of food intake and weight gain. Through the process of generalization, the covert response of even the *thought* of food eventually resulted in an avoidance process manifested as a psychological and physiological feeling of disgust or nausea. At the point where Janet cognitively did not wish to continue her dieting, she was unable to eat normally because the avoidance conditioning to food had become so strongly established and so generalized. Therefore, one can see the conditioning rationale of Janet's statements that something inside of her prevented her from eating.

The behavior modification program that proved effective in un-learning this generalized habit pattern involved a treatment procedure that probably resulted in the extinction of the anxiety response to food intake, and also extinguished the concomitant feelings of nausea and disgust. Janet consented to a treatment program in which the conse-quences of not eating apparently were more aversive than eating, i.e., the restriction to a barren and uninteresting room on the days that she did not gain weight. Janet progressed extremely well on the behavior modification program designed for her. The reinforcement derived from being allowed outside of her room, and the associated privileges on and off the ward proved potent enough to extinguish over time the condi-tioned aversion to food. The initial technique of placing a tray of food in Janet's room and not commenting on her food intake removed whatever reinforcement she had gained from the excessive attention others paid to her eating behavior. Over the course of treatment, different learned habits in relation to food were established. These new eating patterns became self-reinforcing because of their association both with certain hospital privileges and a change in her physical appearance. A further reinforcement might have been the greater feeling of well-being she experienced as her health improved with weight gain.

The individual and family sessions with Dr. C. seemed extremely helpful in dealing with Janet's interpersonal relationships and in pre-paring the family for her return from the hospital. Family counseling enabled Janet and her siblings to explore many aspects of their relation-ships with each other and their parents. Further, the entire family felt a part of the treatment process. The additional step of closely monitoring and adjusting the contract procedures after Janet returned home were important in maintaining the new eating patterns in the natural environ-ment. The eventual reinforcement of balanced and controlled eating behavior rather than eating as much as possible was effectively ac-complished at home because the Caldwells were familiar with the process of monitoring and reinforcing specific behavior patterns.

Recent reports indicate that there has been an increase in persons hospitalized with a diagnosis of anorexia nervosa, and that these admis-sions are predominantly of young, adolescent females (Bemis, 1976). The American preoccupation with slimness has been pointed to as a significant element in the increased incidence of anorexia nervosa (Bruch, 1973) and, indeed, the factor that many cases have in common is the youngster's desire to lose weight in order to overcome a perceived state of obesity. Whether this is a particularly American phenomenon or a phenomenon of affluence interacting with the body image ideals of various cultures can be debated. A dissatisfaction with body appearance is fairly common in both sexes in our culture during adolescence. However, the intense preoccupation with and anxiety about physical appearance exhibited by many adolescent females seems to be strongly influenced by the phenomenon of sex-role stereotyping. In many cultures, including the American one, female status is often equated solely with physical beauty, defined in part as a slim body appearance. Although recently there has been a tendency for adolescent girls to receive more reinforcement for academic and other accomplishments than was previously the case (Kaplan and Bean, 1970), interpersonal attraction is still strongly related to physical appearance. The incidence of cases of anorexia nervosa might not diminish until there is a significant change in the inordinate amount of social approval that adolescent females receive for physical attractiveness, and until other kinds of attributes also are strongly reinforced by the social milieu. Further, it would seem necessary to develop prevention efforts through public education in order to teach persons to recognize the first signs of anorexia nervosa. Intervening at this early stage might help to reduce the number of persons suffering from this devastating disorder.

REFERENCES

American Psychiatric Association. *Diagnostic and statistical manual of mental disorders* (2nd ed.) (DSM–II). Washington, D.C.: American Psychiatric Association, 1968.

Bemis, K. M. Anorexia nervosa. Unpublished manuscript, 1976. (Available from text author upon request).

Blinder, B. J., Freeman, D. M. A., & Stunkard, A. J. Behavioral therapy of anorexia nervosa: Effectiveness of activity as a reinforcer of weight gain. *American Journal of Psychiatry*, 1970, *126*, 1093–1098.

Bruch, H. Instinct and interpersonal experience. *Comprehensive Psychiatry*, 1970, *11*, 495–506. (a)

Bruch, H. Eating disorders in adolescence. *Proceedings of the American Psychopathological Association*, 1970, 59, 181–202. (b)

Bruch, H. *Eating disorders: Obesity, anorexia nervosa and the person within.* New York: Basic Books, 1973.

Cohen, D. Constitutional law–civil commitment: A patient involuntarily committed to a state mental institution who has not been adjudicated incompetent may refuse treatment based on his First Amendment right of free exercise of religion. *Brooklyn Law Review*, 1971, 38, 211–222.

Coleman, J. C. *Abnormal psychology and modern life* (5th ed.). Glenview, Ill.: Scott, Foresman and Co., 1976.

Feighner, J. P., Robins, E., Guze, S. B., Woodruff, R. A., Winokur, G., & Munoz, R. Diagnostic criteria for use in psychiatric research. *Archives of General Psychiatry*, 1972, 26, 57–63.

Halmi, K. A. Anorexia nervosa: Demographic and clinical features in 94 cases. *Psychosomatic Medicine*, 1974, 36, 18–25.

Halmi, K. A., & Sherman, B. M. Gonadotrophin release to LHRH in anorexia nervosa. *Archives of General Psychiatry*, 1975, 32, 875–878.

Kaplan, A. G., & Bean, J. P. (Eds.). *Beyond sex-role stereotypes. Readings toward a psychology of androgyny.* Boston: Little, Brown, & Co., 1976.

Leitenberg, H., Agras, W. S., & Thomson, L. E. A sequential analysis of the effect of selective positive reinforcement in modifying anorexia nervosa. *Behavior Research and Therapy*, 1968, 6, 211–218.

Mental Health Law Project. *Basic rights of the mentally handicapped.* Washington: 1973.

Schiele, B. C., & Brozek, J. Experimental neurosis resulting from semi-starvation in man. *Psychosomatic Medicine*, 1948, 10, 31–50.

Waller, J. V., Kaufman, M. R., & Deutsch, F. Anorexia nervosa: a psychosomatic entity. In M. R. Kaufman & M. Heiman (Eds.), *Evolution of psychosomatic concepts.* New York: International Universities Press, 1964. Pp. 245–273.

10

Obesity, Diet, and Environment— The Case of Irene Wintertree

Irene was a 14-year-old Native-American girl who was seen at a community health clinic in a large city in the Upper Midwest. At that time, she was five feet three inches tall and weighed 198 pounds. Irene was referred to the clinic by her school nurse for treatment of a persistent bad cold. The health nurse at the community clinic who talked with Irene was also of Native-American background. The youngster remained relatively expressionless throughout the discussion, and her movements seemed slow and effortful. When asked about her weight, she indicated that she had been bothered by her physical appearance for some time, but she had not specifically tried to lose weight. The nurse asked Irene if she would be willing to come to the clinic on a regular basis and work with a psychologist on ways to lose weight, and Irene readily agreed to do so. However, she indicated that she did not want her mother involved in the weight problem at that time.

Both Irene's mother and father had been born on Indian reservations of the Chippewa tribe. They had experienced a great deal of hardship from lack of money and inadequate housing to provide protection from the severe cold in winter. Irene's parents remained on a reservation for several years after they were married. They had three children during that period; the third youngster was Irene. When Irene was four years old, the family moved to a large city in the same state and two more children were born after the move to the city. Mr. and Mrs. Wintertree eventually separated, although both continued to live in the same urban area. At the time Irene was seen at the clinic, she was living with her mother and her 16-year-old sister. Her older brother no longer lived at home and the two younger children, ages 9 and 8, had recently been placed in foster homes. The family was on public assistance.

FAMILY BACKGROUND

Irene was interviewed by Dr. M., the psychologist at the clinic, who was a white woman of middle-class background. The information Irene related about her family history evolved over the five-month treatment period with Dr. M. Irene recalled her family life as one of great turmoil and occasional violence. She reported that both of her parents drank heavily, and occasionally got into physical fights with each other. She felt that life on the reservation generally had been quieter and happier than her experiences in the city, but she observed that she had been too young when the family moved to remember many of the details of her early life. However, when she periodically got a ride back to the reservation to stay with relatives for varying periods of time, she noticed that there were not many jobs available, and drinking to excess was often a problem. The young people tended to leave the reservation, although they often came back for short periods of time when they were in some kind of difficulty in the city. However, a special treat in the fall was for persons living in the city to return to the reservation during a festival period, and feast on venison, wild rice, and fried bread.

Irene described her father as a well-meaning person who did not talk a great deal, therefore making it difficult to know when he was angry. He had no particular urban job skills, and he was frequently unemployed when they moved to the city. He tended to spend his days at home or drinking with other Indian men in the low socioeconomic, primarily Native-American area in which they lived. Mrs. Wintertree worked from time to time at some type of unskilled labor, but usually she also was at home. Irene indicated that her mother had a severe problem of alcoholism and had been through both inpatient and outpatient alcoholism treatment programs in the city. However, she often did not stop drinking when in treatment or invariably began drinking again after the termination of a particular program. The Wintertree children occasionally saw their relatives in the area, but more or less got on the best they could by themselves during the periods when Mrs. Wintertree was hospitalized for treatment of alcoholism.

Irene's father moved out of the house when she was nine years old. His departure was a culmination of a period of intense arguments and physical fights associated with heavy drinking by both parents. Irene described this time as an extremely frightening one. She and her siblings tried hard to stay out of their parents' way, but they were tired from lack of sleep and hungry because there was little food in the house. Irene has continued to see her father from time to time, but she did not think that they were particularly close. He had been living in a common-law relationship with a white woman and her family for several years.

Irene described her relationship with her mother as changeable. She said that her mother expressed an intense interest and concern for her children when she was not drinking, and she would try hard to see that the family had enough food and were in good health. Irene felt that her mother could be characterized as overconcerned during these periods. However, Mrs. Wintertree was frequently dazed or argumentative as a result of excessive alcohol use, and it seemed to Irene that her mother forgot about her family as soon as she started drinking. After Mr. Wintertree moved out, Irene would sometimes wake in the morning and find a man in the house who had spent the night with her mother. However, since similar episodes sometimes had occurred when her father was living at home but away somewhere for several days, Irene did not find this situation unusual or disturbing.

Irene indicated that she and her 16-year-old sister Mary fought with each other a great deal of the time they were together. The disputes centered on many issues, such as sharing the household chores, caring for the younger children, and each sister wanting to wear some article of clothing belonging to the other. Nonetheless, Irene felt that she and her sister had a close and caring relationship. Irene's brother had moved out of the house when he was 16 years old and was living with some friends in another part of the city. Irene rarely saw him. At the time of the interviews at the community health clinic, the two younger children were placed by the State Child Protection Agency in foster homes. This action had been taken since there was no adult at home to care for them; Mrs. Wintertree had been in the hospital for a number of weeks with physical problems related to alcoholism. Irene and Mary were technically under the supervision of their father, but they rarely saw him and they lived on and managed together the money the family received from public assistance. Mary did not spend much time at home and she was often out with her friends and boyfriend. She recently had dropped out of school, but she had not as yet found a job she was interested in. Previously, she had been in various types of school-related difficulties such as disruptive behavior and truancy, and she had also been detained by the police for several hours for suspected shoplifting. However, this charge had not been substantiated.

SOCIAL HISTORY

Irene indicated that she had no friends in school or in the neighborhood, and she more or less kept to herself. Even as a child, she had rarely played with the other children in the neighborhood. She found it difficult to initiate conversations with the youngsters in her junior high school classes, and she did not belong to any clubs or participate in any athletic activities. However, she stated that she enjoyed the subject matter presented in her classes, and she always studied and kept up with her school work. She attended school regularly except for episodes of family crises.

Irene related that she was often teased and called names by the other youngsters at school because of her large size. She sometimes argued back, but usually did not respond to their taunts. She said that she made it a practice to leave the school area just as soon as classes were over. When she got home, she generally spent the afternoon watching television.

PRESENT PROBLEM

Her weight had become a problem to Irene when she was about 12 years old. She indicated that in thinking back about her weight, she realized that even as a child she had been somewhat overweight. However, her weight had not really concerned her or been commented upon by others until she started junior high school. She said it was only when she had experienced the teasing of her classmates in school that she began to consider attractiveness to be the same as skinnyness.

Irene related that although many times there had been little food in the house, usually there was something she could eat that would be temporarily filling. The family could not afford to buy meat regularly, and the bulk of the foods they customarily bought consisted of items such as corn meal, macaroni, spaghetti, and potatoes. They also ate a great deal of bread that was fried in either lard or any other fat that was available in the house. She recalled that on the reservation her grandmother always had served the children fried bread with meals and as snacks, and Irene and her family continued the custom of eating fried, homemade bread.

When Irene was around 12 years of age and her body began to mature sexually, she also experienced a rapid and sustained weight gain. She continued a pattern of eating very little for breakfast, snacking on fried bread during the morning if she was at home, or consuming only the parts of the school lunch she liked (primarily the potatoes, bread, and dessert). She then snacked again on fried bread at home in the afternoon. Her supper usually consisted of a spaghetti or macaroni dish, sometimes with some meat in it, and fried bread. Since Irene spent a great deal of time in the house when she was not at school, she often watched television and ate, or consumed food while she did her homework. Her mother was frequently unable to cook because of her drinking behavior and Irene usually cooked for the family. She made meals that were easy to prepare, making use of whatever food was in the house. There was no regular schedule for grocery shopping, and the amount and type of food the family bought depended on whether there were food stamps or money available.

Irene indicated that staying home and eating throughout the day and evening had become a strongly established pattern. She often felt lonely and bored, and she would find herself wandering around the house and rummaging through the kitchen looking for something to eat. She also said that she tended to eat whenever she was upset. She related that she was quite bothered when her peers or family called her names or ridiculed her while she was eating. However, she had not really tried to limit the amount of food she ate and their taunts only resulted in her eating still more. She felt rather helpless and unsure about whether she would ever be able to lose weight, and she said that she had not really thought about going on a weight reduction program until the health nurse had discussed this possibility with her. Irene acknowledged to Dr. M. that she was quite unhappy about her physical appearance, and she said that she was willing to try to lose weight.

Irene was given an MMPI to complete and her scores on all of the scales were within normal limits except for the depression scale. The moderate elevation of this scale in combination with a relatively low score on the defensiveness scale suggested that Irene was experiencing a great deal of unhappiness in her life situation and was indicating a "cry for help."

TREATMENT PROGRAM

Dr. M. described to Irene the basic strategy of a behavior modification program for weight reduction. Before going into the specific details of the program, Dr. M. stressed that a crucial aspect of success in weight loss and the maintenance of that loss was a decision and commitment on Irene's part that changing her eating habits was something she really wanted to do. Dr. M. pointed out the difference between wanting to lose weight and wanting to change one's eating patterns, and that successful weight loss could only be attained by working hard to modify longstanding behavior patterns. Dr. M. said that she would work directly with Irene and that Mrs. Wintertree would not have to be involved for the time being, since Mrs. Wintertree was in the hospital and Irene was the primary person who did the food shopping and cooking.

Dr. M. gave Irene some forms to fill out each day until their appointment on the following week. The purpose of filling out the forms was to obtain detailed information about Irene's typical eating patterns, in order to effectively plan a program to modify these behaviors. Irene was instructed to record, for each meal and snack, the time that she ate, the amount of food eaten, the place of food intake, and any emotions she might have been experiencing prior to food intake. An appointment was also scheduled for the following week with the clinic's nutritionist. The latter would explain to Irene the nutritional value and amount of calories in various foods, and give her a series of menus that were low in cost and also low in calories. Several additional meetings with the nutritionist were scheduled over the five-month treatment program in order to explore possible ways of changing Irene's high carbohydrate diet pattern, so typical of low-income families.

A primary focus of the behavior modification program was to teach Irene to avoid skipping meals and then filling up between meals. A token system was therefore instituted in which Irene could earn points for eating a balanced breakfast, lunch, and dinner each day (Leon, 1974). She also earned points for not eating in between meals, or for eating low-calorie snacks at that time. Additional points were earned for eating reduced portion sizes, and engaging in some form of daily exercise. At first, Irene decided that her daily exercise would be a brisk, 20-minute walk. However, as she began to lose weight, Dr. M. encouraged her to participate in some type of exercise that would involve her in social interactions with other persons, such as athletic activities after school or at a community club. Dr. M. and Irene talked about the number of points Irene could realistically earn on a daily basis, and also the weekly point total she would be required to earn for an additional reinforcer. The point requirements were set high enough so there would have to be some change in eating patterns in order to earn a reward, but were not set so high that it was unlikely that Irene would obtain a reinforcer. Since there was very little money that Irene could use for herself or treat herself to as a reward, Dr. M. set up a reinforcement system with clinic funds whereby Irene would earn five cents on each day that she met or exceeded her daily point requirement. Irene also earned an additional 25 cents a week whenever she met or exceeded her weekly point total requirement. Three months after the start of the program, Irene had made good progress on the modification of her eating patterns and the monetary reinforcer was gradually phased out. Social praise and assigning a letter grade for progress were now strong enough reinforcers to maintain the new eating patterns.

Irene reported that at first it was extremely difficult for her to cut down on her snacking and eat three balanced meals a day. However, she tried to follow the program and in so doing learned that she felt hungrier when she woke up in the morning if she had not been eating heavily the evening before. Irene also switched to low-calorie snacks such as carrots and celery instead of the fried bread she had typically snacked on.

An extremely difficult time for Irene to refrain from eating was immediately after she got home from school. Usually, she would be upset because her classmates had either ignored her or made fun of her. Dr. M. explored with Irene alternate ways she could deal with her problems with her peer group than by eating. She suggested activities that Irene could gradually get involved in so that she would not come directly home and be tempted to eat. Dr. M. also role played and had Irene rehearse more assertive ways of dealing with her classmates than the pained silence or occasional verbal counterattacks Irene usually resorted to. An added encouragement for Irene's efforts at weight loss was the knowledge that as she became less deviant in body build, she would have to spend less time and effort dealing with taunts about her weight.

Irene's progress in weight loss was somewhat uneven, but she showed a general decrease in weight over the five months of weekly appointments. On some weeks, Irene's weight remained stable or else she had regained some of the weight she had previously lost. The reasons for the failure to progress in weight loss over that particular week were explored, and usually the associated factors were an excess of foods that Irene had eaten between meals. Dr. M. again suggested strategies for weight reduction including low-calorie snack foods or, preferably, remaining out of the house and getting involved in club activities with her peers. Dr. M. provided Irene with encouragement to keep trying to change her eating patterns, and expressed her opinion that over time Irene would lose weight if she modified her food habits.

Irene lost 32 pounds over the five-month treatment period. At that point, the visits with Dr. M. were scheduled for once every two months since Irene was making satisfactory progress in weight loss. These bimonthly visits provided Irene with social support for maintaining her new eating patterns, and they also dealt with any type of peer or family problem that might have arisen. Irene indicated that, as she lost weight, she also began losing the self-conscious feeling of being ugly and unattractive.

An important aspect of the treatment program was the opportunity that Irene had to discuss with Dr. M. problems in addition to those of excessive food consumption. At first, the weekly discussions focused on an evaluation of issues related to eating behavior. However, after Irene became more comfortable with Dr. M., she began to bring up other problems as well, particularly her unhappy and disordered family situation. Dr. M. talked with Mary on several occasions, at first about ways that Mary could help and provide social reinforcement for Irene's efforts to lose weight. Later, Dr. M. explored with both girls how they could remain living at home, receive a greater degree of social support from relatives in the area, and cope with their mother's and their own problems. Irene and Mary began to spend more time in activities together, and both agreed that for the present, the younger children would receive better care if they remained in their foster homes. Irene was given further information about social groups for adolescents in the community, and she was encouraged to get involved in them. She also was strongly encouraged to continue with her studies and reinforced for her academic achievements. As her weight loss progressed and she became more active with her peers, her life did not seem quite so unhappy.

Additional follow-up indicated that Irene occasionally regained some of the weight she had previously lost, but in general her weight continued to decline over the next year. Eventually, she was able to stabilize her weight at approximately 135 pounds. At that time, she indicated that she no longer viewed herself as clumsy and fat.

DISCUSSION

Obesity, like anorexia nervosa, can be classified as a special symptom (DSM-II, 1968), indicating no evidence of psychosis or other type of mental disorder. The point at which an individual is labeled as obese is to a great extent arbitrary and culturally determined. Standards of physical attractiveness in relation to weight status vary from country to country, and in India and other societies in which there is a great deal of poverty and little food, being overweight is valued as a sign of wealth. Life insurance tables of ideal body weight are often used in the United States to assess obesity, and generally persons who are 20 percent to 25 percent or more above ideal body weight are considered obese. Seltzer and Mayer (1965) have popularized a technique for assessing subcutaneous fat through measuring the triceps skinfold thickness, and they define obesity as the amount of subcutaneous fat that is one standard deviation above the norm for a particular sex and age. Genetically, females have a greater degree of subcutaneous fat than do males.

Obesity is an extremely prevalent problem among urban individuals of low socioeconomic status, and this is particularly true for females and for children as compared to adults. Obesity was six times more prevalent in New York City and twice as prevalent in London among women of lower socioeconomic class than women of upper socioeconomic class (Goldblatt, Moore, and Stunkard, 1965; Silverstone, Gordon, and Stunkard, 1969, respectively). By the age of six, obesity was nine times as prevalent among lower-social class girls than girls of the upper class (Stunkard, d'Aquili, Fox, and Filion, 1972). A similar but less marked relationship was found for males in the studies with adults and with children.

Juvenile onset obesity appears to have serious physiological as well as psychological implications. Hirsch (1971; 1972) reported that there are marked differences in the size and number of adipose cells in obese and normal weight persons. Adipose cells increase in number up to early adolescence, but apparently the total number of cells do not change after that time (Hirsch and Knittle, 1970; Hirsch, 1972). Weight reduction during adulthood results in a decrease or shrinkage in the size of the fat cells, but there is no decrease in the number of adipose cells (Salans, Horton and Sims, 1971). The permanence of the number of adipocytes after adolescence might be a factor in the extreme difficulty obese persons have in maintaining a weight loss. Lloyd, Wolff, and Whelan (1961) found that 80 percent of overweight children and adolescents continued to be overweight as adults.

Research findings demonstrate that the experience of being obese can have an important influence on one's body image. Adults with juvenile onset obesity indicated that they continued to think of their bodies as grotesque and loathsome even after weight reduction (Stunkard and Mendelson, 1967). Stunkard and Burt (1967) found that the critical age for developing this enduring concept of one's body was during the adolescent period. Massively obese persons with juvenile onset of obesity continued to overestimate their body size on a perceptual measure of body size estimation, even after they had lost a substantial amount of weight (Glucksman and Hirsch, 1969). Age of onset of obesity also has been shown to influence the adult individual's emotional response to weight reduction; juvenile onset massively obese persons manifested a significant number of signs of emotional disturbance as weight loss progressed (Glucksman and Hirsch, 1968). These emotional disturbances were not found in severely obese persons with adult onset of obesity (Grinker, Hirsch, and Levin, 1973).

The psychoanalytic conception of obesity involves the classification of overeating as an oral fixation or a regression due to unresolved dependency needs (Jones, 1953). Other psychodynamic theorists have posited that obesity is a symptom of a deep-seated emotional disturbance, and have indicated that removal of the symptom will result in symptom substitution or a deterioration in the individual's emotional functioning (Alexander and Flagg, 1965; Bruch, 1963; 1973; Fenichel, 1945).

From a social learning perspective, excessive food consumption can be viewed as an overlearned habit that has generalized to diverse environmental stimuli (Leon and Chamberlain, 1973a, b). However, one cannot overlook the possibility that obesity also is influenced by constitutional factors such as body build or an overabundance of fat cells. The child who is overfed develops a constitutional tendency toward obesity because of the production of a greater than average number of fat cells. In addition, the overfed child is highly likely to gain the strong social approval of one or both parents for patterns of excessive eating. The finding that obese adults reported a high frequency of obesity and overeating in one or both parents (Leon and Chamberlain, 1973a) suggests that in addition to possible genetic influences, the factors of modeling and imitation learning also play a vital part in the development of patterns of excessive food consumption. Thus, obesity can be considered as a complex interaction of the factors of constitution, reinforcement, and imitation learning. These factors may result in the observation and the learning of behaviors related to consuming food in a variety of situations, including in many cases situations associated with emotional arousal.

Schachter, Goldman, and Gordon (1968) have strongly suggested that obese persons do not eat a greater amount of food when emotionally aroused than they do in more relaxed situations. A laboratory study by McKenna (1972) indicated that food intake did not result in anxiety reduction in an experimentally induced fear situation. However, a comprehensive review of the literature on the psychological aspects of obesity (Leon and Roth, 1977) generally substantiates the long-held clinical notion that obese persons do tend to eat more when emotionally aroused. In addition to a possible anxiety reducing aspect of overeating, excessive food intake also could be learned and be maintained by the positive reinforcement derived from food consumption. Further, eating may function as a response incompatible with anxiety. However, an overall consideration in interpreting the results of obesity studies is that it may not be relevant to generalize from artificially contrived laboratory situations to eating behavior in the natural environment.

An analysis of the efficacy of the various techniques for treating obesity has indicated that behavior modification procedures are more effective than any other non-surgical method of treatment in sustaining a weight loss over a period of time (Leon, 1976). The greater efficacy of behavior modification techniques seems likely to be due to the fact that systematically teaching and reinforcing habit change results in the learning of new skills in relation to eating. The individual can then apply these skills to future eating situations long after the treatment program is over. Emphasizing and reinforcing habit change has been shown to be more effective than reinforcing the number of pounds lost in maintaining a weight loss over an extended period of time (Mahoney, 1974).

The strategy of reinforcing changes in eating patterns is reasonable if one considers that specific diets, fasting, or appetite suppressants function primarily by taking food away from an individual. The majority of persons participating in these procedures eventually regain the weight they had lost (Leon, 1976), probably because the program had not taught them new behaviors for dealing with the urge to consume food. In contrast, changing one's eating patterns may result in the extinction of a highly overlearned habit of consuming food in response to emotional arousal and to diverse environmental stimuli. Therefore, the individual has the opportunity to learn new behaviors in relation to the cues previously associated with food intake that can generalize to future situations. Leon (1975) found that obese persons who lost a substantial amount of weight over a six-month period responded to a lesser number of inappropriate stimuli with food intake than they had before the weight loss program was initiated. This group also reported a higher frequency of eating in response to cues of hunger after substantial weight reduction. A recently completed study by the author and her colleagues (Leon, Roth, and Hewitt, 1976) indicated that persons who were successful in losing weight, during the weight loss period developed patterns of reading, knitting, ironing, housecleaning, or exercising in response to the urge to eat. These behaviors apparently functioned as a distraction, a behavior incompatible with food intake, or as a means of physically getting away from the environmental cues that signalled food consumption.

The pattern of excessive eating that Irene developed does not appear to have been highly determined by parental reinforcement patterns. However, Irene had ample opportunity to observe her parents engage in another type of excessive consumption pattern, that of alcohol intake. Thus, overeating, as a generalized consummatory response, might have developed in part through imitation learning. In addition, the high carbohydrate diet eaten by the Wintertree family also contributed strongly to Irene's obesity problem.

The sudden and continued weight gain that Irene experienced from the time of puberty possibly was influenced by a learned association between emotional arousal and food intake. The onset of puberty proves difficult for many adolescents, and Irene's relative lack of social skills and disordered family situation might have become especially salient as she became a teenager and was expected to be socially active with both boys and girls. She then learned, or continued a previously learned, pattern of dealing with her emotions by consuming food. While Mary tended to leave the house and spend time with her peers when stressful circumstances occurred, Irene stayed home. When she was at home, she ate; and the more obese she became, the more difficult it was for her to establish rewarding social relationships with her schoolmates. Apparently, the primary reinforcements Irene experienced during puberty were doing well academically and eating at home. This situation changed markedly when she began to lose weight and was taught more flexible ways of interacting with her peers and others in her social milieu. Irene's obese body state functioned as an aversive stimulus to other persons, but this aversive stimulus was gradually removed through weight loss. The concomitant development of more satisfying ways of relating to her peers provided Irene with a great deal of reinforcement for maintaining her new eating patterns. There was no evidence of symptom substitution or a deterioration in functioning with weight loss. On the contrary, Irene exhibited an increase in self-esteem and a more favorable body image as she experienced success in weight reduction.

Irene came from a cultural background that did not tend to define obesity as a problem, and also did not equate physical attractiveness with excessive thinness. The ridicule she experienced in school was in part a result of her exposure to and involvement in the white culture and its propensity to equate thinness with physical beauty. Irene apparently had not been obese long enough to develop a stable body image of herself as a fat and ugly person. The fact that her body image changed realistically as she lost weight might have been a significant factor in the maintenance of her weight loss. Her interest and cooperation in monitoring her food intake and following the token program were also crucial factors in the success of that particular treatment method. In addition, adequate nutritional instruction and help in planning low-calorie meals that could be purchased on a low-income budget were important in the success of the program.

Many of the problems with which Irene had to cope and with which she continued to be confronted were outside of her control and that of her therapist. The stresses in her family situation due to a broken home and her mother's continued drinking could not be solved by losing weight, developing more effective social skills, and receiving reinforcement for good academic progress. However, Irene had learned to deal with emotional arousal in ways other than through eating. As she grows older and more independent, her adverse home conditions should become less of a daily influence on her life. Further, she will have the opportunity to continue to develop and apply her intellectual ability.

REFERENCES

Alexander, F., & Flagg, G. W. The psychosomatic approach. In B. J. Wolman (Ed.), *Handbook of clinical psychology*. New York: McGraw-Hill, 1965. Pp. 855–947.

American Psychiatric Association. *Diagnostic and statistical manual of mental disorders* (2nd ed.) (DSM-II). Washington: American Psychiatric Association, 1968.

Bruch, H. Disturbed communication in eating disorders. *American Journal of Orthopsychiatry*, 1963, *33*, 99–104.

Bruch, H. *Eating disorders: Obesity, anorexia nervosa and the person within*. New York: Basic Books, 1973.

Fenichel, O. *The psychoanalytic theory of neuroses*. New York: Norton, 1945.

Glucksman, M. L., & Hirsch, J. The response of obese patients to weight reduction: A clinical evaluation of behavior. *Psychosomatic Medicine*, 1968, *30*, 1–11.

Glucksman, M. L., & Hirsch, J. The response of obese patients to weight reduction: III. The perception of body size. *Psychosomatic Medicine*, 1969, *131*, 1–7.

Goldblatt, P. B., Moore, M. E., & Stunkard, A. J. Social factors in obesity. *Journal of the American Medical Association*, 1965, *192*, 1039–1044.

Grinker, J., Hirsch, J., & Levin, B. The affective responses of obese patients to weight reduction: A differentiation based on age at onset of obesity. *Psychosomatic Medicine*, 1973, *35*, 57–63.

Hirsch, J. Adipose cellularity in relation to human obesity. *Advances in Internal Medicine*, 1971, *17*, 289–330.

Hirsch, J. Can we modify the number of adipose cells? *Postgraduate Medicine*, 1972, *51*, 83–86.

Hirsch, J., & Knittle, J. L. Cellularity of obese and non-obese human adipose tissue. *Federation Proceedings*, 1970, *29*, 1516–1521.

Jones, E. *The life and work of Sigmund Freud.* New York: Basic Books, 1953.

Leon, G. R. A behavior modification approach to the treatment of obesity. *Minnesota Medicine*, 1974, *57*, 977–980.

Leon, G. R. Personality, body image, and eating pattern changes in overweight persons after weight loss. *Journal of Clinical Psychology*, 1975, *31*, 618–623.

Leon, G. R. Current directions in the treatment of obesity. *Psychological Bulletin*, 1976, *83*, 557–578.

Leon, G. R., & Chamberlain, K. Emotional arousal, eating patterns, and body image as differential factors associated with varying success in maintaining a weight loss. *Journal of Consulting and Clinical Psychology*, 1973, *40*, 474–480. (a)

Leon, G. R., & Chamberlain, K. Comparison of daily eating habits and emotional states of overweight persons successful or unsuccessful in maintaining a weight loss. *Journal of Consulting and Clinical Psychology*, 1973, *41*, 108–115. (b)

Leon, G. R., Roth, L., & Hewitt, M. I. Eating patterns, satiety, and self-control behavior in obese patients during weight reduction. Unpublished manuscript, 1976.

Leon, G. R., & Roth, L. Obesity: Psychological causes, correlations, and speculations. *Psychological Bulletin*, 1977, *84*, 117–139.

Lloyd, J. K., Wolff, O. H., & Whelan, W. S. Childhood obesity: A long-term study of height and weight. *British Medical Journal*, 1961, *2*, 145–148.

Mahoney, M. J. Self-reward and self-monitoring techniques for weight control. *Behavior Therapy*, 1974, *5*, 48–57.

McKenna, R. J. Some effects of anxiety level and food cues on the eating behavior of obese and normal subjects. A comparison of the Schachterian and psychosomatic conceptions. *Journal of Personality and Social Psychology*, 1972, *22*, 311–319.

Salans, L. B., Horton, E. S., & Sims, E. A. H. Experimental obesity in man: Cellular character of the adipose tissue. *The Journal of Clinical Investigation*, 1971, *50*, 1005–1011.

Schachter, S., Goldman, R., & Gordon, A. Effects of fear, food deprivation, and obesity on eating. *Journal of Personality and Social Psychology*, 1968, *10*, 91–97.

Seltzer, C. C., & Mayer, J. A simple criterion of obesity. *Postgraduate Medicine*, 1965, *38*, A-101–A-107.

Silverstone, J. T., Gordon, R. P., & Stunkard, A. J. Social factors in obesity in London. *The Practitioner*, 1969, *202*, 682–688.

Stunkard, A., & Burt, V. Obesity and the body image: II. Age at onset of disturbances in the body image. *American Journal of Psychiatry*, 1967, *123*, 1443–1447.

Stunkard, A., d'Aquili, E., Fox, S., & Filion, R. D. L. Influence of social class on obesity and thinness in children. *Journal of the American Medical Association*, 1972, *221*, 579–584.

Stunkard, A., & Mendelson, M. Obesity and the body image: I. Characteristics of disturbances in the body image of some obese persons. *American Journal of Psychiatry*, 1967, *123*, 1296–1300.

11

A Study of
Sexual Deviation—
The Case of
Michael Boland

Michael Boland was 21 years old when he phoned for an appointment at a local guidance clinic. He indicated that a woman friend had suggested that he call. His problem, as he stated it on the phone, was that he tended to attract and be attracted to members of his own sex. He also felt that he was too shy and anxious.

Michael came from a white, lower middle-class environment. At the time the client was seen, his father was working in a small welding shop, and his mother had died of cancer six months previously. Michael was the youngest of three children and the only boy in the family. His sister Patricia was 26, and another sister Carol was 23. Both were married and lived in the area. The members of the family all practiced the Catholic religion and attended church regularly.

Michael looked younger than 21 years of age. His tall, slim appearance, with wavy hair, long lashes and even features, gave him an air of prettiness. Michael wore conspicuously stylish clothes and jewelry, with every article carefully matched. He spoke in an extremely low tone of voice during the interviews, which made it difficult to hear him across the desk.

FAMILY BACKGROUND

Michael described his mother as a sweet, kind, and sensitive person, and he said that he had been very close to her. Even though she had become progressively ill over a number of years, Michael found it difficult to get used to the fact that she was dead. He said that his mother had always been very protective in her relationship with him, and he missed not having the guidance and concern that his mother had continually provided.

Neither parent had given Michael any sexual information. He reported that sex was a taboo subject in his household, except for comments by his mother that premarital sexual relationships were sinful. Michael had never told his mother about his attraction for males. However, on a number of occasions he had related to her his discomfort in social situations with girls, particularly those his own age. Mrs. Boland had always responded by assuring Michael that he was still too young to worry about girls, and that it was more important for him to be concerned about his future career. She said there was plenty of time for him to go out on dates and think of marriage, and that eventually he would find a nice girl. In the meantime, Mrs. Boland felt that it was important that Michael did not get mixed up with "the wrong crowd," and she encouraged him to participate in family rather than peer group social activities.

Whenever Michael went out in the evening, his mother stayed awake until he got home and she expressed relief that he had returned without any mishaps befalling him. Michael would then feel extremely guilty because his mother was ill, and she had been kept awake because of worry and apprehension about his welfare. Michael said that his mother had not been as overprotective with his two sisters as she had been with him. He remembered that his mother had not discouraged Carol from going out on dates, as long as Mrs. Boland knew the persons with whom Carol was going to be out. Michael felt that his mother was genuinely pleased when Carol got married at the age of 19, and he recalled that the courtship and wedding period of his eldest sister Patricia was also a happy and exciting time. The client stated that both of his sisters were happily married, but he did not feel very close to either of his brothers-in-law.

Michael characterized his relationship with his father as one of coolness and distance, rather than open conflict. He said that he had never felt a deep emotional bond with his father, and they rarely had any extended conversations. The client reported that his father had been aware of Mrs. Boland's overprotectiveness toward Michael, but Mr. Boland had never commented on this relationship nor attempted to change it.

Mr. Boland had no hobbies, and he spent a great deal of time watching television. He rarely saw the few acquaintances he had, and Michael felt that his father did not really like people that much. The client said that his father did not enjoy being with others because he was bitter that he had not been more successful economically. Michael never discussed vocational plans with his father. Mr. Boland made no comment about Michael's ambition to become a fashion designer, nor did he express an interest in the special courses Michael was taking in fashion design.

Since Mrs. Boland's death, Mr. Boland had become even less communicative with Michael. Although they both shared the same house, Michael and his father hardly talked to each other. Michael prepared meals for the two of them, and several times a week they ate dinner at either Carol's or Patricia's house. Michael usually went out in the evenings, and his father rarely asked him where he was going or commented on what time it was when Michael returned.

INTERPERSONAL BACKGROUND

The client reported that his sisters had related to him in a protective manner ever since he was a child, and they still frequently pampered and fussed over him. He felt very close to his sisters, and said that he thought of Patricia as a second mother. When he first started school, Carol took him to class every day and made sure that he got there on time. Mrs. Boland told Carol to be certain that Michael was neat when he got to school, and Carol always combed his hair or tucked his shirt in before she let him enter the classroom. The client stated that he was well behaved and somewhat shy throughout his school career, and he rarely got into difficulty with any of the teachers. Most of his teachers were women, and he frequently became the "teacher's pet" because of his good behavior and cooperativeness.

Michael was nonassertive with his peers, both outside of school as well as in school. He said that he never felt accepted by the other boys because he was not good in sports. Michael stated that he had never possessed the skills necessary to play baseball or running games well, and no one had ever coached him in these games. He reported that he had always been slender of build and frequently ill with colds. He found it more comfortable to follow along with one of his sisters and her friends, or play alone, rather than play games with children his own age. His sisters were expected to watch him, and they encouraged him to stay with them. As a child, there was usually one particular boy that he would play with from time to time, but he often played with girls when he did interact at all with peers.

The adolescent period was a time of great turmoil for Michael. He began to masturbate frequently, and he felt guilty because he thought he was doing something that was wrong or could harm him in some way. Michael was troubled with a skin problem during adolescence, and he was very self-conscious about the pimples on his face. Although he recognized that most teenagers have this problem, he felt that his skin condition was more severe and noticeable than any other youngster's.

At the time of the clinic interviews, Michael still felt that he had a poor complexion, even though there were no blemishes apparent to the interviewer. Michael stated that he was always conscious of his physical appearance, and had never thought that he was physically attractive to girls. He had lifted weights while in high school, in order to build himself up to be an acceptable male. However, he felt that he was not strong enough to fight over and win a girl, and that it was much easier to attract males because he did not have to prove his strength.

Michael did not go out with girls very often. Dating had always been a struggle for him, and he did not feel comfortable being with a girl. However, he had occasionally gone out with one young woman over a period of seven months during his junior year in high school. She was three years older than he, and they had kissed each other on occasion. Michael stated that eventually he stopped calling her because he was not interested in girls, and he was not aroused sexually by females. He had never attempted heterosexual intercourse.

During the high school period, Michael had maintained a relationship with another boy from school. They appeared to have been initially drawn toward each other because both lacked interests similar to those of the other youngsters in the class. At a period when many of the boys were talking about real or fantasied sexual exploits with girls, Michael and his friend Tom had little to offer to this conversation. They tended to become embarrassed or anxious by the other boys' comments. Through being friends with each other, Michael and Tom could avoid the general discussion about girls, and they were less likely to become the target of the other boys' teasing. Tom introduced Michael to mutual masturbation, and at a later period, to fellatio.

Michael stated that he and Tom still felt a warm affection for one another, but after graduation, each had gone his separate way. Michael began to frequent homosexual bars at irregular intervals, but his mother did not allow him to spend every evening out of the house. He stated that many of the men he met at the bars were physically attracted to him, and this was a very enjoyable experience. Michael also said that he derived a great deal of physical pleasure from homosexual activity. The client engaged in a number of homosexual encounters when his mother was still alive, and these relationships increased in frequency after her death. He said that he was not in love with any single person, but he enjoyed receiving attention and flattery from the many men he met at gay bars.

Michael reported that he often felt greatly troubled by the rights and wrongs of his sexual behavior, and thought that he was committing a sin. He had never been able to discuss these concerns with his parish priest, or with any members of his family. At the time Michael was seen, he had several female friends who were fellow students at the school of fashion design, and mostly older than he. He maintained friendly, platonic relationships with these woman, and they appeared to enjoy his company. Michael had confided to one of them that he felt guilty about his sexual orientation, and this woman was the one who suggested that Michael contact the clinic.

PSYCHOLOGICAL EVALUATION

Michael was seen by a female psychologist, Dr. T. The client appeared to be quite anxious during the first interview, and he tended to speak in a quavering and barely audible tone of voice. He found it difficult to maintain eye contact with the examiner, and often looked off to one side or down at his hands. He stated that one of the reasons that he had come for evaluation was to find out why he was so nervous and high-strung. The client also complained of a lack of self-confidence and of being socially naive and immature. His major concern, however, was that he was attracted to members of the same sex. Michael cooperated readily with the examiner and performed the tasks asked of him during the psychological evaluation. After his initial anxiety lessened, he smiled more frequently and began to initiate some conversation. He also helped the examiner put away the test materials at the end of the testing session.

The client completed a general personality inventory, the MMPI. He was asked to give stories to a number of cards from the Thematic Apperception Test (TAT), in order to gain more information about social relationships and interaction patterns. Michael also completed the Assertive Questionnaire (Lazarus, 1971).

There was evidence on the test material of anxiety, depression, and repetitive and bothersome thoughts. The client, however, was not overwhelmed by his personal difficulties. On the contrary, a number of his responses indicated an expectation that he would eventually be able to solve his problems and be a success in life.

Michael expressed a continued concern about behaving as one is "supposed to" or "ought to." He depicted many of the persons on the TAT cards as being punished for wrongdoings, and the punishment was viewed as an expected and justified retribution. Another theme evident in the stories he told was that of an individual who had a number of weaknesses beyond his personal control. In spite of these weaknesses, the person is able to be successful and proud of himself. The following excerpt from one of the TAT stories illustrates this theme: "he is very strong and muscular, but he has other weaknesses of which he has no control. But he still thinks that he is a great person and he ends up to be a success."

The client's responses to the test material suggested an uncertainty about sexual identification. Some of the figures on the TAT cards were initially labeled as female, and then seen as male. A number of other percepts that were seen as human figures were not delineated as either masculine or feminine, but were described in the neuter gender. Older male figures were pictured as helpful persons, but individuals to whom one could not get close. He tended to view females his own age as physically unattractive and artificial, but recognized that other men might see women as desirable. The client responded in a very negative manner to concepts about his own body, and he described himself as physically awkward and in need of improving his appearance. He also indicated that he sometimes wished that he were a girl.

The client's responses to the Assertive Questionnaire indicated that he typically interacted with others in a nonassertive manner. For example, he responded "yes" to the following items: "Are you always very careful to avoid all trouble with other people?" "When a person is blatantly unfair, do you usually fail to say something about it to him?"

"Would you be hesitant about asking a good friend to lend you a few dollars?"

In general, the test results confirmed the information about the client that had been gained from the interview.

COURSE OF THERAPY

Therapy was recommended in order to help Michael deal with his inner turmoil and guilt feelings about his sexual orientation, and to aid him in modifying his shy and dependent behavior. The goal of therapy was to enable the client to make future decisions, including the selection of a sexual partner, on the basis of a more open choice, rather than because of poor interpersonal skills. Therapy with an older man was recommended, so Michael would have a male to model his behavior after. The therapist would also be available to provide counseling to the client on the techniques of heterosexual activity, if the client expressed an interest in obtaining this information. Michael responded quite favorably to the advice that he enter therapy, and accepted the suggestion that he be seen by a male therapist. He expressed disappointment that he would not be continuing with Dr. T., but he was able to establish good rapport with the recommended therapist.

The initial therapy sessions were devoted to a discussion of Michael's feelings of guilt about his homosexual behavior, and his attitude that he was inferior and unattractive. Dr. E. encouraged Michael to express his feelings, and asked him to cite specific situations in which he had felt inadequate. It was apparent from Michael's comments that his feelings of inadequacy stemmed in large part from a lack of social skills in interacting with other persons, male as well as female. Dr. E. and Michael examined in detail the social events where Michael had acted in a manner the client considered inadequate. Dr. E. pointed out to Michael the effect of his behavior on other persons, and how the responses of others in turn shaped the way Michael subsequently interacted with them.

The client brought up a recent event that was troubling him, and the therapist was able to demonstrate to Michael the functional relationship between Michael's behavior and the response of those around him. The client described a situation that had occurred at school when he was doing some sketches of fashion designs. A girl in his class asked to see his book of drawings, and he readily gave the book to her to look at. The young woman later handed in some sketches which were quite similar to the ones Michael had done. When the class as a whole evaluated each other's work, a number of students commented on the similarity between Michael's drawings and those of Susan's. Michael felt that Susan had then implied that her sketches were done first, and that he had copied from her. Michael did not make any comment to Susan or to any of the other class members during the discussion and evaluation of the sketches. Further, he did not tell anyone that Susan had looked at his sketches before she had done her own.

Michael said that he was very upset by this episode, and he felt that Susan had taken advantage of him by asking to see his notebook. He thought that his sketches were quite good, and felt that they had been devalued because of the suggestion that he had obtained his ideas from Susan. Michael reported that he was very angry at Susan and humiliated by the episode. He went directly home after class and stayed there for the rest of the day. His father did not notice that Michael was upset, and Michael did not say anything to Mr. Boland about the incident. When Michael saw Susan in class the next day, he made it a point to sit at the opposite end of the room from her, and in general, tried to ignore her.

Dr. E. pointed out to Michael how this incident was a good illustration of Michael's typical nonassertive, compliant behavioral style. Dr. E. discussed how the client's passive compliant behavior could encourage others to take advantage of him, particularly when Michael made no overt response to assert himself. Michael's habitual response to a difficult interpersonal situation was to withdraw from that environment. The withdrawal functioned to reinforce Susan's behavior and also prevented Michael from engaging in more effective and mature ways of dealing with other persons.

Dr. E. employed the behavior therapy technique of assertive training (Wolpe and Lazarus, 1966) to teach Michael how to deal with others in a more effective and satisfying manner. He asked Michael to suggest other behaviors which he might have employed to handle the situation that was troubling him. Client and therapist then role played a number of Michael's suggested alternatives, and the inadequacies of some of the client's initial solutions were quickly apparent in the role playing situation. Eventually, Michael made a suggestion which seemed to both client and therapist to be an adaptive, assertive response. Michael acted out this role, while Dr. E. role played the reciprocal changes in Susan's behavior. Michael then assumed Susan's role, and Dr.

E. role played the assertive behavior Michael had suggested. This latter procedure enabled Michael to gain a better understanding of how a change in behavior on his part would in turn affect another person's behavior. Dr. E. advised Michael to continue practicing the more assertive behavioral role when he was at home, and he also encouraged the client to act more assertively in interpersonal situations. The therapist pointed out that an individual's feelings of self-esteem and self-worth are dependent on the way other people respond to him or her.

The issue of Michael's sexual orientation was discussed at length in therapy. The client reported that he experienced a great deal of physical gratification from engaging in homosexual behavior, and he had no interest in sexual activity with someone of the opposite sex. He said that the problem that troubled him most was his guilt feelings because of a religious belief that his sexual behavior was sinful. He also recognized the attitude of the majority of persons in our society that homosexuality is a behavior pattern to be scorned, or viewed as a sign of emotional disorder. Many of the therapy sessions were devoted to discussions about Michael's guilt feelings, and the need to differentiate between the motivation for changing his sexual orientation and the desire for societal acceptance of his behavior.

Dr. E. actively encouraged Michael to participate in social activities and dates with women. He suggested that one of the ways that Michael could overcome his feelings of inadequacy was through practice in the social skills necessary for interacting with members of the opposite sex. The therapist also suggested that Michael go out with a woman whose company he enjoyed, and he should not be concerned about whether he was becoming sexually aroused by that person. If the client felt that he was physically attracted to one of the girls he enjoyed dating, Dr. E. could then counsel him on heterosexual techniques.

During the course of therapy, Michael continued to frequent homosexual bars, and he engaged in homosexual activity about once or twice a month. He tended to go out with different men, rather than gravitating to a relationship with one particular individual. However, he followed the therapist's suggestion and also went out on dates with a number of girls his own age. The client reported that he did not experience anxiety and these occasions were somewhat enjoyable, but he had not become sexually aroused by any of the girls he had been with. He had kissed one of his female dates good night and had held her hand, but that was the extent of physical contact. Michael noted that he felt more relaxed being out with a girl than he had previously.

However, he continued to express a preference for homosexual activity.

At the end of one year of treatment, Michael said that he wished to continue in therapy for a while longer. He stated that he felt more confident and less anxious than he had when he started therapy, but his major problem was still his feelings of guilt about his homosexual behavior. Although he could now enjoy himself on a date with a woman, he was not interested in heterosexual behavior. Therapy was terminated approximately two months later because Michael felt that he was able to deal with other persons in a more comfortable and satisfying manner.

DISCUSSION

This case presents a number of difficult questions about the role of the therapist in modifying behavior that most members of a society label as deviant. Is the role of the therapist that of "curing" a troubled individual by shaping that person to conform to society's standards of normal behavior? Or, on the other hand, is the therapist's role that of "curing" an individual by shaping the person to conform to the therapist's standards of normal behavior, irrespective of whether the therapist's definition of normality agrees with the definition of the greater society? Also, how does one define what is normal and what is abnormal behavior? One can also ask whether the therapist is justified in using the label "pathology" to describe behavior that might be quite acceptable in other contexts or in other cultures.

Perry London's book, *The Modes and Morals of Psychotherapy*, presents an excellent discussion of the effect of the therapist's moral values on the practice of therapy, and on the type of change one strives for in treatment. London's thesis is that every therapist brings to the therapy session a set of values and standards, and it is impossible to interact with the client without these values entering in. Moral standards influence the course of treatment and the judgments made about the client's progress. London states that each therapist must examine his or her own moral standards, see himself or herself as a moral agent, and thus acknowledge that moral principles do influence the therapy process.

In treating an individual manifesting a sexual deviation, the theoretical system as well as the values of the therapist can be extremely crucial in formulating treatment goals. Psychoanalytic theorists, for example, view homosexuality as a pathological disorder where the normal object is replaced by an unnatural sexual object (Alexander and Shapiro, 1952). Therefore, homosexuality, by definition, is abnormal and a change in sexual object would be crucial for treatment to proceed. Other theorists may consider homosexual behavior to be sinful, or a reflection of a deterioration of the standards of a society. Thus, irrespective of the changes seen in the client during the course of therapy, the client would not be considered a treatment success as long as he or she continued to engage in homosexual behavior.

An increasingly shared belief among therapists of a number of theoretical persuasions is that each person should be free to live his or her own life as long as that person does not hurt or interfere with the freedom of another individual (Rogers, 1961; Szasz, 1965). In this context, a client who continues to express a preference for homosexual activity while otherwise becoming reasonably free of conflict would not be influenced by the therapist to change to a heterosexual mode of behavior. The criterion of therapeutic success would be based on whether the client was able to interact with others in a comfortable way, and in a way that did not hurt another individual.

Homosexual behavior can be considered either as a pathological process, or as a behavior that is a deviation from a cultural norm. Definitions of normal and abnormal behavior based on the medical model suggest that abnormal behavior is analogous to a pathological disease process. One cannot cure the patient unless one treats the cause of the problem, i.e., the pathological inner dysfunction. It is assumed that the external symptom will disappear when the underlying disease process is cured (Buss, 1968).

The psychoanalytic formulation of homosexuality falls within the framework of the medical model, because homosexual behavior is considered to be a symptom of an underlying psychic disturbance. Sexual deviation in males is seen as a symptom reflecting a defense against a strong fixation on the mother or a fear of the father. According to psychoanalytic theory, the Oedipus complex causes the youngster to have intense castration anxiety because of the fear of the father's retaliation for sexually desiring the mother (Alexander and Shapiro). The homosexual individual resolves this conflict by replacing the incestuous sexual object (the mother) with a sexual object of the same sex. Homosexual behavior is therefore a symptom of interrupted sexual development due to pathological psychic conflict centering around strong libidinal attachments to the mother and an inability to identify with the father.

A statistical model of normality suggests that what is defined as normal is that behavior which conforms to the conventions of the majority of a population. Any behavior that is unexpected or unusual is labeled abnormal (London and Rosenhan, 1968). The concept of homosexuality as deviant behavior follows from the statistical definition of normality. Homosexual behavior is deviant in the sense that most members of our society are not predominantly or exclusively homosexual in orientation, although as Kinsey, Pomeroy, and Martin (1948) have shown, many males have at some time between adolescence and old age had some homosexual experience. The concept of deviation suggests that a given behavior is different from what most members of a society engage in. However, the statistical definition does not imply that because a behavior is different, it is by definition a result of underlying conflict and tension and thus pathological. Further, in 1973 the American Psychiatric Association, with the strong backing of the American Psychological Association, removed homosexuality from the Diagnostic and Statistical Manual's (DSM-II) official classification of mental disorders. Thus, there has been an official recognition of homosexuality as an alternative life style, rather than by definition, a symptom of abnormal behavior. Nonetheless, the prejudices existent in our culture suggest that it might take some time for the viewpoint of a large segment of the population, including many members of the mental health professions, to change to the official attitude that homosexuality is not a sign of pathology.

In other cultures, including classical Greece, homosexual behavior was socially recognized as a highly valued form of behavior between males (West, 1967). Even within the present culture, homosexual behavior may not be considered to be unusual in situations where members of the opposite sex are not present, such as in prison or at boarding school or camp. The concept of deviation, rather than pathology, allows one to analyze a given behavior within a specific social or cultural context. What is labeled as normal in one culture might well be considered abnormal in a different culture or another era. Universal standards of normality are rarely found.

A social learning interpretation of homosexual behavior is oriented around a deviation concept of abnormality. Homosexual behavior would not, in and of itself, be considered a sign of severe emotional disturbance. Both normal individuals and those society labels as deviant learn to behave in a given manner because of particular patterns of reinforcement and imitation. One would have to analyze the reinforcement patterns associated with specific social interactions and the models that were available to a given individual in order to understand how that person's behavior was shaped. However, all persons will tend to repeat behaviors they are reinforced for, particularly if these behaviors are modeled by other persons in the environment. The homosexually oriented individual most likely had an opportunity to observe, and be reinforced for, different types of behavior than the heterosexually inclined individual.

An analysis of the interpersonal relationships in Michael Boland's life experience illustrates that deviant as well as normal behavior may be learned through the same general processes of reinforcement and modeling. Michael was in continual contact with his mother and sisters while he was growing up. He saw very little of his father, and communicated with him still less. His father did not present a strong model of traditionally masculine interests and behavior for Michael to imitate, in contrast to the continually present feminine role models provided by his mother and sisters. Since Michael was in frequent interaction with the female members of his family, they were very potent sources of reinforcement. Michael was given attention and social approval for engaging in the behaviors they approved of, and their social approval become particularly important to him. He apparently did not view his father as an important source of reinforcement. However, Michael learned that he would gain reinforcement from his mother and sisters when he acted in a passive and dependent manner.

Michael had very little opportunity to interact with his peers, due to Mrs. Boland's overprotectiveness. He was therefore deprived of the chance to regularly observe the role behavior of male members of his peer group, outside of the school setting. Similarly, Bieber (1962) found that less than one fifth of the male homosexuals he studied had participated in typically masculine games. The majority of Bieber's subjects reported that during childhood they were excessively fearful of physical injury and they avoided physical fights.

Michael was not able to learn the social and physical play skills necessary for peer acceptance, because he did not play very frequently with youngsters his own age. As Michael grew older, there was a greater and greater discrepancy between his behavior and what his peer group considered acceptable behavior. Peer group interactions did not seem to function as an important source of reinforcement until Michael was in high school. However, Michael had always been able to gain social reinforcement from his mother and sisters. Throughout Michael's life history, they reinforced him for behaving in a nonassertive, home-oriented manner.

In the case presented, the factor of body build appears to interact with the factor of social relationships in the development of the homosexual behavior pattern. Michael was very thin and somewhat sickly as a child. These problems might have caused his mother to be more protective of him and reinforce dependency behavior more than she might have if Michael had been stronger and more active. Michael's thin stature made it difficult for him to compete in sports, and he was ridiculed because of his body build. One of the reasons why he withdrew from playing with other boys was because of this ridicule. As Michael grew older, he was acutely aware that his physique was not as muscular as most boys his age, and he attempted to compensate for this by lifting weights. He was not successful in changing his physical appearance, and eventually Michael gave up trying to make himself stronger, i.e., with a body build that he thought would be appealing to members of the opposite sex.

Michael expressed the idea that one had to be strong and prove oneself in order to date girls. He equated the process of dating with a contest where the strongest male was awarded the prize of feminine company. In order to keep the girl's companionship, one had to be constantly alert and fend off the advances of the other males. In addition, Michael was never comfortable dating girls because of a general lack of skill in interacting with persons his own age. When he did go out with a girl, his choice was someone a number of years older than he. Michael seemed more able to relate to a companion who was similar in age to his sister, a predictable and nonthreatening person in his life existence.

Michael's first adolescent friendship and sexual experience with his friend Tom proved to be a pleasurable encounter. In contrast to the feelings of inadequacy and discomfort he experienced when interacting with members of the opposite sex, Michael's relationship with another boy was quite satisfying. Michael did not have the attitude that he had to prove himself physically, and he felt accepted as he was. His friend was more sexually experienced than he was and able to provide Michael with a gratifying homosexual encounter. During later sexual relationships between the two boys, Michael found even greater reinforcement from homosexual activity. Michael did not become sexually aroused by members of the opposite sex, perhaps because of anxiety about his physical appearance. Further, he had never interacted with a woman in a way in which he could learn the behaviors leading to heterosexual arousal. The women Michael felt most comfortable with were older than he and did not expect a sexual relationship with him.

When Michael was in high school, the persons that he associated with were homosexually oriented males, and they became the role models that he emulated. When he modeled his behavior after the homosexual behavior he observed, the others gave him social approval for doing so, which served to reinforce and maintain this behavior. The high school period was also the first time that Michael had interacted with members of his peer group for any duration.

Michael continued to think of himself as unattractive, of poor complexion, and inferior in body build. He stated that he felt more attractive when he wore highly styled clothes and jewelry, because he received a great deal of attention from others when he was elegantly dressed. The client's highly ambitious pursuit of a career in fashion design may also have been related to the approval he received from others for activities related to clothing.

Although Michael received a great deal of immediate sexual gratification from his homosexual encounters, he felt very guilty afterwards. The guilt feelings stemmed from his strict and moralistic upbringing, where issues were continually viewed in terms of a choice between good and evil or right and wrong. The client's mother emphasized that there were certain ways in which one "ought" to behave. Sexual activities, in general, were termed sinful and the result of bad peer influences. Michael was also sensitive to the attitude that most persons in our society have toward homosexual behavior. When he frequented gay bars, he experienced a feeling of belonging to a group which was estranged from society. This feeling of estrangement was uncomfortable, because the rules Michael learned during his strict upbringing had always stressed the importance of acting in a "good" or socially acceptable manner.

When Mrs. Boland died, Michael felt her loss quite keenly and thought of her a great deal. These thoughts included recollections of his mother's moral principles, and Michael felt very guilty because he was continuing to engage in homosexual behavior. However, the reinforcement associated with sexual gratification was intense and immediate, and the guilt feelings did not occur until after the homosexual encounter. Michael therefore became anxious and depressed, but did not change his behavior pattern.

If homosexual behavior is a response that is deviant rather than pathological, is the goal of therapy to make the client less anxious and guilty about his sexual orientation, or should the therapist attempt to change a homosexual behavior pattern to a heterosexual one? Many therapists would leave this decision up to the client. The therapist would function to help the client resolve overall difficulties in relating to other persons, so that eventually the client could become more skilled and less anxious in communicating with others. At this point, the client might state that it is his choice to continue in a homosexual behavior pattern, because this is the most gratifying sexual experience for him. Szasz (1965) and others would feel that the client has a right to decide, and would abide by whatever decision the client made.

The therapy procedures that Michael participated in were determined in part by his complaints of discomfort because of feelings of inadequacy, anxiety, and depression. The client showed little motivation to change his sexual orientation, and wanted help primarily for his feelings of guilt and inadequacy. The therapy sessions were therefore oriented around the general interpersonal problems the client brought up.

Behavior therapy techniques can be employed when the client is motivated to change to a different pattern of sexual functioning. Feldman and MacCulloch (1971) have reported positive results using a procedure of aversive conditioning to homosexual stimuli, with relief experienced when heterosexual stimuli are presented. The individual is given an electric shock when a slide of a nude person of the same sex is presented, and the shock is terminated when a slide of an individual of the opposite sex is shown. Further, Masters and Johnson (1970) have described a technique of utilizing an experienced sexual partner to gradually induce sexual arousal in a member of the opposite sex. The person in treatment undergoes a conditioning process whereby pleasurable sensations and sexual arousal become associated to heterosexual stimuli. The Masters and Johnson procedure has important implications for teaching a heterosexually inexperienced or anxious individual the skills of sexual behavior. However, the client must be motivated to change his or her sexual orientation before any of these techniques can be effective. In Michael's case, his previous social conditioning, as well as the gratifying nature of his homosexual experiences, proved too strong to motivate him to change his sexual behavior.

REFERENCES

Alexander, F., & Shapiro, L. B. Neuroses, behavior disorders, and perversions. In F. Alexander & H. Ross (Eds.), *Dynamic psychiatry*. Chicago: U. of Chicago Press, 1952. Pp. 117–139.

American Psychiatric Association. *Diagnostic and statistical manual of mental disorders* (2nd ed.) (DSM-II). Washington: American Psychiatric Association, 1968.

Bieber, I. *Homosexuality: A psychoanalytic study*. New York: Basic Books, 1962.

Buss, A. *Psychopathology*. New York: Wiley, 1968

Feldman, M. P., & MacCulloch, M. J. *Homosexual behaviour: Therapy and assessment*. Oxford: Pergamon Press, 1971.

Kinsey, A. C., Pomeroy, W. B., & Martin, C. D. *Sexual behavior in the human male*. Philadelphia: Saunders, 1948.

Lazarus, A. A. *Behavior therapy and beyond*. New York: McGraw-Hill, 1971.

London, P. *The modes and morals of psychotherapy*. New York: Holt, Rinehart, & Winston, 1964.

London, P., & Rosenhan, D. (Eds.), *Foundations of abnormal psychology*. New York: Holt, Rinehart, & Winston, 1968.

Masters, W. H., & Johnson, V. E. *Human sexual inadequacy*. Boston: Little, Brown, 1970.

Rogers, C. R. *On becoming a person: A therapist's view of psychotherapy*. Boston: Houghton Mifflin, 1961.

Szasz, T. S. *The ethics of psychoanalysis*. New York: Basic Books, 1965.

West, D. J. *Homosexuality*. Chicago: Aldine, 1967.

Wolpe, J., & Lazarus, A. A. *Behavior therapy techniques*. Oxford: Pergamon Press, 1966.

12

A Lifetime Exposure to Alcohol— The Case of Maria Valdez

Maria Valdez, a 40-year-old Mexican-American, had been employed as an assembly line worker for a number of years. She was referred from an alcohol rehabilitation clinic to a state mental hospital so she could receive more intensive care for her problems of alcoholism. Maria voluntarily admitted herself to the hospital in order to participate in a special alcohol abuse program. This was her first admission to a mental hospital.

The patient had used alcohol freely for the past twenty years and had manifested an episodic drinking pattern over that time period. She typically got drunk for one or two days on the weekend, drinking at home or in bars, and she then stayed sober for the rest of the week. Until the previous year, Maria had never reported to work drunk nor did she drink while she was working. However, the patient estimated that over the past ten years, she has never stayed sober for longer than two weeks at a time. Maria's only legal arrest occurred one year previously when she was charged with drunken driving.

At the time of the evaluation, Maria was separated from her husband and the youngest of her three children had recently been placed in a foster home. Maria had been fired from her job four months previously because she had become unreliable about appearing for work. She subsisted on welfare support after she lost her job, and she was referred to an outpatient clinic for alcoholism by her welfare worker. However, Maria continued to have great difficulty remaining sober and she was then referred to a state mental hospital for inpatient treatment.

CHILDHOOD BACKGROUND

Maria's father was born in Mexico, and her mother was a first generation Mexican-American. When Mr. Valdez was a young man, he emigrated to the United States in search of a better job. Maria's parents were tenant farmers and they had lived and worked in the same rural area since Maria was a child. Maria was the second youngest in a family of nine children.

Maria revealed that she had never felt close to her mother. She described her mother as a stern and religious person who rarely showed affection toward any of her children. Mrs. Valdez also had a long history of engaging in periodic drinking bouts, and Maria clearly remembered many occasions during her childhood when her mother was drunk. The children learned to stay out of her way at this time because Mrs. Valdez would become physically and verbally abusive toward her family.

Maria recalled that her father was quite affectionate toward her and he rarely punished her when she misbehaved. He usually drank wine throughout the day, but she could not remember ever seeing him drunk. Maria indicated that Mr. Valdez also responded to his wife's drinking bouts by trying not to interact with her when she was intoxicated. However, after the drinking episode, he chided her about her behavior and her neglect of the children.

Maria said that she was fond of her brothers and sisters and she remembered that they always had fun together when they were growing up. An older sister took over the household chores and made sure that she had enough to eat whenever their mother was drinking.

The way of life in the rural area where Maria lived alternated between boredom and physical exhaustion during the work season. The Valdez children had very little formal schooling because they toiled in the fields during planting and harvesting time and they went to school only when they had no work obligations. Each of the children stopped attending school at the age of 14.

Maria went to live with a married sister in a large city nearby when she was 15 years old. A number of her brothers and sisters had also moved to the same city and they kept in contact with each other. However, she rarely saw one of her brothers because he was continually in jail on charges related to drunkenness. Maria was able to find work on an assembly line at an electronics factory. She occasionally went back to visit her parents, but she saw less and less of them as she established an independent life in the city. Maria indicated that no one in her family attended church very often, but she frequently prayed at bedtime.

YOUNG ADULTHOOD

Maria began spending her free time with the persons she met at work and at local dances rather than with her relatives in the city. She said that she tried to make friends with persons of many ethnic groups and she had few friends who were Mexican-American. She indicated that her Chicano acquaintances reminded her too much of the old-fashioned ways of her parents and she wanted to lead the kind of life in which she could have more fun.

Maria's first sexual experience occurred at age 15 when she met Bill Harper, who was employed at the same factory where she worked. Maria stated that she had several other sexual relationships before marriage, but she liked Bill very much because he was so much fun to be with, and they were married when she was 17.

Maria reported that Bill was a carefree and happy person during the first year of marriage. He enjoyed drinking with other persons and Maria and Bill usually drank quite heavily on the weekend, either at someone's house or at a bar. Maria stated that they often drank to the point where they both had severe hangovers the next day, but this discomfort was forgotten when they began drinking again. She indicated that after several years of following this type of drinking pattern, her hangovers no longer seemed as severe.

Bill was not continuously employed because he failed to appear at his job if he did not feel like working that day. However, Maria was able to obtain fairly regular employment on an assembly line or doing simple clerical work and she was often the sole financial provider for the family. Maria said that she was not terribly upset with her husband when he quit or was fired from a job, because she was usually employed at the time. She enjoyed Bill's companionship and the lively people they met and she did not nag him about working. Instead, she tried to humor him when he was in a bad mood or feeling the effects of drinking too much.

Maria and Bill had two children during the first three years of their marriage. These pregnancies were unplanned and Maria revealed that she had never really enjoyed taking care of her two sons. After each child was born, she arranged for a neighbor to look after the youngsters and she went back to work as soon as she felt physically able to do so. Maria stated that it was fortunate that she could find work because otherwise the family would not have had enough money to live on.

Three years after their marriage, Bill was arrested on a robbery charge and sentenced to four years in prison. Maria said she was surprised to find out that her husband had been burglarizing stores, but she had never questioned him about his activities or the money he spent when he was out of work. While Bill was incarcerated, Maria continued to drink on the weekends, at first with her friends and then with new acquaintances. She occasionally had sexual relationships with some of the men she met, but she did not establish a long-term alliance with anyone else.

Maria described Bill as a changed man when he came out of prison. He was bitter and angry and no longer fun to be with. When they drank together, the evening usually ended in arguments and an occasional physical beating. Maria and Bill separated about six months after his release from prison and she eventually obtained a divorce. Maria then engaged in a series of liaisons with a number of men she met at bars or through mutual acquaintances. None of these relationships lasted very long and Maria usually found herself providing all of the financial support until she tired of that person and told him to move out.

Maria indicated that she had lived for six months with a man who was a heroin addict, although she did not realize that he was addicted when they first met. They were already living together when she found out and she stated that she maintained the relationship for a while longer because he was pleasant to be with. However, Maria said that he suddenly "cracked up." He began shouting and talking irrationally and he threatened to kill her. The bizarre behavior he manifested was extremely frightening and she called the police. Soon after this episode, he was committed to a mental hospital.

Maria got married for the second time when she was 33 years old to someone she became acquainted with at a bar. She stated that she felt Phil was the kind of person she could depend on and he was also fun to be with. Phil was employed in the produce department of a supermarket and he had previously worked as a cab driver. He also had a drinking problem, but he started drinking each day in the afternoon and his drinking did not markedly interfere with his job. Maria continued her well-established drinking pattern of staying sober during the week and drinking heavily on the weekend. Maria and Phil had lived together continuously for four years and they have been separated off and on for the past three years.

Maria said that her sons had always been quite unruly and difficult to discipline, and she or the man she was living with attempted to control their behavior by hitting them with a strap. She generally encouraged the boys to play outside so she would not be annoyed by their actions. She rarely asked her sons about their outside activities, even when they came home extremely late at night.

Maria indicated that there were continual arguments between Phil and her sons. Michael and Charles usually formed an alliance with each other in order to oppose Phil's directions and they generally ignored Maria's attempts to persuade them to obey. Two years after their mother remarried, the boys moved out of the house following a prolonged family argument about their behavior. According to Maria, all persons agreed that the move would be beneficial. Michael and Charles were then 16 and 17 years old, respectively, and they supported themselves by working in factories.

Maria did not see her sons very often after they moved out, except for occasions when either Michael or Charles needed some money. Maria indicated that she always gave them whatever funds she could spare, whenever they asked for money. Maria reported that both of the boys enjoyed drinking beer, but she did not think that either of them had a drinking problem. When she was admitted to the alcohol abuse program at the hospital, she had not seen Michael or Charles in several months and she had no idea where they were living or working.

Shortly after Michael and Charles moved out, Maria gave birth to a daughter. Phil, of Jewish background, voiced strong suspicions that he was not the father of this child because her complexion was so dark.

Even though Maria swore that Susan was Phil's child, he was not completely reassured until the youngster grew older and began to look like him.

The continual drinking and the accusations of infidelity made Maria and Phil's marital situation quite difficult. Phil was fired from several jobs because of incidents related to the fact that he began drinking at work. He also became very argumentative at home when he was intoxicated and his drinking behavior was particularly annoying to Maria during the week because she did not drink then. Phil eventually moved out of the house, but he continued to give Maria money for Susan's support when he was working. Maria said that she was sorry that Phil's drinking behavior had become so severe that they could not live together. He was the first man she had lived with who tried to support her and who took an interest in her at times other than when they were drinking.

Maria started seeing another man a few months after Phil moved out, and she said that Phil often spied on them. Phil subsequently went to a social worker and claimed that Maria was not taking adequate care of their daughter. During the following year, Susan was placed in a foster home and Maria was given visitation rights. Maria was told that her daughter would be restored to her when she stopped drinking and was more competent to care for her. Maria indicated that she was glad that Susan was well taken care of in the foster home and she hoped that she would be able to terminate her drinking and eventually regain custody of Susan.

Phil sought help for his drinking problem after Susan was taken from Maria's custody, and with support of Alcoholics Anonymous, he has been quite successful in abstaining from alcohol use. Maria revealed that she and Phil recently made an agreement to get back together again if they could both stop drinking and straighten out their lives. Phil has continued to visit Susan at the foster home and he has also helped persuade Maria to seek assistance for her drinking problem.

TREATMENT HISTORY

Maria accompanied Phil to several meetings of Alcoholics Anonymous at his insistence. She did not attend any further meetings because she was reluctant to stand up in front of the group and tell them about her personal life. However, at this point Maria was unable to remain sober for longer than a few days at a time and could not keep a job. Several weeks after she stopped attending AA meetings, she experienced a blackout after a two-day drinking period. She could not remember anything that had happened over that time span and she was very frightened by this incident. Maria told her welfare worker about the blackout, and the latter helped her to enroll in an outpatient alcohol rehabilitation clinic.

Maria participated in group therapy sessions at this clinic for about three months, but there was little change in her drinking behavior. The staff recommended that she receive more intensive treatment. Maria was told that she might benefit from a program of Antabuse therapy in combination with other forms of treatment, which could be started in the supervised environment of a hospital. Maria agreed to sign into a state mental hospital in order to participate in a special alcohol abuse program.

PSYCHOLOGICAL EVALUATION

Maria was seen by a psychologist on the staff of the mental hospital. The patient was neatly dressed when she appeared for the interview and her dyed red hair was well combed. She spoke in a quiet tone of voice and her conversation was free flowing and relevant to the questions asked of her. Her memory of past and current events appeared to be quite adequate. Maria conversed in a somewhat detached manner, as if the many unpleasant interactions she related had happened to someone else.

Maria became more emotionally expressive as she discussed the reasons why she had signed herself into the hospital. She said that she was unable to control her drinking sprees and she found it impossible to deal with the many problems brought on by her indulgence in alcohol. She stated that she did not want Susan to grow up in foster homes and she sincerely wanted to be able to take care of her daughter. Maria expressed the hope that eventually she and her husband would be able to live together again.

The patient also revealed her fear that if she kept on drinking, she would "crack-up," like the heroin addict with whom she had lived. She realized that whenever she had a day off, she could not keep herself from drinking. She was also spending a greater proportion of her time drinking alone rather than in the company of others.

The patient became quite agitated as she told Dr. C. that she had not realized when she signed up for the alcohol abuse program that she would be confined to a mental hospital. This realization had occurred only after her admission on the previous day, when she observed some patients from other wards at the evening movie. She again recalled how frightened she had been when the man she had lived with became severely disturbed.

Dr. C. told Maria that persons come to the kind of hospital she was in for many different reasons and her drinking problem did not mean that she was insane. The patient was also reminded that she was on a special ward, participating in a program just for alcoholics. Despite further reassurance, Maria became visibly anxious when the psychological tests were administered to her. She felt that the reason she was asked to respond to something as peculiar as the Rorschach inkblot test was because she was indeed mentally disturbed. She thereupon asked Dr. C. if the testing session could be terminated because she felt ill and wanted to lie down. When the patient appeared the next day to continue with the evaluation, she stated that she hoped she would not have to take any more tests. Dr. C. explained that the information gained from the tests could be helpful in determining the best course of treatment for her and Maria agreed to complete the psychological testing.

The patient performed at a level indicative of average intellectual functioning. Despite rather limited formal schooling, Maria was able to correctly answer information questions about literature and geography, and she manifested adequate arithmetic skill. There were some indications that she occasionally found it hard to differentiate between her covert thoughts and the events around her. However, this report of confusion appeared to be descriptive of her drinking episodes and was not suggestive of psychotic thought processes. There was no evidence of organic brain pathology.

On the TAT cards, the patient described relationships between men and women in terms of battles to be won. Women were portrayed as acting in a passive and dependent manner, but the function of this behavior was to manipulate the man to do what the woman wanted. In addition, these relationships were superficial in quality, with little communication of significant personal feelings. Alcohol consumption was depicted as a means of meeting people and providing a vehicle for conversation. The ingestion of liquor also functioned as an escape from the expression of strong feelings of anger, frustration, and anxiety.

COURSE OF HOSPITAL TREATMENT

Maria participated in an alcohol abuse treatment program for individuals who have been unsuccessful in staying sober during some type of outpatient treatment. The program is ten weeks in duration and the patient cannot leave for a home visit without the permission of the hospital staff. The alcoholic's entire day in the hospital is structured and through the help of specially trained ward personnel, the patients are encouraged to develop greater skill and comfort in expressing their feelings. All participants in the program attend group therapy sessions and lectures about the psychological and physiological effects of alcohol. A number of patients also receive Antabuse therapy.

The Antabuse treatment procedure consists of the administration of daily doses of this drug, with the dosage adjusted to an optimum level for that person. The medication usually has little overt effect on the individual as long as there is no alcohol in the bloodstream. However, the person will become violently ill if alcohol is used when the drug is present in the body, i.e., during the four or five days subsequent to the ingestion of Antabuse. The symptoms of Antabuse in combination with alcohol include nausea, vomiting, dizziness, headache, and heart palpitations (Strecker, Ebaugh, and Ewalt, 1955).

Antabuse treatment must be initiated in a carefully controlled setting because of the strength of the physiological reaction to the drug when alcohol is ingested. For ethical as well as safety reasons, the helping professional must make sure that the patient undergoing Antabuse treatment does so voluntarily. Further, the effects of the drug must be fully explained and demonstrated to the individual.

In order to promote this understanding of the drug's effects, the alcoholic, while in the hospital, is given a small amount of alcohol after taking Antabuse. The individual then experiences an attenuated version of the physical symptoms associated with drinking while Antabuse is present in the body. This procedure may be repeated several times during the individual's hospitalization in order to clearly demonstrate the association between Antabuse and alcohol. For many alcoholics, Antabuse treatment has been a successful means of preventing further alcohol consumption. However, Antabuse therapy may have a suppressive rather than an extinguishing effect, i.e., the alcoholic will not drink after taking Antabuse but may skip the medication and consume liquor when the Antabuse is no longer present in the bloodstream.

Maria was placed on an Antabuse treatment program in order to help her terminate her drinking. She participated in the ward activities and responded well to the group milieu once she got over her initial turmoil in acknowledging that she was a patient in a mental hospital. Maria also began to take an active part in the group therapy sessions. She talked about the kinds of men she had been attracted to and how her expressed dependency on another person functioned as a means of controlling a good part of his activities.

Maria continued to express the hope that she and Phil would eventually be able to solve their marital difficulties. Phil agreed to come to the hospital each day and they participated together in a therapy group for couples with drinking problems. After two months of sessions in the couples' group, Maria and Phil appeared to be somewhat more sensitive to each other's feelings and they were able to discuss alternatives to the way they usually interacted with each other.

At the end of the ten-week treatment program, Maria was hopeful that she would be able to control her drinking behavior. She also agreed to continue on Antabuse medication as an outpatient. She and her husband decided to live together again and they planned to petition the court to have Susan restored to them. Maria and Phil were referred to a mental health center in their area, where they could continue together in group therapy.

In light of the longstanding nature of Maria's drinking problem, the hospital staff felt that there was only a fair chance that she would be able to permanently terminate her excessive drinking. However, much could be gained if she could substantially curtail her consumption of alcohol. The prognosis for this latter possibility seemed more promising.

DISCUSSION

Alcoholism is categorized in the psychiatric literature as personality disorder, i.e., a maladaptive behavior pattern of long-standing duration qualitatively different from a neurosis or a psychosis (DSM-II, 1968). Personality disorders such as alcoholism, drug addiction, and antisocial personality have traditionally been conceptualized as a behavioral response to anxiety. Instead of internalizing anxiety through the use of defense mechanisms, the individual responds to these feelings by engaging in particular maladaptive behaviors.

Physical dependence on alcohol has been considered an important factor in diagnosing an individual as an alcoholic. Many excessive drinkers are physiologically addicted to alcohol and manifest physical withdrawal symptoms when the alcohol supply is suddenly removed (Himwich, 1956). However, the diagnosis of alcoholism is usually made when the pattern or amount of alcohol intake interferes with interpersonal functioning, irrespective of whether physiological addiction is manifested. In addition, alcoholism can fall within the separate diagnostic classification of a brain disorder when the chronic use of alcohol results in damage to the brain and central nervous system. Further, alcohol ingestion may be a part of a group of symptoms associated with other types of deviant behavior.

Psychodynamic theorists have suggested a number of predisposing personality traits as relevant to the etiology of chronic alcoholism. Included among these factors are unfulfilled oral dependency needs, latent homosexuality, and self-destructive impulses. However, studies comparing alcoholics with nonalcoholics have failed to reveal any consistent personality traits or problem configuration in the etiology of alcoholism (Jellinek, 1962; Bandura, 1969). It appears quite likely that many of the personality traits noted in alcoholic individuals are the result rather than the cause of the drinking behavior.

Alcohol has a depressant effect on the central nervous system, manifested by an inhibition of the cortical brain centers dealing with judgment and foresight. During alcohol consumption, the subcortical centers exciting strong affect are gradually released from the inhibitory control of the cortex. As a result, an individual who has ingested a large amount of alcohol may begin to express intense emotions and generally behave in a manner in which he or she would not behave when sober. Consistent with these processes, Nathan and O'Brien (1971) found that chronic alcoholics manifested a greater level of depression and a higher frequency of deviant behavior when they were drinking than when they were sober.

Bandura surveyed some of the experimental research dealing with the effects of alcohol on physiological functioning and behavior. He found substantial evidence that alcohol ingestion can lessen the autonomic arousal and emotional behavior resulting from aversive environmental situations, thereby reducing anxiety. This attenuation of autonomic arousal is probably mediated by the inhibition of the cortical centers dealing with judgment and reasoning. Thus, alcohol consumption can function as a learned behavior maintained by the strong positive reinforcement associated with rapid anxiety reduction. Events such as the next day's hangover and the unfavorable evaluation of one's drunken behavior are contingencies that occur at a much later point in time than the immediate reduction in emotional arousal through alcohol ingestion. These future negative events may therefore have little effect on one's immediate drinking behavior.

A number of studies have indicated that there is a high incidence of alcoholism among family members of alcoholics (Fort and Porterfield, 1961; Tahka, 1966). As Bandura pointed out, family members can model a particular pattern of drinking and in this manner teach other persons in the family to associate alcohol consumption with various environmental events. In addition, the consumption of liquor can be highly gratifying if alcohol intake occasionally results in anxiety reduction. An individual with this type of learning history may therefore develop a behavioral repertoire dominated by drinking behavior.

Ethnic group membership is also an important factor in the development of particular drinking patterns. Ethnic groups vary in the extent to which alcoholic beverage consumption and drunken behavior is sanctioned, and the reported incidence of alcoholism is related to this attitude of social tolerance. For example, although alcoholic beverages are consumed in Italian and Jewish households, the rates of alcoholism among members of these two groups is extremely low (Jellinek, 1960; Bandura, 1969). This lower incidence of alcoholism appears to be related to the traditional practice of confining the use of wine and other forms of liquor to clearly prescribed social and religious functions. The individual may drink a glass of wine with a meal or partake of an alcoholic beverage during ceremonial or festive occasions, but liquor consumption at other times or in intoxicating amounts is negatively sanctioned.

It is significant to note that there has been a rise in the incidence of alcoholism among Jews who have ceased to adhere to many of the traditional religious practices of their faith (Snyder, 1962). This increase in alcoholism is most likely related to the assimilated Jew's greater opportunity to observe and be reinforced for following the drinking norms of the majority group. Excessive or more generalized drinking patterns therefore gain the social approval of persons outside of the ethnic group, or the approval of other members of the Jewish group who are imitating the drinking norms of the greater society.

Socioeconomic status is another variable that has a significant influence on the prevalence as well as treatment of problems related to alcohol. Opler (1967) found that the incidence of alcoholic psychosis was 3.4 times higher for black individuals than for white persons. However, the black persons in the study were primarily of lower socioeconomic class, while the white persons were of varying socioeconomic classes. In general, socioeconomic class, rather than race, was the significant contributing factor in the differing rates of mental illness in black and white populations (Srole, Langner, Michael, Opler, and Rennie, 1962). Alcoholic psychotic disorders occurring in members of the lowest socioeconomic class were handled primarily in state hospitals rather than in private hospitals or clinics, and a greater proportion of the lower socioeconomic group received custodial care rather than some form of treatment (Hollingshead and Redlich, 1958). The rate of fatalities due to alcoholism was significantly higher in lower socioeconomic urban areas (Srole, et al.).

Social class variables were also related to attitudes about alcohol consumption. Lawrence and Maxwell (1962) reported that women of lower socioeconomic status showed a lesser approval of moderate social drinking and a greater abstention from alcohol consumption than did women of other socioeconomic groups. All classes showed less tolerance for drunken behavior in women than in men.

Jellinek (1960) has described a number of distinct alcoholic behavior patterns, some of which reflect differences in the use of alcohol among members of various social and cultural groups. His findings refute the belief that alcoholism represents a specific type of drinking pattern. The drinking behavior described in the case presented in this chapter closely parallels the type that Jellinek labeled "epsilon alcoholism." This pattern of alcoholism is characterized by periodic drinking bouts that last from a few days to several weeks, with complete abstinence from liquor occurring between these episodes. Epsilon alcoholism apparently does not result in physiological dependency and withdrawal symptoms.

The case of Maria Valdez illustrates the importance of social and family factors in the development of a particular drinking pattern. Maria grew up in a cultural setting in which there were no strong proscriptions against the consumption of liquor, although alcohol indulgence by women was less socially acceptable than in higher socioeconomic groups. Nonetheless, Maria had had the opportunity to observe both men and women engaging in excessive drinking since the time of her early childhood. Alcoholic beverages were in plentiful supply in the Valdez household, and Maria's mother provided an early model of alcohol abuse. She engaged in the type of periodic drinking that Maria also adopted when she was older. Mr. Valdez usually did not drink to the point of inebriation, but he also modeled the use of liquor as an integral part of his life activities.

Because of the high frequency of drinking behavior that Maria was exposed to, it was inevitable that alcohol would be consumed during times of emotional stress. Maria therefore had the further opportunity to observe the reduction in aversive arousal that generally accompanies alcohol intake. As Maria began drinking socially, there was a high probability that at some time she also would experience a reduction in aversive arousal as a result of the ingestion of alcohol. Liquor consumption therefore became a highly overlearned behavior because of the intermittent reinforcement of alcohol consumption, through anxiety reduction, in association with the continual observation of drinking behavior.

The local bar was an important recreational facility in the lower socioeconomic urban neighborhood where Maria lived. Lower social class areas also tend to be inhabited by a large proportion of alcoholics and this further increased the likelihood that the persons she met would drink excessively. One of Maria's brothers who moved to the city also centered his social activities around drinking and became an alcoholic.

Maria stated that she felt affection for her parents and family, but there was little evidence that she made an effort to maintain her family ties. She rarely saw her father whom she said she particularly cared for, and the longer she lived in the city, the less she saw of her other relatives. She did not attempt to develop a warm interpersonal relationship with her sons, either, and they grew up with very little supervision and guidance. Although Maria related in a warmer and more involved manner with her daughter, her prepotent behavioral repertoire consisted of work, superficial relationships with male companions, and heavy drinking on the weekends. The strength and inclusiveness of this repertoire left little room for extensive interactions with any family members.

With the exception of her husbands, the liaisons that Maria formed were quite transitory in nature. Her basic criterion for male companionship was that the person should be fun to be with and should spend most of his free time with her. Maria was able to control the activities of the men she lived with because she usually provided the money for food and alcohol or drugs. The threat of withholding funds until her demands were submitted to was a potent means of controlling the behavior of these individuals.

During the year before she was hospitalized, Maria's drinking behavior became a generalized response to many environmental stimuli that had not been previously associated with liquor consumption. The intensification of her drinking may have been due to the emotional stress generated by her husband's continued attempts to intrude on her life and remove their daughter from her custody. Concomitant with the change in drinking behavior, Maria's life situation changed markedly: she lost her job, her daughter was placed in a foster home, she suffered a blackout, and she realized that she could not curtail her drinking. The previously reinforcing pattern of periodic heavy drinking had therefore lost much of its reinforcing effectiveness because alcohol consumption was now interfering with a great many of her everyday activities. At this point, she began to consider seeking help for her drinking behavior.

Maria was further motivated to seek treatment by the example of her husband. Phil had been a heavy drinker like herself, but he had been able to terminate his drinking behavior and lead a more satisfying life. Maria found gratification in Phil's social as well as financial support and she was not permanently alienated from him by his role in having Susan placed in a foster home. Maria was influenced by Phil's pleas that she seek treatment and she eventually applied for inpatient therapy.

Although Maria entered the hospital voluntarily, she did not label the place she was in as a mental hospital until she was confronted with the obviously psychotic behavior of some of the patients from other wards. It is possible that Maria was genuinely unaware of the nature of the hospital she came to, but it is also apparent that she did not pay attention to the stimuli suggesting that she was entering a mental hospital. Maria therefore continued to behave in a manner consistent with a lifelong pattern of not attending to or avoiding aversive environmental stimuli. When she first realized that she was in a mental hospital, she became extremely agitated because she was afraid that she would also be considered insane.

Since none of the patients on Maria's ward behaved in a disturbed manner, she gradually began to feel more comfortable in the hospital. With Phil's emotional support and shared participation in the couples' group, Maria started to make some progress in therapy. She gradually learned how to relate to others socially without liquor consumption being a part of this relationship. She also began to verbalize and communicate her feelings, an important skill that could serve as an alternative to drinking alcohol when emotionally aroused.

Formal group therapy and other group situations such as Alcoholics Anonymous have proven helpful in modifying the behavior of excessive drinkers (Garitano, 1969). The opportunity to interact with others manifesting similar problems is an important source of social support. The group can serve as an extremely powerful source of reward for sustained abstinence, as well as a source of disapproval for continued alcohol indulgence.

It is possible that Maria will be able to substantially curtail her drinking behavior if there is a change in her social interaction patterns. Therefore, it is extremely important that she avoid the discriminative stimuli that previously elicited alcohol intake, such as spending the evening at a bar. The use of Antabuse to suppress alcohol consumption should be particularly helpful in providing Maria with the opportunity to learn new social skills unrelated to drinking behavior.

Maria did not exhibit the depressed behavior often observed in alcoholics who have recently stopped drinking. Although she no longer had available the reinforcement associated with alcohol consumption, she was provided with a new source of reinforcement. She gained the social approval of the other group members and there was an overall improvement in her life situation. For Maria and her husband, the continuation of group therapy on an outpatient basis would seem to be a crucial factor in sustaining the modification of their longstanding drinking patterns.

REFERENCES

American Psychiatric Association. *Diagnostic and statistical manual of mental disorders* (2nd ed.) (DSM–II). Washington: American Psychiatric Association, 1968.

Bandura, A. *Principles of behavior modification.* New York: Holt Rinehart & Winston, 1969.

Fort, T., & Porterfield, A. L. Some backgrounds and types of alcoholism among women. *Journal of Health and Human Behavior,* 1961, *2*, 283–292.

Garitano, W. W. Group therapy with alcoholics. In H. M. Ruitenbeek (Ed.), *Group therapy today*. New York: Atherton Press, 1969. Pp. 336–341.

Himwich, H. E. Views on the etiology of alcoholism. I: The organic view. In H. D. Kruse (Ed.), *Alcoholism as a medical problem*. New York: Hoeber-Harper, 1956. Pp. 32–39.

Hollingshead, A. B., & Redlich, F. C. *Social class and mental illness*. New York: Wiley, 1958.

Jellinek, E. M. *The disease concept of alcoholism*. New Haven: Hillhouse Press, 1960.

Jellinek, E. M. Phases of alcohol addiction. In D. J. Pittman & C. R. Snyder (Eds.), *Society, culture, and drinking patterns*. New York: Wiley, 1962. Pp. 356–368.

Lawrence, J. J., & Maxwell, M. A. Drinking and socioeconomic status. In D. J. Pittman & C. R. Snyder (Eds.), *Society, culture, and drinking patterns*. New York: Wiley, 1962. Pp. 141–145.

Nathan, P. E., & O'Brien, J. S. An experimental analysis of the behavior of alcoholics and nonalcoholics during prolonged experimental drinking: A necessary precursor of behavior therapy? *Behavior Therapy*, 1971, *2*, 455–476.

Opler, M. K. *Culture and social psychiatry*. New York: Atherton Press, 1967.

Snyder, C. R. Culture and Jewish sobriety: The ingroup-outgroup factor. In D. J. Pittman & C. R. Snyder (Eds.), *Society, culture, and drinking patterns*. New York: Wiley, 1962. Pp. 188–225.

Srole, L., Langer, T. S., Michael, S. T., Opler, M. K., & Rennie, T. A. C. *The midtown Manhattan study* (Vol. I). *Mental health in the metropolis*. New York: McGraw-Hill, 1962.

Strecker, E. A., Ebaugh, F. G., & Ewalt, J. R. *Practical clinical psychiatry* (7th ed.). New York: McGraw-Hill, 1955.

Tahka, V. *The alcoholic personality*. Helsinki, Finland: Finnish Foundation for Alcohol Studies, 1966.

13

A Study of Borderline Psychosis—The Spirit in the Candle Flame

Martha Stewart was referred to the psychiatric section of a large city hospital after she had undergone a thorough evaluation in the hospital's medical unit. Martha was 16 years old, and her chief complaints were severe pain in the lower abdomen and genital areas, and chronic anxiety which had intensified during the past few months. Additionally, she reported that on several occasions she had seen a spirit in the flame of a candle, and these episodes had frightened her considerably.

The client was white and of lower-class background. Her brother John was 18 and her sister Betty was 15 at the time of the evaluation. Martha's parents separated when she was 13 years old. Mrs. Stewart had worked part-time as a waitress for many years, and the family received welfare assistance to supplement their low income. Mr. Stewart was a carpenter by trade, but he had not worked for the past five years because of chronic and severe alcoholism.

Martha and her mother were seen by staff members of the hospital's psychiatric unit. A social worker interviewed Mrs. Stewart, and Martha was seen by a psychiatric resident and a psychologist.

FAMILY HISTORY

Martha described her family life during the period when her father lived at home as "terrible" and "awful." Her earliest memories of her family were associated with incidents related to her father's drinking, and she vividly recalled occasions when Mr. Stewart began hitting his wife and the police had to be called. The client related that her father frequently stayed in the house, drank heavily, and became more and more abusive as he drank, until he eventually passed out.

Mr. Stewart's behavior became quite bizarre about six months prior to when he left his family. At times while drinking, he would suddenly pick up any available object and throw it at whomever was close by, barely missing that person. He then laughed uproariously as the individual ran out of reach. On several occasions, Mr. Stewart reported that voices were bothering him, and it sometimes appeared as if he were carrying on a conversation with someone who was not physically present. On the other hand, Martha stated that Mr. Stewart was usually very quiet and mild when he was sober, and would help around the house.

Mrs. Stewart was extremely nonassertive in her relationship with her husband. She did not comment on his drinking or make any effort to induce him to change his behavior. When he began to shout at or hit her, her usual response was to try to stay out of his way. It was generally a neighbor who called the police when Mr. Stewart became extremely belligerent.

Mr. Stewart was abusive toward the children also, and he frequently responded to John's presence by forcefully hitting him with a belt. It was difficult to predict when these beatings would occur. Occasionally, when John did not comply with an order his father gave him, nothing happened, while at other times and for no apparent reason, Mr. Stewart would hit him. John would then run out of the house and stay out until his father drank enough to fall asleep.

Both Mrs. Stewart and Martha indicated that Mr. Stewart had sexually molested his two daughters on a number of occasions. All of these episodes occurred at times when Mr. Stewart had been drinking and Mrs. Stewart was away at work. Martha stated that she was about 10 years old the first time her father "bothered her." She reported that he came into the bedroom she shared with Betty and proceeded to sexually molest her. At the same time, he threatened her with a knife to prevent her from calling for help or telling anyone. Martha later related the incident to her mother and said that she had pleaded with Mrs. Stewart to retaliate against her father in some way, and protect her and her sister from a possible repetition of this behavior. Mrs. Stewart said that it would not help matters if she spoke with him because she thought there was nothing she could do to prevent a similar incident from happening again.

Martha indicated that she had observed Mr. Stewart molest her sister Betty a number of times, too. The client said that she had told her mother about these events also and begged her to intervene, but to no avail. Martha further related that on three or four occasions during the year prior to her father's moving, when no one else was in the house, Mr. Stewart had forced her to "go all the way." She stated that she felt both angry and ashamed after each of these episodes, and was puzzled by the fact that she also felt very guilty. Martha did not tell her mother or Betty that her father had forced her to have sexual intercourse with him, and she never asked Betty the specific details about the extent to which he had molested her.

Mrs. Stewart told the social worker that there was nothing she could have done to prevent her daughters from being sexually abused, and further, she did not think that her husband's behavior was so unusual or harmful. It was apparent from Mrs. Stewart's comments that she did not ask questions about what took place at home on the evenings when she was working. She maintained a noninvolved attitude, and even when her daughters complained to her, she did not confront her husband about his behavior.

On his own initiative, Mr. Stewart moved out of the house and into a rooming house in the same neighborhood. He told his wife that he did not want to be bothered with the family any more. Mr. Stewart was not employed at the time he moved out, and he lived on welfare assistance for a number of years. He continued to visit the family from time to time, and Mrs. Stewart said that she bore no hard feelings toward him. Martha reported that her father's physical condition had deteriorated as a result of his drinking behavior, and that he had frequently been hospitalized or arrested for drunkenness.

Martha indicated that she got along quite well with her sister and she felt there was a strong bond of mutual affection between them. However, the two girls rarely discussed their father or other family matters. They usually participated in social functions together and they had a number of mutual friends. The client said that she and Betty did not get along with their brother John. He frequently started arguments and then began punching one of them. They found it difficult to defend themselves because John was bigger and stronger than they were. Martha indicated that she generally tried to be protective of her sister, but she appeared to be ineffective in preventing Betty from being hit by their brother.

Mrs. Stewart also reported that John frequently acted in a physically aggressive manner. A number of teachers told her that her son was a severe behavior problem at school, and he was often sent to the principal's office as a disciplinary measure. When John was about 10, he was referred to a school psychologist for evaluation, and Mrs. Stewart said she was told that her son was emotionally disturbed. John was then placed in a special class and he remained there until he dropped out of school at age 16. John did not attempt to find a job, and he spent his time wandering around with a group of boys his age. He had not had any difficulties with the police, but Mrs. Stewart felt that this situation would not last for long. She noticed that John sometimes came home with small items that apparently were stolen from department stores. Mrs. Stewart said that she did not make an issue about where he got these items, because she felt helpless about what she could do to control John's behavior.

SOCIAL AND EDUCATIONAL BACKGROUND

The client's parents had no friends, nor did they maintain ties with any of their relatives in the area. Martha's maternal and paternal grandparents had been dead for some time, and she did not remember any of them.

The client reported that she was quite active as a child, and she had always had a number of girl friends to play hopscotch and running games with. She indicated that she had played with girls exclusively, because boys were too rough and were constantly in trouble. As an example, she cited the difficulties in which her brother John and his friends were frequently involved.

Martha seemed to behave quite differently when she was at home compared to when she was with her friends. She stated that she was often tense and anxious at home, yet she behaved very exuberantly and was the "life of the party" when she was with her girl friends. The client said that this alternating behavior style became more pronounced when she was around 13 years old and her friends began to be interested in boys. Mrs. Stewart also commented on Martha's changeable behavior, and said that she felt this was just Martha's nature. The client reported that she began to smoke when she was about 14, and she smoked quite heavily when alone as well as when she was with her friends. She attributed the heavy smoking to her nerves.

Martha stated that she enjoyed being with her girl friends so she spent as much time with them as she could. Their conversations were usually about favorite entertainers and boys they knew, or about teachers and events at school. The girls very rarely discussed personal matters, and the client never mentioned her father. Martha said that she listened when her friends talked about sex but she did not join in the conversation. She usually did not complain to her friends about the persistent pain and cramps she was having. Betty was also part of this peer group, and when she and Martha were in the house, they continued the conversations they had participated in with their friends.

The client said that she and her girl friends occasionally went places together with a group of boys, but she never went out alone on a date. She indicated that she was very strict with the boys she was with and discouraged any sort of physical contact. She stated that she never let any boy hold her hand or put his arm around her. Martha said that she wanted to wait until she was married before she had any further sexual experiences.

Mrs. Stewart reported that several months before the hospital visit, some neighbors had complained to the police that Martha and Betty were having a loud party while Mrs. Stewart was away at work. The group dispersed when they realized the police had been called, and the police did not pursue the matter any further when they found out that everyone had gone. A neighbor told Mrs. Stewart that it sounded as if the group were drinking, and Mrs. Stewart discovered that the beds were in a state of disarray. Consistent with her behavior in the past, Mrs. Stewart did not ask the girls what had occurred nor did she say anything about the disordered house. Mrs. Stewart commented to the social worker that it was natural that teenage girls would get noisy at times. She made no other evaluation of the incident.

Martha also brought up this episode during one of her interviews, and she indicated great annoyance that the neighbors had called the police. She said that she and her friends had only been talking, although she recognized that their conversation might have gotten a bit loud and therefore disturbing to others. She firmly maintained that the neighbors were only trying to cause trouble and there was no justification for their calling the police. She stated emphatically that there were no drugs or liquor at the party.

Martha revealed that she was not really interested in school, but she wanted to do better scholastically so she would graduate. The client had been getting only marginal grades for the past few years, and at the time she was seen, she was failing in all of her subjects. Martha indicated that she did not spend a great deal of time doing homework and she was always behind in her school subjects. She stated that her "nervousness" and abdominal pains interfered with her ability to concentrate and study for examinations. She also stated that she did not think she was very smart, and this made her even more anxious when a test was pending. √

Mrs. Stewart reported that she often woke up in the morning and found Martha sleeping in bed with her or on the floor beside the bed. Martha explained this behavior by saying that she always felt much better sleeping near her mother, and she had maintained this pattern ever since Mr. Stewart moved out of the house. Mrs. Stewart said that she never commented on Martha's sleep activity, and she neither encouraged nor discouraged Martha from sleeping near her.

PRESENT STATUS

Martha related that she still experienced a number of conflicting emotions whenever she thought of her father's sexual assaults. She was extremely angry at him because of his sexual advances, but she also felt ashamed and guilty. She thought that if she had tried harder, she could have prevented him from having intercourse with her. In addition, she told the interviewer that she was very concerned that her mother would find out the full extent of what had happened. It appeared to Martha that none of her girl friends had undergone similar experiences, and she did not want any of them to find out about her father's behavior.

Martha said that she was often in extreme discomfort because of pain and cramps in the abdomen and genital area. She indicated that her menstrual cycle was quite irregular and that she had a great deal of pain whenever she had her period. On numerous occasions over the past few years, Martha had been sent to the school nurse or had stayed home from school because of severe pain. She frequently cried at home because of her discomfort, and the pain intensified her feelings of nervousness. Her family was solicitous to her when she said she was in pain, and Betty often did some of Martha's share of the household chores when Martha complained of feeling ill.

It was difficult for the client to locate precisely where the pain emanated from. She described the pain as a generalized sensation which seemed to spread out in waves inside of her. The pain often felt as if some outside force had invaded her body and traveled inside her from place to place. Sometimes these sensations were pleasurable, but at other times the pain was so severe that it seemed as if she would be unable to get out of bed. However, if she got involved in watching a program on television or if one of her friends called, the pain would suddenly disappear.

Martha was given a complete medical examination and underwent a number of special diagnostic procedures, but no physical basis for her reports of pain could be found. Previous medical examinations were also negative.

The client indicated that she was quite troubled about some events that had recently occurred. For amusement, she and her girl friends sometimes sat in a circle in a darkened room and stared at a candle burning in the center of the room. The girls told ghost stories or related frightening incidents, generally trying to scare each other. These occasions were marked by a great deal of giggling and by exclamations of fright and interest. Martha stated that there was no drug or alcohol consumption associated with these games.

The client reported that several months previously, when she and her friends were playing this game, she suddenly saw what appeared to be a spirit in the candle flame. This image was very clear to her, and she said that she sat transfixed at this vision, feeling awed and frightened by what she saw. Her friends noticed that she had suddenly become very quiet, and several persons asked her what was the matter. The client said that the spirit disappeared when her friends started asking her questions. Martha denied that anything was wrong, and she did not share this experience with Betty or with anyone else. She reported that she heard a constant ringing sound for several days after this episode, and this further terrified her. She stayed at home and cried frequently, but she still told no one about the experience that was frightening her.

When her friends repeated the candle game about two weeks later, Martha again participated with them. She once more saw a spirit in the flame, and on this occasion, she immediately became quite frightened and asked that the game be stopped. She was extremely anxious for several days after this second episode, and she indicated that she was concerned about the reason why she had seen the spirits. The client was sure that the spirits were not products of her imagination, and she wondered whether she had a special ability to experience visions. Martha said that the spirits seemed to look like an older person, neither male nor female. She stated that on both occasions, the spirit appeared to look at her questioningly, but the figure did not say anything to her.

PSYCHOLOGICAL EVALUATION

Martha was seen by a female psychologist for diagnostic evaluation. The client was neatly dressed and attractive in appearance. She sat at the edge of her chair, fidgeted with a button on her sleeve and smoked one cigarette after another. She answered questions promptly and spoke rapidly in a great rush of words. She spontaneously told about the sexual episodes with her father, and when she talked about these incidents, she diverted her gaze from the examiner and looked down at her hands. The client also spoke readily about the spirits she had seen.

Martha scored in the average range of intelligence and gave evidence that she had the intellectual skills necessary to pass her courses at school. Some of her responses on the projective tests indicated that she was intensely preoccupied with themes of victimization and sexual assault by men. The central figure in a number of her stories was a girl who was concerned about religious condemnation and maternal rejection. This concern was due to a violation of the rules for appropriate sexual behavior between members of a family. The tests further revealed a strong wish for and a mourning of lost innocence. The content of the stories on the projective cards was strikingly similar to the actual events of the client's life history as described to the interviewer.

The client gave a number of responses to the projective cards that suggested a confusion and breakdown in reality testing. Some of the percepts on the Rorschach ink blot test were quite different from those given by the majority of persons taking the test, and the description of these percepts was quite personalized in nature. For example, on a card that is commonly interpreted as a bat or a butterfly, the client said "it looks like someone who is hurt and calling for help. She's looking out of a dark room." One of the cards with an assortment of colors on it was seen as "the messed up insides of a person. She must of been in an accident. There's her blood smeared all over."

Responses of this type are indicative of a breakdown in reality testing, in the sense that the client is not responding to the test material in a similar way to how the average person responds to these stimuli. One of the assumptions of projective testing is that a subject will respond to ambiguous test material in a manner that is analogous to how the subject responds to other current environmental stimuli. In Martha's case, there was evidence of some confusion between her experiences of the past and the situations she had to deal with in the present.

The impairment in reality testing was not consistently seen on all of the test material, and for the most part, Martha's responses provided evidence that she was able to function adequately in her social environment. However, the occasional breakdowns in reality testing may have been predictive of further difficulties in functioning if environmental pressures became too great. The solutions the client gave to many of her TAT stories similarly suggested that she did not possess the skills necessary to effectively handle interpersonal difficulties, particularly sexual matters. Her most frequent solution to her problems was to avoid thinking about them by means of withdrawing into fantasy, or engaging in a great many social activities with other persons.

RECOMMENDATIONS FOR BEHAVIOR CHANGE

Mrs. Stewart and Martha were seen individually to discuss the results of the evaluation. Each was told that it was the consensus of the persons handling Martha's case that she be seen in individual psychotherapy. Martha accepted this recommendation and agreed that it would be beneficial for her to have a chance to talk over her problems with someone. She strongly requested that she be seen by a female psychotherapist.

Mrs. Stewart also appeared to accept the advice that her daughter enter into a program of psychotherapy. However, she said that she did not understand how "talking" would change Martha's behavior, or why "nerve pills" would not be as effective. It was difficult for Mrs. Stewart to accept the concept that problems at the present time could be related to negative experiences in the past. However, Mrs. Stewart agreed to follow the recommendation for treatment.

Since there was a long waiting list for outpatient psychotherapy at the hospital, Martha was referred to a family counseling center nearby which handled many adolescent cases. A routine follow-up several months after Martha was seen at the hospital indicated that neither Mrs. Stewart nor Martha had contacted this agency.

DISCUSSION

Although the term borderline psychosis is used frequently in clinical practice, it is not an official diagnostic category of the American

Psychiatric Association (DSM-II, 1968). Labels such as latent schizophrenia, pseudoneurotic schizophrenia, and incipient psychosis have also been applied to behaviors similar to those categorized as borderline psychosis. Grinker, Werble, and Drye (1968) have written that the borderline category often functions as a repository for uncertainty, and as a wastebasket category denoting a lack of agreement among diagnosticians. Since the behavior of many individuals falls within the broad framework of the borderline category or some variation thereof, it is important to examine some of the criteria used in applying this label.

Borderline psychosis refers to a pattern of functioning characterized by the presence of both neurotic and psychotic symptoms. At times the person's behavior will more closely approximate neurotic functioning, while at other times psychotic symptoms will predominate. However, the borderline person is generally able to function in society, although he or she may be regarded by others as somewhat strange or peculiar.

Neurosis and psychosis have been viewed as quantitatively different from each other according to degree of severity, or qualitatively different, i.e., two distinctly separate psychological processes (Buss, 1966). If interpersonal functioning is conceptualized as a quantitative continuum ranging from normal to neurotic to psychotic, then the behavior of the borderline individual would fall in the range between neurosis and psychosis. A quantitative viewpoint of deviant behavior implies that the greater the stress or the more divergent the individual's learning experiences are from those of the majority, the more abnormal will his or her behavior appear.

Proponents of a qualitative distinction between neurosis and psychosis argue that these categories reflect two different types of processes, and there is some research that supports this point of view. Eysenck (1955) administered a large number of tests to normal, neurotic, and psychotic individuals. The test scores were compared by means of discriminant function analysis, a complex statistical procedure. The analysis revealed two independent dimensions: a Neuroticism factor differentiating neurotics from normals, and a Psychoticism factor differentiating psychotics from normals. These results suggest a qualitative difference between the responses of neurotics and those of psychotics. The borderline individual would then be viewed as a person who has mixed symptoms, i.e., symptoms characteristic of two different processes. However, a definitive statement on the respective merits of the quantitative-qualitative positions cannot be made at the present time; this issue must await further research findings.

Knight (1953) pointed out that individuals diagnosed as borderline behave quite adequately in a well-structured situation or during nonstressful circumstances. A characteristic of the borderline syndrome is that habitual behaviors and superficial relations with other persons are not impaired. The individual's behavior pattern may remain quite similar throughout his or her life existence, as long as no severe environmental stresses are encountered.

Grinker, Werble, and Drye employed an ego-psychology theoretical orientation in studying 51 persons diagnosed as borderline. These individuals were systematically observed and their behavior was assessed in terms of ego processes. Findings indicated that the borderline syndrome was a result of arrested development of ego functions. The ego dysfunction consisted of the following: the main affect expressed was anger, and there appeared to be a defect in affectional relationships, an absence of indications of self identity, and depressive loneliness. The investigators reported that they could find no specific etiological conditions that could have produced the borderline syndrome.

From a social learning point of view, the Grinker, et al., results suggest that the syndrome of borderline psychosis refers to individuals who have difficulty in interacting with, and in establishing positive emotional responses to, other persons. The finding of depressive loneliness similarly points to a difficulty in communicating with others. Because of this lack of skill in interpersonal relationships, the individual's response repertoire is quite limited. Anger may be the affect highest on the response hierarchy because this type of behavior has a high probability of being immediately reinforced by the attention of other persons. Angry behavior is therefore a response that occurs with great frequency in a number of diverse situations.

The development of a positive self-concept and feelings of self-identity also depends on one's interaction with others. The concept of oneself as a worthwhile or as an incompetent individual is formed by having evaluations placed on one's behavior by other persons. The individual then uses these evaluations as a comparison standard for judging present behaviors. A person who judges most of his or her behavior as bad or inadequate is typically described as having a poor self-concept. If one has not had much opportunity to interact with others and learn the labels placed on one's behavior by other persons, one may not be sure whether one is competent, or a good or bad person. This results in a deficiency in one's labeling repertoire, or as Grinker, et al., term this, an absence of self-identity.

The social learning approach to deviant behavior focuses on analyzing the contingencies of reinforcement operating in the present environment that maintain given behaviors. The development of the present behavior pattern can also be understood in terms of the individual's previous interpersonal history. Rotter (1954) postulated that an individual's behavior is determined by the expectancy that a particular reinforcement will occur as a result of a specific behavior being emitted. The value of the reinforcer to the individual is also considered to be important. Bandura and Walters' (1963) version of social learning theory also stresses the role of reinforcement in shaping behavior, and particular attention is given to the process of observational learning in the acquisition of novel responses. In borderline psychosis as in other types of behavior, one must assess the reinforcers available in the environment and the types of behaviors the person has had an opportunity to observe and be reinforced for, in order to understand the present behavior pattern.

Martha grew up in a family environment where parental reinforcement or attention occurred only infrequently. Her mother interacted with her in a nonpunitive but distant manner and reinforced very little positive or negative behavior. For example, she took the time to bring Martha to the hospital for evaluation, but she did not appear to the interviewer to be greatly concerned about becoming involved in changing Martha's behavior. The behavior that Mrs. Stewart modeled consisted of a benign pattern of minimal emotional involvement with others, and Martha observed and imitated this interaction pattern with her peers. The client related to others on a fairly superficial level. She could be talkative and the life of the party, but she was not able to develop the personal emotional involvement necessary to form a close friendship with another individual.

Despite Mrs. Stewart's minimal involvement with her daughter, she was still the major source of positive adult attention available to Martha. The client learned that when she became anxious, anxiety reduction would occur if she left her bedroom and slept in closer proximity to her mother. Mrs. Stewart was a discriminative stimulus for anxiety reduction because she was not part of the aversive stimulus configuration associated with the molestations. The sexual assaults all took place when Mrs. Stewart was out of the house. Martha therefore became conditioned to get out of bed at night and sleep in her mother's room or on the couch, away from the scene of the early frightening events.

Martha's most important source of interpersonal reinforcement was her sister, and Betty served as a stimulus that evoked protective responses from Martha. There were few alternative sources of reinforcement available to either girl when they were children, so their relationship with each other was quite important. The opportunity that Martha and Betty had to relate to each other provided both of them with some of the skills necessary to interact with persons outside of the family. However, in spite of the close emotional bond between them, they did not tell each other about many of their experiences.

The masculine role that Martha observed from her father's behavior was one of belligerence, physical abuse, or else noninvolvement. Mr. Stewart was at various stages of inebriation during most of the time that Martha interacted with him. He often became argumentative and physically violent when he was drinking, but most of his behavior was quite unpredictable. However, Mr. Stewart was not a consistently aversive stimulus, since he tended to act in a passive and somewhat positive manner when he was sober. Although the majority of Martha's emotional responses toward her father were quite negative, the infrequent positive interactions functioned to sustain a small amount of positive affect toward him.

The interaction patterns of the Stewart family resulted in a very low probability that there would be a positive relationship between John and his sisters. Martha generalized from her negative, anxiety-provoking relationship with her father, and responded primarily in a negative manner to her brother. John, in turn, imitated many of the behaviors he observed in his father. He was very belligerent toward Martha and Betty, and he frequently punched them. John had little opportunity to observe positive male-female relationships, and he learned from his father's behavior that women were not highly valued objects. John did not respond to his mother in a positive manner either because of the attitude toward women he learned from his father's behavior, and because of the low frequency of Mrs. Stewart's interactions with John.

The client was extremely confused and anxious about the entire subject of sexual relationships. After the sexual assaults, she reported that she did not feel negatively toward her mother for failing to protect her. Instead, she was very concerned that her mother should not find out the details of the assaults. This attitude suggests that the sexual encounters were not entirely aversive experiences for Martha. Her father's attention had some reinforcing value to her, and she probably also gained some physical gratification from the sexual experiences. Martha's statements that she felt she could have stopped her father if she had tried hard enough may have had some basis to them. Nonetheless, Martha's early sexual experiences were primarily aversive and anxiety provoking. The client's initial concept of sexual relationships was most likely based on her own learning history, and she may have generalized from her previous experiences to her expectation of what sexual interactions were like with someone her own age.

Martha's report of the party she had when the police were called was inconsistent with the neighbors' complaints and her mother's description of the state of the house. In spite of Martha's anxiety about sexual relationships, as she matures physically and more sexual demands are made on her, she might indiscriminately engage in sexual activity, following a pattern of passively submitting to the advances of others. It is possible that she has already been involved in sexual relationships with boys of her peer group, because Martha did not have an opportunity to observe and learn that affection and interest can be expressed in ways other than through sexual intercourse.

The behaviors that Martha expected from males were physical aggression and forced sexual activity, and the response highest on her repertoire for interacting with men was passive submission. Martha also had the opportunity to observe members of her peer group interacting with each other, and she was able to learn some additional social skills from them. However, her earlier sexual experiences occurred at a time when her interpersonal repertoire was quite limited, and the behaviors that became strongest were those which reinforced aggressive sexual behavior by males.

The question of the adequacy of Martha's reality testing is relevant to a discussion of her somatic complaints and to an understanding of the occasions when she saw a spirit in the flame of a candle. The client persisted in her complaints of pain and cramps in the abdomen and genital region, despite several thorough medical examinations which indicated that there was no physical basis to her experience of pain. The complaints of pain may have been a result of the client labeling a variety of normally occurring bodily processes, such as a mild bladder distention, premenstrual uterine contractions, or the genital manifestations of sexual arousal, as painful stimuli. The labeling of sensations in the abdomen as painful may have been due to the close proximity of the abdominal and genital areas.

Martha apparently was failing to discriminate between nonpainful and painful stimuli in the genital and abdominal regions. The genital region of the body was associated with a great many negative experiences in her life, and the complaints of pain served to focus her attention on a perceived physical problem in this region of the body. The complaints also allowed her to avoid dealing with the problems of sexual arousal and the greater issue of adult sexual relationships.

Martha's somatic complaints were persistent and incapacitating. She described these pains in a way that suggested that they sometimes seemed to her like forces invading her body. The quality of the descriptions of pain and the bizarre perceptions of body organs on the projective test point to an impairment in reality testing, involving misinterpretations of bodily processes.

The images that Martha reported seeing in the candle flames raises the issue of whether Martha was extremely suggestible and thought she saw something that the other girls also expected to see, or whether she had actually experienced an hallucination. An hallucination is a perception which is not consensually validated, i.e., other persons in the environment, exposed to the same stimuli, do not give the same response. The difference between an hallucination and an overactive imagination is one of degree, based on how many other persons, responding to the same stimuli, apply a similar perceptual label. One must also take into account the individual's certainty that the sensory misinterpretation was an actual behavioral event and not just an embellishment of ordinary sensations.

McGuigan's research (1966) supports the notion that hallucinations are the result of a misinterpretation of sensory stimuli. He found that there was an increase in covert oral language responses such as chin muscle action, whispering, and breathing, just before a psychotic person reported an auditory hallucination. The person who reported hearing voices was apparently labeling his own subvocal speech as the voices of other persons.

Martha was quite sure that the vision she experienced was not a product of her imagination, but was something "really there." The client gave evidence of breakdowns in reality testing on some of her responses to the psychological tests, and apparently a similar process occurred in relation to the stimuli she reacted to while viewing the candle flame. She labeled the stimuli associated with the candle flame as an actual object, and not as a reflection of her imagination. This suggests that at times Martha's interpretation of the environment was quite different from the interpretations of other persons. It is important to note, however, that these deviant interpretations were infrequent, and Martha usually functioned in a manner that indicated adequate reality testing.

The client had difficulty learning from her parents the discriminations necessary for labeling perceptual or social events in a consensually validated manner. However, she had ample opportunity to observe and imitate her parents' deviant interpretations of environmental events. Mr. Stewart modeled misinterpretations of sensory processes when he experienced hallucinations as a result of the advanced stages of alcoholism. In a similar manner, Martha on two occasions also interpreted ambiguous stimuli as distinct visual perceptions. Mrs. Stewart, on the other hand, modeled deviant interpretations of social interactions. She verbalized the attitude that her husband's sexual assaults on his daughters was a harmless activity, which is quite different from the way most persons in our society would interpret these events.

The diagnosis of borderline psychosis was decided upon because Martha's symptoms varied in their deviance from socially accepted norms of behavior. Many of the client's symptoms could be labeled neurotic manifestations, while other symptoms were more unusual and indicative of occasional breakdowns in reality testing. Overall, Martha's level of functioning was not highly deviant. The client learned enough from engaging in social interactions with persons outside of her family to realize that her social learning history was quite uncommon. She therefore did not discuss her family experiences with anyone else, and she tried to model her behavior according to the norms of her peer group.

As Martha matures, persons outside of the home will become more important agents of reinforcement. The client could manifest a positive behavior change if she is reinforced by others for less deviant behavior. Therapy could also have provided a source of reinforcement for positive behavior change. However, it is difficult to predict exactly what modifications will occur in her behavior over time, because one does not know the types of interpersonal situations she will encounter.

Since there was no follow through on the recommendation for therapy, it may be quite difficult for Martha to learn more adequate ways of interacting with other persons. The fact that the therapy recommendation was not pursued points to the difficulty in persuading

persons who are not familiar with psychological services to seek prolonged treatment. The issue of providing adequate mental health
services to the poor is part of this complex problem.

REFERENCES

American Psychiatric Association. *Diagnostic and statistical manual of
mental disorders* (2nd ed.) (DSM–II). Washington: American Psychiatric Association, 1968.

Bandura, A., & Walters, R. H. *Social learning and personality development.* New York: Holt, Rinehart & Winston, 1963.

Buss, A. H. *Psychopathology.* New York: Wiley, 1966.

Eysenck, H. J. Psychiatric diagnosis as a psychological and statistical
problem. *Psychological Reports*, 1955, *1*, 3–17.

Grinker, R. R., Werble, B., & Drye, R. C. *The borderline syndrome.*
New York: Basic Books, 1968.

Knight, R. P. Borderline states. In R. Lowenstein (Ed.), *Drives, affects,
behavior.* New York: International Universities Press, 1953.
Pp. 203–215.

McGuigan, F. J. Covert oral behavior and auditory hallucinations.
Psychophysiology, 1966, *3*, 73–80.

Rotter, J. B. *Social learning and clinical psychology.* New York: Prentice-Hall, 1954.

14

Psychophysiologic Disorder—A Gut Reaction to Environmental Stress

Edward Polowski was examined by a specialist in internal medicine, and then referred to a clinical psychologist for further evaluation. The patient complained of a longstanding problem of severe cramps and diarrhea whenever he ate highly seasoned foods or encountered any type of stressful situation. This problem was diagnosed as an irritable colon when the patient was a child. Since that time, he had been treated by a series of physicians, all of whom confirmed this diagnosis. The patient reported that the medications prescribed for him had varied in effectiveness, and he had recently been in severe discomfort.

Edward was 35 years old, married, and the father of a six-year-old boy and a two-year-old girl. He was a college graduate with a degree in library science and had been a librarian in the same city library since he graduated from college. Edward stated that he began having unusually severe gastrointestinal symptoms at the time that a new director was appointed to the library a number of months ago. Recently, he had been sexually impotent on occasion, and this problem also concerned him.

CHILDHOOD HISTORY

Edward was an only child. His parents were working class first generation Americans of Polish origin. Their formal education concluded at the grade school level, and both were employed in factories. Edward's father had worked on the night shift for many years, and throughout Edward's childhood, he had little contact with his father except on weekends. Edward portrayed Mr. Polowski as a well meaning but gruff person who usually let his wife handle disciplinary matters. He occasionally spanked Edward for misbehaving, but if he intervened at all, it usually involved shouting at his son. If Edward continued the negative behavior, his father did not follow through with any further disciplinary action.

Mr. Polowski generally stayed around the house when he was not working, but from time to time he took his son to a sporting event. Edward said that he felt affection for his father, but they had never had common interests, nor had there been much communication between them.

Edward described his mother as a tender and affectionate person. She was usually quite cheerful and she spent a great deal of time with her son when she was home. Mrs. Polowski was very pleased when Edward helped her with the household chores, and she was extremely solicitous to him when he was ill. Edward felt that his parents were able to establish a good marital relationship. They sometimes had loud arguments, but these incidents did not last for long and there was no carry-over of negative feelings.

Edward attended Catholic parochial schools until he went to college, and his parents were very pleased with the good grades he received. He particularly enjoyed reading, preferring this activity to playing with other youngsters. If his parents got into a dispute with each other or with him, he habitually withdrew to his room and read.

Edward related that he had had numerous occurrences of intestinal difficulties ever since childhood. These episodes were associated with circumstances such as his mother or teacher insisting that he do something he did not want to do. He also became ill when he had to make a public appearance such as participating in his First Communion or in a play at school. His mother tended to be quite concerned about making him comfortable when he had intestinal symptoms, although she always told him that it was just a "nervous stomach." She said that she knew how he felt because she was also troubled with a "nervous stomach" when she was anxious or upset.

When Edward was nine years old, his mother took him to her physician because Edward was in severe discomfort. He was in the midst of an episode of cramps and diarrhea that lasted for about a week. The onset of the symptoms was associated with Edward's complaints that his new teacher was too strict and forced him to keep going over material he had already mastered. Edward stayed home from school during the latter part of that week, and the physician prescribed some medication which relieved a great deal of the discomfort. Mrs. Polowski pleaded with the doctor to call the school principal and explain the reason for Edward's symptoms. This was done and Edward reported that his teacher became somewhat more flexible in relation to his school activities. Edward had other occurrences of cramps during that school year, but none as severe as the earlier occasion.

Edward also had periodic intestinal problems while he was growing up, but these attacks usually lasted for just a few hours at a time. In high school, he experienced another prolonged occurrence of intestinal symptoms during a final examination period. Edward generally received good grades in school, but he was always quite anxious before a test because he was afraid that he would not do well. He was very anxious during these particular examinations because he had received lower grades than he had expected on some of his previous tests. He therefore studied a great deal and ignored his mother's assurances that he would do well on the exams.

Edward began having intestinal symptoms during the examination period, and the symptoms did not subside, even with medication, until ten days later when he went to a physician. He was given a complete medical examination, including a number of special tests of the gastrointestinal tract. These tests revealed no structural defects or damage, and the problem was again diagnosed as chronic irritable colon. Edward was given a new medication to take when he felt that the symptoms were about to recur.

EARLY ADULT YEARS

Edward lived at home while he attended a city college. The first friends he ever had were some students he met at college. He had always been shy and somewhat detached from others, and before college, he had never met any persons his age with whom he felt comfortable. Because of his interest in books, he decided to major in library science, and he eventually got to know some of the other students majoring in similar fields. There were relatively few males in most of Edward's classes, but he did meet two or three young men he became friends with. They sometimes went to movies or concerts, and occasionally they went out together with some girls they knew from school.

Although Edward found it pleasant to be part of a group that included females, he was a senior in college before he decided to go out alone with just one girl. At that time, he met a girl he was attracted to, and he eventually asked her out. Edward said that he enjoyed being with Mary, and they spent a great deal of time together over the next several months. Mary was also of the Catholic faith, and they sometimes went to church together. Mrs. Polowski told Edward that Mary was a nice person, but Edward felt that his mother did not really encourage or discourage his friendship with Mary.

Edward had not had much sexual experience before he met Mary. He had begun masturbating prior to adolescence, but he felt this activity was sinful and would harm him. He recalled that he tried to control this urge as best he could, but he was not always successful. Edward's physical approach to Mary was tentative and unsure. Mary told him that she believed it was wrong to engage in premarital sexual activity, and Edward stated that he felt the same way, too. Edward said that they lost interest in each other after about five months, and they eventually drifted apart to other friendships.

Edward met Jean, a college sophomore, two months before he graduated. As Edward phrased it, "we got used to spending our time together." Jean had also been brought up in the Catholic faith, and she and Edward began to attend church together on Sundays. Jean's immediate family was quite large, and each time Edward went over to her house, there were a number of persons at home. Edward said that he did not feel at ease with Jean's family, but he made an effort to converse with whomever happened to be home.

After they had known each other for about a year, Edward and Jean decided to get married. They agreed that it would be best to postpone marriage until Edward was more financially secure in his position at the library. Edward said that both his parents and Jean's were pleased that they were going to get married, and they approved of the plan to wait until Edward and Jean had saved some money.

Jean told Edward that she felt they should wait until they were married before having any sexual relationships, and Edward said that he respected this wish. He related that his sexual relationship with his wife proceeded from a stage of mutual inexperience to one of satisfaction. However, he still felt that the sexual drive was a reflection of man's baser instincts. Jean and Edward decided that it would be best to delay having children for a few years, and the rhythm method of birth control was followed.

Edward reported that he had not been greatly troubled with irritable colon symptoms during college and when he first started to work at the library. He expected that he would have a "nervous stomach" during examination periods, and he took medication accordingly to keep these symptoms to a minimum. Jean knew of these problems so she tended to go out of her way to maintain Edward's good humor during these episodes. She watched the food that he ate when they were together, and she encouraged him to rest rather than be with her. Edward also had some difficulty with intestinal symptoms during the period before their wedding. However, Edward recalled that he was able to function reasonably well and he did not have to miss any of the social activities planned, as long as he took the prescribed medication.

MARITAL AND EMPLOYMENT HISTORY

Edward stated that reading was one of the most gratifying activities he could think of. Jean had seemed pleased with his interest in books before their marriage, but her attitude later changed. She indicated to Edward that she had come to feel that his constant reading was a means of avoiding interactions with her and with others. Especially after the children were born, Jean repeatedly told Edward that it was important for him to spend less time reading and more time with his family.

Edward said that he had never really been with other children for any length of time when he was young, because he was an only child. He revealed that he did not feel any more comfortable interacting with his own children than he had trying to relate to other youngsters during his childhood. He left disciplinary matters to his wife, and generally spent his time at home reading. Edward sometimes played ball with his son Matthew, but he engaged in this activity very infrequently, and only after his wife had asked him to do this for some time. His daughter Julie was two years old, and Edward commented that she was more verbal than Matthew had been at the same age. He occasionally interacted with Julie by teaching her to say new words.

Edward described his marriage as "reasonably good." Jean was on good terms with Edward's parents, and she and Edward's mother joined together in their efforts to prevent him from having episodes of intestinal difficulties. Edward said that Jean was a good homemaker, and she tried hard to please him. When they were first married, Jean did not seem to mind spending most of their evenings at home. She was very proud of the vocational advances Edward had made at the library, and she accepted his statements that he could not participate in various social events because the reading he did at home helped him with his work. They currently had some friends they saw from time to time, but they generally did not attend as many social activities as his wife would have liked to.

Edward indicated that his relationship with his wife had seemed to deteriorate after the children were born. He felt that he and Jean did not communicate with each other as much as they used to, and he recognized that many times he purposely withdrew from social interactions by reading. It appeared to Edward that most of his wife's time was spent taking care of or nagging him about the children, and she did not seem as interested in his work as she used to. He also realized that he was not sharing with her as many of the events that happened at work as he had previously. Edward said that he did not agree with his wife's belief that it was important for a father to interact with his children. He pointed out that his own father had spent very little time with him, but he cared for his father nonetheless and felt this lack of companionship had not hurt him.

Edward described his vocational situation as quite satisfactory until a number of months ago. He enjoyed working with books, and he found it gratifying to aid persons in finding the materials they were looking for. He eventually advanced to the position of head of the reference department, and two female librarians worked under his supervision. He stated that he had no difficulty interacting with them, and he generally ignored any attempt either of them made to influence the way he ran his department. Edward always avoided open confrontations. He typically listened without comment to what others said, then went ahead and did what he thought was best. Edward said that he generally behaved in this manner with his wife also, whenever they had a difference of opinion on some matter.

A new library director had been hired a few months previously, and Edward found it extremely difficult to get along with this man. The director tended to issue statements to the library staff about policy changes without consulting with them first. Edward said that he was not able to ignore these orders and continue doing whatever he wanted to do, as had been his practice with the previous administrator. Further, Edward felt that he should have been offered the director's position, and he found it especially difficult to take arbitrary orders from a man whom he felt was not as qualified as he was.

Over the past few years, Edward's intestinal difficulties had gradually become more severe and incapacitating, and there was a marked intensification of his problems during the previous year. The medication prescribed for him had been reasonably effective in controlling his symptoms, but lately he found it necessary to stay home in bed whenever he had an episode of bowel spasms. The intestinal cramps had become extremely painful, and he often had spells of diarrhea lasting for almost a week. These bouts came on suddenly, with little advance warning, and were generally associated with negative events that had occurred at work or at home.

Edward stated that his wife continued to be very solicitous and helpful, encouraging him to rest at home when he was in discomfort. He said that she went out of her way to see that he was not disturbed by the children or upset by outside events. Edward indicated that his mother also became greatly concerned when he was ill, and brought over special foods that she had found through her own experience to be good for "settling your stomach."

Edward related that there had been a number of instances since his marriage when he was impotent. He stated that his wife was very understanding during these infrequent occurrences, and he noted that each of these occasions had been subsequent to a prolonged period of intestinal difficulties. During the past several months, the episodes of impotence had increased in frequency, and Edward said that there were times when he wanted to have sexual intercourse, but he was not sure whether he would be able to have an erection. He felt that his wife was also becoming more concerned about this problem, but she was purposely not saying anything for fear of making the situation worse.

In order to make sure that the irritable colon disorder had not developed into something more serious, Edward heeded the pleas of his wife and mother and made an appointment for a complete medical examination. He also hoped that the doctor would prescribe a stronger medication to control the distressing bowel symptoms. While in the process of the medical evaluation, Edward told the physician about the occasions of impotence.

MEDICAL EVALUATION

The physical examination and blood tests were all within normal limits. X-rays of the gastrointestinal tract revealed an irritability and hyperactivity of the bowel, but there were no indications of obstructions, ulcerations, or other organic changes.

The diagnosis of chronic irritable colon made at this time was consistent with earlier diagnoses of Edward's condition. His problem was viewed as psychophysiological in nature, i.e., changes in bodily function were associated with emotional stress. The internist referred the patient for psychological consultation in order to further explore the problems with interpersonal relationships and to learn more about the episodes of impotence. Edward was continued on antispasmodic medication.

PSYCHOLOGICAL EVALUATION

Edward was tall and thin in appearance, and slightly balding. He was neatly dressed in a conservatively styled suit and tie. He met on two occasions with Dr. R., a male clinical psychologist. Edward readily answered the questions asked of him, speaking of his problems in an impersonal, emotionless manner. It was apparent that Edward spent a great deal of time ruminating about his difficulties, and he indicated that he was aware of a relationship between environmental events and the onset of his physical symptoms.

Edward completed a comprehensive personality inventory, the MMPI. He scored in a range that was higher than the population norm on the scale measuring an interest and concern with bodily processes. However, all of the other scale scores were within normal limits, and the client's general response pattern indicated good reality testing. There were no suggestions of psychotic processes. (See Chapter 13 for a general discussion of the issues involved in defining reality testing.)

The client's responses on the Assertive Questionnaire (Lazarus, 1971) strongly indicated that he typically responded to interpersonal situations in a passive, nonassertive manner. This behavior pattern was exemplified by the client responding "no" to the following items: "If a friend betrays your confidence, do you tell him how you really feel?" "If someone keeps kicking the back of your chair in a movie, would you ask him to stop?"

Edward responded to the TAT cards in a highly formalized and intellectual manner. His perceptions and stories were very imaginative, but the responses functioned to draw attention to the structural details of the cards rather than dealing with interpersonal relationships. For example, on one of the cards commonly described as an interaction between some women and a man plowing a field, Edward said that the scene was similar to a painting he had seen. He depicted the man as a symbol of an earth god. A response of this nature avoids dealing with any kind of affective interaction, just as Edward's habitual response in his social milieu was to avoid emotional encounters.

The client's noninvolved, intellectualized response style was also evident on a sentence completion test. Edward responded with Biblical and other quotations to words such as "I," "A child," and "A mother." This is consistent with Edward's report that he engages in philosphical, rather than problem solving, introspection about his problems.

Some of the responses to the various tests suggested that Edward was ambivalent about sexual matters. A dichotomy was presented in his stories between love as a romantic, good, and noble emotion, and sex as a base and ignoble instinct. Strong religious overtones were associated with this distinction between sacred and profane love.

COURSE OF THERAPY

In addition to the prescribed medication, Dr. R. recommended that Edward engage in a behavior therapy program of assertive training (Wolpe and Lazarus, 1966). Dr. R. explained that Edward's interpersonal relationships would be more satisfactory if he learned to actively express his feelings and rights in a socially acceptable manner. There might also be an associated diminishment of the psychophysiological symptoms with assertive training. Edward agreed to these recommendations, and he participated in assertive training for approximately five months. (See Chapters 7 and 11 for other descriptions of assertive training.)

Although medication is important in treating psychophysiological disorders, it is also essential for the individual to learn to respond to interpersonal events in a more flexible manner. In assertive training, specific situations are dealt with in which the client is taught the difference between acting in an aggressive and an assertive manner. In circumstances where acting assertively could result in negative consequences, alternative behaviors are suggested and rehearsed.

During the initial therapy sessions, the client was encouraged to talk about any past events that had been particularly distressing. Through a discussion of these events, Dr. R. was able to point out the typical way that Edward interacted with other persons. It was quickly apparent that ever since childhood, Edward responded to aversive situations with physiological over-activation and passive withdrawal. As the therapy sessions progressed, Edward also became more aware of the relationship between his typical nonassertive behavior style and the negative behavior of others.

Edward brought up a recent situation that he still found extremely troubling. The library director had arbitrarily ordered some books for Edward's department without consulting him first. Edward stated that he was very upset by this action, but he said nothing to the director. He came home from work feeling extremely agitated and beset by intestinal cramps which became more severe as the evening progressed. He told his wife that he was not feeling well, but he did not tell her the details of the events at work. He ate very little at dinner, and soon afterwards, he went to his room and read in bed. Edward said that Jean made a special effort to keep the children out of the bedroom so they would not disturb him. Despite medication, the cramps continued sporadically the following day as well, and Edward said that he was forced to stay home from work that day because of his discomfort.

Dr. R. asked the client to think of some other ways that he could have interacted with the library director, which allowed Edward to express his opinions without provoking retaliatory behavior. Eventually, a more assertive alternative was suggested and the ramifications of this new approach were discussed. Edward thought that he could have calmly but firmly told the director that it was a clearly acknowledged part of Edward's job to order books for his department. Since funds were available, the director should have given Edward the opportunity to submit his own purchase order.

Edward felt that his job would not have been in jeopardy if he had behaved in this manner. Therefore, a behavioral rehearsal took place, with Edward practicing the more assertive role, and the therapist playing the role of the library director. Next, Edward assumed the role of the library director, and observed the model of assertive behavior provided by the therapist's actions.

Edward eventually became more comfortable acting in an assertive manner, and he discussed with Dr. R. the changes in the behavior of others which resulted from the modification of his behavior. Edward showed greater awareness of how his typically detached behavior functioned to avoid family responsibilities and involvement with other persons, and he expressed a desire to change this behavior pattern. Dr. R. reinforced Edward for acting more assertively with his wife and for communicating his feelings to her. Near the end of the course of therapy, Dr. R. felt that it would be beneficial if Edward and Jean were seen jointly for a number of sessions. Dr. R. discussed with them the contingencies between Edward's prolonged somatic distress and detachment and the strong reinforcement Jean's solicitude provided for this behavior.

As Edward began to act more assertively, he was very pleased to discover that there was a gradual diminishment in the frequency and severity of the episodes of somatic distress. There was a general improvement in his physical condition as well, and he experienced enhanced gratification from interacting with his wife and children. Associated with these changes, there was a termination of the occasions of sexual impotence. Although from time to time Edward still reacted to stressful situations with somatic difficulties, these episodes markedly lessened as he began to gain the necessary skills and be reinforced for acting in a more assertive manner.

DISCUSSION

A psychophysiologic disorder involves a dysfunction of a single organ system innervated by the autonomic nervous system. The organ system is therefore not under full voluntary control (Gregory, 1968). An individual with a psychophysiologic disorder does not behave in an abnormal manner, and there is no evidence of language or memory disturbances. According to the American Psychiatric Association's definition (1968) of this diagnostic category, the physiological changes that occur are those that normally accompany certain emotional states, but the changes are of greater intensity and duration. Further, the individual may not have a conscious awareness of the emotional state.

Cannon (1939) divided the basic biological patterns of reacting to stress into two major categories, the fight-flight and withdrawal-conservation patterns. These patterns were delineated on the basis of whether the primary site of activation is the sympathetic or parasympathetic portion of the autonomic nervous system. The fight-flight patterns represent a variety of active modes of coping with stress. The physiological processes involved are the result of sympathetic innervation, and the modifications in function are similar to the changes that occur in an emergency situation. Startle movements, tremors, and altered respiration are some of the behavioral manifestations of these patterns. The withdrawal-conservation patterns involve a reduction of activity and a conservation of resources. These patterns result in a stimulation of gastrointestinal functions, which are primarily under parasympathetic control.

Alexander and Szasz (1952) presented a psychoanalytic interpretation of gastrointestinal disturbances that was biologically aligned with the withdrawal-conservation patterns. They postulated that the wish to be taken care of is associated on the physiological level with an increase in gastric secretions. The authors pointed out, however, that not all persons with conflicts of dependent receptive urges develop a gastrointestinal disorder. Alexander and Szasz theorized that there is a characteristic physiological response pattern associated with every emotional state. However, before an individual can develop a psychophysiological disorder, there must also be a vulnerability of the affected organs. It is assumed that the emotional factors related to diarrhea are either anal-erotic impulses, or an inhibition of oral needs because of guilt feelings about the sadistic nature of these impulses. These emotional states are presumed to be associated with an increased stimulation of the sacral parasympathetic nerves supplying the colon and rectum, resulting in diarrhea.

Engel (1963) employed Cannon's dual system of categorization in his explanation of various psychophysiologic dysfunctions. He also posited that there was an interaction between a particular type of emotional pattern and a somatic weakness or vulnerability. According to Engel, the emotions associated with the withdrawal-conservation patterns consist of a giving-up because of feelings of helplessness and hopelessness. In the case of irritable colon, the psychological stress is symbolically responded to as a need to rid one's body of a noxious situation or agent. The result is a defensive reaction involving intestinal over-activity.

There is some evidence supporting the notion of somatic vulnerability, if this concept is defined in terms of genetic or constitutional differences in autonomic response patterns. Richmond and Lustman (1955) demonstrated stable individual differences in the autonomic response patterns of newborn infants to environmental stress. If this differential autonomic response to stress continued throughout life, each person would show a stimulation and sensitivity of different organs in reaction to emotional arousal. Thus, an individual who characteristically responded to stress with a rise in blood pressure would manifest a sensitivity of different body structures than would an individual whose habitual response pattern to stress involved activation of the gastrointestinal tract.

Ullmann and Krasner (1969) presented a variety of learning formulations of psychophysiological disorders. They cited evidence suggesting that certain behavioral roles have emotional concomitants that lead to physiological changes. If these physiological changes are of long duration, they may eventually result in structural damage. For example, strong anger and fear are both associated with a rise in systolic blood pressure (Ax, 1953). Therefore, a person who had learned to consistently interact with others in an angry or fearful manner may, over time, begin to show organic changes resulting from the chronically elevated blood pressure. In this particular case, hypertension is the result of a learned and consistently repeated way of reacting to specific situations.

Ullmann and Krasner also pointed out that an individual's particular autonomic response pattern may be a direct result of classical conditioning processes. Although various types of stress may initially evoke a number of different autonomic responses, the individual with a psychophysiologic disorder may have been conditioned to respond with a dysfunction of one particular organ system.

The Russian studies demonstrating interoceptive conditioning provide a laboratory example of how this process could occur. Interoceptive conditioning is a classical conditioning procedure in which either the unconditioned stimulus, the conditioned stimulus, or both are delivered directly to an internal organ of the body. For example, a dog was conditioned to exhibit a wide variety of respiratory and other bodily changes in response to stimulation of the intestinal tract (Razran, 1961). The inhalation of air with a high composition of carbon dioxide was the unconditioned stimulus which naturally resulted in respiratory changes. In the described procedure, intestinal stimulation was carried out just before the air was inhaled. Through the process of classical conditioning, after a number of trials the intestinal movements became the conditioned stimulus for the pattern of respiratory changes (the conditioned response). When the dog's intestine was stimulated, the animal was conditioned to respond with a particular respiratory pattern. Thus, an organism may learn through repeated pairings to respond to various internal or external stimuli with a specific visceral response. Since interoceptive conditioning involves the conditioning of a particular autonomic response, this process could eventually result in a psychophysiological disorder.

Operant or instrumental conditioning procedures have also become relevant to a discussion of psychophysiological disorders. Until recently, it was thought that autonomic responses were basically involuntary and could not be brought under voluntary control. However, recent studies have indicated that autonomic responses can be modified through instrumental conditioning procedures. Di Cara and Miller (1969) reported that rats could learn to increase or decrease their heart rate in order to avoid or escape from a shock. It is likely that humans can also be instrumentally conditioned to emit a particular physiological response, because of the reinforcement history associated with that response.

Observational learning may also be important in the development of psychophysiological disorders. Berger (1962) demonstrated that the opportunity to observe a model responding emotionally to environmental stimuli resulted in a vicariously instigated emotional response in the observer. A child may thus learn to respond to aversive situations with intestinal symptoms, because of having repeatedly observed a parent respond in this manner to unpleasant events. The somatic response may then serve as an operant that is reinforced by the attention of others and the opportunity to escape from the aversive situation.

The question of why a given individual develops one particular psychophysiologic disorder rather than another has been the subject of much debate. The conditioning studies just described clearly indicate that learning processes are involved in an organism's physiological response to environmental stimuli. However, research findings have not substantiated the theory that particular psychophysiological disorders occur only in individuals with a specific type of personality constellation (Ullmann and Krasner, 1969). The organ system involved in psychophysiological disorders appears to be a complex function of constitutional and learning factors. Mirsky (1958) demonstrated this point in his study of persons who developed ulcers. The combination of given personality factors and elevated pepsinogen secretion levels were highly predictive of later ulcer formation, while neither factor in isolation was strongly related to the development of ulcers.

It is impossible to determine at this point whether or not Edward had exhibited a gastrointestinal response to stress from the time he was a newborn. However, it is apparent in Edward's case that modeling cues were important in the formation of the psychophysiological response. Edward reported that as a child, he observed his mother responding to aversive situations with intestinal dysfunction, and he was reinforced by his mother's attention and concern when he exhibited similar somatic difficulties. The irritable colon syndrome may also have developed because the client became conditioned to respond to stressful situations and the associated emotional arousal with symptoms of intestinal dysfunction.

Antispasmodic medication was an important component of the treatment process because the drugs blocked or lessened the intensity of the conditioned response. A gradual extinction of the conditioned physiological response was made possible by the simultaneous acquisition of more effective behaviors for dealing with aversive situations. The physiological concomitants of the new assertive behaviors were apparently antagonistic to the physiological components of the previous role behaviors.

Edward Polowski's social learning history illustrates how a person's behavior can be shaped by the lack of opportunity to learn the skills necessary for interacting with other persons. Edward led a fairly isolated existence from the period of early childhood until he went to college. He did not see his relatives very often, and prior to college, he rarely interacted with members of his peer group. His father worked on the night shift and spent a minimal amount of time with him during the weekends. Edward therefore had very little opportunity or encouragement to learn to act in a more socially outgoing and assertive manner.

Edward's mother reinforced passive and quiet behavior, and both of his parents were pleased that Edward took such a great interest in reading. His parents encouraged him in this activity, and Edward also received a great deal of attention from them when he complained of intestinal discomfort. Mr. and Mrs. Polowski rarely modeled or reinforced more assertive ways of behaving with others.

When they were first married, Edward's wife interacted with him in a manner that was similar to how his mother related to him. Jean made few demands on Edward, pampered him when he was ill, and reinforced him for his interest in reading. Jean apparently did not interact with her mother-in-law in a competitive manner, but instead, the two women formed a coalition aimed at catering to Edward's wishes and preventing him from being disturbed when he was ill.

Edward's habitual interaction style became less reinforcing when his children were born. He was no longer the center of his wife's and mother's attention. Caring for the children was time-consuming and fatiguing, and Matthew and Julie also demanded attention and concern. Edward found it extremely difficult to form a positive relationship with his children. As a child, he had never learned the social skills necessary for interacting with his peers, and as a father, he was similarly unable to talk to or play with his children on their level. He interacted with Julie in a way that was consistent with his enjoyment of reading: he taught her to say new words.

Edward stated that many times he felt that his wife was imposing on him when she pressed him to relate to the children. The need to assume a behavioral role of responsibility and involvement with his family was quite aversive to Edward, and he avoided or escaped from this situation by withdrawing and reading. The bouts of irritable colon similarly allowed him to withdraw, and his discomfort served to divert his wife's attention away from the children and back to him.

With assertive training, Edward began to learn and practice more effective social skills for dealing with interpersonal problems. He gradually began to act in a more assertive manner, and he was reinforced for changing his behavior because he was able to establish a more harmonious relationship with the new director. If there had been no reciprocal change in the director's behavior, Edward might have eventually been able to be assertive enough to look for a job at another library.

There was also an important change in Edward's relationship with his wife. Although Edward still obtained a great deal of pleasure from reading, he no longer used this activity as an escape from interacting with others. He began to communicate with Jean more than he had ever done previously, and this was reinforcing for both of them. As his relationship with his wife improved, he also began to take a greater interest in household events, and this interest generalized to more frequent interactions with his children. When some event occurred at home that disturbed him, Edward learned to talk over his feelings and reactions with Jean, instead of withdrawing and reading.

Edward's new assertiveness required a change in Jean's habitual style of interacting with her husband. Rather than discouraging this assertiveness, Jean found it reinforcing to have her husband relate to her in a more interested and active manner. Through the joint therapy sessions, Jean was able to see how she was reinforcing Edward's noninvolved, sick behavior, and she subsequently began to modify her excessively solicitous interactions with him. With these modifications in their personal relationship and the lessening of the episodes of intestinal difficulties, the problem of sexual impotence was alleviated.

Edward's somatic reaction to stressful situations was a highly conditioned response. However, it was possible for him to learn alternate ways of dealing with aversive situations. Edward acquired some of the skills necessary for positive interpersonal relationships, and he eventually learned to find these activities reinforcing. The new, assertive behaviors may have been antagonistic to the previously conditioned gastrointestinal reaction. In time there was a marked reduction in the painful and inconvenient symptoms of irritable colon.

REFERENCES

Alexander, F., & Szasz, T. S. The psychosomatic approach in medicine. In F. Alexander & H. Ross (Eds.), *Dynamic psychiatry.* Chicago: U. of Chicago Press, 1952. Pp. 369–400.

American Psychiatric Association. *Diagnostic and statistical manual of mental disorders* (2nd ed.) (DSM-II). Washington, D.C.: American Psychiatric Association, 1968.

Ax, A. The physiological differentiation between fear and anger in humans. *Psychosomatic Medicine,* 1953, *15,* 433–442.

Berger, S. M. Conditioning through vicarious instigation. *Psychological Review,* 1962, *69,* 450–466.

Cannon, W. B. *The wisdom of the body.* New York: Norton, 1939.

Di Cara, L. V., & Miller, N. E. Heart rate learning in the noncurarized state, transfer to the curarized state, and subsequent retraining in the noncurarized state. *Physiology and Behavior,* 1969, *4,* 621–624.

Engel, G. L. *Psychological development in health and disease.* Philadelphia: Saunders, 1963.

Gregory, I. *Fundamentals of psychiatry.* Philadelphia: Saunders, 1968.

Lazarus, A. A. *Behavior therapy and beyond.* New York: McGraw-Hill, 1971.

Mirsky, I. A. Physiologic, psychologic and social determinants in the etiology of duodenal ulcer. *American Journal of Digestive Diseases,* 1958, *3,* 285–314.

Razran, G. The observable unconscious and the inferrable conscious in current Soviet psychophysiology: interoceptive conditioning, semantic conditioning, and the orienting reflex. *Psychological Review,* 1961, *68,* 81–147.

Richmond, J. B., & Lustman, S. L. Autonomic function in the neonate: I. Implications for psychosomatic theory. *Psychosomatic Medicine,* 1955, *17,* 269–275.

Ullmann, L. P., & Krasner, L. *A psychological approach to abnormal behavior.* Englewood Cliffs, N.J.: Prentice-Hall, 1969.

Wolpe, J., & Lazarus, A. A. *Behavior therapy techniques.* Oxford: Pergamon Press, 1966.

15

Psychosis Associated with Chronic Drug Abuse— The Trip Too Many

Dennis Bancroft was committed to a mental hospital for observation after he suddenly smashed a wine bottle and tried to strike his father with the jagged edge. The police were called for aid in taking Dennis to the emergency room of the psychiatric hospital. The attending physician did not feel that Dennis was under the influence of a drug at the time of the assault and he recommended that Dennis be hospitalized for an observation period.

Dennis was 23 years old when he was committed, and of white middle-class background. He had been attending a college near his home for the past seven months. The patient reported that he had tried a wide variety of drugs, but he indicated a preference for hallucinogenic drugs such as LSD, mescaline, and psilocybin. He indicated that he had experienced hallucinations on innumerable occasions, but only when he was under the influence of a psychedelic drug. He also revealed that he had used alcohol extensively since he was 15 years old.

Dennis was extremely angry with his parents for committing him to a mental hospital. He repeatedly challenged their right to have him "put away" and he accused them of saying that he was crazy so they would not have to be bothered with him or embarrassed by his behavior.

CHILDHOOD HISTORY

Mr. Bancroft was an executive in a large engineering company. When Dennis was a child, the family moved quite frequently to different locations both in the United States and abroad. Until recently, the Bancrofts had rarely lived longer than a three-year period in any one city. Dennis attended many different schools, so he did not have the opportunity to form long-term friendships with any youngsters his age. His only sibling was a brother Walter, who was ten years his senior. The family was of Catholic religious affiliation, but had never attended church regularly.

Mr. and Mrs. Bancroft were interviewed together by a social worker. Mrs. Bancroft stated that she definitely had not wanted a second child because of her vivid memories of the intensely painful and prolonged labor she had undergone during Walter's birth. Throughout her pregnancy with Dennis, she was extremely frightened that she would have to go through another unbearable ordeal, and she blamed her husband for the fact that she was pregnant.

Mrs. Bancroft said she was surprised that Dennis's delivery was not as painful as Walter's had been. However, she indicated disappointment that she had given birth to a second boy, because she felt that boys were too active and difficult to discipline. Mrs. Bancroft openly stated that she had never felt particularly close to Dennis, because he always acted in a sullen and unloving manner.

Mr. and Mrs. Bancroft both agreed that Dennis's behavior had been a severe problem to them since his childhood. When he was just three years old, the other parents in the neighborhood would not allow their children to play with him because he was rough. He constantly hit and kicked his brother, even though Walter was ten years older than he. Mrs. Bancroft indicated that Walter usually tried to push Dennis away without hitting him, but occasionally Walter hit him back quite hard. This seemed to infuriate Dennis and caused him to fight back even more vigorously.

The parents stated that it had always been difficult to compel Dennis to obey them. Mrs. Bancroft reported that Dennis invariably ignored her threats and scoldings and even when she spanked him, there was no change in his behavior. She recounted an episode when Dennis, at four years of age, had run outside without any clothes on. She chased him down the block until she caught him, then she carried him home while he struggled and screamed. In the process, Mrs. Bancroft got kicked in the abdomen. She indicated that she was so angry with Dennis she could have killed him. She gave him a sound spanking, but she said that the next day he was just as mean and difficult to handle as he had always been.

Mrs. Bancroft felt that Dennis had a constant need to be the center of attention in any setting he was in. Since the time of his early childhood, he had tried to dominate social situations by talking constantly and running around the room. Further, he did not stay in the house when he was told to do so. Walter and his parents were continually looking for him even though he was supposed to be home. Dennis refused to go to sleep at a set hour, and ever since he was nine or ten years old, he could be heard walking around the house when the rest of the family was in bed.

The parents reported that Walter had always been more quiet and congenial than Dennis and he conformed more readily to parental discipline. Mrs. Bancroft said that it had always been easier for her to feel affection toward Walter. She was not constantly involved in arguments with him, and Walter was willing to help her discipline Dennis. Mrs. Bancroft sometimes asked Walter to hit Dennis when he misbehaved, and Walter always obeyed her request.

Dennis's parents were in agreement that it was Mrs. Bancroft who assumed the responsibility for disciplining the children. Mrs. Bancroft told the social worker that she blamed her husband for Dennis's continuing behavior problems, because she felt that Mr. Bancroft had not been strict enough with Dennis. Mr. Bancroft in turn, complained that when he came home in the evening, his wife always presented him with a list of Dennis's wrongdoings for that day. She then expected him to deal with these problems immediately, and if he did not, she accused him of spoiling Dennis and a loud argument ensued.

Mr. Bancroft felt that it was important to talk and reason with children rather than to react to every situation by shouting and hitting. He acknowledged that his approach to Dennis's misbehavior resulted in continuous disagreements with his wife. He indicated that he resented her attitude that he alone was at fault for Dennis's constant problems.

Both Mr. and Mrs. Bancroft used some type of external substance reportedly to help them cope with the arguments they had about Dennis's behavior. Mrs. Bancroft indicated that her husband drank liquor as an escape from dealing with family problems and his use of alcohol had already begun to affect his liver. She also stated that Mr. Bancroft sometimes became very hostile and verbally abusive while he was drinking, and Mr. Bancroft agreed that this was so. However, he pointed out that his wife's heavy use of tranquilizers and sedatives was her own means of escaping from family difficulties.

SCHOOL HISTORY

Dennis had experienced numerous academic and behavioral difficulties throughout his school career. On two occasions in elementary school, he failed the grade he was in. Both times, Mr. Bancroft went to the school and persuaded the principal to pass Dennis on to the next grade, arguing that Dennis would be even more of a problem if he were in a class where he was bigger and older than the other children. In addition, Mr. Bancroft promised to spend more time helping Dennis with his studies.

The Bancrofts had received continual complaints from the school because Dennis had great difficulty getting along with female teachers, and he would not listen to their directions. When Dennis was in the eighth grade, his teacher reported that he was still reading at a second-grade level. Reports from Dennis's high school teachers indicated that he disrupted his classes by laughing, wandering around the room, and picking fights with the other students.

Dennis rarely completed his homework assignments, and his standard comment was that he had already done the work in school. Mrs. Bancroft said that on many occasions she stood over Dennis and tried to force him to work at his desk, but to no avail. If Mr. Bancroft sat down and went over the assignments with him, he sometimes got his work done. However, what often happened was Mr. Bancroft ended up completing the homework assignment for Dennis.

Because the family moved so frequently, Dennis was often enrolled in schools where he was not previously known. Mr. Bancroft typically went to the school that Dennis was going to attend and was successful in having Dennis placed in classes commensurate with his age, rather than with his academic skills. Mr. Bancroft also blocked any attempts to transfer Dennis to a class for emotionally disturbed youngsters.

CHILDHOOD TREATMENT HISTORY

Dennis was taken for evaluation to numerous psychiatrists, psychologists, and neurologists. The results of these consultations consistently indicated that Dennis was not suffering from any type of neurological disability. His hyperactive behavior was therefore considered to be psychogenic in nature.

Dennis was periodically in treatment with a psychologist or a psychiatrist throughout his childhood, but his parents reported that there was no change in his behavior. At one point, the Bancrofts and Dennis participated together in family therapy, but Mrs. Bancroft terminated these sessions after three months because she felt that they were not making any progress. The longest interval that Dennis remained in therapy with any one professional was four months. At some point with each new therapist, Dennis refused to continue in therapy and Mrs. Bancroft acceded to this refusal.

ADOLESCENCE

When he was 14 years old, Dennis stole a car and drove it over to his house. As soon as his mother found out about the theft, she called the police and had him arrested. Dennis was held in police custody for several hours until his father came to the precinct station. Mr. Bancroft promised the police that he would see to it that a similar incident would not happen again and the case was dropped. However, Mr. Bancroft indicated that on a number of occasions in other cities, he was forced to intervene again because for one reason or another Dennis was in police custody.

Dennis had periodically run away from home from the time he was 10 years old. At age 12, he was missing for over a week before he was located by the police. When Dennis was found, he was staying with a farmer who had provided him with food and shelter. Again, his father talked with the juvenile authorities and persuaded them to drop the case and release Dennis in Mr. Bancroft's custody.

Dennis was sent to a military academy upon entering the ninth grade, because his parents hoped that he would benefit from the strict discipline at the school. The Bancrofts revealed that Dennis was furious when he found out that he had been enrolled in the school and he promised that at the first opportunity, he would cause trouble and run away.

Mr. Bancroft was eventually able to calm Dennis and talk him into attending the school on a trial basis. However, Dennis soon got into difficulty with the school administration because of smoking and drinking liquor on the premises. The parents also received a report that

Dennis was found with a pocket knife belonging to one of the other boys. Dennis ran away from the school after he was punished for stealing the pocket knife, and he was not found until several days later. He was then expelled from the academy and he went back to the school in his neighborhood.

Dennis dropped out of high school at age 16. He then spent his time in the company of an older group of boys who drank together quite frequently and drove around in cars. Mr. Bancroft did not pressure Dennis to obtain a job after he left school, because he felt that Dennis should have a chance to "find himself."

Dennis was 18 years old when he told his father that he was getting bored with sitting around the house and he wanted to join the armed forces. Mr. Bancroft said that he was delighted with Dennis's decision and he accompanied him to the recruiting station. Mr. Bancroft spoke with the military personnel and persuaded them to approve his son for enlistment, despite Dennis's past difficulties in school and with the police.

After he had been in the service for three months, Dennis was confined to quarters following a bar fight with some other recruits. He attempted to slash his wrists with a piece of glass several hours after he was restricted. The suicide attempt was noticed almost immediately and Dennis was taken to the psychiatric ward of the base hospital. However, he slipped out of the hospital two weeks later when he was given permission to go to the canteen.

Dennis was listed as AWOL for a period of one year.

YOUNG ADULTHOOD

Dennis was interviewed and tested when he was committed to the mental hospital. The rest of the details of the life history were provided by the patient during his interviews with the psychologist.

Dennis reported that he began smoking marijuana and experimenting with drugs when he was in high school. He sometimes used drugs and liquor at the same time, which made him act in a "pretty far out way." He indicated that his suicide attempt in the army occurred because of strong feelings of depression due to a combination of an alcohol and amphetamine hangover.

Dennis hitchhiked around the country during the year that he was AWOL. He was usually able to find someone to provide him with a place to sleep for a few nights, and when he tired of one location, he drifted somewhere else. He stated that he used drugs quite frequently during this time period. Whenever he was short of funds, he contacted his father, who always sent him some money. Dennis ignored Mr. Bancroft's pleas to come home and turn himself in to the military authorities. However, about a year after he left his unit, he rather impulsively hitched a ride and went to his parents' house.

Dennis stated that his parents were shocked by his appearance when he arrived home. His hair had grown quite long and the clothes he was wearing were dirty and torn. He also had lost about twenty pounds since the last time his parents had seen him. Dennis said that his mother was quite angry because he had just suddenly appeared at the door one day. Before she let him into the house, she made him wash and change in the basement and she insisted that he throw his old clothes into the garbage can.

Mr. Bancroft talked Dennis into reporting to military headquarters and he also persuaded Dennis to have his hair cut before giving himself up. Mr. Bancroft then convinced the authorities to discharge Dennis from the service without any kind of disciplinary action, on Mr. Bancroft's promise that Dennis would seek psychiatric help.

However, soon after Dennis was discharged, he decided to move on to a larger city where the drug scene was more active. He said that he was not interested in nor did he need psychiatric treatment. He felt that his mother was probably quite pleased when he decided to leave, because all she did was yell at him to find a job and stop lying around the house. Dennis felt that working at a meaningless job was society's means of controlling people and he wanted no part of that process. Mr. Bancroft gave Dennis some money when he decided to leave and drove Dennis out to the highway so he could hitch a ride.

Dennis reported that he spent most of his money on drugs. He worked at odd jobs when he was in immediate need of funds, but he generally relied on his father to support him. Dennis was jailed for vagrancy on two occasions over the next few years. Each time he was arrested, his father sent him money for bail.

Dennis stated that he had probably tried every available drug except heroin. He said that he had not used heroin because he had seen too many junkies during his travels and he was genuinely afraid of getting hooked. He indicated that he liked the "cool" feeling he experienced with cocaine, but he enjoyed the psychedelic drugs most of all.

Dennis revealed that he had used LSD, mescaline, and psilocybin quite frequently over the past five years and had had innumerable hallucinatory experiences. He estimated that he had taken some type of hallucinogenic drug on at least three hundred occasions. He indicated a feeling of excited anticipation before each trip and he commented on how beautiful many of the visual experiences were. Colors became very pronounced and vivid, and he sometimes perceived exquisitely beautiful spinning pinwheels of color. Shiny objects seemed to glitter and tree limbs appeared to move with a gentle, undulating motion. Occasionally, objects became blurred and wavy, like heat rising off a black top road. Dennis described visual illusions in which persons or objects in the center of the visual field looked disproportionately large and round, while those persons or objects at the edge of the visual field seemed smaller or stretched out. He further stated that the persons he was with seemed more beautiful and loving when he was under the influence of an hallucinogenic drug.

Dennis indicated that he enjoyed the special social communion that came from living with persons who were also into the drug scene. He said that he was more relaxed and he could relate better to others when he was under the influence of a drug. He also revealed that he had had intercourse for the first time while he was high on marijuana, and his sexual pleasure was always enhanced if he was "stoned" at the time.

Dennis reported that, over the course of his experimentation with hallucinatory drugs, he had had approximately ten or fifteen bad trips. He indicated that it was impossible to predict when a bad trip would occur. He described these episodes as extremely nightmarish in quality, with the world and the people in it very grotesque and threatening. Dennis said that his usual response to these fearful visions was to become panic-stricken and run from place to place. He often struck out at anyone who tried to come near him, and occasionally he injured himself. It was usually a day or two after a bad trip before he was able to feel relatively calm. However, he said that he disregarded the memories of these frightening and sometimes violent hallucinatory experiences the next time he obtained some drugs. In addition, he continued to drink whisky fairly often, a practice maintained since adolescence.

Dennis sometimes felt extremely depressed and let down after an hallucinatory episode, irrespective of whether the experience had been a pleasant or an unpleasant one. However, he continually sought out further opportunities to use drugs because there was always the potentially beautiful trip to look forward to.

CURRENT SITUATION

After five years of drifting from place to place, Dennis began to tire of wandering around. Every time he came home for a short while, his father pleaded with him to continue his education, and eventually, Dennis agreed to try to get into a college near his home.

Mr. Bancroft accompanied his son to the school and arranged for Dennis to take a high school equivalency examination. Dennis received a borderline score on the examination, but his father talked with the dean of admissions and the school eventually agreed to admit Dennis on a probationary status. Mr. Bancroft paid the tuition fees and provided money for Dennis to rent a room on campus.

Dennis said that he had had no difficulty becoming acquainted with some students who were interested in taking drugs, and he associated primarily with these persons. He met a young woman who was part of this group and they spent a great deal of time together. Janet was intensely interested in social problems and her conversations with Dennis stimulated him to become more sensitive to political and social issues.

Janet belonged to a student organization whose avowed philosophy was the revolutionary overthrow of the present form of government. Dennis also became quite active in this organization, because he felt that he had found a purpose in life through helping to change the social system. Dennis said that he pictured himself as a social prophet and a reformer, and he stated a personal belief that one should be able to do as one pleases, as long as one's actions do not hurt others. However, he revealed that he had helped to plan the bombing of a building, although the group later abandoned these plans. The members of the organization also precipitated a strike action that forced the college to close down for several days.

Dennis indicated that the use of drugs was not a regular part of the organization's activities, although sometimes the group members smoked marijuana together after the meetings. Janet and Dennis usually associated with a different group of persons when they wanted to take drugs. However, Janet gradually started to lose interest in drugs, and she told Dennis that she did not like the fact that his entire life revolved around drug use. As Janet became involved in a greater variety of activities with other persons, she and Dennis spent less time together.

Dennis reported that his classes were not particularly interesting or relevant to his life, and he generally did not attend lectures. His grades were very poor at the end of the first semester and he was placed on final probation. Dennis failed to appear for the second semester midterms in any of his courses. A short time thereafter, he was committed to the mental hospital.

ADMISSION HISTORY

The patient stated emphatically that he was not under the influence of any kind of drug at the time he attacked his father. He reported that the two of them had been drinking together at home and the next thing he knew, he had smashed a bottle and tried to hit Mr. Bancroft with the jagged edge. He recalled struggling with his father while the latter shouted for Dennis's brother to come and help him. Walter, who had never married, happened to be home and he managed to force Dennis to drop the bottle. Dennis said that he did not understand why he had tried to injure his father. He was puzzled by the combination of angry and panicked emotions he had felt at the time of the struggle.

Dennis was enraged because Mr. Bancroft committed him to a mental institution for observation. He repeatedly stated that no one had the right to deprive another person of his freedom. The patient said that he despised his father and had never been able to respect him. He emphasized that he was not mentally ill and he viewed the attack on his father as an unexplainable event, which sometimes happens in the life of every normal person.

Dennis claimed that his parents were having him put away so they would not have to bother with him. He insisted that he was not dangerous and he did not need to be protected from himself and others, as his father had indicated. Dennis did not feel that his use of drugs had in any way changed his personality or caused him to behave in unusual ways. He denied experiencing hallucinations or delusions except when he was under the influence of psychedelic drugs.

A staff physician tried to explain to Dennis that he was being hospitalized for an observation period in order to gain a clearer picture of his behavior patterns. Dennis, however, maintained that there was nothing wrong with him and he repeated that he was forced into the hospital against his will. During the admission procedures, Dennis was told that his long hair would have to be cut for health and sanitary reasons. He refused consent and despite his vehement protests, he was forcibly restrained while an attendant cut his hair.

PSYCHOLOGICAL EVALUATION

A psychology intern administered a battery of tests to Dennis while he was hospitalized. The intern was in his late 20's and he was able to establish good rapport with the patient. Dennis behaved in a subdued and cooperative manner, but at times his emotional expression was not congruent with the topic of conversation. He sometimes smiled fleetingly while he described an unhappy circumstance, and he maintained a neutral expression as he described how angry he was that he had been committed. Dennis spoke freely about his past life and his drug experiences. He provided details about the effects of the drugs he had experimented with and he gave information about the frequency with which he had taken various drugs.

Dennis's test scores indicated that he was able to function in the average range of intelligence. His responses further suggested that he had the capability to perform at a superior level in certain areas of verbal ability. However, his performance was consistently poor on a number of tests measuring perceptual motor functioning and memory.

The numerous errors Dennis made on the tasks involving the visual processing of information and visual-motor coordination raised the question of whether he might have suffered minimal brain damage as a result of the long term use of psychedelic drugs. However, the data supporting this inference were largely circumstantial in nature, i.e., the signs of cortical impairment were primarily visual dysfunctions, and the most characteristic perceptual changes occurring with hallucinogenic drugs are also primarily in the visual sphere.

The patient was administered the Rorschach test and he showed evidence of disturbances in thought and behavior that are generally considered to be psychotic in nature. His responses to the test stimuli were highly unusual and bizarre and he verbalized peculiar thoughts that seemed to intrude on him while he was engaged in the testing activities. There were indications of feelings of confusion, difficulties in concentrating, and an intense depressive affect. His TAT responses suggested that he tended to react to interpersonal relationships in a suspicious and aggressive manner. There was no indication of any plans or strivings for future goals.

The patient gave evidence of a longstanding behavioral disturbance, with a probable deterioration in functioning due to the chronic use of hallucinogenic drugs. One could diagnose Dennis's difficulties as a "drug-induced" psychosis only in the sense that his previously marginal state of functioning became more deviant as a result of drug abuse.

HOSPITALIZATION RECORD

Dennis's parents visited him the day after he was admitted to the hospital, and he became very agitated and destructive when they appeared. He threw a chair at his father and blamed him for the fact that his hair had been cut against his will. Mrs. Bancroft commented that he looked much better with shorter hair and Dennis then directed a verbal tirade at his mother as well. Eventually, a staff member suggested that it might be best if the parents ended their visit for the day, so Dennis could calm down. The patient was given a sedative subsequent to his parents' departure and he went to sleep.

Dennis behaved in a depressed manner during the entire six weeks he spent in the hospital. He slept a great deal during the day and he interacted only minimally with the other patients. When he did converse with others, he expressed his belief that his parents were to blame for all of his problems. He also said that the only hope for the world was in starting a new society, free from the false values of the present social system.

Dennis received no treatment other than mild sedation. Six weeks after his admission, he was released in his father's custody, with the understanding that outpatient psychiatric care had been arranged.

There was no followup information available on Dennis Bancroft.

DISCUSSION

The drugs that Dennis used most frequently were LSD, mescaline, and psilocybin. The effects of mescaline and psilocybin are reportedly similar to LSD, but there is relatively little research information on these drugs, as compared to the number of studies evaluating the action of LSD (Barber, 1970). The research available suggests that the behavioral effects of psilocybin can be observed for a period of approximately four hours after drug ingestion. The influence of LSD and mescaline is often noticeable for eight to twelve hours after the drug is taken.

Some of the initial effects of LSD ingestion are trembling, dizziness, and difficulties in breathing. These symptoms appear to be due to the stimulation of the sympathetic nervous system (Barber). Another consistently reported effect is a change in body image, i.e., the body or a limb feels heavier or lighter than usual, or feels as if it had changed shape in some way. Alterations in tactile sensitivity have also been frequently noted, e.g., the texture of clothing, the skin, or various objects seems to feel different than usual (Hoffer and Osmond, 1967).

The most vivid and most characteristic perceptual changes associated with LSD intake are visual in nature and result in alterations in colors or in the size and form of objects. Hoffer and Osmond stated that subjects whose eyes were closed often described varied patterns of light and color. A distortion in three dimensional space also was commonly indicated. However, the nature of the psychedelic experience is importantly related to the dosage level of the drug, and the reported symptoms increase in magnitude as the potency of the drug is elevated.

The changes in mood or emotions associated with LSD intake are dependent on factors besides drug potency. An important variable is the individual's reaction to the many somatic and perceptual changes produced by the action of the drug. Depending on the individual's expectations and anxiety level, one may respond in a happy or ecstatic manner, or become extremely anxious and panic stricken (Barber).

The setting in which LSD is taken is also of importance. In a group setting with familiar persons, many individuals become talkative and report a feeling of elation. However, if the person is in an unfamiliar setting and is somewhat anxious before drug use, a negative, extremely frightening reaction may ensue even with low or moderate doses of LSD. Many individuals have reported a vivid memory of the perceptual and emotional changes that occurred during hallucinogenic drug use (Hoffer and Osmond). Linton, Langs, and Paul (1964) found that on the day following LSD intake, there was a high degree of recall of the drug experience. However, many of the subjects who reported a feeling of loss of control during the LSD trip did not tend to accurately recall this feeling on the following day. Katz, Waskow, and Olsson (1968) found that a number of subjects indicated an unusual change of mood after LSD intake. Some individuals reported that they experienced opposing emotions which existed simultaneously or almost simultaneously, such as feelings of intense happiness and intense anger. Often, there was no cognitive counterpart to these contradictory emotions, i.e., the subjects reported strong affect, but they could not say why they felt so elated and so hostile at that particular moment. Katz et al. concluded that this particular "ambivalent" state produced by LSD ingestion could be an extremely bizarre and upsetting experience for many individuals.

Barber presented evidence suggesting that the naïve user who becomes frightened by the effects of LSD or manifests a prolonged adverse reaction has a generalized difficulty in tolerating strangeness and ambiguity. This individual might have functioned quite adequately in his or her usual environment. However, under the influence of LSD, the person may fear that he or she is becoming insane and the perceptual changes being experienced will continue indefinitely. The feeling of panic is therefore the result of discovering that one's usual sense of competence and mastery has been disrupted by the uncontrollable LSD experience. Barr, Langs, Holt, Goldberger, and Klein (1972) similarly found that superficially well-adjusted persons who were experiencing a great deal of inner turmoil and conflict responded to the effects of LSD by becoming extremely anxious and fearful that they were going crazy.

For the experienced LSD user, bad trips apparently occur when the individual takes an unusually large amount of the drug. Since LSD is so potent, a very small increase in dosage level seems to produce an extremely negative and frightening psychedelic experience.

Barber reviewed a number of studies of individuals who manifested long term adverse reactions following LSD use. It was evident that the great majority of these individuals had a history of psychiatric problems long before they used drugs. The current disturbance seemed due to an interaction of chronic psychological conflicts and current environmental stresses.

Glickman and Blumenfield (1967) suggested that the psychoses, homicides, and suicides reported as LSD reactions would have occurred without the frequent use of this drug. Further, many persons who are hospitalized because of psychotic reactions associated with LSD use report the indiscriminate use of a wide variety of drugs. Therefore, the adverse reactions occurring in these individuals cannot be attributed solely to the action of LSD.

Flashback experiences have been reported by some individuals subsequent to LSD use. This experience appears to involve a spontaneous recurrence of part of an hallucination after the original psychedelic experience took place. Flashback episodes seem to occur more often in high frequency LSD users, particularly when the individual is under stress. However, Smith (1969) found that some persons reported a flashback experience up to three years after an LSD trip, even though there was no further use of the drug during this time interval. He indicated that the flashback often involved the recall of unpleasant psychedelic experiences. For example, if during an LSD episode a person imagined that someone was about to harm him or her, this memory might be a part of the flashback experience. Louria (1971) also found that the unpleasant aspects of a trip seemed to dominate the reported hallucinatory recurrences.

The flashback experience may possibly be due to physiological and structural changes in brain function resulting from chronic LSD use. However, there is no confirming data on this hypothesis at the present time, and the flashback phenomenon is still poorly understood. In addition, the precise mechanism through which LSD produces perceptual distortions remains to be established by future research.

In assessing the relationship between Dennis's past history and his present behavior problems, it is apparent that he was rarely reinforced for socially acceptable behavior by anyone in his social milieu. There is little indication that he was ever able to establish a lasting and satisfying relationship with another person. His mother was severely rejecting in her attitude toward him even before he was born, and she constantly criticized him no matter what behaviors he was engaging in. Dennis's efforts to approach her in a nonaggressive manner were probably met with continual rebuff. In addition, she encouraged her other son to act aggressively toward Dennis, and she regularly berated her husband for not punishing Dennis severely enough for his alleged misbehaviors.

Mr. Bancroft's response to Dennis's behavior also reinforced his son's aggressive and antisocial activities. He did not punish Dennis for negative behaviors, even when some type of disciplinary measure seemed justified. Mr. Bancroft tended to minimize his son's misdeeds, perhaps in response to his wife's over-reaction to these same activities. Mr. Bancroft was extremely successful in preventing Dennis from facing the usual consequences of his actions. Ever since Dennis was a child, his father had made excuses for him or supplied money to get him out of trouble. Mr. Bancroft interceded at school, with the police, and with the military authorities.

Dennis had little opportunity to observe his parents engaging in positive social behaviors. Mr. Bancroft generally related to his wife in a passive and compliant manner, but he became belligerent and abusive when he was drinking. Mrs. Bancroft continually belittled her husband and criticized his behavior. Both of Dennis's parents modeled the use of external substances as a means of producing mood changes. Mrs. Bancroft was a conspicuous user of tranquilizers and sleeping pills and Mr. Bancroft drank so heavily that he was having serious liver complications.

Dennis imitated his father's pattern of excessive drinking and he may have used alcohol to reduce the aversive emotional arousal generated by interactions with persons in authority. Consuming liquor with persons his age was also reinforcing, because he gained their companionship while they were drinking together. Dennis also began experimenting with drugs in the context of peer group social activities. Drugs, even more than alcohol, were a gratifying escape from the unpleasant realities of his life existence. Further, the use of illegal substances gave him the gratification of knowing that he was defying the rules set by adults.

Dennis became acceptable to a particular peer group because he was a drug user, and as a result of this acceptance, a new way of life opened up to him. As a member of the drug subculture, he was able to hitchhike across the country and find food and shelter with persons he had never met before. This type of existence was additionally gratifying because Mr. Bancroft supplied Dennis with the funds for his wanderings without requiring Dennis to get a job or go to school.

Dennis's enlistment in the armed forces was consistent with his learned pattern of escaping from environmental problems. Joining the service allowed him to physically remove himself from his social milieu, just as using drugs provided him with a psychological flight from his everyday existence. Dennis quickly became acquainted with persons in his unit who were also drug users and he associated primarily with these individuals. However, the overall rules and restrictions of military life were too strict and confining for him. He responded to this situation as he had to so many pressures and unpleasant circumstances in the past. He tried to leave the scene of his difficulties. First he attempted suicide, then he went AWOL.

Dennis made the suicide attempt at a time when he was experiencing strong feelings of depression following drug and alcohol use. This gesture was another example of the extremely maladaptive way that he had learned to deal with his environment. Whether or not Dennis fully intended to kill himself, the attempt may have had reinforcing consequences for him because he gained the attention and concern of the military personnel. Dennis's decision to run away from these surroundings may have occurred when the hospital routine became dull and the staff was no longer as attentive. Therefore, he again physically removed himself from a displeasing situation. Further, he repeated a long established pattern of terminating treatment. Dennis had learned through many previous experiences that his father would reinforce this escape from pressure pattern by using his influence to prevent aversive consequences from happening.

After five years of drifting from place to place, Dennis apparently became satiated with wandering. Therefore, he accepted his father's offer to go to college and live on campus. Dennis was further attracted to college life because he knew that he would have money for drugs and he would have the opportunity to relate to persons who also found it reinforcing to use these substances.

When Dennis entered college, Janet acquainted him with the activities of the student organization she belonged to, and he found that the philosophy of this group was consistent with his own feelings of anger and discontent. However, Dennis's personal formulation of revolutionary ideals seemed highly determined by his extremely aversive family experiences and his subsequent difficulties with other agents of society. As Janet became more involved in this political organization and less involved in taking drugs, her relationship with Dennis deteriorated. Although Dennis was enthusiastic about discussing social injustices and participating in strike actions, his strongest reinforcement came from the use of hallucinogenic drugs. The use of drugs apparently took precedence over all of his other activities and relationships.

When Dennis was committed to the hospital, he manifested a number of symptoms generally considered to be psychotic in nature. He had just engaged in unprovoked, highly aggressive behavior, he showed a confusion in thought processes, and at times he manifested intensely depressed affect. However, it is difficult to label Dennis's behavior at the time of hospitalization in accordance with accepted diagnostic categories. The Diagnostic and Statistical Manual of Mental Disorders (DSM-II, 1968) describes a category of "Psychosis with Drug or Poison Intoxication," which includes disorders caused by psychedelic drugs. Since Dennis had an extensive history of highly deviant behavior, it does not seem likely that his current difficulties in functioning could be attributed solely to the use of psychedelic drugs.

Nonetheless, the continued use of these substances over a five-year period undoubtedly exacerbated interpersonal problems already in existence. Some of the reported short-term side effects of the hallucinogenic drugs are confused thought processes and various mood changes. Since Dennis frequently used these drugs and suffered from alterations in thought and mood, these side effects may have contributed to his difficulty in relating to other persons. In addition, the sudden attack on his father may possibly have been provoked by a flashback of an earlier unpleasant hallucination involving Mr. Bancroft.

At this point in our scientific knowledge about hallucinogenic drugs, one can only speculate about the intriguing question of whether Dennis suffered brain damage as a result of prolonged drug abuse. Repeated psychological and neurological evaluations during childhood failed to reveal any definite signs of cerebral dysfunction. However, when Dennis was evaluated as an adult, there were a number of indications of perceptual problems that may possibly have been the result of drug use, or perhaps the result of the combination of drug and alcohol use. Further research is obviously needed before this issue can be fully resolved.

One must use caution in interpreting some of the psychological test responses of persons who have used drugs, particularly the hallucinogens. In evaluating the findings on particular tests, it is important to distinguish between responses that could be descriptive of a drug experience and responses that indicate a more generalized deviance in functioning. For example, an individual might have differing grounds for answering "yes" to the following question: "I sometimes have peculiar thoughts or see things that no one else sees." A "yes" answer might be reflective of severely disturbed thought processes or it might indicate that the respondent has had experience with various kinds of drugs. Therefore, the responses to many test items cannot be interpreted without gaining information about the individual's drug experiences.

An extremely troubling factor in this case is Dennis's loss of liberty and his civil rights through the process of being involuntarily committed to a mental hospital. As Szasz noted:

> The committed patient suffers a serious loss of civil rights. In many jurisdictions he is automatically considered legally incompetent: he cannot vote, make valid contracts, marry, divorce, and so forth . . . the committed person is incarcerated against his will, must suffer invasions of his person and body, cannot communicate' freely with the outside world, usually loses his license to operate a motor vehicle, and suffers many other indignities as well. (1963, pp. 40–41)

Szasz pointed out that the legal justification for commitment generally centers around a judgment that the person is psychotic or is otherwise mentally ill, but does not understand his or her condition or the need for treatment. A further criterion is whether one is considered dangerous to oneself or others. However, Szasz felt that the social disturbance created by the individual's behavior may be a crucial factor in determining whether an individual is committed or not. He also stated that another important consideration is the social role of the deviant person, in comparison to the individuals making the judgment that a particular person should be removed from society.

In Dennis's case, the behavior that provoked commitment was obviously dangerous to another person. Dennis's attack on his father was apparently the first known episode of behavior that was dangerous to others, where commitment on this basis could be legally justified. The psychiatrist and the judge evaluated the attack on Mr. Bancroft in the context of Dennis's continuing history of behavior problems. The fact that Dennis had used drugs for a long period of time was also taken into consideration. This information apparently was sufficient for the professional persons in authority to make a determination that commitment for an observation period was in order. Dennis's hospitalization was clearly involuntary, and since he was admitted for observation, he received no treatment except for the administration of sedatives. Dennis quickly learned that he had no civil rights when he was physically restrained and had his hair cut against his will.

One is faced with the dilemma of how to preserve Dennis's civil rights at the same time that other members of society are protected. The possibility exists that at a future time Dennis might engage in further outbursts of aggressive behavior. However, commitment in a mental hospital is not a realistic or humane solution to his behavior problems. Although Dennis may never be more than a marginal member of society, one cannot lock up everyone who has the potential for harming oneself or others.

A residential group setting appears to be a promising treatment approach for individuals with drug problems. Like Dennis, many of these persons share a history of noncompliance to authority, and their peer relationships have centered around the use of drugs. In organizations such as Synanon and Odyssey House, the person is in continual interaction with others who are learning to live without drugs. Strong peer pressure to completely abstain from taking drugs exists, and social reinforcement is provided for conforming to these group norms. However, an individual must learn to find this group experience more reinforcing than the gratification derived from using drugs. Whether Dennis Bancroft will ever reach this point is an open question.

REFERENCES

American Psychiatric Association. *Diagnostic and statistical manual of mental disorders* (2nd ed.) (DSM–II). Washinton: American Psychiatric Association, 1968.

Barber, T. X. *LSD, marihuana, yoga, and hypnosis.* Chicago: Aldine, 1970.

Barr, H. L., Langs, R. J., Holt, R. R., Goldberger, L., & Klein, G. S. *LSD: Personality and experience.* New York: Wiley, 1972.

Glickman, L., & Blumenfield, M. Psychological determinants of "LSD reactions." *Journal of Nervous and Mental Diseases,* 1967, *145,* 79–83.

Hoffer, A., & Osmond, H. *The hallucinogens.* New York: Academic Press, 1967.

Katz, M. M., Waskow, I. E., & Olsson, J. Characterizing the psychological state produced by LSD. *Journal of Abnormal Psychology,* 1968, *73,* 1–14.

Linton, H. B., Langs, R. J., & Paul, I. H. Retrospective alterations of the LSD–25 experience. *Journal of Nervous and Mental Diseases,* 1964, *138,* 409–423.

Louria, D. B. *Overcoming drugs.* New York: McGraw-Hill, 1971.

Smith, A. E. W. *The drug users.* Wheaton, Ill.: Harold Shaw Publishers, 1969.

Szasz, T. S. *Law, liberty and psychiatry.* New York: Macmillan, 1963.

16

Simple Schizophrenia— An Indifference to Other Persons

John Fraser's high school guidance counselor referred him to a local counseling center because of John's uninterested and shy behavior at school, and because it appeared that he was constantly daydreaming in class. John was 18 years old and in the tenth grade when he was seen.

John was black, and of lower socioeconomic class background. He had a sister Ann, who was three years older than he. Both of his parents were born in southern rural areas and they had only elementary school educations. His parents separated when John was 4 years old, and his mother worked as a hospital orderly for many years. Mr. Fraser was a musician, and, according to Mrs. Fraser, he had never worked steadily because of a drinking problem.

Mrs. Fraser accompanied John to the counseling center. She was interviewed by a social worker, and John was seen by a psychologist. Mrs. Fraser described John as a good boy who had always been quiet and dreamy. She was surprised that the school now considered his behavior a problem.

DEVELOPMENTAL HISTORY

Mrs. Fraser reported that her pregnancy with John was uneventful. He was born at full term and weighed about 6½ pounds. The period of labor and birth were free of complications, and John did not have any feeding problems during infancy or childhood. He had the measles at age five, but no other childhood diseases.

Mrs. Fraser stated that John was a quiet and generally satisfied baby. He was easy to take care of, and he did not cry very much. Mrs. Fraser indicated that John's development progressed smoothly, but she thought that he was a little slow in talking. He did not say words or phrases until he was almost three years old.

FAMILY HISTORY

John's parents grew up in the South, and they moved to a large city in the Midwest soon after their marriage because Mr. Fraser thought he could find a better job there. John's sister was born a year later. When Ann was three months old, she was taken back to the South to live with her maternal grandmother so that Mrs. Fraser could go back to working full time. Ann continued to live with her grandmother and saw her parents only infrequently.

The Frasers' marital history was one of numerous separations and reconciliations. Mrs. Fraser stated that she and her husband constantly quarreled because of incidents related to her husband's job as a musician and the persons he met at work. Both Mr. and Mrs. Fraser had received a strict Baptist upbringing, and Mrs. Fraser did not approve of the behavior of her husband's friends or the bars he played in when they came to the North. Mr. Fraser's working hours were irregular, and he was continuously exposed to drugs and alcohol. He frequently got involved with other women, and many times he did not come home for a period of several days.

The Frasers moved from a rooming house to an apartment in a low-income housing project after John was born, and John and his mother still lived there. Mrs. Fraser said that she did not want to send John to live with her mother because she was having severe marital difficulties, and she wanted to have someone near her. She worked on the 3 to 11 P.M. shift at the hospital, and she was able to arrange for one of her neighbors to take care of John while she was at work. Mrs. Fraser said that she could not rely on her husband to watch John, and Mr. Fraser's job also involved evening hours when he was working.

Because John was such a quiet child, he needed only minimal attention when Mrs. Fraser was away at work. After supper, the neighbor took John back to the Frasers' apartment and put him to sleep. She locked the door, and then returned to her own apartment. Mrs. Fraser stated that she did not have to worry about John being left alone, because the walls in the apartment building were so thin that if John started to cry, the neighbor was able to hear him from her own apartment. When John no longer required a neighbor's supervision, Mrs. Fraser made him promise that he would stay in the house by himself whenever she was away at work, and she spanked him if she discovered that he had been out of the apartment while she was gone.

Mrs. Fraser said that she and her husband fought loudly and frequently when John was small, and John often started to cry when his parents began arguing. Mrs. Fraser stated that John had been afraid of his father ever since the violent arguments he witnessed when he was a child.

John's parents separated permanently when John was four years old. Mr. Fraser still lived in the area but he rarely saw his son, and his drinking problem apparently became more severe. Mrs. Fraser indicated that the way of life in the urban area they were living in was drastically different from the life style she knew in the rural South. She said that the city ways were rough and often sinful, but the only alternative was to go back to a poverty-stricken area where there was little one could do to earn a living.

Mrs. Fraser felt that it was especially harmful for a girl to grow up in an urban ghetto environment because of the loose standards of behavior. This was another reason why she sent her daughter Ann to live with her mother. Mrs. Fraser noted that when she decided to have John remain with her, she vowed to shield him as much as possible from the bad influences of the neighborhood.

Mrs. Fraser took John to church with her quite regularly. She indicated that she tried to stress to him the importance of staying on the good path and avoiding bad companions. She was very concerned that John would be exposed to narcotics, and she constantly preached to him about the evils of trying heroin and other drugs.

Mrs. Fraser stated that John was used to being by himself, and he usually did not play with other children or go out of the house while she was at work. John occasionally played with some boys younger than he, when he was about 9 or 10 years old. However, Mrs. Fraser ended these relationships because she said that she did not want other children in the apartment when she was away. She punished John by spanking him with a belt if she noticed that some children had been over.

Since that period, John had not had any friends, either at school or in the neighborhood. Mrs. Fraser indicated that John got used to being either with her or by himself, and they both found this to be a comfortable arrangement. She said that she was not interested in becoming friends with another man, and she was content just to take care of John. Although she and John did not talk to each other very much, she felt they were content in each other's presence.

Mrs. Fraser stated that John had never expressed an interest in girls, nor had he asked questions about sexual matters. She also reported that she had to constantly fuss at John to get him to bathe or change his clothes. She felt that he would continue wearing the same things day after day if she did not keep track of when he had last changed.

Although John was 18 years old when he was seen, he had never expressed any thoughts about what he would like to do when he finished high school. Mrs. Fraser said that she had never brought this topic up either, because she felt there was no use in planning things too far ahead.

Mrs. Fraser noted that as John got older, he became quieter and seemed less interested in what was going on around him. John spent a great deal of time watching television, but sporting events were the only type of program that he seemed to enjoy.

SCHOOL HISTORY

John's school records showed that he did passing work in grammar school, but his performance was becoming progressively poorer each year. He had repeated the ninth grade and was in the process of repeating the tenth grade as well. His high school teachers felt that he was not working up to his capacity and they reported that he appeared to be uninterested in the events in the classroom.

Throughout John's school career, his teachers consistently described him as a shy and nonaggressive child, who seemed to spend a great deal of time daydreaming and never got into trouble. One of his teachers commented that he frequently seemed to be in a world of his own, oblivious to the activities ensuing in the classroom. He was often unresponsive to comments directed to him by his teacher and fellow pupils, and he made no attempt to follow the clothes styles of his peer group.

The school personnel labeled John's behavior as a problem one year prior to his referral. However, the comments about John's behavior from grade school on made it evident that he had been detached and withdrawn ever since he started school. During the previous year, there was a noticeable increase in the frequency of incidents where other youngsters made fun of John and called him odd. These incidents served to focus greater teacher attention on John's behavior.

PSYCHOLOGICAL EVALUATION

Mr. S., the psychologist, entered the waiting room and introduced himself to John and Mrs. Fraser. John got up readily from his chair and followed the psychologist to the interview room. As they walked down the corridor, John responded to the examiner's comments with either a "yes" or "no" answer, or else he did not reply at all.

John was of average height and slightly overweight. He was neatly dressed, but he made no attempt to maintain an orderly appearance. For example, when a shirt tail pulled out of his pants as he was reaching for something, he did not tuck his shirt back in. After he took a handkerchief from his pocket, he rather haphazardly stuffed the handkerchief back in his pocket and left it, half in and half out.

John never looked directly at the psychologist, even when he was answering questions. He tended to look down at his hands or off to one side of the room. He gave short answer responses in a flat tone of voice, and he stared silently at the floor after each response. John did not gaze around the room or look at any of the objects on the desk in front of him. His facial features rarely changed, and he maintained a blank, expressionless look throughout the testing sessions.

Mr. S. asked the client if he had any special interests or if there was something he especially enjoyed doing. John's response was "nothing." The psychologist inquired about what John did after school each day, and John's reply was "not much." John affirmed that he liked school, and when asked whether he had any problems there, he said "no."

The test results indicated that John was able to perform within the dull normal range of intelligence, and there was evidence that he had the capacity for higher intellectual functioning. The client scored relatively poorer on those questions measuring social awareness and social judgment, and he scored equally as poor on items measuring the ability to think abstractly.

The client gave one word responses to many of the Rorschach ink blots, and he said that he did not see anything on several of the cards presented. Some of the perceptions that he verbalized were quite different from those of most persons taking the test. These unusual responses were not indicative of the use of imagination or creativity, and they were not bizarre in nature. They suggested, rather, an impoverishment of cognitive processes reflecting a limited response to one's environment.

The descriptions to the TAT cards were also quite short, and represented a very superficial account of the interactions that could be depicted. An example of the type of story the client gave is the following: "Two people. Just there." There was no description of conversation or emotional expression, nor was there any suggestion that the persons might be engaging in unusual thoughts or behavior.

The general impression gained from the testing and interviews was that the client typically responded in a minimal way to his social environment. There were indications that at times his behavior might appear unusual or peculiar to other persons. The test material showed no evidence of organic brain damage.

COURSE OF PSYCHOTHERAPY

The staff of the counseling center agreed that John's behavior was consistent with a diagnosis of simple schizophrenia. The prognosis for behavior change in a disorder of this type is usually quite poor. However, it was decided that family therapy could effect a modification of the interactions between John and his mother. In turn, there might also be some change in John's behavior with his peers.

Because of the research findings on family influence in schizophrenia, family therapy appeared to be a promising treatment approach. A number of studies of schizophrenic families have suggested that schizophrenic disorders are associated with deviant family communication and interaction patterns (Bateson, Jackson, Haley, and Weakland, 1956; Lidz, Cornelison, Fleck, and Terry, 1957). An often repeated finding indicates that the mothers of schizophrenics tend to be more controlling, restrictive, and fostering of dependency than the mothers of normal persons (Buss, 1966). The child who becomes schizophrenic may also be under the control of an individual whose own perception of reality is deviant, and who limits the interpersonal contacts the child has with persons other than family members. In order to be loved by the parent, the child must accept the parent's distorted view of reality (Lidz, Cornelison, Terry, and Fleck, 1958).

The technique used with John and his mother centered on teaching them to openly communicate their feelings and attitudes to each other. The nature of the perception of reality that Mrs. Fraser transmitted to John could then be brought out and discussed. Further, it was hoped that John could eventually be encouraged to interact more with other persons.

Mrs. Fraser was initially skeptical about the recommendation for treatment. She stated that there was nothing really the matter with John, except that he was too quiet. However, the social worker explained the seriousness of John's behavior problems, and reminded Mrs. Fraser that John was approaching the time when he would be finished with school. The social worker pointed out that it was essential that John learn to communicate with others if he expected to find a job. Further, it was important for John to be able to take care of himself and be somewhat independent, in case something happened to Mrs. Fraser and she was unable to take care of him. Mrs. Fraser eventually agreed to participate in family therapy with her son.

The therapy recommendation was discussed with John also. The client made no comment about the suggested need for therapy, and he indicated that he did not feel strongly about whether he came for treatment or not. John remained silent when Mr. S. told him he would like to meet jointly with John and his mother on a once a week basis.

The initial therapy sessions seemed rather uncomfortable for both John and his mother. John did not say anything spontaneously; he spoke only when he was asked a direct question. The sessions were marked by long silences, followed by Mrs. Fraser's attempts at conversation. However, it was difficult for Mrs. Fraser to talk about her feelings, and she was quite vague in discussing why John should be kept away from his peers. Nonetheless, she firmly stated that John was a good boy because she had prevented him from being exposed to environmental influences.

The series of therapy sessions assumed a pattern where at least half of the appointments were not kept. The explanations for not appearing varied, and sometimes Mrs. Fraser did not call to cancel a missed appointment. There was very little progress in therapy in terms of guiding John to become more communicative, and helping Mrs. Fraser to modify her interactions with her son. John continued to spend most of his time in the house, and he expressed no interest in establishing interpersonal relationships.

Three months after the therapy sessions began, Mrs. Fraser and John stopped coming to the counseling center. Mrs. Fraser did not respond to any of the letters sent to her inquiring about why they had terminated their visits. The family made no further contact with the center.

DISCUSSION

The diagnosis of simple schizophrenia is made on the basis of observable symptoms and information gained from the life history of the individual. The official definition of the American Psychiatric Association states in part:

> This psychosis is characterized chiefly by a slow and insidious reduction of external attachments and interests and by apathy and indifference leading to impoverishment of interpersonal relations, mental deterioration, and adjustment on a lower level of functioning. (1968, p. 33)

The individual appears apathetic and manifests a gradual withdrawal from interactions with other persons. Hallucinations and delusions are rarely seen.

A distinction has been made between process and reactive types of schizophrenia, based on studies of the life history and test performance of persons diagnosed as schizophrenic. The process classification refers to those individuals whose behavior shows a gradual and progressive deterioration over time. The personality functioning of the individual is characterized by a longstanding inability to adequately deal with the environment, and the family history is marked by poor adjustment of multiple family members. The prognosis for the process schizophrenic is poor, and there is a continuous deterioration in functioning over time (Herron, 1962).

The reactive type of schizophrenic manifests a relatively good history of personality functioning prior to the sudden onset of psychotic symptoms. A more favorable premorbid family adjustment is evident, and there is a better prognosis for the alleviation of the psychotic disorder. Brackbill and Fine (1956) concluded from their research that process schizophrenia is determined by organic factors, while reactive schizophrenia is primarily related to psychological factors. Other studies have reported negative findings on the issue of organic etiology, and Herron suggested that it might be better to conceptualize the process-reactive distinction as two end points on a continuum of personality functioning, rather than two qualitatively distinct types of disorders.

The criterion for the diagnosis of simple schizophrenia closely parallels the definition of the process type of schizophrenia. Irrespective of whether a genetic or constitutional component is part of this disorder, a progressive deterioration in the effectiveness of dealing with the environment is evident. However, it is important to consider that as a person matures, societal expectations change. Therefore, a schizophrenic individual may behave in much the same manner over a long period of time, but have greater difficulty in coping with the environment as he or she grows older. More independent and assertive behaviors are usually expected with age and the person may show an inability or disinterest in learning new role behaviors. The progressive deterioration in functioning may therefore refer to the increasing inappropriateness of a particular behavior pattern as the person matures, as well as referring to a disintegration of social behavior over time.

In John's case, the school defined his behavior as a problem, but the school personnel did not make this judgment until he was in high school. However, the client's records indicated that his behavioral repertoire had always been extremely limited and he had behaved in a similar manner throughout his school career. His quiet and withdrawn demeanor did not function to gain the teacher's attention, because this behavior was not disruptive to the class. As is the case with many simple schizophrenics, John's behavior was relatively unnoticed as long as few environmental demands were placed on him and he could exist in a sheltered environment. When societal expectations changed, it became apparent that John had not learned mature role behaviors.

The difficulty of using traditional verbal psychotherapy to modify the behavior of persons classified as simple schizophrenic is well documented. In John's case, there is an additional variable: the different race and cultural background of the clients and of the therapist. Jones and Jones (1970) have written about the special problems of dealing with persons of a minority group and termed these individuals "the neglected client." The authors stated that it was imperative that the counselor know the culture and jargon of the clients, not only to understand the client's role in the family situation, but also to establish rapport by being able to speak in the same idiom.

Wilson (1971) stated that counselors must understand how clients coming from a different culture relate to the helping professional, and they should also explore the client's expectations about the counseling process. He further pointed out that many minority group clients, who are not upwardly mobile because of their life experiences, expect to be told what to do. He suggested that it would often be helpful for the therapist to assume a directive role, actively advise the client on how to change his or her behavior, and give the reason why this particular behavior change would be of benefit. Wilson also stated that the most effective type of treatment would be short and frequent counseling sessions geared toward short-range planning and immediate change.

Roberts (1950) noted the high rate of mental illness among minority persons, and stated that the adjustment problems of many black individuals stem from their attempts to exercise, despite strong opposition from the majority cultural group, those cultural habits, skills, and values which are an important part of their cultural heritage. Roberts also stated that minority persons will be capable of developing the type of family life and emotional security necessary for normal personality development only when they are sufficiently removed from economic and cultural marginality.

Fleck (1966) and Grier and Cobbs (1971) cautioned against a therapeutic approach that interprets all of the client's problems in racial or cultural terms. These authors indicated that one must take into account the likelihood that some of the family interactions and behavior patterns of the disturbed individual are independent of racial or ethnic patterns. Further, even though minority group persons would probably feel most comfortable talking with a member of their own group, this is not a panacea for all problems of therapy with culturally different individuals.

In order to understand the type of deviant behavior that John Fraser manifested, one must evaluate the particular relationships that occurred within his family, and also assess how these interactions were influenced by racial and cultural factors. Mrs. Fraser did not act in a rejecting manner toward her son, but there was relatively little verbal communication between them. She was out of the house much of the time when John was home from school because she worked the 3 to 11 P.M. shift at the hospital. When Mrs. Fraser was with John, the behavior she modeled was that of someone with limited interpersonal relationships. Mrs. Fraser did not have any friends and she generally stayed in the house when she was not at work. There was very little contact with John's sister and grandparents, and Mr. Fraser did not visit John at all. Mrs. Fraser had discouraged John's father from visiting, for fear of losing her firm control over John's behavior.

Mrs. Fraser's restriction of John's activities prevented him from having the opportunity to closely observe a variety of adult and peer models. His mother reinforced him with praise and approval when he stayed at home, and she punished him when he interacted with other youngsters in the neighborhood. Mrs. Fraser's description of the hazards in the environment structured the outside world as a dangerous and nonreinforcing place.

There was very little for John to do in the house except watch television, and he found it gratifying to observe athletic contests. These events can elicit attention and excitement if there is a fast pace of activity occurring. An individual who is uncomfortable relating to others can learn to find reinforcement in watching an attention-getting game, where set rules of behavior are followed and few social interactions occur.

John rarely had a chance to experience reinforcement from his social environment. He did not have the opportunity to play ball or go to a movie or dance with his peers, and he never learned the interpersonal skills appropriate for these situations. By the time John was a teenager, he already had an extensive learning history where reinforcement was not gained from interpersonal sources.

The lack of opportunity to experience and derive gratification from social relationships resulted, over time, in an indifference to the stimuli that many persons find reinforcing. Positive emotional responses were not evoked by the opportunity to relate to other persons. Two of the common symptoms of simple schizophrenia are apathy and withdrawal from social interactions. These symptoms can be viewed as the result of a limited environment and a lack of reinforcement in social situations. The unimaginative, rather peculiar verbalizations the client gave to the test material were also related to his limited opportunities to speak with other persons and his inattention to social stimuli.

John was not totally isolated, because he went to school and he occasionally attended church meetings. However, he did not interact a great deal with others during these events. The classroom situation was quite structured, and the youngsters were expected to follow specific rules of behavior. John made no attempt to approach the other children, and they usually ignored him at recess and at lunch.

John always attended the church meetings with his mother. Mrs. Fraser interacted only minimally with the people around her, but she listened intently to the preacher. The message of these religious meetings was that one must be alert to worldly temptations and not act in a sinful manner; one must strive very hard in life to be good, or else suffer the eternal consequences. The present life was expected to be difficult and unhappy, and salvation and happiness would be found in the next world. The picture of reality that was transmitted to John as a result of these meetings was that the outside world was a dangerous place where a strongly aversive event could happen at any time. John's home appeared to be the only safe place where he could gain reinforcement.

Mrs. Fraser was brought up in an environment that was quite different from the urban ghetto she encountered when she moved to the North. Many of Mrs. Fraser's disagreements with her husband stemmed from their differential reaction to the urban environment. Mrs. Fraser probably acted in a restrictive and controlling manner long before she moved North. This type of behavior is more congruent with a rural southern environment, where there are relatively few outside activities and clearer rules of conduct are prescribed. In a large city, however, there are many external sources of stimulation, and the rules of conduct are not as rigid.

Mrs. Fraser was not able to control her husband's behavior in the city because he had many sources of gratification available to him. However, she was able to control and restrict her son's behavior, and John learned at an early age that the external environment is dangerous, and he should not seek stimulation outside the home.

There was a completely realistic aspect to Mrs. Fraser's fear of the environment. An urban ghetto can be an extremely dangerous place to live in, especially if one has limited social supports and contacts. Exposure to crime and violence is a very real concern. When Mrs. Fraser had to go to work, she was justifiably concerned about her son's safety. Thus, one can see an interaction between Mrs. Fraser's restrictive and controlling behavior toward her child and a realistic environmental situation necessitating control for reasons of safety.

In John's case, the therapy that was employed was not effective. It is difficult to judge whether there might have been some positive behavior change if Mrs. Fraser had not terminated the contacts with the center. An unresolved problem that was not directly dealt with was the fact that Mrs. Fraser was never totally convinced that John's behavior should be modified, because he met her criterion of how a good boy should act. Further, the therapy did not focus on alleviating some of the realistic environmental problems that necessitated concern for John's safety.

In line with the recommendations made by M. E. Wilson (1971) for therapy with minority group persons, a more effective approach might have been one that dealt specifically with behavior change rather than the expression of emotions. Individuals of any group who are not accustomed to verbalizing their feelings may find a treatment centering on the expression and analysis of emotions quite aversive. The client must also be convinced that long term benefits can be gained from continuing with these techniques.

Mrs. Fraser's lack of conviction that a behavior change in her son was necessary should also have been directly discussed. The Frasers would probably have discerned more relevance in a problem oriented therapy approach, with behavior changes programmed to occur in small stages. Eventually, these techniques might have provided John with an expanded behavioral repertoire for dealing with the environment.

REFERENCES

American Psychiatric Association. *Diagnostic and statistical manual of mental disorders* (2nd ed.) (DSM–II). Washington, D.C.: American Psychiatric Association, 1968.

Bateson, G., Jackson, D. D., Haley, J., & Weakland, J. Toward a theory of schizophrenia. *Behavioral Science*, 1956, *1*, 251–264.

Brackbill, G., & Fine, H. Schizophrenia and central nervous system pathology. *Journal of Abnormal and Social Psychology*, 1956, *52*, 310–313.

Buss, A. H. *Psychopathology*. New York: Wiley, 1966.

Fleck, S. An approach to family pathology. *Comprehensive Psychiatry*, 1966, *7*, 307–320.

Grier, W., & Cobbs, P. *Jesus Bag*. New York: McGraw-Hill, 1971.

Herron, W. G. The process-reactive classification of schizophrenia. *Psychological Bulletin*, 1962, *59*, 329–343.

Jones, M. H., & Jones, M. C. The neglected client. *The Black Scholar*, 1970, *5*, 35–42.

Lidz, T., Cornelison, A. R., Fleck, S., & Terry, D. The intrafamilial environment of schizophrenic patients. II. Marital schism and marital skew. *American Journal of Psychiatry*, 1957, *114*, 241–248.

Lidz, T., Cornelison, A. R., Terry, D., & Fleck, S. The intrafamilial environment of the schizophrenic patient. VI. The transmission of irrationality. *Archives of Neurology and Psychiatry*, 1958, *79*, 305–316.

Roberts, S. O. Some mental and emotional health needs of Negro children and youth. *Journal of Negro Education*, 1950, *19*, 351–362.

Wilson, M. E. The significance of communication in counseling the culturally disadvantaged. In R. Wilcox (Ed.), *The psychological consequences of being a Black American*. New York: Wiley, 1971. Pp. 416–427.

17

Chronic Schizophrenia— "I Can't Think or Talk Straight"

A young woman appeared one evening at a walk-in crisis intervention center and told the person interviewing her that she had come to the center because "I've been feeling really weird. I can't think or talk straight, and it's really a scary feeling.... It seems like everything is falling apart in my head. I hear voices telling me I'm 'no good'." The person was disheveled in appearance; her long brown hair hung down to her shoulders and was uncombed and matted. She looked at the interviewer with an open-eyed, fixed stare and, throughout the discussion, her gaze never moved from the interviewer's face. She indicated that she had heard of the center from the staff and fellow residents of a half-way treatment house she had recently been in.

The young woman's name was Diane Franklin and she was 22 years old. She revealed that she had been in a number of psychiatric treatment facilities since the age of 14, and she had learned to seek help of some type whenever she felt as if she could not cope with life on her own. Diane indicated that her family lived in the same city, but she had been trying to be somewhat independent of them. She currently shared a small apartment with another young woman whom she had met at the half-way house.

Diane was the youngest in a family of three children; her sister, age 29, was a college graduate who was married and had two children;

Diane's brother was 26, also a college graduate, and employed as an accountant. Diane's mother had been hospitalized periodically over the past 20 years and was diagnosed as paranoid schizophrenic. Mr. Franklin divorced his wife 11 years previously and subsequently remarried. The family was white, of middle-class, Protestant background.

The counselor at the walk-in clinic suggested to Diane that she sign herself into an acute psychiatric care facility associated with the center. Diane readily agreed to do so and she was hospitalized on a psychiatric inpatient ward of the hospital.

FAMILY BACKGROUND

Diane was interviewed by a psychiatry resident. She described her childhood as unhappy and sometimes scary, and recalled the many arguments her parents had had. She indicated that often the heated verbal exchanges between her parents escalated to the point where her mother would grab her father by the shoulders and begin shaking him until her father would have to forcefully push his wife away from him. Diane remembered her mother as being extremely unpredictable, one moment calm and conversing quietly, the next moment becoming quite angry and shouting. Diane felt that her mother had almost always provoked the arguments with her father, often for no reason apparent to Diane.

Diane recalled that when she was a child, her mother was periodically away from home for varying periods of time. There always seemed to be something mysterious about these absences, since her father typically would only state that Mrs. Franklin had gone for "a rest," and was vague about where his wife had gone to or how long she would be away. These absences increased in frequency and length during the time that Diane was in elementary school. Generally, Mr. Franklin's sister came to the house and helped with the family chores when Mrs. Franklin was away. However, she usually did not come to visit when Mrs. Franklin was at home.

Diane indicated that she was generally "babied" by the other members of her family. She described her father as quite warm and indulgent with her during her childhood when he was not preoccupied with personal problems relating to his wife. She remembered that her older sister made sure that Diane ate properly and she also helped Diane prepare her clothes for school the next day. She felt that her sister and brother generally made extra efforts to be nice to her. They often let her get her way and even took care of some of the household tasks that she was supposed to do, if Diane did not feel like doing them. She said that her aunt also tended to give in to her whims.

The family situation became even more confusing to Diane around the time of her tenth birthday. She recalled that her mother had been particularly argumentative and suspicious, and her parents had engaged in a series of intense arguments. Diane's maternal grandparents, whom she had not seen in several months, came to the house unexpectedly one day. More arguments ensued, and then her parents left with them. Her father returned home later in the day and told Diane and the other children that their mother had been hospitalized for her "nerves" and would be in the hospital for some time. Diane stated that, as it turned out, her mother did not come back to live with them. Mr. Franklin's sister and his parents became more involved in caring for the family, but the children rarely saw their maternal grandparents.

Several months after Mrs. Franklin left the house, Mr. Franklin told his children that he and their mother were getting a divorce. Diane recalled that this period of time was an extremely bewildering one for her. She became even more confused when a number of months later her father brought a woman named Betty Sanders to the house, and told the children that he would like them to meet her. Diane said that Betty seemed rather distant and uncomfortable with her, and Diane felt the same way. This mutual feeling did not change as Betty became a more frequent visitor to the home. Diane recalled that when her father told the children that he and Betty were going to be married, she quietly accepted this announcement. However, she felt very frightened and perplexed because she had not seen her mother since she had been hospitalized, and Diane did not know what was going to happen to her mother.

Diane mentioned that she was around 13 years old when she saw her mother for the first time since she had been hospitalized. Diane described this visit as extremely upsetting because her mother had seemed very distant and uninterested in being with her children. The visit took place at some sort of boarding home, and Diane remembered that a number of the other persons there had stared at her and her sister and brother but had not attempted to converse with them. Diane said that she had felt frightened and uncomfortable for several weeks following this visit, and none of the children had gone out of their way to see their mother after that time. Further, Mr. Franklin discouraged these visits because he felt that they were too upsetting for all persons involved. Their mother rarely called them or made overtures to be with her children.

A social worker conducted several interviews with Mr. Franklin while Diane was hospitalized. Diane's father indicated that it had become impossible to live with his first wife. For the children's benefit as well as his, he had obtained a divorce and custody of the children. Their mother has continued to alternate between the hospital and being maintained on medications in community treatment settings. She apparently was having increasing difficulty communicating with others, and at the time of the evaluation, the Franklin children had not seen their mother in some time. Mr. Franklin revealed that he was content in his second marriage, but wished that his second wife could have been more affectionate and less strict with the children.

Mr. Franklin could recall nothing unusual in Diane's birth or early development, and he indicated that she had never had any unusual medical diseases or significant injuries. Mr. Franklin appeared to be genuinely concerned about his daughter and frustrated and uncertain about how he could help her. He expressed the fear that Diane had fallen into the same pattern of repeated hospitalizations that her mother exhibited. Mr. Franklin stated that his two eldest children were happy and functioning quite adequately, and did not manifest the emotional instability that Diane did. Mr. Franklin confirmed that Diane had been treated as the baby of the family and had not been encouraged to be as independent and self-reliant as she might have been. He recalled that he always was somewhat bewildered by Diane's behavior and had difficulty deciding how to deal with her. As a child, she seemed especially sensitive and hurt by criticism or verbal reprimands, while as an adolescent she sometimes seemed impervious to reprimands or the loss of privileges. Diane and her stepmother had frequent arguments, and the latter accused Mr. Franklin of being too lenient with his daughter. In retrospect, Mr. Franklin felt that the family pattern that had developed in dealing with Diane was one of inconsistency and indulgence.

SCHOOL AND PEER RELATIONSHIPS

Mr. Franklin indicated that Diane did fairly well in school, although she occasionally went through periods when she appeared confused and "didn't seem to have her two feet on the ground." Her several hospitalizations during adolescence interfered with her school progress, but she nonetheless graduated from high school and had taken some further course work. However, she generally seemed to lose interest in her college courses about half-way through the semester, and often did not appear for the final examination.

Diane had a number of male and female friends during high school and she seemed to enjoy being with them. However, Mr. Franklin felt that Diane often did not take a stand about her own wishes and ideas, and she sometimes followed the poor judgment of the persons she was with. In addition, she seemed to go through periods of confusion and inefficiency that often required some type of professional help. During these periods, she seemed to lose interest in her friends and surroundings.

Diane also mentioned that she had enjoyed interacting with other teenagers "when my head was straight." She said that during adolescence she had used marijuana in group settings with her friends and had tried some "downers," but these experiences usually made her feel "weird" afterwards. Her first heterosexual experience occurred when she was 16. She had intercourse on a number of occasions with a boy she had known and liked for some time. She stated that she had found these experiences satisfying. She did not feel guilty about sexual relationships before marriage as long as there was affection involved in the relationship. She occasionally has had sexual relationships with other young men since that time.

SYMPTOM HISTORY

The information gained from Diane and her father indicated a longstanding pattern dating back to the period of elementary school in which Diane exhibited poorly organized thinking and behavior, confusion, and inefficiency. Diane periodically experienced difficulties in concentrating and completing her school assignments, and she was evaluated a number of times by a school psychologist. These several evaluations were consistent in finding that Diane was of above average intelligence, but her responses to the test material were often quite unusual and bizarre in comparison to the ideas and associations exhibited by most persons her age. Her uneven concentration on the tasks she was working on also interfered with her performance on the tests.

When Diane was 14 years old, she was seen by a psychologist for several months because her complaints of feeling "weird," her forgetfulness, and her confusion about recent events had become quite noticeable. For example, she had taken a test in school the previous week and had received a C– on this examination. Diane later told her father that she could not compete academically with her classmates and she was certain she was not going to pass. She said that the test she had taken was a college entrance examination, and her failing grade would prevent her from continuing in school. However, the teacher indicated to Mr. Franklin that the examination had only involved a class assignment.

The weekly sessions with the psychologist did not result in an improvement in Diane's behavior and her confusion continued to intensify. Diane was then hospitalized for six weeks in a psychiatric hospital. Under a structured schedule including daily classroom activities, her confusion and feelings of unreality gradually decreased and she was able to return to her regular school.

A similar episode of confusion and concentration difficulties occurred when Diane was 16, and she was hospitalized again. Mr. Franklin was told that Diane was exhibiting many of the signs of a schizophrenic process. She again complained that she could not think straight, that she had difficulty following through on tasks she was involved in, and that she felt extreme anxiety because it seemed as if she were unable to control the things she said or did. The structured hospital milieu, set up so that events happened on a routine schedule, plus the anti-psychotic medication she was placed on, proved helpful. Diane was discharged from the hospital three months later, maintained on the medication. She was enrolled in a different high school and did well for the next year.

After graduating from high school, Diane seemed to drift for a period of over a year. She saw her friends from time to time and was involved in activities with them, but she could not decide whether to go to college full-time or get a job. She had stopped taking the anti-psychotic medication prescribed for her because she felt the drugs masked her true personality. She again experimented with marijuana and on a number of occasions, cocaine. She was hospitalized at age 20 for several months when her confusion and feelings of unreality intensified again. At this time, she was placed on a different kind of anti-psychotic medication. When she had improved to the point where she could be released from the hospital, arrangements were made for her to live in a half-way treatment facility in the community. She stayed at the community facility for a number of months and then moved into an apartment with an acquaintance from the half-way house. She functioned reasonably well in this arrangement for approximately six months, and regularly participated in activities with persons her age. She then stopped taking the prescribed medications, and gradually the confusion and feelings of unreality returned. At this point, she sought help at the walk-in clinic.

COURSE OF HOSPITALIZATION

Diane was under the general treatment supervision of a clinical psychologist, Dr. G. He met briefly with Diane on a daily basis, and saw her for more intensive discussions once a week. When first admitted, Diane indicated that she heard voices talking to her, telling her that she was bad and worthless, and that she might be better off dead. She would look at Dr. G., but then suddenly glance in the opposite direction, almost as if she were checking to see whether there was someone behind her. Her body movements at other times during the initial interviews appeared somewhat hesitant. She was quiet and cooperative but, when she tried to answer questions, she was unable to get words and coherent sentences out. She would then become confused and unable to talk. Diane eventually was able to state that she did not believe that she was trying to get better. She felt that she was not letting herself think clearly or get straightened out. She also indicated that she did not feel that Dr. G. could understand what she was trying to say because even she could not understand herself.

Psychological testing corroborated that Diane was functioning at a psychotic level, with poor reality testing, unusual and bizarre thought associations, and an impaired ability to concentrate and communicate with others. She was diagnosed as suffering from a schizophrenic reaction, chronic undifferentiated type. However, the occasional evidence of delusions of persecution and ideas of reference were suggestive of a paranoid schizophrenic dimension.

Dr. G. worked in consultation with the ward psychiatrist, and various types of medications and combinations of drugs were tried and evaluated in terms of their effectiveness in improving Diane's concentration and lessening her feelings of unreality. A structured daily activity plan also was initiated, with special events and privileges used as reinforcers for being involved in ward activities such as housekeeping chores, serving meals, interacting with others, and attending group meetings. Diane gradually became more involved in the daily activities on the ward. She began to participate in group therapy sessions and contribute to decisions about ward procedures. She also began establishing positive relationships with the staff and other patients, and exhibited less helplessness and dependency.

Diane's difficulties in memory, concentration, and processing information began to lessen. Her comprehension and abstract abilities improved, and she was able to function with much less external structuring. She still exhibited occasional misperceptions of the events happening around her, but she became increasingly able to recognize her own inappropriate thought processes. When she became aware that her thinking was confused, she was capable of redirecting her attention to the concept she was trying to formulate. She no longer heard voices inside of her, and her anxiety level decreased markedly as her functioning improved.

Diane indicated to Dr. G. that a long-standing and still present problem was a personal sense of emptiness and a lack of awareness of her own preferences, goals, and personal strengths. She questioned the continued use of medication and indicated again that the medication prevented people from perceiving her as an individual person. However, Dr. G. explained that the medication was quite important in helping Diane to concentrate, think clearly, and generally function more effectively. He expressed his belief that, without the medication, it would be difficult for Diane to maintain her considerable improvement.

Arrangements were made for Diane to return to a structured half-way house setting in the community. She would reside at this home and work during the day with the other persons living there on jobs in the local area. The prognosis for the maintenance of her improved functioning was considered poor, because of the chronic nature of her thought disorder and her tendency to stop taking whatever anti-psychotic medication she was on as soon as she began to function more effectively. In the past, she had been unable to deal with the stresses of the ordinary environment when she moved outside of a sheltered, structured setting, and this pattern did not bode well for her future life existence.

DISCUSSION

The diagnosis of chronic undifferentiated schizophrenia was made on the basis of Diane's manifestation of a long-standing thought disorder and the associated history of increasingly impaired functioning over time. The psychotic nature of this difficulty was suggested by the depth of her confusion and inability to concentrate. Her stated feelings of unreality and the hallucinations and misinterpretations of events in the world around her were also considered. Diane was diagnosed as suffering from chronic undifferentiated schizophrenia since she showed mixed schizophrenic symptoms, rather than the more specific behavior patterns and lesser personality disorganization associated with paranoid schizophrenia. To a great extent, one can view the thought disturbance as a primary factor, and her interpersonal and school difficulties as secondary to her problem of processing information and thinking in an organized manner. Her feelings of anxiety and poor self-esteem appear to be largely a result of her inability to control her thoughts and communications with others.

A number of studies have been conducted on the interaction patterns of parents with a schizophrenic child, based on the theory that disturbed family relationships and communications result in the development of schizophrenia in the offspring (e.g., Bateson, Jackson, Haley, and Weakland, 1956; Farina, 1960; Lidz, Cornelison, Fleck, and Terry, 1957). However, Fontana (1966) reviewed the research in this area and challenged the conclusions of the various studies because of questions about methodology and the generalizations made from the data. Liem (1974) found that difficulties in communicating with a schizophrenic son in an experimental situation were the result of the poor verbal communications and inappropriate conceptualizations of the youngster, rather than of the parents. This finding suggests that the disturbed communication processes noted in some family interaction studies might be a result of the child's thought disorder, rather than the cause of it.

A large number of long-term research projects have recently been started evaluating the life histories and fate of youngsters growing up in an environment in which one or both parents are schizophrenic (Garmezy, 1974). The study of children at risk for the development of psychopathology has focused on the study of genetic predispositions in combination with specific stress factors and their consequences. These follow-up studies developed from the general hypothesis that the interaction of predisposition and environment will provide the foundation for adaptive or maladaptive personality development (Garmezy, 1975). One extensive project at the University of Rochester is currently involved in a long-term longitudinal study of vulnerable children, i.e., those children at risk for the development of psychopathology because the mother was diagnosed as mentally ill (Cromwell and Wynne, 1974). On the other hand, another long-term project at the University of Minnesota is focusing on the invulnerable child, i.e., the competence qualities of children at risk due to psychiatric problems of the mother. In this latter project, an attempt is being made to isolate the response patterns on a number of measures that differentiate between adaptive and maladaptive high risk children (Garmezy, 1973). Both of these long-term projects are in their relatively early stages, and the valuable information they undoubtedly will provide about children at risk should unfold in the next few years.

The study of the development of schizophrenia in children of schizophrenic mothers was begun in Denmark in 1962 (Mednick, Schulsinger, and Schulsinger, 1975). By 1967, two subgroups of these high risk children could be distinguished: one in which the high risk subjects already had been admitted to psychiatric hospitals or had received psychological treatment, and a matched, second high risk group in which some improvement in functioning had been shown over the five-year, follow-up period. Analysis indicated that the mothers of the sick group manifested a greater severity of the schizophrenic disorder and had been hospitalized earlier in the child's life than the mothers of the well group. The sick group youngsters, on the initial testing, had manifested a greater physiological overreactivity than had the members of the well group. Further, a large majority of the youngsters in the sick group had been subjected to serious complications during pregnancy or birth. However, it takes a long time to assess whether young persons who look deviant or not continue to do so in young adulthood. This point is highlighted by Schulsinger's report (1976) of a subsequent re-assessment of the subjects in the Mednick, et al. study which indicated that in 1972–1974 a significant proportion of subjects in the total high risk group exhibited clinical manifestations of schizophrenia or borderline states. This project is still in progress and continued follow-up of these individuals would seem particularly important in light of the failure of other investigators to confirm Mednick, et al.'s psychophysiological findings (Erlenmeyer-Kimling, 1975) or the findings of a high frequency of pregnancy and delivery complications (Hanson, Gottesman, and Heston, 1976).

Several studies have indicated that some high-risk children manifest various attentional and information processing impairments not found in groups of low-risk children. A follow-up study of high-risk children by Hanson, Gottesman, and Heston (1976) found that 17 percent of the schizophrenic offspring groups and none of the control group youngsters manifested enduring patterns of maladjustment. A number of children in the high-risk group also exhibited several of the signs often associated with the premorbid histories of schizophrenics, such as poor motor skills, large intraindividual performance inconsistencies on cognitive tasks, and apathy and emotional instability. Marcus (cited in Garmezy, 1975) found that the children of schizophrenic mothers manifested attention and reaction time deficits. These deficits were not manifested in the children in the low-risk groups.

The evaluation of a possible genetic contribution to the development of schizophrenia has been approached from the study of the incidence of schizophrenia in identical (monozygotic) and fraternal (dizygotic) twins, and in families (Gottesman and Shields, 1976). In a careful and extensive investigation, Gottesman and Shields (1972) found that the concordance rate for schizophrenia in monozygotic twins varied between 40 percent and 58 percent. The concordance rate also was affected by the level of severity of the disorder in the proband. For dizygotic twins, the concordance rate varied between 9 percent and 12 percent. Rosenthal (1970) summarized a number of family studies and concluded that the morbidity risk for schizophrenia was higher in the families of the index cases than was the morbidity risk for the general population. Heston (1966) did a follow-up of the children of severely schizophrenic mothers who had been separated from their natural mothers within three days of birth and reared in various types of foster homes. This group was compared with a group of early adoptees born to mothers without psychiatric problems. An evaluation of the adult status of these adoptees indicated that there was a high degree of psychiatric and sociopathic disability in the group with schizophrenic mothers. All cases of schizophrenia in the adoptees were located in the schizophrenic mother group. The age-corrected rate for schizophrenia in this group was 16.6 percent, clearly above the one percent expectancy rate for the general population.

Some years ago, Meehl (1962) postulated that clinical schizophrenia was the endpoint of a process involving both genetic and social learning factors. He used the term schizotaxia to refer to an integrative neural defect, which he felt was the only thing inherited. The imposition of any type of social learning history on a schizotaxic individual resulted in a personality organization which he called the schizotype. However, if the interpersonal situation was favorable and the person also inherited a low anxiety readiness, the schizotaxic individual would function reasonably adequately. Meehl stated that only a subset of schizotypic personalities would decompensate into clinical schizophrenia, and he felt that the most crucial factor in this decompensation was a schizophrenogenic mother. Other constitutional weaknesses also were posited but the necessary condition for the manifestation of clinical schizophrenia was the inheritance of the integrative neural defect. Current research has failed to substantiate the universality of that much maligned lady, the schizophrenogenic mother (Fontana, 1966; Hirsch and Leff, 1975). However, Meehl's concept of the interaction of inherited neurological deficits and environmental stress factors in the manifestation of clinical schizophrenia appears quite appropriate in light of the initial findings of the follow-up research on high-risk children. (See Chapter 19 for further discussion of the diathesis-stress model of abnormal behavior).

The history of the development of Diane's schizophrenic disorder strongly suggests that genetic influences operated in conjunction with environmental stresses in the onset and course of her difficulties. If schizophrenia could be explained entirely as an inherited disorder, one would expect to find a monozygotic twin concordance rate of 100 percent. However, there is little evidence for a concordance rate that high. Therefore, Diane's case will be formulated and analyzed under the assumption that she inherited a biological predisposition to schizophrenia, and the social learning influences in her life interacted with this biological dysfunction in the development of clinical schizophrenia.

The presence in the home of a schizophrenic mother during Diane's formative years of personality development suggests both genetic and social learning influences. As the research literature strongly indicates, Diane was at a higher than normal risk for the development of a schizophrenic disorder because of genetic factors. These genetic influences, possibly in the form of a deficit in neural transmission or in neural integration, could have been manifested by difficulties in concentrating, processing information, and thinking in an organized fashion. In addition, environmental pressures were plentiful. The family was subjected to an intense degree of emotional stress because of the arguments between the parents, the mother's unpredictable behavior, and the frequent verbal abuse she directed toward her children. Diane had ample opportunity to observe her mother's behavior and perhaps adopt some of her mother's poor reality testing and confused view of the motives of other persons.

Although Diane reported that she engaged in friendly interactions with her peers, she seemed to drift from person to person and group to group. The lack of enduring friendships might have been partly a result of Diane's poor social skills. Further, Diane's mother was an inadequate female role model for teaching her child how to relate harmoniously with other persons. Mr. Franklin's second wife was described as cool, aloof, and authoritarian, and also might not have provided Diane with a role model from which she could learn how to relate to others in a positive way. On the other hand, Diane learned some social skills and during adolescence was able to function well enough to graduate from high school, despite two hospitalizations. Although her mother's behavior resulted in emotional stress and poor learning opportunities for prosocial behavior, it is possible that other adequate role models were present in Diane's life, particularly her sister and brother. She also was able to gain social reinforcement from interactions with her father, who seemed to be genuinely concerned about his daughter and appeared to interact with her in a warm and supportive manner. Diane's siblings and paternal aunt also appeared to be supportive figures in her life.

Diane related to her family in a highly dependent manner, and this dependency behavior was reinforced by all of the persons around her except for her mother and, later, her stepmother. Diane's relatives attributed the reinforcement of her dependency behavior to the fact that she was the youngest in the family and certainly, this might have been a significant factor. However, an interesting question is whether the family's avoidance of reinforcing independent behavior was the cause of Diane's dependency or the result of their observation of Diane's early difficulties in processing information from the environment. If Diane, from birth on, had exhibited an inappropriate and confused coping style, then the family's initial efforts to protect her and act for her might have been elicited by Diane's own behavior. However, over time these early family interactions became a highly learned pattern of relating to one another and, later in life, Diane was reinforced for continuing to act in a helpless manner. This dependent and helpless behavior pattern also was noted in the hospital and was changed in that setting through the use of medication and a behavior modification program.

An unknown factor is why Diane's schizotypic personality decompensated into clinical schizophrenia, while her brother and sister, if they were schizotypes, remained competent and functioned quite well.

Controversy exists about whether the mode of inheritance of schizophrenia is monogenic or polygenic (Gottesman and Shields, 1973).
Therefore, from a monogenic point of view, one could say that either
one inherits or does not inherit the possible neurological deficits associated with schizophrenia. A polygenic view suggests that one can
inherit a greater or lesser degree of a particular deficit or syndrome of
deficits. Therefore, Diane's brother and sister might not have inherited
a neural deficit, or inherited a lesser degree of the deficit than Diane
did. From the social learning perspective, the timing of Diane's birth
could also have been crucial. Her mother's symptoms were reported to
have become markedly worse around the time of Diane's birth and in
the ensuing years. Therefore, Diane's siblings were older when their
mother showed a deterioration in functioning, and they had a longer
opportunity to develop more effective social skills. If they already had
been able to establish some relationships with peers, they would have
been less dependent on interacting with their mother than Diane was
when Mrs. Franklin's behavior became quite deviant. Therefore, their
relationships with other persons could have remained essentially normal. The association of Diane's birth and the intensification of the
mother's symptoms suggests that Mrs. Franklin might have been quite
rejecting of Diane and particularly unsupportive in her interactions with
her youngest daughter.

The question remains, "What about Diane's future?" Her history
is consistent with Phillips' (1953) designation of the individual with a
poor adjustment prior to the development of schizophrenia. Her stressful family history, difficulties in school and in forming enduring relationships with peers, and the gradual worsening of her symptoms over
time are all suggestive of the poor premorbid history that is associated
with an unfavorable prognosis.

Diane's treatment history indicated that various kinds of anti-psychotic medications were helpful in alleviating the symptoms of her
thought disorder. This improvement in communicating with others was
associated with a greater responsiveness to material and social reinforcement, and the development of more assertive and independent behaviors. However, a continuing problem with the use of anti-psychotic
medications is the tendency for the individual to stop taking these
drugs once he or she is functioning better. As the thought disturbance
once again becomes more severe, there is a related unresponsiveness to
social or other types of reinforcement. This statement does not mean
that the behavior of schizophrenic individuals can be modified only

when they are on medication. There has been ample demonstration that behavior modification programs can increase the social skills of institutionalized chronic schizophrenics (Ullman and Krasner, 1965). However, the preceding discussion is germane to persons who are in the midst of acute distress generated in part by various internal processes, e.g., those associated with mania or acute schizophrenic episodes. Those individuals might be unable to pay attention to and learn or, might be uninterested in, the kinds of reinforcement contingencies they would be responsive to if they were in a less agitated state.

Therefore, it would seem that an appropriate treatment strategy was chosen for Diane when she left the hospital. Her behavior could be monitored in a half-way house setting and she could receive social approval for taking her medication. Long-term placement in this structured community facility would also seem extremely important in increasing her social skills and in alleviating some of the stresses of coping with an unpredictable environment. Further, the vocational training and job placement with others from the half-way house could give her a sense of accomplishment and self-esteem. However, it is unlikely that Diane would be willing to remain in this setting for an indefinite period of time. Therefore, Diane might experience repeated hospitalizations throughout her life due to the stress of interacting with persons in the natural environment, plus the insidious nature of the chronic schizophrenic process. The ultimate hope, of course, is that the studies of competence and vulnerability in high risk children will result in the development and application of more effective prevention and treatment techniques.

REFERENCES

Bateson, G., Jackson, D. D., Haley, J., & Weakland, J. Toward a theory of schizophrenia. *Behavioral Science*, 1956, *1*, 251–264.

Cromwell, R. L., & Wynne, L. C. The University of Rochester Child and Family Study: Development of competence and vulnerability in families at high-risk for schizophrenia. Rochester: mimeographed, 1974.

Erlenmeyer-Kimling, L. A. A prospective study of children at risk for

schizophrenia: Methodological considerations and some prelimi-
nary findings. In R. D. Wirt, G. Winokur & M. Roff (Eds.), *Life
history research in psychopathology* (Vol. IV). Minneapolis: University of Minnesota Press, 1975. Pp. 23–47.

Farina, A. Patterns of role dominance and conflict in parents of
schizophrenic patients. *Journal of Abnormal and Social Psychology*, 1960, *61*, 31–38.

Fontana, A. F. Familial etiology of schizophrenia: Is a scientific methodology possible? *Psychological Bulletin*, 1966, 66, 214–227.

Garmezy, N. Competence and adaptation in adult schizophrenic pa-
tients and children at risk. In S. R. Dean (Ed.), *Schizophrenia:
The first ten Dean award lectures*. New York: MSS Information
Corp., 1973. Pp. 168–204.

Garmezy, N. Children at risk: The search for the antecedents of
schizophrenia. Part II: Ongoing research programs, issues, and
intervention. *Schizophrenia Bulletin*, 1974 (Summer), No. *9*, 55–
125.

Garmezy, N. The experimental study of children vulnerable to psychopathology. In A. Davids (Ed.), *Child personality and psychopathology: Current topics* (Vol. II). New York: Wiley, 1975. Pp. 171–
216.

Gottesman, I. I., & Shields, J. *Schizophrenia and genetics.* New York:
Academic Press, 1972.

Gottesman, I. I., & Shields, J. Genetic theorizing and schizophrenia.
British Journal of Psychiatry, 1973, *122*, 15–30.

Gottesman, I. I., & Shields, J. A critical review of recent adoption,
twin, and family studies of schizophrenia: Behavioral genetics
perspectives. *Schizophrenia Bulletin*, 1976, *2*, 360–401.

Hanson, D. R., Gottesman, I. I., & Heston, L. L. Some possible
childhood indicators of adult schizophrenia inferred from children of schizophrenics. *British Journal of Psychiatry*, 1976, *129*,
142–154.

Heston, L. L. Psychiatric disorders in foster home reared children of
schizophrenic mothers. *British Journal of Psychiatry*, 1966, *112*,
819–825.

Hirsch, S. R., & Leff, J. P. *Abnormalities in parents of schizophrenics.* Maudsley Monograph No. 22. London: Oxford University Press, 1975.

Lidz, T., Cornelison, A. R., Fleck, S., & Terry, D. The intrafamilial environment of schizophrenic patients: II. Marital schism and marital skew. *American Journal of Psychiatry,* 1957, *114,* 241–248.

Liem, J. H. Effects of verbal communications of parents and children: A comparison of normal and schizophrenic families. *Journal of Consulting and Clinical Psychology,* 1974, *42,* 438–450.

Mednick, S. A., Schulsinger, H., & Schulsinger, F. Schizophrenia in children of schizophrenic mothers. In A. Davids (Ed.), *Child personality and psychopathology: Current topics* (Vol. II). New York: Wiley, 1975. Pp. 217–252.

Meehl, P. Schizotaxia, schizotypy, schizophrenia. *American Psychologist,* 1962, *17,* 827–838.

Phillips, L. Case history data and prognosis in schizophrenia. *Journal of Nervous and Mental Disease,* 1953, *117,* 515–525.

Rosenthal, D. *Genetic theory and abnormal behavior.* New York: McGraw-Hill, 1970.

Schulsinger, H. A ten year follow-up of children of schizophrenic mothers. Clinical assessment. *Acta Psychiatrica Scandinavica,* 1976, *53,* 371–386.

Ullmann, L. P., & Krasner, L. (Eds.). *Case studies in behavior modification.* New York: Holt, Rinehart, and Winston, 1965.

18

Paranoid Schizophrenia— The Case of Carlos Rivera

Carlos Rivera, a 47-year-old Mexican-American, was committed by the court to a maximum security hospital for the criminally insane. This was his sixth commitment to a state mental hospital in the last fifteen years, and his fourth stay at a hospital for the criminally insane. The present commitment procedures were initiated after Carlos was apprehended for burglarizing a cocktail lounge and pistol-whipping the owner when the latter attempted to resist. A patron in the bar recognized Carlos, and the patient was arrested shortly thereafter.

Carlos stated that he was hazy about what happened in the bar, and he could not remember the details of the burglary. He only remembered that he had taken benzedrine and wine before the alleged event, and "my mind blanked out. You lose your reasoning power. I took all that wine and I woke up in jail." He did not recall repeatedly shouting, "you're not going to control me; you're not going to control me."

The police report indicated that Carlos had "gone berserk" when the police officers attempted to arrest him. He struggled forcefully with them and threatened to kill anyone who came near him. He was eventually overpowered when a policeman came up behind him and knocked the gun he was brandishing out of his hand. Carlos and several other persons received minor injuries as a result of the struggle.

Carlos had been married twice. His first marriage lasted for five years, and a daughter born during this time was the patient's only child. His daughter was approximately 19 years old at the time of the evaluation. Carlos and his second wife separated after they were married for two years, and at the time of the arrest, Carlos was unsure of where his wife was living.

Carlos had an arrest record that dated back to when he was 12 years old. He was apprehended on numerous occasions for various types of theft, and he was also arrested several times for assault with a dangerous weapon. Since his first arrest at age 12, Carlos had spent a total of 23 years in either penal institutions or mental hospitals.

SOCIAL HISTORY

Carlos grew up in a poverty-stricken Mexican-American area in a large city on the West coast. His parents emigrated from Mexico to the United States in hopes of bettering their economic status. Carlos was the youngest in a family of five boys and two girls. All of the children were born in the United States.

The Riveras' standard of living had always been marginal because Mr. Rivera was never able to obtain steady employment. He was only hired for seasonal jobs that involved unskilled, manual labor. Mrs. Rivera was employed occasionally as an assembly line worker, but her time was limited by family responsibilities, and in addition, there were frequent layoffs at the factories.

Carlos described his father as a stern man with a quick temper. His father often expressed bitterness and disappointment because of the difficult life the family had in the United States, and he spent much of his time talking and drinking with the other men in the neighborhood. Mr. Rivera reacted quickly when any of his children misbehaved, and he frequently punished Carlos and his siblings by hitting them with a strap. Mrs. Rivera rarely punished the children for misbehaving. She usually waited until her husband came home, then told him about any problems with the youngsters. Mr. Rivera would then administer some form of physical punishment.

The patient was born with a deformed foot and had always walked with a limp. Carlos had a dark complexion, and he said that he was constantly teased by his siblings and the neighborhood children because he was skinny and black, and because he had a crippled foot. He stated that his parents rarely intervened when he was teased by his siblings, and his mother did not give him any special treatment because he was the youngest child. On the contrary, it seemed that his mother was preoccupied with so many problems that his difficulties were always overlooked in the usual turmoil at home.

The patient revealed that he was tormented by the children's taunts about his physical appearance, and he was also distressed by the harsh punishment he received at the hands of his father. There was little he could do to prevent his father from hitting him, but he found that he could make the other youngsters stop teasing him if he fought back or gave them some food. Carlos quickly developed a skill at fighting, and he indicated that he began to enjoy the knowledge that some of the children were afraid of him.

Having enough to eat was a real problem in the Rivera household. Carlos related that he often was hungry when he left the table after a meal. He began stealing food from stores in the neighborhood when he was about 6 or 7, and he occasionally shared the food with his siblings or other children. Carlos's first official difficulty with the police occurred in relation to stealing food: he was arrested at age 12 for breaking into a food store. As a result, he was sent to Juvenile Hall and was kept there for two weeks.

The patient said that some older boys taught him how to masturbate when he was about six years old, and he had continued this activity since that time. His first heterosexual experience occurred when he was about 14. According to Carlos, this episode was the result of a dare by some boys because they expected that he would be unable to perform sexually. Carlos revealed that he had surprised the other boys because he had been able to attract a girl and then successfully engage in sexual intercourse.

The patient indicated that he had had many heterosexual experiences since adolescence, during the times when he was out of institutions. He stated that these experiences were pleasurable, but he did not feel that sex had ever been a strong necessity in his life. Carlos stated that he had also had a number of homosexual propositions over the course of his life. He occasionally submitted to homosexual advances when he was in prison, because he feared for his physical safety if he did not submit. However, he stated that homosexual encounters nauseated him and he tried to avoid these experiences if at all possible.

EDUCATIONAL BACKGROUND

Carlos quit school when he was 15 years old. He was in the eighth grade at the time, and he felt that he had not learned much in school. Carlos said that his teachers never took the time to listen to the ideas he was trying to express, and they failed to help him when he was having difficulty with a particular subject. Carlos also indicated that he disliked standing up and reciting in front of the class. He was ashamed that he was so skinny, and the other youngsters made unfavorable comments about his physical appearance when he spoke in class. Carlos said that no matter what he did in school, he could not win. If he knew the answer to a question the teacher asked him, the children called him "smarty," and if he was unable to answer the question, they called him "burro."

DELINQUENCY RECORD

During his adolescence and young adulthood, Carlos was in and out of juvenile detention homes, reform schools, and prisons. He was confined to a state mental hospital for several days when he was 14. According to the patient, he was hospitalized briefly for observation because he faked a suicide attempt in order to get out of reform school. On another occasion, he escaped from a police station while he was being charged with possession of marijuana, and the police never traced him. Carlos was made a ward of the Juvenile Court at age 15 because of his numerous arrests.

The patient stated that he was unruly and drank a great deal when he was a teenager. He said that he has frequently been intoxicated, and during these periods, he "feels like a zombie. No reasoning power. I go to sleep." The patient also stated that he had taken benzedrine for many years because the drug pepped him up and he enjoyed this feeling. He denied ever using heroin.

Carlos became a member of a neighborhood antisocial gang when he was 17. The gang members drank a great deal and they participated in various criminal activities including burglary and physical assault. Carlos said that he had to go out of his way to be daring and tough, because he had to continually prove to the others that he was not a weakling. Carlos and some other gang members were caught in the midst of a burglary, and Carlos sustained a bullet in his arm in a shootout with the police. He was 19 years old at the time.

Carlos reported that he continued to engage in antisocial activities each time he was released from prison. He said that he was not frightened by the prospect of imprisonment, because the food was good, and he had a chance to continue his education. Carlos indicated that he spent his free time in prison reading, and for the first time in his life he felt that he was gaining important knowledge. Carlos read many books dealing with metaphysical and religious subjects, and he also had become very intrigued with occult topics.

MARITAL HISTORY

Carlos got married when he was 20. His wife was three years younger than he, and Carlos stated that they got along fairly well, except for a constant concern about financial matters. After his marriage, Carlos continued to steal cars and other objects in order to gain money for his daily needs. He said he was too skinny to earn a living by any other means.

Carlos had been married for two years when he received a five-year prison sentence for auto theft. His wife divorced him while he was in prison, because she had found another man with whom she wanted to live. She also told Carlos that this person would be a good father to Carlos's daughter. Carlos agreed to the divorce and he had not seen his wife or daughter since.

The patient remarried when he was 28 years old. He indicated that he and his second wife, Maria, had a good relationship and they were sexually compatible. Carlos said that they enjoyed living in some rooms of their own, even though the house in which they resided was quite dilapidated. Carlos continued to steal cars and burglarize stores because he was always short of funds. He stated that employers still would not hire him for manual labor, and he had no skills for any other type of job. Carlos was apprehended again after he and Maria had been married for two years, and this time he was sentenced to a four-year prison term for theft. When Carlos was sent back to prison, his wife went to visit some relatives in the Midwest. Carlos had not seen or heard from her since.

RELIGION

The patient was raised as a Catholic and attended church regularly with his mother and siblings until he was 14 years old. Carlos indicated that for a period of time after he remarried, he considered himself a Protestant because he felt that the Catholic church had too many sins. He said that he still did not believe in different churches because there is only one God.

The patient decided to regard himself as a Catholic again when he was 34 years old, just after his release from prison. He began to attend church from time to time, and he indicated that he continued to pray every night, which he believed was more important than going to church. Carlos related that he usually prayed to God to help him overcome the evil forces which made his life so full of misery and sadness. He stated that he had been confused many times during the past few years, because it seemed to him that God and the Devil were one Being, or that God had joined with the Devil in tormenting him. Carlos felt that the only defense he had was prayer, even though he was not sure whether God's intentions toward him were good or evil.

LATER ANTISOCIAL RECORD

Carlos reported that his activities over the past few years had become increasingly associated with heavy drinking, and he was frequently arrested. While he was drinking, he became very angry about his current situation, because he felt that other persons were preventing him from having the kind of life he wanted. Carlos indicated that if he then got into a fight or was caught stealing something, he "went crazy" and had to be forcibly subdued because he wanted to kill anyone who annoyed him.

Carlos was 35 years old when he was sent to a state hospital for the criminally insane for the first time. He was apprehended while in the process of armed robbery, and he became physically violent and incoherent when the police attempted to arrest him. He had spent the previous few hours drinking, and he indicated that he did not clearly remember what he did after he had left the bar.

When Carlos was confined for the second time to a hospital for the criminally insane, he was described as disoriented and physically violent, and he was given a total of thirty electro-convulsive treatments. A marked improvement in his behavior was noted after the course of shock therapy. Carlos revealed that the shock treatments were quite frightening to him, and during that time period, he believed that the doctors were trying to kill him. The patient was confined to the same hospital for varying periods over the course of the next ten years.

INTERVIEW AND PSYCHOLOGICAL EVALUATION

The patient was referred for psychological testing in order to determine whether he was mentally competent to stand trial. Carlos appeared to the examiner to be younger than 47 years of age and of more robust build than the patient's descriptions indicated. Carlos looked directly at the psychologist during the interview, and he spoke to her in a forceful tone of voice. Although the patient completed the tests administered to him, he repeatedly commented that he did not like taking the tests because everyone would then be able to read his mind.

The patient had difficulty remembering a number of past events that were documented in his files. He was also unable to remember the name of the hospital he was confined in, and he was disoriented about what season, month, and year it was. His conversation was hard to follow at times because he tended to interject comments that would appear to a casual listener to be irrelevant to the topic discussed.

Carlos scored within the dull-normal range of functioning on an individually administered intelligence test. There was evidence of an impairment in abstract reasoning due to the intrusion of distracting thoughts. Also, the patient's responses on items measuring judgment in social situations was quite deviant from the responses given by persons on whom the test was standardized. Carlos was also asked to draw a picture of a person. He drew a figure with long hair and said that the picture was "Jesus Christ. Full of suffering."

Several other tests were administered and the results substantiated the clinical impression that Carlos had difficulty distinguishing between reality and fantasy. There was also evidence that Carlos experienced a great deal of anger that he did not overtly express. Further, he attributed hostile intentions to the persons around him. There was no evidence of organic brain pathology.

Carlos told the examiner that as he became more aware of how other persons lived, he became more certain that he would never be able to change his life existence. He stated that the forces in the world around him seemed too strong and powerful for him to fight. When he tried to overcome his problems by stealing or fighting, he found himself in further difficulty. In addition, Carlos saw no hope for himself in terms of a job, and having enough money to buy food was a very real problem for him. The patient stated that there was no path that he could see that would allow him to rise above the misery of his present existence.

Carlos attributed his problems primarily to "the Gringoes." He felt that white persons were in control over him; they owned the factories or fields he worked in, the house he lived in, and the stores he bought food and clothes in. The laws were made by Gringoes, and it was the white lawyer and the white judge who conspired to sentence him to jail. It seemed to Carlos that no matter where he turned, he could find no evidence of Mexican-Americans having control over their own fate. It was outsiders who did not understand or care about him who were causing him so much difficulty.

The patient also felt that members of his own ethnic group were persecuting him. Carlos stated that early in life he had learned never to trust anyone and always to rely on himself. He had to be constantly on the alert so he would not be cheated or hurt by others. Carlos said that his parents and his brothers and sisters were against him too, and they would hurt him also if they had the opportunity to do so. He remembered numerous occasions during his childhood when he was teased or hit by another youngster and none of his siblings came to his aid. Instead, they joined in the teasing and added further to his misery. Carlos recalled that his mother never intervened to help him either, even though some children might have been hitting him, or his father severely beating him.

Carlos became extremely agitated as he related these events. He spoke in an increasingly louder tone of voice and he gesticulated with his hands and arms in large sweeping movements. He ignored the examiner's questions and comments and in his discourse began to mix Spanish words with the English. He repeated over and over again that he was intelligent and resourceful and he deserved more in life than to be locked up in hospitals and prisons because persons were purposely tormenting him. Even God, he felt, had allied Himself with the Devil in order to persecute him.

The patient reported that he could hear voices laughing at him and telling him to do evil things. The voices also made fun of him because he was so skinny and ugly, and they told him that it was impossible for a woman to be attracted to him. Many times he became enraged by the voices he heard, and before he knew it, he was involved in a physical dispute with someone. Carlos indicated that the voices seemed to bother him more when he was in his home environment than when he was confined in a hospital. The patient revealed that he also had special powers that made it possible for him to hear what other persons were thinking about him. He said that he knew some of the doctors were trying to kill him.

On the basis of the interview and test material, the psychologist concluded that Carlos Rivera was not able to take care of himself and his property, and therefore he was not mentally competent to stand trial (California Probate Code Annotated, 1971).

WARD BEHAVIOR

The patient was described as "suspicious and hostile" because he interpreted many of the ward procedures as in some way an attempt to control his mind. The nursing personnel noted that even though Carlos was confused at times about what day it was or why he had been committed, he was extremely alert to his immediate environment. He promptly noticed any change in the hospital routine and became angry whenever a modification in procedure occurred. He also questioned very closely any new persons admitted to the ward, in order to find out why they were there and if they had heard of him in some way. No one came to visit Carlos while he was at the hospital.

The patient often muttered to himself in Spanish, and when he was asked what he was saying, he replied that he was talking to the voices. However, there was a decline in the patient's reports of auditory hallucinations the longer he stayed in the hospital. Carlos was maintained on heavy doses of tranquilizer medication, and he became less agitated and suspicious over time.

After he was hospitalized for several months, Carlos was assigned to an indoor paint crew. He appeared to enjoy this job, and it was noted that he learned quickly, worked carefully, and took pride in his work. His supervisor commented that the patient was agile, despite his limp.

Carlos had a very poor relationship with the other members of the paint crew. An incident was recorded in which another patient accused Carlos of being careless with the paint equipment, and Carlos reportedly became enraged and threatened to kill the other person. Carlos also accused the other worker of being unfair to Mexicans, even though the latter was himself a Mexican-American. Carlos had to be forcibly brought back to the ward after this incident, but several days later he was allowed to rejoin the work crew. There was no further mention of the altercation when Carlos went back to work.

COURSE OF THERAPY

Three months after Carlos was admitted to the hospital, the staff physician recommended that Carlos participate in group therapy. The patient regularly attended the meetings of an ongoing therapy group, but he did not participate very often in the discussions. He became extremely disturbed if someone criticized him, and he would then start shouting vehemently in Spanish until the session ended, or until the focus of attention was diverted to someone else.

The therapist reported that there had been little change in the patient's attitudes or behavior in the group in the course of four months of therapy sessions. However, Carlos attended the meetings regularly, and the therapist felt that eventually Carlos would learn how to communicate more effectively with the other group members. The patient also remained on the paint crew. This work was considered beneficial because he was kept active and involved with other persons, and because the job provided him with an occupational skill should he be discharged from the hospital. However, the prognosis for a long-term improvement in functioning was considered poor because of the extensive nature of the patient's interpersonal difficulties.

DISCUSSION

Paranoid schizophrenia is a psychotic disorder manifested by delusions of persecution or grandeur, often in association with hallucinations (DSM-II, 1968). Individuals manifesting this syndrome tend to be quite verbal in expressing their ideas, and they may be hostile, aggressive, and therefore dangerous if a particular delusion involves the belief that other persons or uncontrollable forces will harm them. The delusional system of the paranoid schizophrenic is not as consistent and organized as in cases diagnosed in the separate category of paranoia. In paranoid schizophrenia, interpersonal functioning is relatively more impaired.

Individuals diagnosed as paranoid schizophrenic are generally older and more intelligent than persons manifesting other types of schizophrenic disorders (Wolman, 1965). There is also less evidence of a general disorganization of personality. However, after an individual has been hospitalized for a number of years, the symptoms which differentiate the various categories of schizophrenia are often not as pronounced, and many persons progress to a chronic undifferentiated state.

Psychodynamic formulations of the development of paranoid schizophrenia place strong emphasis on the individual's use of the defense mechanism of projection. The paranoid individual ascribes to others characteristics that cannot be accepted in the self, particularly strong sexual and aggressive impulses (Wolman). A commonly held belief since the writings of Sigmund Freud (1959) is that the paranoid employs the defense mechanism of projection to guard against homosexual impulses. The projection of these impulses to other persons is assumed to be unconscious and an indication of an impairment of reality testing.

An analysis of Carlos's ability to relate to other persons is important in assessing the traditional psychodynamic viewpoint that paranoid schizophrenia, particularly in males, is a result of latent homosexual impulses. The patient exhibited a general orientation, based on an aversive life experience, of viewing all persons in the environment as hostile and devious. There was no one with whom Carlos had ever been able to establish a warm emotional relationship. His description of his two marriages indicated that very little shared communication had occurred.

Carlos successfully engaged in heterosexual activity when he had the opportunity to do so, despite his feelings that his body was unattractive. He at times submitted to homosexual advances in prison, but he did not find these experiences gratifying. Carlos had never learned the interpersonal skills necessary to form a close relationship with any person, male or female. His sexual behavior was dependent on availability, and he chose female partners when he had the opportunity to do so. It therefore seems more parsimonious to interpret the patient's deviant behavior as the result of an inability to communicate with others, rather than resulting from the influence of latent homosexual impulses. However, there is no obvious way to clearly accept or refute either theory.

Carlos Rivera's life history indicates that his deviant behavior fell into two somewhat different patterns. Antisocial activities associated with adequate reality testing were more typical of the earlier part of his life, and stealing and physical violence in conjunction with confused reality testing was a pattern that developed at a later period.

Theft became an established behavior pattern when Carlos was still a young child. He was reinforced for stealing by the gratification he received from the food he ate when he was hungry, and by the esteem he earned from his peers when he stole something they valued. The persons in his social environment communicated the attitude that there was little one could do to improve one's life, because the rules and regulations that governed one's existence were in the hands of fate or the Gringoes, and therefore outside of one's personal control. Any act which flaunted the establishment's rules, such as skipping school or taking things that did not belong to one, was highly reinforcing because it made fun of or contradicted the perceived hold institutional forces and alien persons had on one's life existence.

When Carlos was 35 years old, there was a change in the quality of his antisocial acts and he was then confined for periods of time in mental hospitals rather than in prisons. The thefts that he carried out became more interpersonal in nature. Instead of stealing cars or appliances, he began to burglarize establishments when other persons were present, and he frequently engaged in physical violence during these burglary attempts. His reality testing was less adequate because he began to attribute hostile intentions to all persons he came into contact with, as he became more emotionally involved in the conviction that everyone was against him. This belief system eventually became delusional in quality because it was so pervasive and it aroused such intense affect. As Carlos began to pay more attention to his covert thoughts and less attention to objective aspects of the environment, he also began to report that he heard voices talking to him.

The psychologically crushing effect of an economically deprived environment has been documented in a number of studies demonstrating a strong relationship between socioeconomic class and mental illness (Hollingshead and Redlich, 1958; Kleiner, Tuckman, and Lavell, 1960; Pasamanick, Roberts, Lemkau, and Krueger, 1964; Srole, Langner, Michael, Opler, and Rennie, 1962). Individuals of the lowest socioeconomic stratum were confronted with physical and psychological stresses that were due to continual economic insecurity. Their childhood environment contained little love, protection, and stability so that many of these persons grew up experiencing a lifetime of neglect and rejection, first by parents and siblings, and later by society as a whole.

The problem of severe emotional disturbance in persons who are economically and socially deprived is therefore one of immense proportion. The adverse environmental conditions which lower socioeconomic class persons are forced to deal with may result in these individuals being less resistent to stress. Their life experiences may have conditioned them to expect that no one will help them in time of need, or they may feel that they will be personally unable to overcome their problems. Langner and Michael (1963) reported that lower status persons tended to agree with statements suggesting feelings of futility, resignation, alienation from group and society, and social isolation. Psychological difficulties and antisocial behavior would therefore be likely to result from these conditions.

Many individuals express an attitude that they are not the masters of their own destinies, and that the events which happen to them are a matter of luck or a result of forces outside of their personal control. Rotter (1966) categorized this attitude as an external control orientation, and he considered the locus of control factor an important personality trait. Phares (1972) suggested that many instances of criminal behavior may be the result of behavior motivated by an attitude of external control. Since diligence and hard work have not been viewed by many minority group persons as attributes leading to success in life, then taking what they can get might result in an improvement in status. Therefore, antisocial behavior would very likely be reinforced by peers, if these individuals shared an external control orientation.

Lefcourt and Ladwig (1972) studied a group of white and minority group inmates who came from similar socioeconomic backgrounds and who were imprisoned for similar crimes, generally car theft. Their findings indeed indicated that the minority group inmates exhibited a relatively greater expectancy that their fate was controlled by forces outside of their personal control than did the white inmates.

Carlos was born with a number of physical characteristics over which he had no personal control, and his life experiences seemed consistently outside of his control from that point on. He discovered that because he had a darker skin and was more vulnerable than others around him, his family and peers imitated the behaviors and attitudes they had learned from the majority group. Through ridicule, they behaved toward Carlos as the majority group behaved toward them.

Carlos was able to protect himself and actively gain social approval from persons in his social milieu only through imitating the aggressive behavior he observed around him. The patient's environment was one in which aggression was reinforced and modeled by his father, siblings, and peer group. Bandura and Walters (1959) had similarly found that the fathers of delinquent boys modeled physical aggression and reinforced their youngsters for acting in an aggressive manner toward other children.

The haven that Carlos eventually found from the realities of his life existence was the sheltered world of the prison and the mental hospital. During his first stay at Juvenile Hall, Carlos enjoyed the food, and he found the sleeping accommodations more comfortable than what was available at home. The routine of prison life may have been monotonous and at times violent, but Carlos also derived a great deal of reinforcement from being confined. He also had the opportunity to further his education and he found this to be a gratifying experience.

The increasing deviance of the patient's behavior as he grew older was associated with a worsening of the interpersonal and economic circumstances of his life. When Carlos was released from prison at age 34, he was separated from his second wife, and he had lost contact with his daughter. He rarely saw his parents or any other family members. There was no one who could offer him emotional support, and there was no one to converse with as a means of testing social reality. Carlos increasingly believed that life was unjust, and that the persons existing in the world had hostile intentions toward him. These beliefs could not be compared to an external standard of judgment or tested for social consensus, because Carlos spent so much of his time alone. He interacted with other persons generally while he was drinking heavily in a bar, and these occasions were not conducive to rational evaluations of social reality. As his life became more unhappy, the patient turned to religion, in a confused interaction between himself and a deity.

As Carlos grew older, he also experienced a greater need to obtain a job where he would be regularly employed and be able to live above the poverty level. The patient therefore became more and more frustrated as he compared his present existence with his aspirations for a happier and more comfortable life. He was faced with the realization that his life would never be any better than it was at the present time. Carlos responded to these feelings of isolation and economic frustration in the way that he had learned to respond to negative emotions in the past: he became extremely angry and he was frequently involved in fights. He found some relief from the emotional arousal associated with his life situation when he consumed liquor and took pills. He therefore drank until he reached a state in which he was amnesic about his activities during the drinking episode.

The patient's response to alcohol and benzedrine was shaped by his bothersome thoughts and individualized interpretations of his surroundings. Physical aggression and theft were the dominant responses in Carlos's repertoire for dealing with his problems, and he did not discriminate between his fellow Mexican-Americans or white persons in the expression of antisocial behavior. Carlos frequently became physically violent while drinking, and he engaged in burglary as a means of enhancing his economic situation. These behaviors were also self-reinforcing because they functioned as an attack on external society, which Carlos perceived as responsible for his personal plight. A further reinforcement for antisocial behavior was the improvement in his economic and social situation through confinement.

Any discussion of the treatment strategies that might have been effective for Carlos raises many complex issues. The patient's record indicated that he had received a series of electroconvulsive treatments during one hospital confinement, and there was a reduction in physical violence and a diminishment of verbal delusional behavior concomitant with the shock treatments. An interesting question is whether this behavior change was due to a disruption in brain activity as a result of the electroshock, or whether the treatment procedure served as a discriminative stimulus for less aggressive and more socially acceptable behavior.

Dies (1972), discussing the change in a patient's behavior after electroconvulsive treatment, suggested that the patient develops an increasing expectancy for punishment as a function of repeated exposure to shock treatments. Since exhibiting symptoms would be punished by electroshock, the patient eventually would learn that the aversive shock situation could be avoided by engaging in alternate behaviors. Thus, the improvement in Carlos's behavior after electroconvulsive treatment may possibly have been a reflection of this learning sequence, rather than the result of a physical disruption of memory processes.

Perhaps the patient might have been helped at an earlier period of his life by a therapy method such as rational-emotive psychotherapy, which was developed by Albert Ellis (1962). A basic assumption of this treatment approach is that human thinking and emotion are interrelated and are never seen wholly apart from one another. Therefore, the emotional reaction that a person experiences in relation to an event is determined by how the person thinks about and interprets the event, and not by the event itself. The goal of rational-emotive therapy is to recondition the individual's deviant responses by changing the cognitive evaluations the individual makes about particular events. The therapist accomplishes this goal by engaging in an active dialogue with the client in order to persuade the client of the irrationality of his or her ideas.

Many of the ideas that Carlos verbalized about the ugliness of his body and the conspiracy of environmental forces aimed at tormenting him might have been dealt with on a rational basis. Carlos could have been guided to distinguish between ideas about his life existence that were rational, and those ideas that were irrational and in need of change. Guided instruction in more effective interpersonal relationships would also have been extremely helpful. However, with repeated confinements in prisons and in mental hospitals, the patient's interpersonal difficulties became so widespread and overlearned, that no single procedure could be entirely effective. Also, Carlos's behavior was influenced by the fact that he knew that he had been hospitalized in mental institutions. The kind of deviant behavior he engaged in may therefore have been shaped in part by his label of himself as "crazy," and his conception of how a "crazy" person should act.

The patient's reports of auditory hallucinations were relatively recent in origin, and in a sheltered environment, the hallucinatory behavior might have extinguished. A token reinforcement system has proven effective in diminishing delusional verbal behavior in chronic paranoid schizophrenics (Wincze, Leitenberg, and Agras, 1972). This suggests that similar procedures could be employed to control hallucinatory behavior. For example, the patient could be taught to reward himself or herself for each given time interval that an hallucination did not occur, or reward could be made contingent on behaviors incompatible with hallucinations, such as social conversation with another person.

Carlos obviously required help and instruction in many areas of functioning, and group therapy was one method of accomplishing behavior change. However, a treatment strategy which does not deal with the social environment will not be successful. The patient needed training in specific job skills, but he also had to be able to obtain a job so he could use these skills to improve his economic situation.

The interpersonal and environmental difficulties that Carlos Rivera was faced with were many. His problems required modifications in many areas, so the prison and the mental hospital would no longer have to serve as a refuge from the harsh realities of his existence.

REFERENCES

American Psychiatric Association. *Diagnostic and statistical manual of mental disorders* (2nd ed.) (DSM–II). Washington: American Psychiatric Association, 1968.

Bandura, A., & Walters, R. M. *Adolescent aggression*. New York: Ronald, 1959.

California Probate Code Annotated. Sec. 1460 (1959 ed.), 1971 pocket supplement.

Dies, R. R. Electroconvulsive therapy: A social learning theory interpretation. In J. R. Rotter, J. E. Chance, & E. J. Phares (Eds.), *Applications of a social learning theory of personality*. New York: Holt, Rinehart & Winston, 1972. Pp. 491–499.

Ellis, A. *Reason and emotion in psychotherapy*. New York: Lyle Stuart, 1962.

Freud, S. *Collected papers*. Vol. 2. New York: Basic Books, 1959.

Hollingshead, A. B., & Redlich, F. C. *Social class and mental illness*. New York: Wiley, 1958.

Kleiner, R. J., Tuckman, J., & Lavell, M. Mental disorder and status based on race. *Psychiatry*, 1960, *23*, 271–274.

Langner, T. S., & Michael, S. T. *The midtown Manhattan study*. Vol. II. *Life stress and mental health*. New York: The Free Press of Glencoe, 1963.

Lazarus, A. A. *Behavior therapy and beyond*. New York: McGraw-Hill, 1971.

Lefcourt, H. M., & Ladwig, G. W. The American Negro: A problem in expectancies. In J. R. Rotter, J. E. Chance, & E. J. Phares (Eds.), *Applications of a social learning theory of personality*. New York: Holt, Rinehart & Winston, 1972. Pp. 424–429.

Pasamanick, B., Roberts, D. W., Lemkau, P. W., & Krueger, D. B. A survey of mental disease in an urban population: Prevalence by race and income. In F. Riessman, J. Cohen, & A. Pearl (Eds.), *Mental health of the poor*. New York: Free Press, 1964. Pp. 39–48.

Phares, E. J. A social learning theory approach to psychopathology. In J. R. Rotter, J. E. Chance, & E. J. Phares (Eds.), *Applications of a social learning theory of personality*. New York: Holt, Rinehart & Winston, 1972. Pp. 436–469.

Rotter, J. B. Generalized expectancies for internal versus external control of reinforcement. *Psychological Monographs,* 1966, *80,* (Whole No. 609).

Srole, L., Langner, T. S., Michael, S. T., Opler, M. K., & Rennie, T. A. C. *The midtown Manhattan study* (Vol. I). *Mental health in the metropolis.* New York: McGraw-Hill, 1962.

Wincze, J. P., Leitenberg, H., & Agras, W. S. The effects of token reinforcement and feedback on the delusional verbal behavior of chronic paranoid schizophrenics. *Journal of Applied Behavior Analysis,* 1972, *5,* 247–262.

Wolman, B. B. Schizophrenia and related disorders. In B. B. Wolman (Ed.), *Handbook of clinical psychology.* New York: McGraw-Hill, 1965. Pp. 976–1029.

19

Manic-Depressive Psychosis—A Cycle of Repeated Hospitalizations

Bernard Jacobson was 40 years old at the time of his sixth admission to a psychiatric hospital. He had been diagnosed as manic-depressive, circular type, during his last four hospital admissions. Mr. Jacobson was of Jewish background, and had received a bachelor's degree in education. Upon graduating from college, he had been employed for three years as a history teacher. However, his behavior subsequently became so deviant that he could no longer function in a professional setting over a continuous period of time. Mr. Jacobson's wife had divorced him five years ago. The couple had no children.

The present hospitalization was at the instigation of his welfare worker, who felt that the severely depressed behavior Mr. Jacobson was currently manifesting might result in his attempting to commit suicide.

FAMILY BACKGROUND

Mr. Jacobson was interviewed by a social worker and the information he gave was corroborated from the records of his previous hospitalizations. Since Mr. Jacobson was extremely depressed at the time of this hospital admission, most of the facts of his life history came from his past records.

Mr. Jacobson was an only child. His family was of low socio-economic status and he and his parents had always lived together with the maternal grandparents, frequently supported by the latter. His father never had held a regular job and often was gone from the home for long periods of time. Mr. Jacobson remembered his father as aloof and withdrawn. He rarely talked to his son or other family members, although he frequently muttered words to himself. As Mr. Jacobson grew older, he found out that the long periods of time his father was away from home were spent at a mental hospital. (Records at that hospital indicated that the father was diagnosed as a chronic schizo-phrenic.) Mr. Jacobson reported that, at the present time, his father was living in a board and care facility and was being maintained on medica-tion. He apparently was functioning only marginally. Mr. Jacobson indicated that, when his own mood was good, he would visit his father occasionally out of a sense of filial responsibility. However, he said that he could not feel any real affection for his father and he had not visited with him for some time.

Mr. Jacobson felt that his mother was very unpredictable and difficult to get along with. She got angry at him very quickly and often when he was not entirely sure what she was angry about. He indicated that his relationship with her had always been a stormy one. When he was growing up, she frequently shouted at him to get him to obey her, and he characteristically refused to comply despite her threats and spankings. He related that his grandmother also seemed to spend a great deal of time yelling at him and telling him that he was bad. He found it hard to remember occasions when either his mother or his grandmother talked quietly to him. Further, his mother and grandmother also argued with each other quite frequently, often about seemingly minor matters. Mr. Jacobson recalled that his grandfather was rather quiet and passive and did not interfere in the various family disputes. However, he sometimes spent time quietly conversing with his grandson and occa-sionally took him on an outing.

SCHOOL HISTORY

Mr. Jacobson indicated that he had had a great deal of difficulty at school because he was continually arguing with the teachers and would not sit quietly in his seat. His classmates made fun of him because of his disruptive behavior, and he got the reputation of being a bully. The only person he felt comfortable talking to was another boy he became acquainted with in high school. However, he did not engage in any social activities with this youngster after school hours, nor with any other peers.

In a previous hospital admission interview, Mr. Jacobson commented that during high school, he had been able to exert some self-discipline over his behavior. He found that he was genuinely interested in many of the subjects he was taking and he began to study and pay closer attention to the class material. He had learned the basic skills taught in the elementary grades despite his disruptive behavior in school. Therefore, he was not hampered academically when he wanted to learn more about the subject matter he was exposed to in high school. He enrolled in a local college after high school graduation, and eventually received a bachelor's degree in education with a specialization in history. His family helped support him through college as much as they could, and he worked summers at whatever jobs he could find to help pay for his school expenses.

SOCIAL HISTORY

Mr. Jacobson met his wife Sandra when they were both in college. She was also of Jewish background. He stated that he had never had any close friends and he really did not care to participate in social activities with other persons. However, he indicated that he was attracted to Sandra because she seemed to take an interest in him and went out of her way to involve him in activities with her friends and with her family. He said that at first he was unsure about marriage but then he became convinced that he would be happier and more comfortable married to Sandra then he would be alone. The marriage took place one year after they both had graduated from college.

Upon graduating, Mr. Jacobson obtained a teaching position at a local high school. His wife also found a job subsequent to graduation, and she continued to work after they were married. He described his first year of marriage as reasonably happy, but indicated that his sexual relationship with his wife was not very satisfactory. Approximately one year after their marriage, he began to manifest emotional difficulties characterized by bouts of depression and anxiety. He made few attempts to communicate with others during these episodes.

SYMPTOM HISTORY

Over the next year, Mr. Jacobson was absent from work on numerous occasions due to periods of agitated depression, and his teaching contract was not renewed for the following year. He then worked at various jobs whenever he felt able to, and at the same time obtained outpatient therapy. Mr. Jacobson was almost continuously in some form of outpatient treatment over the next eight years, and Mrs. Jacobson's parents provided some financial support to help pay these bills. The treatment he received generally involved supportive therapy and some form of anti-depressant medication. At one point during this time period, Mr. Jacobson had been able to obtain another teaching position. Again, his contract was not renewed because of numerous absences associated with moderately severe depressive episodes.

An interview with Mr. Jacobson's former wife revealed that Mr. Jacobson first began showing signs of bizarre behavior when he was approximately 33 years old. At that time, he became quite hyperactive and agitated and complained of receiving special messages on the radio. He spoke in whispers in the house because he was afraid that some outsider would hear him, and he often stayed up for two or three consecutive nights working without rest on a particular project that had captured his interest. He also was involved in many arguments with his wife and at one point threatened to jump out of the window. He then became extremely agitated and eventually agreed to enter a local psychiatric hospital. He stayed in the hospital for about a week but then signed himself out against medical advice and spent the next several months at home. He gradually became quite depressed, and four months after his previous hospitalization, he swallowed a large number of sedatives. Mrs. Jacobson found him in a semiconscious state, and he was rushed to the emergency room of a local hospital. After his stomach was pumped and he regained consciousness, he was persuaded to return to the psychiatric hospital. He underwent a series of electroshock treatments and was discharged six weeks later, free of depressive symptoms.

Mrs. Jacobson reported that Mr. Jacobson tried to work after his discharge from the hospital, but he was unable to keep a job for more than a week. He spent most of the next few months at home, and his behavior was generally quite belligerent. He also engaged in numerous spending sprees. Mrs. Jacobson said that she was the target of severe verbal abuse, usually precipitated by her objections to the amount of money her husband was spending. She felt that Mr. Jacobson was not in touch with reality during this period and, for the first time, he refused to obtain psychiatric help. After a period of indecision, she finally signed commitment papers so that he could receive treatment again in a psychiatric hospital.

Mr. Jacobson exhibited hallucinatory behavior when he was admitted to the hospital on this occasion, but he calmed down and became rational when placed on the drug, lithium carbonate. He spent two months in the hospital, was given a provisional discharge to a day treatment program, and was instructed to remain on the lithium medication. Mrs. Jacobson indicated that during this hospitalization she finally came to a decision to file for divorce, since she could no longer tolerate the emotional demands placed on her by her husband's erratic behavior. Mr. Jacobson without argument went along with his wife's decision, and the Welfare Department assisted him in making arrangements to live in a boarding home.

Mr. Jacobson functioned reasonably well in the boarding home and day treatment program for about four months, but he stopped taking his medication regularly. One day he suddenly experienced an acute manic episode. He had been helping his landlord paint a room, when suddenly he began painting everything in sight and the landlord had to wrest the paint brush out of his hand. He roamed about the house in his underwear, talked endlessly, and insisted that there was nothing wrong with him. He became extremely argumentative and unpredictable, and the welfare worker then initiated arrangements for Mr. Jacobson's return to an inpatient setting.

When Mr. Jacobson returned to the hospital, the dosage level of lithium carbonate that he had been maintained on was increased. He then became very passive and dependent, complained about his unhappy and ineffective life, and expressed concern when he began exhibiting side effects to the medication. Other anti-psychotic medications were evaluated alone and in combination with lithium carbonate, but the lithium appeared to be the most effective medication for alleviating the emotional disturbance. Mr. Jacobson's mood eventually improved with hospitalization and, two months later, he was discharged back to the day treatment program. However, he resisted participating in this program and then was placed in a board and care facility. He was again hospitalized after another manic episode approximately ten months later. This episode occurred after Mr. Jacobson had once again stopped taking his medication. Upon re-hospitalization, he became quite depressed, refused to get out of bed, and insisted upon having his meals brought to his room. Various anti-psychotic medications were tried, and he then was placed on lithium carbonate in combination with another anti-psychotic medication. He was discharged back to a board and care home when his mood stabilized. However, he eventually discontinued the medication and gradually became increasingly depressed.

PRESENT HOSPITALIZATION

Mr. Jacobson was committed, at his welfare worker's instigation, to a psychiatric hospital in order to prevent the possibility of a suicide attempt. The hospital was a different facility from the one he had been admitted to on previous occasions, and recently had developed a combined medical-behavior modification approach. Psychological testing confirmed a psychotic depression. Mr. Jacobson felt that he was physically damaged and therefore could not work. He communicated that he disliked himself and he also stated that he regretted that he had not killed himself some time ago.

A continuing problem in maintaining Mr. Jacobson outside of the hospital was the numerous side effects he experienced when the dosage level of lithium carbonate or the other anti-psychotic medications he had been placed on was too high. The side effects of lithium included ataxia (staggering gait), mild tremor, dry mouth, and sleepiness. He therefore tended to discontinue the medication when his mood stabilized at a more normal level. Therefore, the hospital treatment program included placing him on a behavior modification program aimed at reinforcing him for taking his medication and for behaving in a more socially appropriate manner. The treatment goal was to eventually extend this program to a day treatment facility.

A token system was set up in which Mr. Jacobson earned points for taking the prescribed medications regularly and without argument. Points could also be earned for behaviors such as getting out of bed in the morning, shaving, combing his hair, getting to meals on time, and not complaining or crying for specific time blocks each day. These points could be exchanged for a variety of reinforcers and privileges both on and off the ward.

Mr. Jacobson was placed on lithium carbonate medication when readmitted, since his previous history suggested that, despite the side effects of this drug, he had been able to function better on this medication than on any other anti-psychotic medication. He did not resist the request that he start taking the medication again. Mr. Jacobson earned very few points during his first week in the hospital and his behavior was observed to cycle between manic and depressed phases. After approximately seven days, at the point at which the blood levels of the drug were sufficiently high to induce a behavioral effect, he also began earning points on the token system. Gradually, more socially appropriate behaviors became established. Mr. Jacobson shaved and showered regularly, was well groomed, and conversed with others about topics other than his symptoms. He also began participating in group therapy sessions. His therapist discussed with him on an individual basis, the necessity of taking the medication indefinitely in order to prevent recurrences of the severe mood swings. They also discussed changes in behavior that Mr. Jacobson should be alert to that might signal that his mood state was beginning to fluctuate more than usual. He was told that, if he noticed the signs of greater than average mood swings, he should contact the hospital social worker. An evaluation would then be made about whether he should be rehospitalized for a brief period of time, or whether some other type of treatment should be initiated.

Mr. Jacobson remained in the hospital for three months. It was possible to maintain him on a lower dosage level of lithium carbonate than had been the case without the behavior modification program. He indicated that he felt a real sense of accomplishment through being able to control his behavior and monitor behavior changes by means of the token system. He was quite pessimistic about whether he would ever be able to function at a job commensurate with his intellectual ability, but he did agree to return to a day treatment program and to continue taking the prescribed medication.

Arrangements were made for the token system to be carried out at the day treatment center. Mr. Jacobson would be able to earn points for social interactions with other persons, such as participating in outings, going to a movie or to the park, or engaging in other group activities. An important aspect of the program was that he continue to take his medication regularly and to communicate to the day treatment and hospital personnel any mood changes. Upon discharge to the day treatment program, it was hoped that the combination of the medication and the behavior modification program would prevent the cycling of emotional behavior to the extremes it had in the past.

DISCUSSION

The manic-depressive disorder is characterized by severe mood swings of psychotic intensity, with a tendency to remission and then recurrence. Generally, this diagnosis is given on the basis of the repeated occurrence of the mood cycles and the lack of apparent environmental events that could have precipitated the mood deviation. The diagnostic criterion of no obvious precipitating events (DSM-II, 1968) implies that manic-depressive psychosis is endogenously determined.

The most common form of manic-depressive psychosis is the manic-depressive, depressed type, characterized by a cycling between normal affect and a progressive decline to a severely depressed state. Other individuals typically cycle between normal and manic behavior. The case presented in this chapter is an example of the circular type of manic-depressive psychosis, in which episodes of both manic and depressed behavior occur, with periods of normal affect in between these mood cycles.

Manic-depressive reactions generally run their course without treatment, although medication or electroconvulsive therapy usually shortens the duration of the mood extremes. The manic phase, if untreated, lasts for about three months, and the depressive phase for about nine months. However, some individuals manifest repeated 24- or 48-hour cycles running the gamut from mania to depression that persists over a period of many years (Jenner, Gjessing, Cox, Davis-Jones, Hullian, and Hanna, 1967). Since a large proportion of persons return to a normal mood state without any type of treatment, there has been a great deal of interest in the possibility of delineating a biological basis to this disorder. Genetic contributions to the development of manic-depressive psychosis have been posited by Elsasser (1952), who found that in cases in which both parents had been diagnosed as manic-depressive there was a 32 percent risk for the emergence of manic-depressive psychosis in the offspring. The expectancy of severe affective reactions in the general population is less than 1 percent (Beck, 1967). In the group that Slater (1971a) evaluated, the frequency of manic-depressive psychosis in the parents of manic-depressives was 11.5 percent, and in the children, 22.2 percent. Slater also found that the concordance rate for affective disorders in identical twins was 57 percent, while for fraternal twins the concordance rate was 29 percent.

Winokur (1969) proposed that there was a likelihood of sex-linked characteristics in the development of affective disorders because of findings of a higher incidence of affective disorder in the daughters than in the sons of depressed mothers. This differential filial incidence was not found in the case of fathers with affective disorders. The possibility that some affective disorders are sex-linked on the X chromosome was suggested by the evidence from two families in which all male members who manifested an affective disorder also were color blind (Reich, Clayton, and Winokur, 1969).

The various studies point to some type of genetic contribution to the development of manic-depressive psychosis. However, the strength of the genetic findings very likely is attenuated by factors such as the reliability of the diagnosis, and the evaluation in some studies of the general category of affective disorder rather than the specific syndrome of manic-depressive psychosis. The influence of imitation learning and a stressful environment on the development of a particular disorder should also be considered. A child growing up in a home in which one or both parents exhibit signs of an affective disorder would certainly be influenced by the parental behaviors and might imitate the behaviors he or she observed.

Stenstedt (1952) found a 15 percent average incidence of manic-depressive psychosis in the parents, siblings, and children of persons diagnosed as manic-depressive. However, when these cases were categorized into good or poor childhood environments, the risk rate for the disorder was 31 percent for persons growing up in an unfavorable environment and 10 percent for those from a favorable childhood environment. These findings are consistent with Slater's (1971b) diathesis-stress model of abnormal behavior. This theory proposes that there is a biological predisposition for the development of various disorders, but the disorder may be manifested only if there is an interaction with environmental stress. The extent of the predisposition and of the stress determines the threshold for the development and the severity of the disorder.

The discovery that lithium salts, used as a substitute for sodium chloride in the diets of cardiac patients, was effective in treating manic-depressive psychosis (Cade, 1949) has increased speculations about biochemical factors in the latter disorder. There has been some interest in the mode of action of lithium carbonate because the drug does not produce a general suppression of behavior as do sedative drugs but, instead, curbs manic and hyperexcitable behavior so that the mood returns to a more normal level. However, it is necessary for lithium carbonate to be accumulated in the blood stream over a period of a week or more before the drug has an effect on behavior (Gershon and Shopsen, 1973). The drug has been reported as more effective in modifying the acute manic phase than the acute depressive phase of the disorder. Recent evidence on a small number of patients suggests that lithium carbonate can be quite helpful in treating the depressive phase as well (Johnson, 1974). Maintenance of individuals on lithium carbonate has proven to be effective in preventing the further recurrence of the extreme mood swings.

Research activity continues in the effort to isolate specific biochemical factors in the etiology of manic-depressive psychosis and in other kinds of affective disturbances. However, in evaluating the biochemical factors associated with a particular disorder, one must be cautious in separating out the specific biochemical effects of various substances on behavior as opposed to the biochemical changes resulting from severe alterations in behavior. Lack of sleep, intense emotional arousal, or depressive stupor, in and of themselves produce changes in biochemistry and in physiological functioning.

It seems appropriate, in light of the research evidence, that a social learning evaluation of manic-depressive disorders should take into account the possibility of a genetic component to this disorder, perhaps manifested in terms of a biochemical abnormality that effects mood. However, heredity is but one of the many ways in which a parent can influence his or her offspring, and the contribution of environmental factors should also be considered. The opportunity that a child has for observing and modeling a parent's deviant behaviors seems likely to have an influence on whether the child also will develop a deviant behavior pattern. Further, the low probability of learning socially appropriate behaviors in an environment in which other persons are acting in a deviant manner also would tend to increase the incidence of disturbed behavior in that particular family. Parents and other family members who are behaving in an unusual and inappropriate way, and are preoccupied with their own problems, would seem unlikely to give attention and social approval to a child when he or she acts in a socially acceptable manner. Thus, the degree of the biological predisposition could determine the amount of emotional stress and deviant environmental factors necessary to produce abnormal behavior in the offspring. However, the type of disordered behavior the child manifests might not necessarily be the same type of disorder as that manifested by the parent (see Heston's study [1966] on the offspring of schizophrenic mothers, discussed in Chapter 17).

The life history of Bernard Jacobson includes the possibility of genetic influences interacting with the factors of an unfavorable environment in the development of a psychotic disorder. Mr. Jacobson's father was diagnosed as a chronic schizophrenic and, throughout his adult life, functioned in society in a minimally effective manner. Mr. Jacobson's childhood experiences were dominated by tensions between his mother, grandmother, and himself, and neither his mother nor grandmother seemed to interact with him in a warm and supportive way. Mr. Jacobson's grandfather was extremely passive and rarely got involved in the arguments among the other family members. The role model he presented to his grandson was also that of an ineffectual and minimally involved male figure.

The persons in Mr. Jacobson's home neither taught nor reinforced him for engaging in the social skills necessary for interacting harmoniously with his peers and other persons. His argumentative behavior in school earned him a negative reputation and as a result he had no friends. Therefore, he was unable to gain gratification through social interactions with his peers. His fighting and verbally abusive behavior also precluded him from having the opportunity to observe how others interact in a cooperative manner, and therefore he did not learn more effective social abilities.

Nonetheless, Mr. Jacobson's life was not completely chaotic and strife-filled and he did acquire some social skills, perhaps in large part from his relationship with his grandfather. Further, his intelligence level was high enough so that he was able to profit from the academic material presented in his elementary school classes despite minimal attention on his part. When he became interested in the subject matter offered in high school, the gratification derived from learning was apparently self-reinforcing. He applied himself to mastering the subject material assigned to him and he did well in school. As he grew more interested in learning and his classroom behavior correspondingly changed, the response of other persons in the environment changed as well. In college, he was able to establish a relationship with both the woman he eventually married and her family. Indeed, the time interval between high school and college graduation was the only relatively tranquil period in his life.

Mr. Jacobson did not appear able to cope with the responsibilities of relating to a wife and interacting with his colleagues and pupils. It is also possible that he was unable to deal with the sexual and social demands of a sustained heterosexual relationship. Within a year after his marriage, he manifested signs of emotional disturbance and sought professional help for his difficulties. Despite eight years of almost continuous therapeutic support and treatment with psychotropic drugs, his functioning gradually became more inadequate and disturbed.

The symptoms clearly characteristic of a manic-depressive disorder first became obvious at age 33, when Mr. Jacobson became hyperactive, hallucinatory, and highly suspicious of others. The first onset of this disorder generally occurs between ages 20 and 30, and in other respects, the natural course of Mr. Jacobson's manic-depressive disorder is similar to the descriptions found in the clinical literature. The episodes of mood swings, although sometimes occurring quite suddenly, followed a consistent escalating or de-escalating pattern in cycling between the manic and depressed phases. Somewhat less usual than the reported normative pattern was the tendency to move through the entire mood cycle in a period of several days. At first, Mr. Jacobson had insight into the fact that he needed help from others to cope with these mood disturbances. However, as these episodes recurred and became more severe he began to blame others for his problems. He became unwilling to be hospitalized for treatment or for his own safety and the protection of others.

Various types of anti-depressant, sedative, and anti-psychotic medications as well as electroconvulsive treatments were ineffective in completely preventing the recurrences of the affective disorder. However, the various treatments did decrease the severity of the symptoms manifested and shortened the episodes of disturbed behavior. Mr. Jacobson functioned somewhat more adequately on the lithium carbonate medication than he had on the other drugs. However, a continuing problem was finding an effective dosage level of lithium while keeping the drug side effects to a manageable level. A further difficulty was to convince Mr. Jacobson to take the medication indefinitely even when his mood was normal.

The incorporation of a behavior modification program with the lithium therapy regimen appeared to increase the probability that further recurrences could be prevented or lessened in intensity. The annoying side effects from the drug functioned to make the indefinite maintenance on medication an extremely aversive experience. Mr. Jacobson could be maintained on a lower dosage level of lithium when the drug was used in combination with the behavior modification program. Therefore, one can be more optimistic that he will continue taking the medication in his present-day treatment setting.

It would be unrealistic, however, to suggest that the behavior modification program served as anything more than a supplement to the drug therapy regimen. Mr. Jacobson did not respond at all to the token program until he had taken lithium for several days. The cumulative effect of the drugs eventually resulted in blood levels of lithium that were high enough to show a pharmacologic effect on mood and behavior. Only then was it possible to modify other aspects of his behavior in a more socially effective direction. Nonetheless, the overall effectiveness of the treatment program was enhanced because Mr. Jacobson was able to earn tokens and gain social reinforcement for engaging in socially appropriate behaviors. His history indicated that he had not had the opportunity to receive social approval for positive behaviors in quite some time.

The extension of the behavioral program to the day treatment center and to other aspects of the nonhospital environment appeared to be a significant step in the treatment process. In addition, training Mr. Jacobson to respond to the early signals of a greater than usual change in affect was important in preventing further recurrences of the disorder. The monitoring procedure also functioned to give him some feeling of self-control and direction to his life. It is hoped that with a lesser number of drug side effects and continued reinforcement for taking the medication and for behaving in a more socially appropriate manner, Mr. Jacobson will be able to stay out of the hospital for longer periods of time and experience a more satisfactory life.

REFERENCES

American Psychiatric Association. *Diagnostic and statistical manual of mental disorders* (2nd ed.) (DSM-II). Washington: American Psychiatric Association, 1968.

Beck, A. T. *Depression: Clinical, experimental and theoretical aspects.* New York: Hoeber Medical Division, Harper and Row, 1967.

Cade, J. F. J. Lithium salts in the treatment of psychotic excitement. *Medical Journal of Australia,* 1949, *36,* 349–352.

Elsasser, G. Ovarial function and body constitution in female inmates of mental hospitals; special referece to schizophrenia. *Archives of Psychiatry* (Berlin), 1952, *188,* 218–225.

Gershon, S., & Shopsen, B. (Eds.) *Lithium: Its role in psychiatric research and treatment.* New York: Plenum Press, 1973.

Heston, L. Psychiatric disorders in foster home reared children of schizophrenic mothers. *British Journal of Psychiatry,* 1966, *112,* 819–826.

Jenner, F. A., Gjessing, L. R., Cox, J. R., Davies-Jones, A., Hullian, R. R., & Hanna, S. M. A manic-depressive psychotic with a persistent forty-eight hour cycle. *British Journal of Psychiatry,* 1967, *113,* 895–910.

Johnson, G. Antidepressant effect of lithium. *Comprehensive Psychiatry*, 1974, *15*, 43–47.

Reich, T., Clayton, P. J., & Winokur, G. Family history studies: V. The genetics of mania. *American Journal of Psychiatry*, 1969, *125*, 1358–1368.

Slater, E. The parents and children of manic-depressives. In J. Shields, & I. I. Gottesman (Eds.), *Man, mind, and heredity. Selected papers of Eliot Slater on psychiatry and genetics.* Baltimore: Johns Hopkins Press, 1971. Pp. 55–67. (a)

Slater, E. A heuristic theory of neurosis. In J. Shields, & I. I. Gottesman (Eds.), *Man, mind, and heredity. Selected papers of Eliot Slater on psychiatry and genetics.* Baltimore: Johns Hopkins Press, 1971. Pp. 216–227. (b)

Stenstedt, A. A. A study in manic-depressive psychosis: Clinical, social, and genetic investigations. *Acta Psychiatrica et Neurologica Scandinavica*, 1952, Suppl. 79.

Winokur, G. Genetic principals in the clarification of clinical issues in affective disorders. In A. J. Mandell & M. P. Mandell (Eds.), *Psychochemical research in man.* New York: Academic Press, 1969. Pp. 329–342.

20

A Progression to Psychotic Depression— "My Life Is Hopeless"

Mary Preston was 64 years old when she was hospitalized because of an overwhelming agitated depression. She expressed the belief that all her efforts were futile and there was no purpose in living. She wished that she were 84 instead of 64, so she would die soon. Mrs. Preston complained that she had difficulty sleeping; she usually woke up early in the morning and then could not fall back asleep again. She also stated that she has been extremely upset and confused over the past few months and she wrung her hands and cried as she related this information to the interviewer.

Mrs. Preston was white and of Protestant working-class background. Her husband had died rather suddenly when he was 53 years old and she had been a widow for the past fifteen years. The patient had two children, a 34-year-old son who lived with her, and a daughter, age 37, who was married and had three children of her own.

Mrs. Preston had first sought professional help for her emotional difficulties when she was 50 years old, one year after her husband died. She was then treated periodically for depression over a fourteen-year period that ended with her hospitalization.

FAMILY HISTORY

Mrs. Preston stated that she had been nervous all of her life. She reported that she never had much confidence in herself and she felt that her low self esteem was due to a lack of happiness and security in her childhood.

Mrs. Preston was an only child and she indicated that she had not had many friends when she was growing up. She described her father as a drunkard whom she hated so much that she could not look into his face. She recalled that her parents were constantly bickering and her mother often complained to her about her father's actions. Mrs. Preston said that she felt close to her mother and sorry for her because she had to contend with such abusive behavior. Mrs. Preston indicated that she had rushed into marriage when she was 18, in order to escape from her intolerable home situation.

ADULT HISTORY

The Prestons had resided for many years in an apartment building in a working class area of a large city. Although they were never able to afford luxuries, they were able to live reasonably well on Mr. Preston's income as a construction worker. The family went to church regularly and the children attended Sunday school. Both youngsters graduated from high school and subsequently obtained jobs.

Mrs. Preston stated that she had always taken great pains to keep her house clean and she had made sure that her children were neatly dressed at all times. She usually spent most of the day doing household chores and each day she prepared a substantial meal for dinner. Mrs. Preston rarely asked either of the children to help her with the housework, because she knew that whatever chore had to be done would be accomplished more adequately if she did it herself. She also felt that her children should have some time after school for themselves or to be with their friends.

Mrs. Preston indicated that her interests had always centered primarily around her family, although she did participate once a week in church-related activities. She had no hobbies and she rarely went out of the house during the week, except for the time she spent shopping or with her church group. Mrs. Preston commented that she didn't need outside activities when her children were growing up, because she had enough to do around the house to keep her busy the entire day. Mr. and Mrs. Preston ordinarily spent Saturday evenings at home watching television, and on Sundays after church, the family visited with relatives.

The patient described her husband in highly positive terms. She indicated that Mr. Preston had always acted in a patient and understanding manner, even though she had often been angry and irritable with him. She expressed regret that she had never given him enough attention, but instead had devoted most of her time to their two children. She stated that her husband had given her the moral support to cope with the problems that came up in everyday life, and fifteen years after his death, she still sorely missed not having his support.

According to Mrs. Preston, ever since she had first been married, she had taken the initiative in making decisions about household matters. She stated that she tended to become quite angry and argumentative when she did not get her way and Mr. Preston typically gave in to her wishes rather than argue with her. She indicated that her husband ordinarily kept his feelings to himself and he rarely expressed strong emotions. He did not interact much with his children and he left disciplinary matters up to his wife. He usually came directly home from work and then spent his free time watching television and reading the newspaper.

Mr. Preston developed a gastric ulcer when he was 42 years old, and he had to follow a strict diet in order to keep this problem under control. He was hospitalized on three occasions for bleeding ulcers and he died suddenly of a blood clot at age 53, several days after his third admission to the hospital.

Mrs. Preston recalled that the period right after her husband's death was one of severe stress and she suffered from insomnia and intense headaches for about a month. She felt that she was alone in the world because her daughter was married and lived in another part of the city and her son was planning to go away to college the following year. She was worried that her health would deteriorate, because she was 49 years old and in the midst of the menopausal period. She feared that if she became ill, she would not be able to provide the financial support necessary for James to go to college.

After her husband's death, Mrs. Preston found a job as an office clerk. She indicated that it was quite difficult for her to get along with the other persons in the office, because she liked to do things her own way and not take directions from others. If she saw any of her co-workers doing their job in a way that she considered inefficient, she tried to point this out to them. However, when she was told on several occasions that she was interfering with the office procedures, she decided that the only way she could keep her job was to do her own work and not pay attention to any other persons. Mrs. Preston subsequently maintained only superficial relationships with her co-workers and she kept her interactions with them to a minimum.

Mrs. Preston reported that it was quite fatiguing to come home from work each day and then take care of the household chores. She was occupied with caring for her son's needs, too, because James had decided not to go to college after all and he still lived at home with her. However, James gave his mother a substantial part of his paycheck to help pay for household expenses.

Mrs. Preston's description of her daughter suggested that Margery, like her mother, was domineering and perfectionistic. They had difficulty relating to each other without getting into arguments. For example, Margery frequently told her mother that she was not allowing James to grow up and she still treated him like a young child. Mrs. Preston strongly disagreed with this assessment and a verbal dispute would then ensue. Both mother and daughter seemed to find it more comfortable to keep their contacts with each other to a minimum and therefore avoid conflict.

Mrs. Preston did not have any close friends and she spent most of her free time at home. She continued to participate somewhat in church activities, but she stated that she went to church functions out of habit rather than because she really enjoyed these events. She typically became involved in tasks that required clerical work, such as sorting foods or clothes collected for charity. She preferred these activities to tasks requiring interactions with other persons. She indicated that everyone knew that she did her best work in jobs where she could do things her own way, without the interference of others.

TREATMENT HISTORY

Mrs. Preston reported that she had been able to recover from the initial shock and grief at her husband's death. She functioned fairly adequately for about a year, but during the following year she went to see her family physician because of extreme "nervousness." He gave her some pills for her nerves and she followed his suggestion and contacted a psychiatric outpatient clinic in the area.

Mrs. Preston's outpatient records indicated that she related her symptoms to the death of her husband. When she was first seen at the clinic, she was unable to sleep well and she was described as anxious, agitated and depressed. She revealed that she was afraid of the future and she was continually bothered by thoughts that she would not be having these difficulties if her husband were alive. She expressed strong guilt feelings about his death and she was convinced that her anger and arguments with her husband had killed him. His death also aroused the earlier memories of her unhappy childhood and she believed that she was now destined to be alone and unhappy again.

Mrs. Preston's conversations with the clinic psychiatrist showed a preoccupation with eyeglasses and optometrists. She had recently started wearing bifocals and she attributed her nervousness to the new glasses. She indicated that she got "the shakes" and felt nauseated whenever she wore them and she reported that the trembling of her body stopped when she took the glasses off. The patient also complained that she was highly sensitive to even minor noises. For example, if she heard the dishes being placed on top of each other, she felt as if she were jumping out of her skin.

Mrs. Preston stated that she had always had great difficulty making decisions and she had been bothered by changes all of her life. Before she was married, she used to throw up when she had to go to a new school or look for a different job. She said that she wanted to move from her apartment house because the landlord was noisy, but she could not come to a final decision on the advisability of moving.

For the next six years, Mrs. Preston came periodically to the outpatient clinic. She talked with a social worker from time to time and a psychiatrist prescribed antidepressant medication for her when she complained of strong feelings of despondency. She had recurring episodes of depression, but the problem was never severe enough to warrant hospitalization.

During this six year period, Mrs. Preston continued to ruminate about her husband's death and she frequently verbalized the belief that her life was empty and meaningless. She was convinced that her son was foolish for wasting his life by living with her and giving her money for expenses. She saw her daughter and the latter's family from time to time, but Mrs. Preston did not appear to derive a great deal of gratification from these interactions. She said that she was too nervous and her grandchildren were too noisy for her to enjoy the occasions when she was with them.

During a subsequent four year period, Mrs. Preston was able to function reasonably well without mood elevating medication. However, when she was 60 years old, she went back to the outpatient clinic she had attended previously. She was troubled with a number of physical ailments and she once more began to experience strong emotional discomfort. She manifested agitated and depressed behavior and she was again placed on antidepressant medication. She was also referred to an internist for treatment of her physical disorders.

Mrs. Preston was able to continue working as long as she was on antidepressant medication. The therapist tried to encourage her to engage in more outside activities, but this effort was not successful. For the next two years, Mrs. Preston came to the clinic at monthly intervals and a maintenance supply of antidepressant drugs was prescribed for her. Her son continued to live at home with her.

At age 62, there was a noticeable deterioration in the effectiveness of Mrs. Preston's behavior in relation to the environment. Her son had convinced her to move to another apartment some distance from where they had previously lived. From the time that she moved, the strong feelings of agitation and depression markedly intensified and she began to come to the clinic on a weekly basis. She quit her job because she noticed that she was making mistakes at work and while paying for items at the store.

In her conversations with the therapist, Mrs. Preston sometimes laughed and smiled inappropriately as she stated how hopeless her life seemed to her. She communicated in a rambling, sometimes hard to follow manner and she often wrung her hands and cried. The patient indicated that she felt that she should be contributing something to other persons, but all she did was take from others. When pressed for details, she could not relate any specific incidents demonstrating why she held this belief. However, she stated that anyone could see that her life was not worthy of notice.

Mrs. Preston also talked about her continued inability to make decisions and how fearful she was that she would decide incorrectly. The decisions she referred to concerned the as yet unresolved matter of whether to buy a new winter coat and her persistent doubts about whether it had been wise to move to another apartment. She said that she relied on her son's judgment in many situations where it was just impossible for her to make up her mind.

The patient's general condition gradually began to worsen. She was suffering from hypertension and other circulatory problems and she underwent surgery for kidney stones. Mrs. Preston stated that she did not feel well, physically or emotionally. She was extremely tired, she had lost weight because of poor appetite, and she suffered from chronic constipation. She frequently had crying spells and was troubled by occasions when it seemed as if her whole body were trembling. She reported that she experienced a feeling of panic after these shaking episodes.

Mrs. Preston revealed that her son had not known that she was coming to the clinic and receiving medication during the past year. He felt that she relied too heavily on taking pills when she was upset. He responded to her complaints of feeling worthless by telling her, "You've got to get hold of yourself." However, after they moved to a new area, she could no longer be active in her church. The distance involved in traveling back to her former neighborhood was just too great for her. She therefore rarely left the house and she felt even more alone and unhappy.

PRE-HOSPITALIZATION PERIOD

Mrs. Preston stopped coming to the clinic during the year prior to hospitalization because she felt that the medication was no longer helping her. She began awakening around four o'clock in the morning and was then unable to fall asleep again. She reported that she was afraid to go outside during the daytime and she sat immobile in a chair or paced the floors until her son came home from work. James would then be annoyed with her because she had not turned on the lights or cooked anything for supper. He was also becoming exasperated with her frequent crying spells and statements that there was no purpose in living.

Mrs. Preston said that she wished she were older, so she would be dead and the misery of this life would be over. Eventually, her depressive behavior became so marked that James took the initiative and brought her to the outpatient clinic. Mrs. Preston and James agreed with the physician's recommendation that she should be hospitalized for more intensive treatment.

HOSPITALIZATION

Mrs. Preston was now 64 years of age. She was very disheveled in appearance on the ward and she made little effort to keep her clothes clean. During the first few days in the hospital, she paced up and down the corridors and muttered to herself, "It's hopeless. It's hopeless."

There was a transition in the patient's behavior during her first weekend of hospitalization. Despite large doses of antidepressant medication, she began to spend the entire day lying stiffly in bed, without crying or talking spontaneously. When asked how she felt, she said that she was dying and that all was futile. She ate very little and she had difficulty sleeping at night. Her son came to visit her every day and her daughter came a number of times too, but Mrs. Preston conversed with them only minimally.

After she had been in the hospital for a week, the physician decided that shock treatments were necessary to alleviate the severe depression. The patient was manifesting symptoms of psychotic proportion, as evidenced by her lying immobile in bed in a depressive stupor. Mrs. Preston and James signed a consent statement agreeing to the treatments.

The patient received electroconvulsive therapy (ECT) over a two-week period, with three treatments given each week. A muscle relaxant was administered in order to lessen the severity of the convulsion. Immediately after each treatment, Mrs. Preston was confused and disoriented about time and place, but these lapses in memory were not noticeable by the next day. The patient reported that she had difficulty remembering some events from the distant past, but this problem diminished a few days after the electroconvulsive treatments were completed.

Mrs. Preston indicated that she was afraid of the procedures involved in getting ready for the shock therapy and she was also frightened by the idea of the shock itself. However, over the two-week period when ECT was administered, she gradually spent less time in bed and she reported that she was feeling much better. She began to move around the ward and she spoke about topics other than how hopeless life seemed.

Mrs. Preston remained in the hospital for five weeks. The progressive change in her behavior continued and she began to initiate conversations with other patients and the ward personnel. She was seen several times a week in brief therapy sessions oriented around teaching her how to interact with others in a more cooperative and gratifying manner. The social work staff arranged for Mrs. Preston to participate in a church group in her present neighborhood and she was aided in contacting other social clubs. A social worker spoke with her son a number of times and he also was given the names of organizations where Mrs. Preston could meet other persons her age.

At the time of her discharge from the hospital, Mrs. Preston indicated that her life did not seem so futile and hopeless. She said that she was glad to be going home and she also expressed the intention of becoming more involved in outside activities.

FOLLOW-UP

Mrs. Preston came back to the outpatient clinic for medication on several occasions during the next few years. However, she was participating in church activities again and her interactions with other persons were on the whole more cooperative. Although she complained of depressive feelings from time to time, her overall affect and behavior was more positive than it had been in quite a number of years.

DISCUSSION

The affective reactions are characterized by a severe disturbance of mood, with alterations in thought and behavior corresponding to the mood changes (DSM-II, 1968). The depressive affect is described as more intense than normal mood variation, or more prolonged than the usual reaction to a distressing environmental situation. There are numerous statements in the psychiatric literature suggesting that individuals who develop depressive disorders manifest an obsessive compulsive premorbid behavior pattern. Various writers have theorized about a relationship between a weakening of obsessive compulsive defenses and the emergence of depressive symptoms (English and Finch, 1964; Freud, 1959; Grigorian, 1970). However, research findings do not consistently demonstrate the presence of an obsessive compulsive personality in persons who later exhibit signs of depression and this issue is still a matter of debate (Buss, 1966).

When a pattern of depression is viewed over an extended time span, it is sometimes difficult to agree on a diagnosis specifying a particular subcategory of depression. Further, different kinds of physical and psychological processes may be in operation at different age periods. Therefore, an individual's deviant affective behavior may change over time and a specific diagnostic label may become more descriptive or appropriate at different periods.

Throughout the long period of Mrs. Preston's affective disturbance, she manifested the somatic complaints, feelings of guilt and unworthiness, and suffering self-righteousness typical of depressed individuals. Her problem of depression might have been diagnosed at various stages of her life as neurotic depressive reaction, involutional melancholia, manic-depressive illness, depressed type, or psychotic depressive reaction. Since the patient was able to function reasonably well for about a year after her husband's death, technically the diagnosis of neurotic reactive depression would have been ruled out. However, the patient might have been depressed since the time that her husband died, but she did not label her depressive affect as a problem until one year later.

The first prolonged episode of intense depression occurred during the menopausal period. A diagnosis of involutional melanchoia could have been appropriate at that time because of Mrs. Preston's age and the lack of a previous history of severe depression. Further, the symptoms of agitation manifested by the patient are often a part of the involutional depressive syndrome. One could question, however, whether the depressive symptoms at that time period were of psychotic proportion.

Mrs. Preston had recurring episodes of depression over the next twelve years, suggesting the diagnosis of manic-depressive illness, depressed type. However, her problem of depression did not appear to be of psychotic intensity during that period either. It was not until two years prior to hospitalization, when she moved to a different neighborhood, that the intensity and all-encompassing nature of the affective disturbance clearly indicated a psychotic disturbance. The diagnosis of psychotic reactive depression then became a possibility.

The issue of diagnosis is germane to the attempt to distinguish between exogenous and endogenous forms of depression. Exogenous depression is defined as a reaction to a specific, highly stressful environmental event. A diagnosis of neurotic or psychotic reactive depression implies that the depressive affect is caused by external stress factors. On the other hand, endogenous depression refers to the concept that certain types of depression are due to biochemical malfunctions within the individual. According to this viewpoint, the depressive state can occur relatively independently of environmental circumstances.

Strecker, Ebaugh, and Ewalt (1955) stated that there is abundant evidence of a constitutional physiochemical predisposition in many cases of manic-depressive psychosis. They also pointed out that involutional melancholia is related to biochemical as well as psychological factors in operation at the change of life period. Therefore, although depression may at times be exacerbated by environmental stress, this state may also be the result of biochemical malfunctions fairly independent of exogenous factors.

Kety (1971) reviewed the research evidence pertaining to biochemical mechanisms and the affective disorders. He concluded that there may be a constitutional factor in affective states related to the inadequate production or action of serotonin, a chemical necessary for proper brain function. This conclusion was based on studies showing low serotonin levels in the cerebrospinal fluid of both manic and depressed patients, which persisted even during remission. Kety postulated that serotonin deficiency may be associated with a predisposition to mania or depression. He further suggested that the actual symptoms of depression may be due to a marked decrease of catecholamine activity, particularly norepinephrine, at receptor sites in the brain.

It is impossible to make a definitive statement about the contribution of biochemical factors to Mary Preston's affective disorder and one cannot rule out this possibility. Nonetheless, it is also abundantly clear that the patient lost a major source of positive reinforcement when her husband died. She was unable to develop other kinds of gratification from her social environment because she had a limited number of interpersonal skills. As her sources of positive reinforcement became more restricted, her depressive symptoms became more severe and incapacitating. (See Chapter 6 for a fuller discussion of the relationship between the loss of sources of positive reinforcement and depression.)

Before the onset of the depressive symptoms, Mrs. Preston manifested several habit patterns that could be described as obsessive compulsive in nature. For example, she was constantly engaged in keeping her house meticulously tidy and she took great pains to make sure that her children were neatly dressed and absolutely clean. However, this behavior pattern could be reflective of the patient's general lack of social skills and confidence in interacting with other persons, rather than being a specific premorbid predisposition for depression. The development of depressive symptoms may therefore occur with any type of behavioral repertoire in which there is a difficulty in establishing alternate sources of positive reinforcement.

Mrs. Preston's range of social interests was quite limited. She related in a superficial manner to the women in her church group but these contacts did not generalize to other kinds of social situations. Mrs. Preston did not establish social relationships with the persons she knew at work, because she believed that the only way she could do her job well was to avoid personal involvements. In addition, there was little evidence of an effort to develop a warmer relationship with her daughter, son-in-law, or grandchildren.

The exception to the noninvolved and superficial way that Mrs. Preston interacted with others was her relationship with her son James. There was a strong emotional bond between them, indicated by the fact that James decided not to go away to college after his father died. He continued living with his mother and he related to her in a generally passive and dependent manner.

Mrs. Preston's description of her relationship with her husband was similar to her account of how James interacted with her. James had ample opportunity to observe his father's behavior and he appeared to imitate his father's interaction style. James, like his father, did not openly react to Mrs. Preston's anger and he tended to avoid verbal confrontations with her. James apparently gained reinforcement from his mother's constant concern and attention and he did not establish any long term involvements with persons his own age. His social interests were centered around the activities and problems of his mother.

Mrs. Preston might have exhibited more severe signs of emotional disturbance at an earlier age if she had not experienced the gratification derived from her relationship with her son. James provided her with a focus for her daily activities and she devoted a great deal of her time to taking care of his needs. This relationship was the major source of reinforcement available to her and because of these interactions, the symptoms of agitated depression did not greatly intensify until other problems occurred when she was in her sixties.

James, on the other hand, reinforced his mother for acting in a depressed manner through his solicitude toward her when she complained of unhappiness and his lack of effort in helping her to become more active outside of the home. When Mrs. Preston verbalized attitudes of despondency and worthlessness, he tried to convince her that she was a valuable individual. James could have avoided reinforcing the depressed behavior he was trying to extinguish if he had ignored his mother's complaints and encouraged her to form closer attachments with other persons. However, the relationship between Mrs. Preston and James appeared to be such that each reinforced the other for home-oriented behaviors, which excluded extended involvement with others.

The marked intensification of the patient's depression at age 62 was associated with two factors: a general debilitation in her physical condition and the change in her environment. When she moved to a different neighborhood some distance from her church, she lost her major source of interpersonal contact outside of the home. Mrs. Preston's new environment required her to engage in active behaviors in a changed social milieu. However, she lacked the skills necessary to establish social contacts with other persons and it was difficult for her to move about because of her physical ailments. Thus, her customary activities were restricted and she again failed to develop substitute behaviors. Because of these additional stress factors, the antidepressant medication was no longer effective and the depressive affect intensified.

Prior to the time of hospitalization, there were relatively few professional attempts devoted specifically to broadening the patient's social repertoire. The antidepressant medication succeeded in altering the patient's mood, which made it easier for her to function in superficial relationships. However, the outpatient treatment she received did not modify her interpersonal deficiencies.

An active and directive therapeutic approach might have prevented the recurrence and intensification of the depressive affect. The therapist could have discussed with Mrs. Preston how she typically interacted with others in either a domineering or noninvolved manner. Specific instruction in how to relate to others more successfully could then have been carried out, enabling Mrs. Preston to establish a greater number of rewarding interpersonal relationships.

The hospital treatment program was oriented toward achieving a rapid alleviation of depression through the use of ECT. Subsequent to this change in behavior, there was an active effort to help the patient become more interested and skilled in social activities. This treatment strategy was apparently effective, in light of Mrs. Preston's infrequent visits to the outpatient clinic following her discharge from the hospital.

The precise manner in which the electroconvulsive seizure acts on the brain is to a large extent still unclear. Nonetheless, many depressed patients show an improvement after this form of treatment when other methods have proved unsuccessful. Tourney (1970) stated that electroconvulsive therapy is the most effective method for treating various forms of psychotic depression. However, before the decision is made to administer ECT, a two week trial period with antidepressants was recommended. Tourney further suggested that following the alleviation of the depression, the patient should receive some form of directive psychotherapy geared toward changing current situational stresses.

Mrs. Preston was helped to function more effectively through the rapid lessening of depressive affect, in combination with an effort to modify her social environment. As she learned to derive more gratification from social interactions outside the home, she was not as troubled with feelings of despondency and worthlessness.

REFERENCES

American Psychiatric Association. Diagnostic and statistical manual of mental disorders. (2nd ed.) (DSM-II). Washington: American Psychiatric Association, 1968.

Buss, A. H. *Psychopathology*. New York: Wiley, 1966.

English, O. S., & Finch, S. M. *Introduction to psychiatry*. (3rd ed.) New York: Norton, 1964.

Freud, S. *Collected Papers*. Vol. 4. New York: Basic Books, 1959.

Grigorian, H. M. Aging and depression: the involutional and geriatric patient. In A. J. Enelow (Ed.), *Depression in medical practice*. West Point: Merck, Sharp & Dohme, 1970. Pp. 109–139.

Kety, S. S. Review: brain amines and affective disorders. In B. T. Ho & W. M. McIsaac (Eds.), *Advances in behavioral biology*. Vol. 1. *Brain chemistry and mental disease*. New York: Plenum Press, 1971. Pp. 237–244.

Strecker, E. A., Ebaugh, F. G., & Ewalt, J. R. *Practical clinical psychiatry*. (7th ed.) New York: McGraw-Hill, 1955.

Tourney, G. The severely depressed patient in medical practice. In A. J. Enelow (Ed.), *Depression in medical practice*. West Point: Merck, Sharp, & Dohme, 1970. Pp. 171–191.

SUBJECT INDEX

NAME INDEX

. . . Much has happened since Case Histories of Deviant Behavior *first appeared three years ago. Events are moving at such a pace that what was a valid reflection of behavior therapy in 1974 has become incomplete and inadequate as a characterization of behavior therapy today. Dr. Gloria Leon, an astute observer as well as a skillful behavioral clinician, chronicle well this progression of events in the second edition of her book.*

from the Foreword by Cyril M. Frar

Photo of woodcut entitled Melancholy *by Edvard Munch reproduced with permission of The National Gallery/Oslo, Norway.*

DATE DUE